WITHDRAWN

THE MINNESOTA EXPERIENCE
an anthology

Frontispiece by Keith Ervin

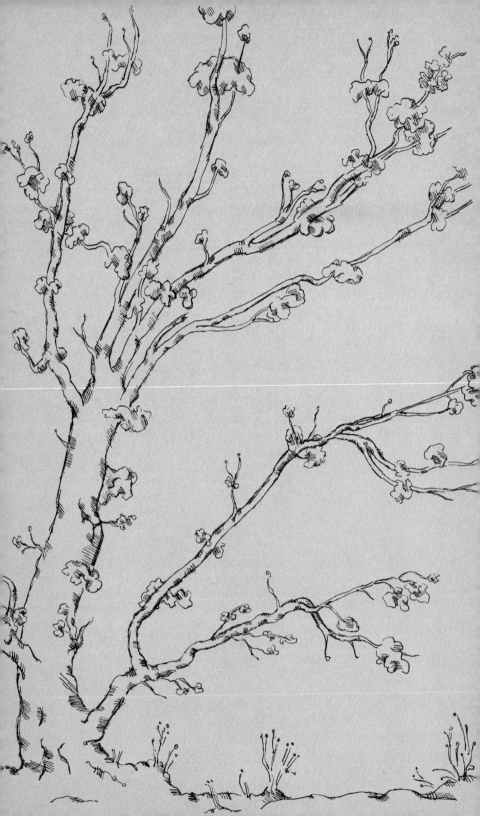

The Minnesota Experience

AN ANTHOLOGY

edited by Jean Ervin

The Adams Press / Minneapolis

PUBLISHED BY THE ADAMS PRESS,
59 Seymour Avenue Southeast,
Minneapolis, Minnesota 55414.

Printed in the United States of America
by the North Central Publishing Company, St. Paul.

Library of Congress Cataloging in Publication Data

Main entry under title:

The Minnesota experience.

    1. American literature—Minnesota. 2. Minnesota—
Literary collections. I. Ervin, Jean.
PS571.M6M52   810'.8'09776   79-10587
ISBN 0-914828-04-5
ISBN 0-914828-05-3 pbk.

PREFACE

S ELECTING WORKS for an anthology of Minnesota literature has reminded me of the maple sugaring I did as a
child. I was fascinated then to see the enormous vats of liquid
gathered with such care boiled down to miniscule amounts of
maple sugar. What my reading for this anthology has boiled
down to will, I hope, suggest the rich variety of prose literature
produced in Minnesota's lifespan. Although I have included a
few essays and some autobiographical material, I have for the
greatest part chosen fiction in the belief that it can convey experience more vividly than other forms. Scott Momaday has said that
telling stories is "a process in which man invests and preserves
himself in the context of ideas. Man tells stories in order to understand his experience, whatever it may be."

The reader will not find an even balance of material from each
period of the state's existence, for neither the quality nor the
quantity of literature from the nineteenth century would justify
such a distribution. Rather, I have tried to arrive at some
semblance of representativeness in terms of location, point of
view, and, where possible, period. Many of Minnesota's diverse
regions are used as settings: the northern wilderness, the prairie,
the farm, the small town, the city. I have included stories of a
number of the ethnic groups who settled the state. The Minnesota
experience in childhood, adolescence, adulthood, and old age is
here. The lives of teachers, priests, a saloon janitor, a businessman, farmers, a peddler, and members of a protest movement are in these stories.

Who qualifies as a Minnesota writer? Someone who was born
and raised in the state, and whose work shows a Minnesota im-
print, is the most obvious candidate. But I have also included
authors who, though not natives, lived here as more than sojourn-
ers and used the Minnesota scene.

In order to illustrate points I wished to make about Minnesota literature, I have at times in the introduction described fiction which was not included in the anthology. Some very good novels were impossible to excerpt, and in other cases a story was omitted because it was similar to one already chosen. I have also appended to the anthology a selected reading list for those in search of a more complete knowledge of Minnesota's literature.

Jean Ervin

Minneapolis, Minnesota
March 1979

CONTENTS

The arrangement of selections in this anthology should be taken as one of many ways to approach Minnesota literature. The reader may wish to invent his or her own order.

CHILDHOOD AND THE FAMILY

OLD AGE

INTRODUCTION

B RENDA UELAND remarked in 1934 that most Middlewestern novels are "as devoid of beauty as a screen porch
duplex on Dupont Avenue South overlooking a gasfilling station." However, for a state with a relatively short history Minnesota has produced a body of fiction whose interpretations of life
have richness and diversity.

But certain strands are prominent in the diversity. In their writing Minnesotans seem to be more aware of the land and climate
than writers from the East, perhaps somewhat less so than those
from the Rockies. One does not have to look far to find geography
and weather woven into a short story or novel either metaphorically or explicitly. The violence of winter blizzards and summer
thunderstorms, the vastness of the prairies, the importance of the
lakes and rivers and of the ever-present wilderness in the
north—all inform the literature of Minnesota.

The sheer size of the state has inspired some writers to contrast
sharply its geographical variations. In Peggy Harding Love's
story "Betrayal" a young woman travels by bus from the northern
lake country to Minneapolis, leaving behind the untainted wilderness. During the early part of the trip she sits beside an Indian
boy. "He was watching the land pass, too, and in his face and
body there was something of its own vital and fierce dignity. . . . This country is his, not mine, Mary thought with a
pang of envy. Why is he leaving it? From somewhere hidden a
cool lake breeze full of the smell of fresh water blew through the
window on her face." As she nears the city on the last leg of the
trip she has an experience which brings her to a recognition of
life's betrayals, her inner journey paralleling her outer one.

Other writers have had a more ambivalent attitude toward the
northern wilderness, seeing it as an echo of the dark side of man.

In John Milton's "An Inner Disquiet" an uneasy relationship between a man and his wife is brought to the surface by a summer in the woods. Kenneth Davis's novel *In the Forests of the Night* makes effective use of the Big Bog country in the 1930's to delineate the wilderness within its protagonist and his double, the narrator. In contrast, the hero of Tim O'Brien's *Northern Lights*, a modern Saul turned Paul, finds himself during a grueling trip through a storm in the woods after years of being unable to make a commitment to other people.

Carol Bly's "Gunnar's Sword" and Emilie Buchwald's "Getting and Spending" use external surroundings to reflect interior states. Both stories are told from the point of view of a woman, one the most vital resident of a retirement home in western Minnesota, the other a woman in early middle age living in a suburb of the Twin Cities. Harriet White in "Gunnar's Sword" is a toughminded realist who is still learning things about herself. Able to accept life's steadily increasing blows, she nevertheless feels the need to see the family farm once more in the face of a late winter storm. "Harriet moved carefully not just because she was exhausted, but because it was borne in on her that she was a very old woman and she would make a fool of herself if she fainted out here in the middle of nowhere with night coming on."

Margaret, in Buchwald's story "Getting and Spending," wonders, "Was this grasping and clutching inherent in the species, this desire for more of everything, more food, more money, and above all, more life?" She is not the tragically miscast housewife of so much contemporary literature, but a woman who meditates on the ephemeral nature of existence on a winter afternoon. "Why do we do it? What purpose does it have?" are age-old questions for anyone living the examined life. Capturing the landscape of a suburban Minnesota community in late winter, Buchwald uses it to mirror an awareness of the fragility of existence.

A young woman returns to her home town, named "Cup" for its location in one of the claustrophobically hemmed-in valleys of southeastern Minnesota, in Mabel Seeley's novel *Whispering Cup*. The incessant whispering of the winds becomes a metaphor for the increasingly sinister events in the human world. "The sound grew and spread in sibilance until it became the sound of a hundred women whispering together, gleeful and malicious."

Early Candlelight, a novel by Maud Hart Lovelace dealing with

Fort Snelling and its surroundings in the 1830's, captures the life of the rivers and their importance to the early settlers. The rivers both give life and bring sudden death. Although violent spring floods can wash away some low-lying settlements, the rivers are a lifeline to the outside world. Jasper Page, troubled by his love for another man's wife, sees black mist rise from the confluence of the Mississippi and St. Peter's rivers. "But on Pilot Knob, that height of land where the Indians placed their dead, the scaffolds stood out against the darkening sky, their grim burdens upon them. Behind him a cloak of rose and vermilion hung from the west, but before him the scene was one of cold desolation. It matched the desolation which suddenly lay in his breast."

In his story "In Loveless Clarity" Norval Rindfleisch sees the Mississippi as an analogue to a family. "The feeling of having been left behind, of having been cheated out of some grand destiny pervades my family's spirit." The river flowing near the West Side of St. Paul is not T. S. Eliot's dark brown god, but "dirty with refuse . . . already senile and shrunk to a rivulet. Its thin trickle is mocked by distant valley ridges which were once the lips of a gigantic flow that drained a continent."

Minnesota's lakes are as much a presence in its literature as the ocean or mountains would be to a Californian. The evanescence of childhood and the difficulty of growing up with a parent who stifles imagination form the theme of Dana Faralla's novel *The Madstone*. During the last summer to be spent at their beloved family lake cottage, three children rebel in different ways against a mother who both overprotects and rejects them. Nine-year-old Theo, feverish from an illness, dreams that his mother, in the form of a cruel child, is chasing him. "The child pushed the boat out into the water as she always did in the dream, and when Theo would follow it she tried to hold him back." In the dream he falls into the water. "He could not breathe, the scum muffling him like a heavy mantle." As the fog drifts in from Lake Superior the human world in the town of Mesabi reflects the external one in R. P. Johnson's novel *A Legacy of Thorns*. "Every man's world was not much more than ten feet all about him, from his eyes to the gray limit of the fog. Every small world was troubled, the sober in idle grinding discontent, the drunk in helpless fury."

Herbert Krause's highly imagistic prose is permeated with the world of farming and nature. In *Wind without Rain*, "wind was like a currycomb ripped across the face and dark a kind of fur along the hand." When an authoritarian pastor lays bare the failings of his flock, he reflects, "All my sins—all our sins, in fact—were dug up and lay open like potatoes rotting on a frozen field."

The farm is central to much Minnesota literature, often serving as a symbol of life itself. Among Minnesota writers there seems to have been little tendency to glorify the farm although some works indirectly suggest the peace of rural life as compared with the anonymity and hectic pace of the city. Other writers have condemned farm life as so overwhelmingly harsh that little remains for the development of the inner self. It is not necessarily the farm itself that stultifies, but the blotting out of compassion and the love of beauty in the day-by-day struggle to survive economically.

Threading the novels of Martha Ostenso is a belief that man is a child of nature, but a child who too often loses sight of his nurturing parent. "A man can break God's laws and be forgiven. . . . But when he breaks Nature's laws there's no forgiveness and there's no escape. . . . Greed is a sin against Nature." Characters in her novels who sin by wanting more than their fellow men frequently find their ambitions the cause of their downfalls. Ostenso's first novel, *Wild Geese*, a melodramatic picture of life in northern Minnesota and Manitoba, depicts the improbable Caleb Gare making virtual slaves of his family while he piles up money and land. Avoiding some of these early gothicisms in subsequent novels, Ostenso developed her themes more subtly. *The Stone Field*, for example, tells the story of a farm girl in northern Minnesota whose pull toward the land is pantheistic.

For some writers the farm has been as fitting an expression of Mammon as the city. In his novel *Pure Gold* Ole Rölvaag tells the bizarre story of Lizzie and Louis Houglam, who live entirely to pile up gold. Their farm becomes a stockade against any intrusion while they devise new ways to make money and to hide their hoard of gold pieces, which they call their "babies." A loving relationship deteriorates into one of suspicion and hatred of each other until they freeze to death with their wealth strapped to their bodies.

But the farm can be a solace to some. In Sheila Alexander's novel *Walk with a Separate Pride*, Nessa McKenna returns to her family's farm in southeastern Minnesota when her husband is inducted into the army during World War II. With the impending birth of her first child, Nessa recognizes the need for "small richnesses: in evenings to carry the basket half-full of straw to the chicken house and to feel the warm shell in the nest, to lift the soft under-body of the hen, touch the egg and put it carefully into the basket, look into the granary and the tool shed and horses' feed boxes. Such a shock of wealth, the fragile egg in the hand."

Adam Webb, the paternalistic farmer in Lorna Doone Beers' novel *A Humble Lear*, finds the land a balm to his uneasy relationship with his family. "Adam, when the ways of man bruised his heart, always fled to the woods and fields. . . . When Martha had turned her shoulder to him in proud and self-contained disdain he had left her in silence and gone to the land, and there grubbing at its tough stumps, uprooting the sycophant vines, hoeing down its thistles and quack grass, he grew calm and soon he rested his hoe in a fence corner and slowly paced over the ground that was his."

Geographical and ethnic variations in Minnesota are reflected within the compass of farm literature. Ava, the protagonist of Shirley Schoonover's *Mountain of Winter*, "was born on a piss-poor farm that scrambled and sprawled on the side of a mountain" in the Iron Range country. Although the Finnish-Americans in her book work hard to achieve a modest material comfort, they know how to play as hard as they work. The vitality of their world is captured by Schoonover—in the Christmas Eve party which lasts until four in the morning and ends then only because it is time to milk the cows, in the Saturday night dances, in the sauna as a social institution, and in the earthy "sharivee" for a newly wedded couple. "Old Big," the mountain that lures and threatens Ava, is a symbol of the world beyond the immediately tangible, firing her imagination and stiffening her resolve not to follow the local custom of marrying at an early age, "like you're nailing yourself down in a box before you really see what's outside of the box." Old Big provides the summer pasture for her cattle and is the source of the fire that nearly destroys her farm. Yet, in the end, the fire clarifies her feelings about herself in relation to the farm.

One of the finest Minnesota novels with a farm setting is Herbert Krause's *The Thresher*. Set in western Minnesota in the late nineteenth and early twentieth centuries, it deals with a second and third generation German-American community. Krause never papers over the harsher aspects of this world, but at the same time he conveys the rich texture of the social life of a farm community facing natural disasters, changes in agricultural methods, and conflicts of opinion over shifting mores. Johnny Black, né Schwartz, is a man consumed with the ambition to succeed in the threshing business. The threshing machine takes on a life of its own. "But hour by hour the cylinder had its greedy fill of stem and fecund head (the strength of summer's sun, the resistless warmth of earth); the straw heaped up; the grain spout belched its kernels into the sack. Stacks vanished, whole settings of them. Straw piles grew. And Johnny threshed and threshed. . . ."

In Emilio De Grazia's "A Minnesota Story" a farmer emerges as a crusader battling the powerful interests that ally themselves against him and his kind, an idealist who spends his life trying to teach his fellow men their own need for cooperation and knowledge. The heroic size of this participant in the protest movements of earlier decades is in stark contrast to today's pygmies who have sold out for the quick fix of self-indulgence. The farmer, who has built his barn well, has thought in terms of generations, not just his own lifespan.

The small town forms the setting for many Minnesota novels and short stories, but it is seldom celebrated. The palette runs from light grey to black, seldom to bright pigments. The boom towns of the nineteenth century and those founded by a single industry, such as the mining company towns in northern Minnesota, tended to attract people who had little in common with one another, and as a result, such communities were without any strong sense of communality. A sense of obligation toward fellow townsmen is lacking. Even though the towns that were settled by residents with a common language and religion offered warmth and security, they too often hedged the citizens with social codes that discouraged individuality and spontaneity. Enforced conformity where everyone is visible, and the corresponding tendency to bury one's true personality, crop up as subjects in a number of Minnesota works. It was this aspect of small town life that produced the "revolt from the village," a nationwide phenomenon in American literature from the late nineteenth century on, peaking during the second and third decades of this century.

Edward Eggleston's *The Mystery of Metropolisville*, based on the actual boom-to-bust Cannon City in southeastern Minnesota, is set during the land fever of the 1850's. The hinge on which Metropolisville turns is speculation in land, with all of its questionable practices—claim jumping, buying up of half-breed scrip, artful dodges to capture the county seat, and diddling of newcomers. When he enters the town Albert Charlton notices "the little claim shanties built in every sort of fashion, mere excuses for preemption. Some were even constructed of brush." As Whiskey Jim tells him, "Taint no land of idees. It's the k'dentry [country] of corner lots. Idees is in the way—don't pay no interest." On the walls of the Sod Tavern is a map of Metropolisville—complete with seminary, depot, courthouse, and other evidences of a settled, civilized community—a map that exists only as a public relations pipe-dream.

Minnesota's most famous questioner of small town life was, of course, Sinclair Lewis, whose Gopher Prairie in the novel *Main Street* is a thinly disguised picture of Lewis's home town of Sauk Centre. Lewis condemned the atmosphere which too often brought to one dead level all imaginations. Carol Kennicott has come from the Twin Cities as the bride of Dr. Will Kennicott, believing that she can awaken the stuffy townspeople. "She had tripped into the meadow to teach the lambs a pretty educational dance and found that the lambs were wolves. . . . She was surrounded by fangs and sneering eyes. . . . She wanted to hide in the generous indifference of cities." Yet in spite of her disgust at the cultural stifling, Carol recognizes that there are many genuinely good people in Gopher Prairie. Her admiration for her husband's dedication to his practice makes her ashamed at times of her own restlessness.

As a young teacher in Borghild Dahl's *Homecoming*, Lyng Skoglund goes to a western Minnesota town for her first job in the early twentieth century. New Stavanger is populated almost entirely by Norwegian-Americans who are resistant to Americanization and highly critical of an outsider's ideas. When she enters her schoolroom for the first time, Lyng finds that "the clock had stopped at twenty-three minutes after four. Even time stood still in New Stavanger." The school superintendent, terrified of crossing the establishment, warns her that she should be content with worn-out and inadequate texts, and must suggest no changes in the curriculum.

James Gray's *Wake and Remember*, published in the 1930's, is told from the point of view of a summer resident in the town of Genesis, a fictional Marine-on-St. Croix. Although the novel is largely concerned with the lives of upper middle class residents, there is an undercurrent of rural violence. Less successful is Gray's *Shoulder the Sky*, which was influenced by *Main Street*. But where Lewis was ambivalent about town life, Gray sees nothing but a sink of debauchery in the town of Nokomis, where young Dr. Eugene Kane has set up his practice. Alcoholism, murder, and incest form the matrix of daily life, and unfortunately the author falls into the sentimental pessimism that had become so fashionable in other 1930's novels about small towns. "Yes, of course. Death is our only trade here. The whole place is dying."

Neil Boardman's *Wine of Violence*, ostensibly a murder story, is most successful as a portrait of a northern Minnesota town too ready to condemn a man who refuses to meet its standards of behavior. Howard Breckwine, a reformed alcoholic who does little to ingratiate himself with his neighbors, has had the audacity to marry a woman supposedly too good for him. Boardman, writing in the 1960's with subtle psychological analysis, avoids the more extreme strokes of earlier writers.

"Why does a town die?" asks a character in Ann Chidester's *The Long Year*. "When it doesn't belong to the people, it dies—and it doesn't belong to the world any more. When the people don't care about being farmers or lumbermen or weavers and become makers of money." Chidester's High Falls is a St. Croix River town in the year 1933, a factory town placed in a dilemma by the owner's willingness to cheapen the products in order to keep the factory open. Chidester's novel, written and published in the next decade, is not an autopsy of a community, but a sympathetic and unpatronizing look at the lives of ordinary people.

In the 1970's Paul Berlin sees the small town not as prying, but as total indifferent to his Vietnam War experience, in Tim O'Brien's story "Speaking of Courage." "The war was over and there was no place in particular to go." Berlin, locked away from life inside an air conditioned car, drives repeatedly around the lake in a flat prairie town. The monotony of the buildings and landscape echo the lack of interest in the war. "Nobody believed it was a war at all."

In 1930 Margaret Culkin Banning published her novel *Mixed Marriage* anonymously, presumably because of its frank examination of then volatile subject matter, a marriage between a devout

Catholic and a Protestant. More interesting today is its view of Carmine, Minnesota, in the Iron Range country. The Reverend Michael Carroll, sent to Minnesota from the East, is appalled at this rootless town filled with parishioners who speak of "home" as always in some other town or country. It seems to him a fantasy. "Huge mines . . . some with lights flickering about their caves far into the night, some closed and with moss growing over abandoned entrances, stripped cliffs, buses speeding to and fro between the town and the near-by cities, great schools extravagantly equipped, miners who spoke little or no English passing on the sidewalk without recognition, shabby Finnish and Scandinavian women, shabbier Italians, wives of company officials driving Packards, secret politics, open vice, priggishness, shooting, snobbishness—all of it couldn't fit together."

The setting for Mary Patterson's novel *Iron Country* is the town of Magrath, Minnesota during the Second World War, not so many years after Banning's novel was published. But unlike Banning's Carmine with its rootless inhabitants, Magrath has a hold upon its townspeople. The heroine, Maxine Johnson, yearns to get away to college, yet at the same time wants to be a part of her town forever. In the last days of high school she tries to leave her mark on everything. "She had put her initials on the back wall of the auditorium stage underneath those of her brother, she had written in class books, in textbooks. . . ." The mosaic of "Italian-Swedish-German-Finnish-Irish-Cornish-French-Norwegian" is "slowly mixing together, not without protest. . . . It was the mining companies, cursed and blessed, that had done that, settling miners' families in locations where the companies owned the houses and the stores."

Magrath is not an ideal community. Its members are "known for a certain lack of sociability, and for their long silences. Silence to the outsider and silence often among themselves." There is, too, a certain readiness to condemn the nonconformist. John Moore, who admits to injuring his foot to escape military service, is too quickly assumed to be the arsonist who set fire to the Catholic Church. But, although the men never swear in front of the women and never "expected women to join in their conversations about baseball, the hunting season . . . and the war," this is not an especially sexist society, at least in terms of its day. Maxine's father has made a companion of her and has, with great difficulty, saved the money to send her to college. On the whole,

Patterson's portrait is more balanced and persuasive than most fictional accounts of small Minnesota communities.

In contrast to Patterson's Magrath is Jon Hassler's Staggerford, a north central Minnesota community pervaded by death. Set in the 1970's, his novel, which bears the name of the town, is an account of one week in the life of a high-school English teacher, Miles Pruitt. A "bone woman" who lives in a gravelike gulch collects discarded animal bones from housewives, wandering in and out of the novel like a medieval emblem of death. The superintendent of schools is so obsessed with his own impending death that he has put his affairs in order years before, living as a virtual prisoner in his own house. The tedium of this nearly moribund community is conveyed by Coach Gibbon's lengthy, detailed accounts of his wrestlers and football players, and the librarian Imogene Kite's encyclopedic monologues. Yet, Hassler does not condemn the town totally, finding hope in a few people, such as Agatha McGee, an elderly teacher who holds the visigoths at bay, as in the selection included in this volume.

Fictional views of urban life in Minnesota have been nearly as varied as the writers' backgrounds. Each author has, in a sense, created his own city. The immigrant Lev Simon in Norman Katkov's *A Little Sleep, a Little Slumber*, must sell his horse to support his family when there is no fruit to peddle during the winter. His is a very different St. Paul from that of Darius Carpenter in Grace Flandrau's *Being Respectable*. While he waits to be driven to church in his Cadillac from his Summit Avenue home in the early 1920's, Carpenter frets because his daughter Deborah has declared that marriage is going out and has put the sign "Live Dangerously" above her table. Marleen American Horse in Gerald Vizenor's story of that name arrives in Minneapolis with "a single change of clothes in a brown paper sack and an old reservation allotment map showing her place on the earth before the flood." She marries a white truck driver who beats her regularly. After alcohol becomes her only consolation her children are taken away from her by the welfare workers.

The parable of the rich man and the beggar in the Lazarus legend forms the theme of Harry Bloom's *Sorrow Laughs*, set in north Minneapolis in the 1930's. The area is a "junction where Jews trying to escape the ever encroaching Negro were creeping into Gentile territory, where Gentile was moving westward or eastward depending on financial status . . . a ring-around-the-rosie made even more haphazard by the iron grip of the Depression." The terror wrought by an unidentified arsonist forces the people of a community to face blind spots in their attitudes toward one another.

Even for a relatively lucky newcomer the city can be a mixed blessing. Dick Malory, protagonist of Grace Flandrau's novel *Entranced*, is determined to rise to the top in St. Paul. From the High Bridge "the city takes on a deceiving and inexplicable beauty. Veiled in the blue and misty gray and rose of its smoke and dust, it has that look of stillness that cities have when they are seen from a distance, that look of being less a city than the dream of a city. . . . Built on hills, it hangs like a mirage above the horizon." But the High Bridge fosters tragedy as well as dreams. Years before, Lydia Malory's grandfather, pushed to produce more and more money to feed the insatiable appetites of an avaricious wife, had leapt over the railing one fine evening, clutching a cane fashioned from a shark's backbone.

Thomas Boyd's *In Time of Peace*, published in 1935, echoes some of Flandrau's feelings about the Twin Cities. Where her shafts were aimed at wealthy St. Paulites, Boyd found a rottenness and hypocrisy in middle class life, with adultery, drunkenness, and increasing materialism the order of the day.

The city is not always seen as a snare in Minnesota fiction. For some writers it is a possible catalyst for communality. Nothing could contrast more strongly with the work of Flandrau and Boyd than the stories of Meridel LeSueur. "A Hungry Intellectual" poses the disengaged Andrew Hobbs, starved for more than food, against the sympathetic narrator who is devoted to her children and to workers' causes during the 1930's. LeSueur's story evokes the days of radical speakers in Gateway Park in Minneapolis and a hunger march to the Capitol.

The St. Paul seen through the eyes of Nessa McKenna pregnant with her first child in Sheila Alexander's *Walk with a Separate Pride* is not the same city as that seen by a man. On her trip to the clinic at the City Hospital she is warmed by the "benign coarseness" of a tired workingman who gives her his seat on the trolley car. But in the early hours of the morning when she goes alone to the hospital to have her baby it is a different city. "Driving through the loop the buildings looked like black rock crowded over the streets. Without their lights they seemed as afraid of night as humans and their cold walls touched."

And lest Minneapolitans take their metropolis too seriously,

Garrison Keillor has provided an antidote in "WLT: (The Edgar Era)." "It was their sandwiches and their magnificent sandwich palace on Nicollet Avenue, not radio broadcasting, that brought the Elmore brothers, Edgar and Roy, to wealth and prominence in Minneapolis." Keillor's picture of a humble restaurant with a lust for local fame has a hilarious crescendo growing out of Edgar's paranoia.

Ostergothenburg was created by J. F. Powers for his witty and incisive tales of politics within the Catholic Church. A city the size of St. Cloud in central Minnesota, it is the heart of "the biggest little parish in the world." Against the background of boosterism in the church and business life of the community, the author gathers up in his story "Keystone" the problems common to many in old age, but magnified for the man at the center of power when he sees that power slipping away.

During the nineteenth century a number of Indian legends were written down by white men and women visiting or living among tribal people in Minnesota. Henry Schoolcraft, a pioneer in Indian studies and the person most responsible for popularizing Indian legends, is probably best known in Minnesota as the discoverer of the source of the Mississippi. While he was an Indian agent at Sault-Ste.-Marie he married a woman who was part Ojibwa and learned her language. Subsequently, Schoolcraft published a number of volumes on the Indians, including myths and legends. In 1821 William Joseph Snelling joined his father, Colonel Josiah Snelling, at Fort St. Anthony (later Fort Snelling) after spending the winter with some Dakota Indians in their wigwams. He learned their language well enough to serve as interpreter on an expedition into the wilderness, and eventually the stories which he heard were collected and published under the title *Tales of the Northwest*. And Mary Eastman, wife of Captain Seth Eastman, translated stories which she heard from Indian women whom she met at Fort Snelling in the 1840's.

Such translators and transcribers seem to have been sympathetic to the cultures with which they came into contact, but inevitably, in transcribing an oral tradition, problems of authenticity arose. Gerald Vizenor has pointed to a number of these problems, which, of course, still exist today. "Translation, who did the telling and listening, was the telling recorded, or later remembered. . . . Of course, there has been the imposition of the dominant cultural values and world views in tribal stories. . . .

Christian influences in the recording of the tribal stories were sometimes obvious, but revisionism is no less a problem in the most accurate telling. Also, consider the difference in oral and written cultures: in the oral tradition there were no single versions of stories. The content was very often determined by the teller . . . and the tellers were many."

Vizenor is a contemporary writer with a foothold in both white and Indian worlds. Often with deft humor, he portrays the clash between two different cultures. In "The Psychotaxidermist" Colonel Clement Beaulieu, "the old mixed blood fur trader and teller of fine tales," recalls the story of Shaman Newcrows, who had been arrested for defiling the Town and Country golf course in St. Paul, by practicing religious rites there. When the prosecutor addresses him as "New Crows" the shaman insists that his name is "Newcrows—one word, one consciousness, one time in all to live on the earth as a bird and animal."

Ironically, the oldest inhabitants of the state are, in a sense, immigrants within their own land. Vizenor has written of the plight of Indians who move to the urban reservation in his book *Wordarrows: Indians and Whites in the New Fur Trade*, summing up the loneliness and confusion of the contemporary Indian facing urban life. Laurel Hole in the Day and her husband move to Minneapolis to escape the violence of the reservation. But they have really migrated to a foreign country. To support their nine children they find work in a glue cap assembly factory where they are instructed in the indecipherable language of a government manual. Their slumlord is delighted to extract an outrageous rent from them, and their fellow Indians "borrow" their household goods.

The immigrant from Scandinavia or from Central or Eastern Europe in the second half of the nineteenth century and the early twentieth century had fewer handicaps than the Indian, but he too found himself an outsider in a strange world. The first generation wanted to retain as much as possible of the old world while at the same time succeeding in the new, and there was the inevitable clash between generations within families as to how far one should go in casting off one's European heritage. Characteristically, the children of immigrants rejected their parents' "outmoded" foreign manners and now useless language. But the first and most compelling need for all was to earn a living and to acquire at least a working use of English.

In Ole Rölvaag's *The Boat of Longing* Nils Vaag lives in a Minneapolis boarding house, appropriately named "Babel" for the mixture of nationalities gathered under its roof. It is a cacophony of clashing wills where poor people experience the worst of the new world. Set in the early years of this century, it tells of an immigrant from a fishing village in Norway whose only knowledge of America had been based on the fictions of a friend's imagination. Minnesota had been painted as a place "where the most beggarly pauper could snap his fingers right in the face of the richest big-bug and do it with impunity." In America, he was told, saloons are more beautiful than the homes of the wealthy in Norway. Nils, now in America and earning his living by cleaning out saloons along Cedar Avenue, finds they are "revoltingly filthy after a ribald Saturday night." The customers, many of them fellow Norwegians, "scarcely resembled human beings any longer—no, not even animals." Torn between his desire for beauty in his life and an equally strong wish to acquire as much money as possible, Nils succumbs to the life of an itinerant worker, never finding a real home in this anonymous society.

Like Rölvaag, Martha Ostenso is concerned with the loss of deeper values in the midst of material temptations. In her panoramic novel about the Red River Valley, *O River Remember*, Magdali Wing exemplifies the grasping side of the pioneer spirit. Ivar, her husband, is truly attached to the land, but not to the extent of living only for his work. When their son Karsten wants to become a painter, his mother firmly turns him to the law and subsequently tramples on any other attempts her children make to develop artistically. Madgi and her brother, Roald Bratland, are schemers, ruthlessly taking advantage of their neighbors' misfortunes in order to speculate in land.

Two St. Paul writers have given interpretations of the immigrant Jew in Minnesota that differ from each other but are complementary. William Hoffman has written wistful and often humorous stories of life on the West Side of St. Paul from the 1920's to the 1960's. The title character of a series of sketches collected in *Mendel*—whose only piece of real estate is his burial plot—is a composite of the many old world Jews who never attain material comfort, but who have spiritual possessions. In his *Tales of Hoffman* the author has gathered together a miscellany of reminiscences of the West Side as it was before the city virtually eliminated the old neighborhood on the Mississippi River flats.

Norman Katkov's *A Little Sleep, a Little Slumber* dramatizes the

22

tensions within the immigrant community. Lev Simon, who is living on the West Side after entering the country illegally during the 1920's, is preyed upon by a fellow immigrant who threatens to report him. Lev's ambition is to see his sons become full-fledged Americans, yet his early years of running from his persecutors in Russia and Western Europe, and his fear of deportation, lead him to suspect anyone not part of his immediate circle. When he ventures out of the West Side to downtown St. Paul, he knows that he must be careful to keep his hands out of his pockets, even though he is desperately cold. "Thieves kept hands in pockets."

The helplessness of a newcomer with scant knowledge of English is vividly portrayed in Margaret Culkin Banning's story "The Perfect Juror," which deals with the court trial of a Finnish immigrant during the Prohibition era. "He was still, still as those who do not comprehend can be sometimes in a kind of self protection." Banning's concern is with the guilt of the community as a whole in its scofflaw behavior, but the allusions and attitudes underlying the fabric of the trial demonstrate that language differences are more than a barrier of words alone.

Monica Krawczyk's stories of Poles and other Eastern Europeans in Minnesota are vignettes of the lives of working class people during the 1920's and 1930's. Sometimes in desperate straits, often working to create some beauty in an existence that would otherwise be sheer drudgery, many of her protagonists are women, people twice displaced: as immigrants and as wives or daughters who are expected to please others, never themselves. In "Quilts" an overworked housewife stays up late at night, incurring her husband's wrath for neglecting the housework in order to carry on the tradition that "every housewife made something new—a feather tick cover, a linen table cloth"—for the holy day of Corpus Christi. There is an inevitable clash between the old and the new in regard to fundamental customs such as making marital arrangements, and in "The One in My Heart" Anulka resists her well-meaning friends when they send the "proposers" to her, offering a man whom she dislikes. Krawczyk's characters are not especially hostile to America, but they are frequently bewildered by what they find. A tension is often set up between what is allowed within their own peasant culture and the possibilities offered by American life. In "For Dimes and Quarters" Antosia impulsively buys an encyclopedia set from a door-to-door salesman, not realizing the enormous cost. But to appease her hunger for learning, she is willing to work as a cleaning woman in spite of her husband's hostility.

Krawczyk, herself a social worker and teacher in Minneapolis, was not without a sense of humor in her observation of two cultures colliding. In "Tokens" Mrs. Futerko uses the Polish custom of a large wedding to rid herself of a deadening job and to acquire a hard-working wife for her lazy, delinquent son.

In 1944 when he was living in Duluth and working on his novel *Cass Timberlane*, Sinclair Lewis stopped his driver, Ace Lyons, in an area about sixty miles southwest of the city. According to his biographer Mark Schorer, Lewis exclaimed, "There's Grand Republic! Look, isn't it beautiful? See that house there—over the hillside! That's where Cass Timberlane lives! Isn't it beautiful?" What Lyons actually saw were a post office, a store, and a Soo Line boxcar. But out of these unpromising materials Lewis constructed Grand Republic, the setting for *Cass Timberlane*, a city much closer to Duluth in size and social structure than to a small town. The city's name reflects the aspirations leading citizens such as Judge Timberlane have for their community, one that is theoretically free of the petty restrictions of older municipalities. "But he knew that for all his talk at public dinners about Midwestern Democracy, the division between the proprietors and the serfs was as violent in Grand Republic as in London. The truckdriver might call Boone Havock, the contractor, 'Boone', when they met in the Eitelfritz Brauhaus . . . but he would never enter Boone's house or his church, and as for Boone's asylum, the Federal Club, neither the truckdriver nor any Scandinavian or Finn with less than $10,000 income nor any recognizable Jew whatever would be allowed even to gawk through the leaded-glass window (imported)."

Lewis's caustic notations of snobbery and deference are surprising in a state that has seen itself as without the sharp divisions of class and wealth found in the East and the South. But other writers have made similar notes. Margaret Culkin Banning, Wanda Neff, F. Scott Fitzgerald, Grace Flandrau, Mabel Seeley, and James Gray all wrote of a society that was far from egalitarian. Class distinctions seem to have been of particular interest to writers of the 1920's, '30's, and '40's. The waves of immigration had been greatest in the decades before that, but many people still bore the stigma of foreign accents and were employed in jobs so unpleasant that only those desperate for work would take them, whereas people from such areas as New England and New York State had the advantages of a longer American lineage and, often, more money, and were not confronted with the most difficult hurdle of all, that of language. Reading Minnesota literature of the period, one frequently catches allusions to the person with an Eastern background as feeling superior to his fellow Minnesotans. Unquestionably the assimilation of the European immigrant and his family and a general filtering downward of income since the Second World War account for the lack of interest in class differences in Minnesota literature of recent years.

In F. Scott Fitzgerald's story "Winter Dreams," published in 1922, Dexter Green, whose father owns the "second best grocery store in Black Bear," determines to climb over the barrier between himself and the wealthy men for whom he caddies in the resort town. Because his family is able to send him to an Eastern university he acquires "that particular reserve peculiar to his university that set it off from other universities. . . . He knew that to be careless in dress and manner required more confidence than to be careful. But carelessness was for his children. His mother's name had been Krimslich. She was Bohemian of the peasant class and she talked broken English to the end of her days. Her son must keep to the set patterns."

Dexter earns the admiration of these men when he becomes an astute businessman, who owns a string of laundries. But wealth was not always the sole social test. Frequently, more subtle forces were at work. In Mabel Seeley's *Woman of Property* Frieda Schlempke, the daughter of German immigrants, hopes to be absorbed into the magic circle of American life, but in the town of West Haven, a fictional Northfield, social obstacles are everywhere. Descendents of settlers from New England and New York have firmly set themselves apart from those who have recently come from Europe. Indeed, the town considers itself "the New England in the West." The barriers are not always tangible and are seldom legal, but they are nonetheless real. And, ironically, the very institutions that should have been most effective in bringing people together are used to foster discrimination. The public schools boast of welcoming poor and rich alike, but the teachers are impatient with the children of immigrants who speak a clumsy English. Organized religion sets up even more subtle walls, but ones that are apparent to a girl of fourteen. "Between ten-fifteen and ten-thirty, on Sundays, the Best People of West

Haven filtered themselves out from the Norwegians and the late-Mass Catholics, also church-bound at that hour, to move by carriage or on foot down Front Street toward the First Congregational Church. She would no more have thought of entering that chaste white-spired edifice than she would have thought of knocking at the gates of heaven dressed as she was in her ignoble flesh. But across Front Street, under the low-hanging maples, anyone, even a foreigner, could linger and look on." Seeley was writing in the 1940's of the 1880's, at a time when traces of class distinctions lingered.

Fourteen-year-old Frieda learns from her employer the word "manipulate" as her key to success, having observed that her mother's endless round of drudgery is unproductive since she gets no money for it. "Only the poor worked. As was only too well known, the poor had no money. Therefore work did not make money."

Margaret Culkin Banning's novels and short stories often dramatize a society where the chasms between wealth and poverty had been created by circumstances beyond the control of the average man. In *The Iron Will* the city of Twin Ports has been built by big money. "Big money had . . . set its ore-docks gleaming with thousands of lights." Banning's novel revolves around a court case during the 1930's Depression in a northern city modeled after Duluth. The problems of running mines that incur losses during a bad period are exacerbated by the bitterness bred in earlier days when big money had bought up and developed the mines after the adventurous but poor men had discovered the ore. There is a sharp contrast between life in the mining towns—where nearly half of the people are on relief, where tax money has been misspent, and where a long-lasting hostility has built up—and the life of the absentee mine owners who live off the mines but have never set eyes on them.

In *Being Respectable* Grace Flandrau etched delicately acidic portraits of upper middle class life in the 1920's in her fictional equivalent of St. Paul, the city of Columbia. "To Louisa, Columbia was a small town. She knew, more or less well, several hundred people. They lived, generally speaking, within a radius of half a mile or so and were connected with the prominent businesses. Especially the older businesses—banking, railroading, manufacturing, wholesale merchandising being among the perfectly respectable. Not retailing."

But it is not quite so simple to ascertain who is respectable at any given moment, and Louisa Denby spends her days trying to chart the shifting sands of respectability. One's likes and dislikes have nothing to do with it. Besides, as her brother said, "one did not invite the people one liked to one's parties, one invited the people other people liked, the people other people invited; the people most in demand who cared least whether they were invited or not."

Less apparent but just as real are the snobberies of the academic world in Wanda Neff's novel *Lone Voyagers*, published in 1929. The shabby genteel lives of university people at Chippewa University in the city of St. Anthony are seamed with false pride and the keeping up of appearances. Though instructors earn less than good mechanics, their wives feel compelled to entertain constantly, but women who work at demeaning jobs in department stores to eke out faculty incomes run the risk of censure from other university wives. When a professor leaves the closed circle of academia to work in a bank he knows he will no longer see his old associates.

Although childhood experiences have been given fictional form by Minnesota writers with varied backgrounds, one sees universal themes appear: fear of the only partially understood world, a wish to escape parental control combined with a deep desire to be within a family circle, an awakening to sexual desires, the diminishing stature accorded parents and other mentors, and a consciousness of adult hypocrisies.

Gordon Parks describes his adolescence in St. Paul and Minneapolis in the 1920's in his autobiography *A Choice of Weapons*. Parks had been born into a tightly knit family in Kansas, but when he was sixteen his mother died and he was sent to St. Paul to live with a married sister. After a difficult time with her irascible husband, Parks lived on a trolley car for several weeks ("the rent was reasonable and there was always some heat") where he nearly made the wrong choice of weapons. Parks' tale is a moving account of an adolescent threading his way among the treacheries encountered by all young people, intensified in his case by color and poverty.

Charles Macomb Flandrau, brother-in-law of Grace Flandrau, recalls his days at a kindergarten in the 1870's. "Mrs. White's" is a delightful account of "the first of Froebel's infantile observatories" in St. Paul, to which he and his little fellow prisoners were carried in a horsedrawn "White Maria" each morning. Flandrau's keen memories of the unconvincing enthusiasms of a too-patient teacher ("the haggard benevolence of the child-gardener in its most indestructible form") serve as a reminder that "progressive education" antedated our own century.

Indian Boyhood tells of Charles Eastman's mid-nineteenth-century childhood in which all children were rigorously trained to meet any contingency. But it was also a life that, at many points, resembled any boy's world, complete with games, both carefree and dangerous. Remembering a hair-raising ride down a river on an unmanageable log, Eastman says, "I cannot speak for my comrade in distress, but I can say now that I would rather ride on a swift bronco any day than try to stay and steady a short log in a river."

The Depression of the 1930's left its mark on a number of Minnesota writers. In Mary Hedin's story "Places We Lost" we read of its impact on a family where economic losses in themselves were small compared to the emotional costs caused by uncertainty. The investment a woman has in her house and a child in a kitten, and the crisis precipitated by a man's feeling of inadequacy, are beautifully conveyed by Hedin.

For the children of immigrants the normal tensions of family life are heightened in other ways. In Borghild Dahl's *Homecoming* Lyng Skoglund, born in America of Norwegian parents, grows up in a household presided over by a mother who resists the Americanization of her children. "I know what happens when children start going around to these Yankee services. It was good-bye to the Norwegian after Gerd Jacobsen had been with that Baptist crowd on Twenty-third Avenue. And it was the same with Valborg Aanerud as soon as she got a taste of those Congregationalists. Both girls became Yankeefied right away. Now the parents of both girls have had to let them prepare for confirmation in the English language. Imagine repeating the Ten Commandments and the Lord's Prayer in a foreign tongue!" At the same time she is anxious for Lyng to be outwardly successful in American terms—to attend the University and to become a teacher. Passionately desiring to become a part of all aspects of American life, Lyng endures a prickly relationship with her mother throughout her childhood and adolescence.

In his Basil Lee Duke stories F. Scott Fitzgerald recreated his own early years in St. Paul, catching the poignancy of male adolescence. "Basil: He Thinks He's Wonderful" recounts the unreliability of girls and their crushes and Basil's own inability to control his garrulousness. In "Basil: A Night at the Fair" a boy in the early twentieth century discovers the supreme necessity of life, a pair of long trousers, after his relationship with his closest friend has been disrupted by the barrier of "two feet of serge."

I have chosen to include in this anthology a work too often overlooked by readers who consider Fitzgerald merely the chronicler of the jazz age. "Absolution," set in a Red River Valley town in the early years of this century, tells of eleven-year-old Rudolph Miller's enduring profound torments about the fate of his soul after he has entangled himself in a web of lies before taking communion. Fitzgerald captures the atmosphere of a farm service town, where the wheat fields stretch endlessly on all sides.

From reading Herbert Krause's novels, *The Thresher* and *Wind without Rain*, it is evident that growing up on a Minnesota farm in the early twentieth century was a demanding, toughening process. The loneliness of orphaned Johnny Schwartz of *The Thresher* is compounded by the opprobrium of having inherited "bad blood" from an immoral father. In *Wind without Rain* a harsh father's absence gives a temporary freedom to the Vildvogel family. When a farmhand brings his violin into their lives, one of the sons learns to play it, but they know their irascible parent would consider it devil's music. "There was something unreal and ghastly about those days, Franz playing, and the music heady as old dandelion brew pushing into our heads but under the round of work a deep dull pounding like a death call, through thin and wakeful sleep, over and over again . . . Father . . . Father . . . if the door opens . . . if the door opens suddenly."

When, as an adolescent, Krause confessed that he wanted to be a writer his father asked what he could find to write about in their rural world of western Minnesota. Krause thought to himself, "Not much doing among our hills, I admitted to myself. Nothing but cornhuskings, housewarmings, baptisings, church meetin's, *schwat suers*, dehornings of cattle, turkey shoots, beer parties, 'coon shoots, shindandies, and lots of work—common everyday experiences. Nothing like the adventures of Arthur or Ali Baba." Like Krause, other Minnesotans have found a world of material within their own state. The following selections offer the reader their versions of the Minnesota experience.

Emilio DeGrazia

A MINNESOTA STORY

Emilio DeGrazia juggles writing, teaching, and editing in Winona, where he has taught at Winona State University since 1969. His short stories and scholarly articles have appeared in a number of periodicals, and in 1977 DeGrazia was one of the founders of Great River Review, *a literary periodical. Born in Dearborn, Michigan in 1941, he received his B.A. from Albion College in Michigan, and his M.A. and Ph.D. from Ohio State University. That DeGrazia's literary roots have been success-fully transplanted to Minnesota can be seen in "A Minnesota Story," which was first published in* Red Cedar Review.

H E HAD NEVER felt such strength before. He held the thick rope tightly in his fists and pulled it taut until his hands slid apart over the rough hemp. It would hold. It would snap a neck as sharply as dead branches broke from the big birches he used to climb as a boy. And the beams would hold. He had cut them from walnut timber dropped with his own axe. They were harder than the steel cable he once had snapped with that same axe.

He also had built the barn with his own hands. "If you build a barn," he told his neighbors, "you've got to do it right. It's got to last." So he didn't settle for pine from the lumber yard. Pine was not heavy enough, and a thumbnail could dig holes in it. When the neighbors told him he was wasting his time and the wood cutting the walnut for the barn, he laughed and said he just had to clear more land. As the barn went up year by year he fell behind, but one day they saw him nailing down the last roof boards. Though the extra coats cost him an extra month's work, he painted it a white as bright as snow on a cold sunny day. He even painted the boards inside. When he was done it was the biggest barn around, and more beautiful than the church in town.

It was this barn he had come to after turning his back on the radar tower near Jason's Mill and walking across the hayfield toward his own house, its boards now wrinkled and greyed by many winters. When was it he decided not to paint the barn or house again? The forties or fifties? And was it because he had no cash or because of some trouble over the price of paint? It was the price of paint, he recalled, the grey house shining again as a memory of the clean white one he had carried his bride into over thirty years ago. It *had* to be the price of paint—the paint made somewhere in Ohio that kept doubling in price until one day, he couldn't remember the year, he told Clarence in the hardware store he wouldn't buy it again because he was waging a boycott to drive the company out of business.

He couldn't remember when he began this boycott because the years passed like a blur under the wheels of his truck. When he was a boy he used to sit on the back of his father's big red hay wagon watching the sunset as the horse pulled it in from the fields. Time in those days passed as slowly as the sun set, his past lengthening out behind him like a shadow. In those days he had a reputation for being fast, whether at haying, running bases, or eating. His father kept telling him to slow down. "Life is short and I'm too old to be on the go," he liked to say, "so I'll go slow." After the family bought its first pickup truck the boy liked to sit in the back, his feet dangling near the road that rushed out from beneath the wheels and then lengthened out until everything in view, like his father walking away from the house in a distant field, stood still on the horizon.

In a sense everything had stood still. Though everyone, even he, had left the old farm, and though the barn and house no longer shined, the place still smelled like the farm he had grown up on as a boy. The once neat rows of corn and grain had been taken over by grass that tossed like long hair in the wind, but he heard the same faint hum of life in the air. If he had the chance to do it over, he no longer would plow the earth; he would send milk cows into the fields once planted in corn and wheat, and each evening he would lead them back to the barn close to the house. We all could have gotten on well enough that way, he thought.

No, nothing here had changed and nothing was likely to

change as long as it remained untouched. Leaving the farm at the age of sixty-two was not the only thing he could do, but it was the smartest. While he remained alive he at least could guard it like a jealous father would his virgin daughter. What would come of it when he was gone he did not know, for its fate lay sealed not in his will, the piece of paper in his shirt pocket containing words scrawled in his own illegible hand, but in the whims of his only son, who had left the farm for college and never returned.

"You know I don't want you to be a radical just for my sake," he told his son the night before he left for college. "I want you to learn what you have to learn, and I know you may never come back." The words forced themselves past the truth, a protest against the other fathers who insisted that their sons not leave, or that they return to take up where they, the tired fathers, had left off. So he let his son go and he did not return, not even to visit the old man on his seventy-third birthday.

Because the roads were bad, the old man told himself, even before the phone call came explaining that the roads were bad. Almost as hot as the weather during the July of '33, when he hitch-hiked and half-walked the hundred miles to Minneapolis to march with the striking truckers who had come from five states to demand a fair day's wages for a fair day's work, and who, after Governor Olson sided with the strikers against the mob organized by the bosses, danced in the streets.

Nothing, not even his wedding the year before, matched that celebration, and only once since the strike had he felt such anger and joy. When after the strike a trucker returning to Iowa dropped him off on a gravel road seven miles from his farm, he waved at the truck until it disappeared over a rise on the highway. He waved not a farewell but tribute to the truckers, the strangers who like new lovers had come together and marched with hearts and arms locked together. As he turned off the main highway to walk the seven miles home, he did not feel the abandonment until his farmhouse came into view, its silhouette black, except for one small light in the back bedroom, against a grey sky sinking into night. His wife did not come down to greet him that evening when he called up to her from the door, and when he reached the bedroom she only half-rose from her pillow to see him. "Are you all right?" she asked without looking at him. "Yes, but I'm tired," he said.

He wanted to say more—wanted her to ask. He had rehearsed

it all as he and the trucker from Iowa sat in silence watching the cornfields drift past. He would not tell her he had walked almost fifty of the hundred miles to the capital before a farmer stopped and picked him up, or that he had not slept in two nights. He wanted to tell her how the men, many with their wives, found each other, how they developed one mind and heart, and how at the end of the second day they were cheered by the soldiers who turned to face not them but the jeering faces along the streets. As he stood before her unbuttoning the only shirt he had worn those three days, the only white shirt he owned, he wanted to tell her what lessons he had learned and what new hope had surged into his life. But as she reached up to turn off the small bedlight, he saw not only weariness on her face but a resentment heavier than that he had left behind in the streets.

When he made his appearance in town the next afternoon to pick up a newspaper, the people turned into doorways or crossed the street to avoid him. The faces were crossed and wary, and later he saw their eyes. They think I betrayed them, he thought; they think that because the truckers got more, the farmers got less. But I know the farmers work harder. I didn't want to say the truckers won. I wanted to tell them what it felt like to have soldiers and workers cheering each other. I wanted to tell them that had never happened here before. I wanted them to know we had started something for all of us.

They never joined him, though he never stopped trying to explain. In the years following the strike he found it hard to lose himself in his chores and began spending more time in town, at first in the cafe and later in its bars. As he entered these places he looked for anyone willing to listen. Even though some admitted he was full of ideas and most couldn't get angry at him, they turned away when he came near, or stopped listening when he caught them at coffee. They let him talk, and in time they admitted he stood up for his beliefs. Besides, he was a good farmer, even though he wasted his time talking and in the city. He had a way with crops, animals, and machines, and if they were sure they could get away in a reasonable time, some of them liked to listen to him talk about farming and now and then even stopped by his place to borrow a tool or his old Fordson, which he kept shined and tuned and which served him until he no longer could get parts.

They repaid him for their talking behind his back. When he ran for the town council they didn't put anyone up against him, and later when he ran for county commissioner they secretly voted for him. He did a good job, they agreed, and he could have kept the job, though a few of them never forgave him for the things he said against religion. He resigned one day in the middle of his second term. "Because you don't really want change, you want a babysitter," he told them. "And besides, I've got better ways to spend my life." After he resigned he began taking trips to Minneapolis during the winter months. "To go to meetings," he told them when they asked. "Do you think things just run themselves? Do you think the world will change without planning? Do you think you can ignore tactics?"

One day word came back from the city with a grain buyer. "They have meetings up there," the buyer told a group of farmers. "They're radicals." For a time everyone watched him carefully, more out of curiosity than fear. Now and then someone called him a communist, and then they backed off. One day he found an effigy of himself hanging from an apple tree behind the cafe, but he just kept on talking. When the things he said were quoted in the newspapers of bigger towns, almost everyone was just a little proud of him.

He was a big grey man. Even before he was married his black hair shined with silver strands, and by the time he was forty it all had turned. He had spent one year at the university before his father, ill and tired, called him back home to farm. Someone said the one year away from home ruined him because he came back full of complaints about religion, the government and the town itself. He carried a book everywhere, and claimed there were no books worth reading in the schoolhouse or county library. He tried to get other people to read his books, but they just shrugged him off. As he grew older he didn't shrink as old men do. He seemed to grow taller and stronger as his hair grew wilder and whiter. Some of the folk thought he could have been a politician if he toned himself down, but when he came back from one of his meetings in the city and ran for state senate right after the Second World War, they didn't vote for him. He was bitter afterward and didn't appear in town for six months, his wife still driving the old pickup in to buy groceries and go to church, as she always did, alone. But one day he walked into the cafe wearing a white shirt and old black suitcoat his father used to wear, and under his arm was a big black book. Someone said he looked like a preacher, and they all laughed.

The old black suitcoat and white shirt became his only suit of clothes, memorials of the three days in 1933 during which he discovered his calling. "If you think I'm a preacher, why don't you listen to my word?" he asked the men in the cafe. "You'd rather give your souls and money to those monkeys dressed in black who pray to their white God every time you have some fun. And when the price of wheat goes down, what do they tell you? Do they let you pray for the price of wheat to go up? Or do they tell you to count your blessings while they pray for you? Your churches are your biggest bosses, and they're so smart they make you feel guilty when I tell you the truth about them."

"That's right," they sometimes said, "that's *damn* right." But later they told each other they only said it to get rid of him. Then they avoided him until his words, and theirs, passed beyond meanings and memories. Before he retired to a room and kitchen above the hardware store in town—to write, he claimed, a book and articles for magazines in Chicago and New York—his moods were like his coming and going from town. Sometimes he spent afternoons denouncing the government, waiting on Sundays for churchgoers to stop in the cafe so he could divine the import of the sermons. Then, as if wearied by his own talk, he did not appear for a week, disappearing into his room above the hardware store until a new headline brought him out again. He'll never burn out, the townspeople told each other, even while they wondered how he could keep up his farm and his talk at the same time.

One winter before he turned seventy he almost died. People didn't notice he hadn't been in the cafe for almost three weeks; they didn't notice, that is, until they saw him alone in a corner booth hunched over a bowl of hot chicken soup and a skinny book. "Poems," he answered when someone asked him what he was reading, and that word kept them away. When that evening they saw him in his corner again drinking soup instead of coffee, someone noticed that he looked pale. The waitress also noticed that the next morning an old woman carrying something covered in white linen went upstairs to his room. That afternoon a doctor arrived from another town and followed the old woman upstairs; they waited four hours for the doctor to come down again and tried to read the tidings on his face. Within minutes the old woman—she had moved to town from a farm after her husband died, and she had been seen many times listening to him in the park the summer before—came down the stairs, made her way through the snow across the street, and entered the cafe. "He's dying," she announced to the faces. "He didn't want me to say anything, but I thought you should know." She stared at them in her own angry silence before someone finally spoke. "Is there anything we can do, Missus?" "You can keep away from him until he dies—that's what you can do. He's angry about dying and he's too honest not to be afraid. He doesn't want you to see him being afraid."

When she closed the door of the cafe that afternoon they all felt as if she had slammed his coffin lid in their faces. They watched her come and go each day, and they waited a week and then two but no word came except more rumors about a radar tower that had fallen. Then in the low hum of the cafe broken only by the nasal wail of a sad song coming from the pink juke box in the corner, they stopped watching for him and almost forgot that his voice once had been the strongest in the room.

One day that winter the door of the cafe opened and a noise like a cheer went up. Though still pale, he looked like a shaggy Moses carved out of white stone. "My god, he's got a beard now too," someone said.

"It's not a sign of old age," the old man shouted back. "It's wisdom you see in these white hairs."

They laughed. "Well, where have you been, old man?"

"You think that just because a body isn't running it's standing still. The same way you think that just because you don't like politicians they'll just go away. No wonder we've got a police state coming. No wonder we don't pull together according to how much we weigh. You think pulling together means being led by the nose. Where have I been? Up in my room working on tactics, where else? I told you what I do up there—I've been writing my book, and right after someone buys me a cup I'll go start the last chapter."

He would not go gentle into his good night. Each night he sat in the cafe waiting for a farmer to come in, and when one settled into a booth the old man advanced on him with a copy of the evening newspaper. "The war," he shouted, "the war isn't over yet. And we just sit here and write our congressmen about the price of milk." He called it the dirty yellow war. That war, on his mind ten years, stirred him to raise his voice with the men who had listened to him for thirty. More than once the owner of the cafe told him to go home, and when he did not go home he went to a bar down the street, concluding the night with a shot of whiskey from his own flask swallowed like a poison to steel him against the grey illness that once had brought him down.

Hostility toward him reached its peak at the same time the dirty yellow war reached its climax. His talk about the war was bad for business and there was talk of barring him from the cafe. The town also was beginning to have second thoughts about what had happened at Jason's Mill, the farm next to his own. When the townspeople had heard of how the radar tower had been chopped down with an axe, they wanted to point the finger at him even though they had seen him almost too weak to walk just two days before the tower fell. No one accused him directly when the federal agents arrived in grey cars, but many told the agents to talk to him. When the agents asked the townspeople whether he had been ill the night the tower came down, they had to say yes, because they had seen the old lady come and go from his place with the doctor. Yet they all knew he somehow was behind it. He had given speeches against the tower in the cafe, and when the big machines rolled up to Jason's Mill to begin work on it they found his old truck parked across the gravel road blocking the way. The younger Jason had forced him off the land at gunpoint and had bought dogs to keep the old man away. "He said I had no right to the property if I was going to let them build on it," the younger Jason told a farmer. "He said *he* had as much a right to my property as I did. He said property is theft. That's when I got the dogs."

"Sellout," the old man told a farmer in the cafe. "The Jason boy is selling the land out from under us so they can grow towers of steel where we once grew corn. No memory. If I asked him whose side the army was on in the strike of '33, he'd think I was talking football, and if I said Wobbly to him he'd think I was talking about weak legs. But I guess he's only like the most of us. First we let them take our boys like lambs to kill in a dirty yellow war, and now they take our land. Someday they'll turn this all into a war zone. They're thinking big these days."

The farmer the old man said these things to claimed there was sadness, not anger, in his voice. He told the agents that he, for one, didn't think the old man did the axe-job on the tower. None of the fuss seemed to matter very much after a while. A new tower was up within a year even though again they found the old man's truck blocking the road, and the agents didn't take the old man away, so, everyone concluded, he was either a lot smarter than they thought or less guilty. So as the dirty yellow war wound down and as the tower took a permanent place in the sky looking down on their lives, they came back to him, this time with a little more respect.

Many years before this had taken place there had been other stories about him—stories spun not from what he did but from what he said. The untold story that everyone wanted to hear was his wife's: the story of the isolated woman who never came to town with him except on business and who on Sundays came to church alone and then waited in the cafe without comment and without a smile for him to finish his commentary on the sermon he had refused to hear and ignore. There was much talk that his wife was unhappy with him, that while he kept up the talk in town she kept up the farm. But like a good wife, she would not permit bad talk about her man. Whenever she detected bad thoughts forming in the faces of the wives of her husband's enemies, she dissolved them with a stare harder than her husband's convictions. Except in her last year, she too was tall, hard and grey, and when she walked men stepped aside in deference not to her burden but to her strength. Her strength began dissolving right after the World War. Unlike other mothers in the town she had not given her son to the War, but he had gone off to college and not returned to the farm. Her husband spent more time in town during these years, and someone said she someday would leave him. She died without warning in the spring of 1949, having failed as fast as the winter turns to spring. With her the people of the town buried her story. When they meandered home with their accusing thoughts, they left her husband standing alone stone-faced at her gravesite.

He was alone on the farm fifteen years after that except for his visits to town. Because he never had a hired hand, and because the farm showed no signs of decline except the fading white paint on the house and barn, the town stopped accusing him of working his wife to death. One day he announced that he was finished with farming, that all he needed was a room in town and fifty dollars a month for the rest of his life. "When I sell my cows and my new tractor I'll be a rich man," he said. "We all make a religion of work. There's some things I want to do before I leave the scene."

So he moved to town, taking a brass bed, an old Victrola, a

library table and an old rocker in his pickup to the room above the hardware store. Except for the old lady and doctor who visited when he was ill, no one, not even his son, entered this room. He had no mysteries to hide in it, but people remained shy of the room as if it were the forbidden interior of a mind not yet spoken; they told each other he wanted to be alone with his thoughts. They knew his son came to visit him at the farm now and then because he told them so. "He's tired of counting someone else's money, and tired of all that traffic," the old man said with smiling eyes. Then on the appointed day he started the old pickup and drove to the farm, the place he still called home, and stayed the day or two until his son drove back north to the city.

One day last year the son parked his Buick outside the old man's room in town, and the people knew something was wrong. Keeping an eye on the hardware store, they went about their business. They did not have to wait long to find out, for everyone could hear the old man shouting, and within ten minutes father and son had brought their quarrel to the street. "Over my dead body," the old man yelled as the son opened the door to his car. "I'll give it away before I see it sold. A hundred years from now my ghost is going to live on that land, even if you won't." Whatever else he said was lost in the roar of the engine as the Buick sped away. Many people turned to watch it disappear over the hill outside town and they knew it never would be back.

"I'll be goddamned," the old man said to a farmer that day, "if they taught him anything at college but how to count other people's money."

* * *

The words he had spoken to his son had been easy to say that day. It was big talk, loud talk, and he knew silence would have said more. Now he had to be sure: he had to go back to the farm to take a final look—to see the land one last time and to stand on it in order to feel whether it was worth the loss of a son. The son could easily be brought back; he was sure of that. A letter, an apology, a hint about a new will, and the son, still full of duty, would return. He knew that he had raised a good son, though the child had left him before he had a chance to make him into a man; and he knew that the son, out of respect, would wait until he died to sell the land.

So in the middle of the afternoon on an October day he climbed into his pickup to return to the farm for one last look. The old truck, rusty on all sides, sputtered haltingly like an old man discharging phlegm. The mailman, who usually noticed little, saw the pickup on the edge of town, and he waved as he did to anyone passing him. Within a minute the town was small in the rear-view mirror, only the grey grain elevator visible on the landscape, and the road behind him disappearing into fields of drying corn. Framed in thick glass, a world of wild flowers rushed by like a golden blur, while an oak in the middle of a cornfield stood in solid silence before drifting out of view. Beyond the oak the hills on the horizon seemed to flow forward like a green glacier returning from the sea.

"Maybe I should have left long ago," he told himself. "Maybe I should have sold the land right after she died and gone to the city. There at least I could have lived with a few of my own kind." His thoughts failed as the pickup slowed to a walk behind a haywagon pulled by a tractor, which straddled the road and shoulder for a quarter mile before turning down a gravel road. As the big wagon turned off, the big grey radar tower became visible on the horizon, as did two human figures standing at the side of the road. The pickup came to a stop, and before saying a word two boys in their late teens threw their bundles in the back of the truck and climbed aboard.

"Where you headed?" the old man asked.

"The city." The one who spoke had hair to his shoulders. "Don't suppose you're goin' that far, are you?" The boy grinned broadly, showing a row of white perfect teeth.

"No sir. I'm just going home—a farm ten miles up the road."

"Hey, old man. You should take us all the way. We ain't gonna get no ride from no hick town like this." This one, dressed in blue jeans and a flannel shirt, did not smile.

"Where you men from?"

"New Pine," the longhaired one said.

"No school these days?"

"We ain't got nothing more to do with *that*," the other said.

"Then you work?"

"Then we're *bored*, old man." The boy with the long hair widened his smile as he said the word.

"Then you're going to Minneapolis?"

"Right, man. The Jefferson Airplane is coming tomorrow night."

The old man's face winced in perplexity. "The Airplane, man," the boy in flannel went on, "they ain't as good as the Association, but they're all we can get in these parts."

"He don't know what you're talking about."

"Hey man, a group. The Airplane's a group."

"A group?"

"A rock group, man. Where you been? You know—sha-boom, sha-boom. You remember now?" They both laughed, and the old man forced a grin, though he didn't remember. "You never listen to rock, old man? Ever hear the Airplane? It's good for your soul, man."

He thought of the old Victrola he had brought with him to the town. "No, I prefer not to," he said. "But I once heard the orchestra play Beethoven. It was many years ago, but that was good for my soul."

"Where did you hear it, old man? In the park in town?" The boy laughed.

"I bet he ain't never been to Minneapolis," the boy in flannel said. "I talked to one old farmer who told me he ain't never been to Minneapolis. That's no lie."

"Yes, I've been to Minneapolis many times," he said, "and once when I was young like you I hitch-hiked up along this road like you." He had begun the story he knew could go on like the road to the city.

"Did you hear blues? They had blues in your day, didn't they, old man?" the longhaired one asked.

"No," he replied, "I went to a strike."

"A *what*?"

"A strike. A protest."

"You mean a demonstration."

"Yes, a demonstration."

"Never had one in our school."

"Why not?"

"I don't know."

"And besides," the boy in flannel said, "the teachers are so dumb they'd call out the National Guard."

"Doesn't that make you angry?"

"It don't do nothing, man."

"You don't like politics?"

"They're all corrupt. As long as they don't bother me. Live and let live—that's what I say." The longhaired boy relaxed in his seat, well-satisfied.

"We don't belong to no party," the boy in flannel said.

"And you didn't like school?" the old man asked.

"Booored. Eight hours a day, five days a week."

"What do you think causes that?" He lifted his foot from the gas pedal slightly.

"These hick towns. There ain't nothing happening here. There ain't no one more interesting than us—and that's because we go the city every chance we get—and there ain't nothing louder than the sound of growing corn."

"You left out my pig," the one with the smile said. "My pig Sally's more interesting than you, and when she's in heat she makes more noise than a county full of growing corn."

"You can stick your pig," the other said, "and someday I'll eat her."

"She'd be better than that fat one you're screwing now." The two of them laughed again, but he didn't hear the laugh, just as he didn't hear the pickup strain under the weight of his foot as it pressed the gas pedal to the floor; and as the truck veered onto the shoulder of the road, he didn't see the ditch until the long-haired boy grabbed his arm. In the next moment the three of them were sitting in silence, looking up at the road from the ditch, all of them too stunned to tremble.

He felt the fear first when he stood next to the truck, his legs suddenly elastic and weak. "You all right, old man? You look pale as a ghost."

"I'm just a little wobbly, but I'm all right." He smiled not at them but at his private joke. "I'd hate like hell to go this way, especially at my age."

"You want me to drive now, old man? You want to let me drive you home?"

"No, I prefer not to." He re-entered the truck and started it. After saying some things to each other outside the truck the two boys got in.

"You slow down now and stay on the road."

"Yeh, man, I ain't got but one life to live."

"You see, old man, my buddy here is scared. He had an older brother killed in a car accident last year. It was a tragedy."

He drove on two miles before anyone spoke again. Then, as if from nowhere, the words came. "It was no tragedy," the old man said. "It may have been sad or too bad, but it was not tragic."

The words were spoken quietly, addressed not to the boys or to himself or even to the air rushing past the window. The boys

42

looked at each other, shrugged. A few minutes later the old man came to a crossroad and the boys climbed out. As the old man drove off he looked into the rearview mirror to see if the boys were waving to him. The boys were facing the road down which they had come and soon disappeared into dots behind him.

He parked the truck in the middle of the gravel drive leading to his farmhouse. Once outside the truck he stood in the grass near the house breathing in the fragrant air and surveying the landscape as if trying to recall the lifetimes that had passed here, and, like the Norway pines surrounding the house, to stand still in it for a moment. To the right he saw his two hundred acres bathed in the soft colors of a setting autumn sun, the yellow grass flowing over the fields like water on a wide river. To his left a quarter of a mile the grey radar station, its legs lost behind a hill and its head slowly scanning the horizon, stood like a steel giant only a hundred yards from the old stones that once had been Jason's Mill. He saw near there the walnut grove where he had dropped the logs for his barnbeams. A fifty year-old shame returned as he recalled the lie he had told his neighbors. "I told them I was cutting the logs to clear that area," he said to himself, "but we all knew I just wanted to have the best barn in these parts." He looked at the barn; even with its weathered boards it looked solid and strong, no sag visible anywhere in the roof. "And it still is the best barn in these parts. They said I'd never finish the thing, but they thought I was too weak to finish another job too."

He began walking across the field toward Jason's Mill and the tower of steel. Halfway to the tower he stumbled across an old hickory fencepost half-lost in the grass. He picked it up, beat the air with it once, then locking it in his fist carried it like a club. When he reached Jason's wire fence he used the post to hack his way through it, and his heart pounded with fury as the tower inched higher and higher into the sky with each step he took closer to it. Then as he came to the top of a rise the whole tower came into view, its steel legs wide on the ground and its superstructure supported by thick cables emanating in all directions toward concrete cubes planted in the field. The old man paused a moment at the summit of the rise, his form outlined in black against the sun setting behind him; then he began walking closer to the tower until he came to the fence surrounding it. At fifteen feet intervals signs were posted on the fence: DANGER KEEP OUT. U.S. GOVERNMENT PROPERTY.

Three years ago, he thought, they didn't have a fence. You could just walk right up to it like it was a big brother who lived next door, and though you couldn't shake hands you could talk to it. Now you can't get near enough to reach one of the wires, and if I touch the fence it'll take my picture. I suppose they're watching me already—suppose they have been for twenty years now. Me—who couldn't keep my wife happy, and didn't have the heart to keep my son on the farm until he was too old to want to leave. And now what? Should I attack it as if it were a windmill? Throw a stone at it? Try talking to it from over here. Write a letter to my congressman? Go home and pretend to forget it when I know damn well it's minding my business and everyone else's too?

He lifted the cedar post over his head with two hands and brought it crashing down against the fence. In that moment a memory flashed through him, blinding him to everything but the few minutes he had spent assaulting a tower like this one three years earlier. He felt the old strength return, the wooden post crashing against the fence feeling as light to him as the axe that with a dozen blows cut the inch-thick cables holding up the tower. Each time he struck the fence he saw again the sparks the axe let off, and he heard the sharp snap the cables made as they burst free into the air. And he remembered that before he felt his hands stung numb from the crash of steel on steel, he saw the superstructure begin to totter like a drunken man, lose its balance against a sky full of stars, and fall. He was surprised that there was no explosion when it hit the ground; the grass muffled the fall and everything went suddenly silent as if the earth were helping him keep his secret. When it was finished he was awed by the ease by which the tower had been brought to its knees, and he rubbed his hands to get some feeling back. Then, careless even of the tracks he left behind, he threw the axe over his shoulder and walked back to his truck.

It was easy then. Even the agents the government sent out were city slickers who didn't bother looking for tracks because they didn't want to get their clothes dirty. But now it was different. The fence around the new tower had a few dents in it, but it had not given and no doubt already had sent its electric warnings. They would come for him this time. The old man took one last look at the tower, threw his post at the foot of the fence, then turned his back to it and began walking home.

By the time he reached the old farmhouse the crickets were

singing in full chorus and the sun had sunk beneath the horizon. He stood a moment looking at a broken window in the old house; a chill passed through him as he thought of the coming winter. I'll have to get back to fix that before the snow starts flying, he thought as he turned and began walking toward the barn. As he walked a vague fear that he had lost something from one of his pockets surged through him, and when his hand found the piece of paper in the pocket of his white shirt the notion struck him for the first time. "It's maybe the only thing left for me to do," he said half-aloud. "What else can I do to make them take it seriously? There's nothing waiting for us but old age and accidents—not tragedy or even political murder. So we'll have to appeal to their pity. Yes, we'll make ourselves pathetic. If no one will crucify us, we'll have to hang ourselves."

He paused before he walked on, his motionlessness as frozen as the notion that had overtaken him like a decision. He looked at the old haywagon still standing outside the barn door like a big wheelbarrow, the oak from which there once hung a swing made of an old tire, and the house itself, once bordered on all sides by two rows of flowers his wife spent hours stooping over. More than the place he would miss his memories of the place, the place he had forsaken for a barren room in town and the people who listened but never heard. A bird flitting overhead broke his reverie, and without thinking he began walking not to the barn but back to the truck.

"No," he told himself before he had taken ten steps. "I can't go back there. They'll listen to me less and less until I make a fool of myself."

He turned and walked toward the barn again, and in a minute stood beneath its thick beams like a child lost in the shadows of a cathedral. He found the rope precisely where he had left it years before, and after checking it for its strength, threw it over the walnut beam in a corner near a white stool that he and his father once had used for milking cows. He was pleased to find in his coat pocket the pen he always carried. He bent down on one knee to write two words on the other side of the will he took from his shirt pocket. "It's hopeless," he wrote in a clear hand. As he folded the paper and returned it to his pocket he saw a frown form on the faceless head of the radar tower. Then before it could turn from him he placed the white stool under the rope, and, testing the balance of the stool, with steady legs stepped onto it.

Paul Gruchow

THIS PRAIRIE, THIS TERRIBLE SPACE

Paul Gruchow was raised on a farm near Montevideo, Minnesota. His formal education began in a one-room country schoolhouse (he and his twin sister made up an entire grade) and ended at the University of Minnesota, where he studied humanities and edited the Minnesota Daily. *His informal education took place at the knees of his father, who knew the name and place of every living thing on the prairie. After stints as a political aide, a radio news director, and a magazine editor in big cities, he retired in 1976 to the country. He lives at Adrian, Minnesota and is managing editor and co-owner of the* Worthington Daily Globe.

A LTHOUGH YOU CAN'T SEE IT on any map, southwestern Minnesota is an island. All rural communities are insular in one sense: we Americans have been boosters for so long that we have by now accepted it as an article of faith that the bigger a thing is, the better, the prettier, the more sophisticated it will be. Everybody wants a richer uncle and a taller apple tree. There aren't any richer uncles or taller apple trees here; we fail the faith.

There *is* a magnificent outcropping of Sioux quartzite here near the city of Luverne. Along the line of the fault which gave it rise lies a high red cliff. Even after years of coming upon it, the first glimpse of it startles, like a pheasant bursting from the slough grass. It is uncharacteristic of the prairie to shift course so abruptly.

Most natives and all visitors will tell you that southwestern Minnesota is as flat as a pancake. But there are greater extremes of terrain here than anywhere else in Minnesota. Here is some of the state's highest ground, along Buffalo Ridge, the backbone of the *coteau*; and here is some of the state's lowest ground, along the

From "Pieces of the Prairie," *Minnesota Monthly*, August 1977, and "The Prairie Is Like a Daydream," *Minnesota Monthly*, March 1978. © Minnesota Public Radio, Inc., 1977 and 1978 respectively. Reprinted by permission of Minnesota Public Radio, Inc.

Minnesota River, in the crests and crevices of which the white men at last won in battle dominion over the land and the Sioux. Only your legs could tell you the extent of the long climb from Redwood Falls to Pipestone.

We are at a dividing point in the continent. Some of our waters flow to the Red River of the North, some west to the Missouri, some east to the Mississippi. The ridge which divides the eastern watershed from the western runs within a few miles of Worthington. If you hadn't been forewarned, you couldn't see it from the cabin of your painted van. But if you approach the continental divide on foot, it is as obvious as the stripe on the highway.

The prairie can't be appreciated anymore. It is too subtle, too vast, too intimate. It isn't accessible by automobile. You've got to get down on your knees to see some of its best features, and even in churches people don't get down on their knees anymore.

Of course it has always been difficult to appreciate the prairies. Charles Dickens went out from St. Louis in 1842 to get a look. He and his companions brought along a picnic lunch, which consisted of roast fowls, buffalo's tongue, ham, bread, cheese, butter, biscuits, champagne, sherry, and lemons and sugar for punch. The meal was delicious, Dickens reported, but the prairie itself was something of a disappointment: "There it lay, a tranquil sea or lake without water, if such a simile be admissable, with the day going down upon it: a few birds wheeling here and there: and solitude and silence reigning paramount around. But the grass was not yet high; there were bare black patches on the ground; and the few wild flowers that the eye could see were poor and scanty. Great as the picture was, its very flatness and extent, which left nothing to the imagination, tamed it down and cramped its interest . . . It is not a scene to be forgotten, but it is scarcely one, I think (at all events, as I saw it), to remember with much pleasure, or to covet the looking-on again, in after life."

James Fenimore Cooper described the scene this way: "From the summits of the swells, the eye (All those detached eyes in Victorian literature!) became fatigued with the sameness and the chilling dreariness of the landscape. The earth was not unlike the ocean when its restless waters are heaving heavily after the agitation and fury of the tempest have begun to lessen. There was the same waving and regular surface, the same absence of foreign objects, and the same boundless extent to the view."

Even Walt Whitman, who loved everything best of all, including in one perfervid passage the prairie, concluded that a few trees would be an improvement on an otherwise quite wonderful thing. "The matter of the cultivation and spread of forests may well be pressed upon thinkers who look to the coming generations of the prairie states," he wrote hopefully in 1882.

Not long ago I drove from my home on the southern border of Minnesota to Gimli, a village on the southern tip of Lake Winnipeg in Manitoba. The drive led me from the heart of the old tall grass prairie to its northern edge. Beyond Gimli the boreal forests of the subarctic shield take hold. Altogether, the journey carried me more than 600 miles northwards, every mile of the distance a deeper excursion into the dimensions of flatness.

I cheated. The route I chose was through the eastern Dakotas, and so it was in the late afternoon, when the light is at its most dramatic, that I approached Sisseton, South Dakota. The Prairie Coteau runs that way. It doesn't look like much on a topographical map of the United States. A thin and rather random scratch of brown on a tan plate. But there aren't any obstructions to the view, no foothills, no forests, no man-made monuments, this being country in which acquiring a mobile home is stepping up in the world. The *coteau* presents itself unadorned and therefore to its greatest advantage. For a time you are not aware that you are approaching it. Then it seems to surround you on all sides; you have the sensation of driving in a gigantic dish and not knowing how you'll ever make it up to the rim and out. Then you are atop the *coteau*, and you can see so far across the prairie that the brown earth looks blue at the edge of the horizon. The distance down from Sisseton to Fargo, North Dakota is so great that your ears pop along the way.

I have been up to mountaintops and down from them. I know that going to the *coteau* is going to the mountaintop, and I know that coming down from the *coteau* is coming down from the mountaintop. I cannot explain why this landscape seems to us so flat.

It is flat, I suppose, as the deserts are flat, as the oceans are flat, as the polar icecaps are flat. It is flat because of the immensity of its distances. The tall grass prairie alone once covered 250 million square miles. It is flat as a grain of sand is flat to a person who owns no microscope. We own no microscopes.

What seems flat seems empty. When we are faced with emptiness, we turn inward. "One might say," the French philosopher

Gaston Bachelard wrote for this reason, "that immensity is a philosophical category of daydream."

The prairie is like a daydream. It is one of the few plainly visible things which you can't photograph. No camera lens can take in a big enough piece of it. The prairie landscape embraces the whole of the sky. The sensation of its image is globular, but without the distortion that you get in a wide-angle lens. Any undistorted image is too flat to represent the impression of immersion, which is central to the experience of being on the prairie. It is a kind of baptism.

The moon is the closest of the celestial objects; it makes the largest image; it affords the best light for prolonged examination; it is visible in the greatest detail. But no amount of walking will get you any closer to it, and you can't reach out and touch it. The prairie, in this respect, resembles the moon. The essential feature of the prairie is its horizon, which you can neither walk to nor touch. It is like the horizon of the sea.

We are helpless as babies about this: whatever we can see and do not understand and must acknowledge, we make over in our own image. The moon, the sea, the prairie all present insurmountable barriers of distance. We cross them on the craft of egocentricity. The moon becomes the marker of time and the dwelling place of desire. The sea becomes the mirror, the bosom. The prairie becomes the breadbasket.

Newcomers to the prairie are at first disconcerted by its nakedness. Later, they will wish it weren't so private.

To live on the prairie is to daydream. It is the only conceivable response to such immensity. It is when we are smallest that our daydreams come quickest.

I drove north across the prairie daydreaming. I am looking at my notebook, and I notice a curious thing. When I get to Winnipeg, my notes stop.

Downtown Winnipeg is an impressive place. Swirls of unmanageable traffic. Swarms of pedestrians. Towering masses of glass and steel. If you don't scurry about you make a nuisance of yourself and invite contempt as a person obviously without gainful employment.

I stayed in a big downtown hotel. The second morning I was in Winnipeg, I was intimidated by the rush of traffic into making a wrong turn, and before I realized what I had done I was out of the city. My feeling about being lost has always been that you might as well enjoy it, so I turned off onto a road that promised to lead through the countryside.

By and by, I happened upon Lower Fort Gary, which was once a provisioning outpost of the Hudson Bay Company and is now a kind of Fort Snelling, a restored historical site in which costumed students enact life in another time. It was a blustery and rather chilly day. I was glad to be inside the walls of the fort. The still warm, coals-baked oatmeal cookie I was offered by a young cook in a bonnet seemed to me as comforting as any cookie I have ever eaten. I was emboldened by it to go out through the gates of the fort and stand, clutched against a tree, along the banks of the Red River of the North. The wind whistled. Even the sea gulls seemed to be having a hard time of it.

I went back through marginal farmlands along what was once the bottom of a great sea to the city. I had no trouble finding it back because it loomed out of the landscape like some enormous tree. I saw the city then as a fortress. I saw what walls we build against the prairie, how timidly we huddle together, how effectively we huddle together, how effectively we close off its vastness of space and make for ourselves another space of more human dimensions.

I can't say what to make of this. I drove the 600 miles home through rain, through mist, through sunshine. What I saw in every light until I was obsessed with seeing it was that nearly every inch of the way had been painstakingly turned over, furrow by furrow. It seemed to me some unknowable comment on the human spirit that we should, despite our walls, have turned ourselves into such an awesome army of Lady Macbeths, rubbing out so relentlessly such a terrible space.

In a great city, when it rains, it rains.

It rained here in Worthington as this was written. You could see the storm coming, as you always can. We have such an unfettered view of the heavens here that, quickly though it changes, the weather never creeps in unawares. Our Mike Micklus, who can direct you to the nearest beaver lodge, and tell where to find a bedded deer in the depth of winter, and name the order in which the wild flowers bloom, says that the first sign of a change in the weather is the tapping of a downy woodpecker.

I didn't hear a downy woodpecker here, although somewhere there may well have been one furiously sounding the alarm. I did see that the morning sky had turned a blue so royal and brilliant that it bedazzled the rising sun. I heard the long calm and the nervous chirping of the birds. I heard the first fingers of the wind fluttering in the cottonwood leaves.

Before the rain, there had been a dry spell. It had been three years since we'd had an adequate summer rainfall, and as the rain falls, so fall our fortunes. It was with more than a little misery that we watched the ground begin again to crack, saw the leaves of the corn curling up again in the heat of the day, felt again in the grit of our teeth the fine topsoil swirling away in the swells of the breeze.

But here it was, seven o'clock in the morning and the wind howling in the corners of the house and rainclouds in the west which would not blow on by.

Some occasions demand to be shared. This was one of them. I rushed down to the office and slipped to shelter just ahead of the first raindrop. It was like the tipping of a bucket. A spit of lightning, a crack of thunder and raindrops so thick and heavy they fell in streams. Water ran from curb to curb in the streets. Inside, the light of the flourescent lamps had turned yellow and warm. We watched the water from the windows. We wore wide grins. There were an uncommon number of us, given the hour of the day. We had all found excuses to come early. It was like the day before a long holiday. What did it matter that lightning had knocked senseless the computer on which our day's work depended?

Even so, there is a mistake we make about ourselves. We imagine that we are close to nature. It is a form of self-flattery: close to God.

We may be intimately acquainted with the elements, but there is hardly anything natural here anymore. Land in the metropolitan Twin Cities is far less intensively exploited, much more of it has been preserved in a natural state than out here on the prairie.

I have the figures in front of me. As a percentage of total space, the metropolitan area has 22 times more forested land, 10 times more marsh land, four times more open water, more than twice as much open undeveloped space as we do. Only 18 per cent of the land in the metropolitan Twin Cities is given over to urban uses, but almost 97 per cent of our land is given over to agricultural uses.

We are in a state which is celebrated for its abundance of water, but here water is our scarcest resource. Of Minnesota's 15,000 lakes, only 150 belong to us, and all of them are dying. Rock county, the southwesternmost county in the state, is the only one in Minnesota which does not contain a natural lake. The prairie is by definition arid.

Such water resources as we had are rapidly disappearing. The squandering of our water began early. Worthington was founded late in the last century on the shores of a pair of lakes. Before the new century was turned, one of the lakes had disappeared. It had been drained to suit the convenience of the Rock Island railroad. In the single decade between 1964 and 1974, 40 per cent of all the wetlands which remained out here were drained. The recent drought did not slow this process. On the contrary, it hastened it.

We are not ignorant of the facts. We know without question that there is no longer enough water to go around. But there is nothing out here which makes people more quickly angry than the suggestion that we ought to begin saving some of it. "Some day maybe farmers will be as important as ducks," is the battle cry.

If water is our scarcest resource, the soil is our most bountiful. In most places out here the topsoil was a foot and a half or two thick when the first white settlers arrived. Staggering as it seems, even that immense resource is turning out to be finite. About half of our topsoil has now blown or washed away. The other half will disappear, too, if we don't change our methods of farming, soil experts warn. It takes, they say, at least a century, perhaps two or three centuries, to make a new inch of it.

Last winter, we woke one morning to discover that we had had a pink snow in the night. The pink was the color of the soil which had drifted our way from Oklahoma, where the dust had blown so thick that traffic stopped and schools closed and some people wore gas masks and goggles against it. Our own black soil floated in the atmosphere 10,000 feet above the surface of the earth, pilots reported.

We are not in any hurry to change our way, nevertheless. The reason is that our farmers are not hicks, as the city romantics would still have it, but businessmen with a considerable stake in an early return on their investments.

Since about 1940 we have been losing ground. Before most of our communities had celebrated their diamond jubilees, the struggle to grow into mighty cities had already been lost.

There were villages which would never have stoplights, towns which would never have shopping malls, cities which would never have freeways.

But we haven't given up hope. Every community big enough to run a contested race for mayor has an industrial park. There is a scrambling for every new enterprise with even one employee. The passion and tenacity which is brought to the crusade for four-lane roads is soul-stirring.

The four-lane roads are like the railroads before them. A community may or may not prosper with one, but without one its fate is certain. If we are islands, the four-lane highways are our links with the mainland, however untravelled, like the railroads, they may be in some future time.

There is a sense in which, despite everything, we have established a solid bridge to the main shore, however. We are all linked by a common commerce.

The edge of Worthington looks now just like the edge of any city whatever size. There is the Interstate, and the Holiday Inn, and the Kentucky Fried Chicken, and the K-Mart and the Standard station: there is a commercial strip without the slightest hint of local character, full of neon and emptiness. How connected it makes us feel!

There is an unexpected circle in this. It was here in Worthington that George Dayton began his career. Not far from here, in Redwood Falls, another pioneer of mass merchandising got his start: his name was Sears.

Our region was from its very earliest days an island. The rivers, on which the first explorers came, ran elsewhere. Later the great wagon trails to the Far West would run north of us and south of us. The main lines of the railroads would do the same. There was never a time when we weren't out of the way.

Fortune seemed to have changed with the construction of that modern river from east to west, Interstate 90. But it wasn't to be so. The Interstate, it would turn out, would not carry traffic to us which intended to stop, except perhaps at one of the chain places along the strip which made us feel so connected.

We were like the little villages which repeat the pattern on a regional scale; we were the places on the map you had to set out for deliberately; the places you would never happen upon. It is not the kind of thing we like to admit to company. We still lay our plans for the day when the roads will cross here.

But there are advantages in islands.

They are, for one thing, secure. We're free from foreign attack. We're safe against earthquakes and hurricanes. We can identify the strangers among us and keep them under watch. There isn't crime here to speak of. Our cruelties, to the not-abnormal extent that we practice them, are more psychological than physical.

There are especially advantages in uncrowded islands.

The lights are dimmer, the noise is softer, the pace is slower. There are some things which will wait until tomorrow.

There are still things here which operate on a human scale. Not long ago a mule died in Kenneth. On one memorable occasion, the mule had danced in the town's bar. On a great many others it had entertained children at town festivals through the region. And to Ras Tweet, its owner, the mule was as dear as a child. So Kenneth had a funeral, a grand funeral with the mule lying on a bed of roses, with a procession by donkey-drawn cart through the village, with speeches in the town square, with tears at the graveyard, with a rollicking wake at the village bar. It elevated everybody's stature.

The death of an ordinary person, or of an extraordinary mule, is still a thing of consequence here. It is still possible to be buried in a cemetery where the gravestone hasn't been chosen by the proprietor for reasons of maximum profit.

When a human being is born or baptized or confirmed or graduated or honored or married or promoted, the news is of general concern here.

Because it is so hard to be anonymous here, it is somehow less important to be somebody. We don't need to scratch and claw so much here to establish our worth. It is possible for the janitor and the bank president to belong to the same country club. There is, after all, only one.

If we are an island, we are also part of a sea. Here the vastness of things in space and in time is apparent to us.

I mentioned that outcropping of quartzite at Luverne. It is known as the Blue Mounds because from a distance it appears to be cast in blue. Atop its modest peak one can see 1200 or 1600 square miles of the surrounding countryside. The sweep of the horizon in any direction is infinite. There is no telling where earth and sky meet. Here one can get some sense of the milieu of the prairie as it was not so long ago, when it was a treeless expanse of waving grass, visited only occasionally by nomads, deathly still because even the wind has no sound except when it is interrupted. It is not clear from this vantage point that the world is ours alone.

On top of the Blue Mounds there is also a stone fence of great length, straight as a carpenter's plumb, which leads to the edge of the cliff. On the floor of the prairie directly below are two circular stone structures. These are not accidental objects. They were self-evidently constructed. By whom? We cannot know. Nothing we know about the Sioux suggests that they might have been the architects. For what purpose? We cannot know. But we can, every spring and every fall, at the hour of the equinoxes, situate ourselves at the high end of the fence and sight down its length to the edge of the cliff and know with certainty that at exactly that spot on only those days will the sun rise. Sitting there in the chill air of a spring morning, it is not clear that time is within our grasp.

It is possible here to be so diminished as to become free.

Nearby, at Kilen Woods, stands quite another monument. There on a hilltop is a small grave, marked only by a headstone and a footstone, both buried level with the surface of the earth.

The grave contains the remains of a young girl who was coming here a century ago with her parents when she was struck down by black fever. Wolves roamed the region in those days, and no grave was safe from them. To safekeep her and so that she might be found again, her survivors piled her grave high with stones from the whole area around.

The mound of stones remained there until 1949, when the woods were opened as a public park. Within a short time, souvenir hunters had carried away every single stone from the girl's memorial.

What is safe from the wolves is not yet safe from us. That we also know here.

Herbert Krause

from THE THRESHER

Herbert Krause was born on a farm near Fergus Falls, Minnesota in 1905. Listening to his blacksmith father's tales of early days in the hills and valleys of his native region, Krause began to store up material for his novels. He began farming with his brother Julius when he was still an adolescent. "I scribbled, and farmed and fell in love and out again." Disaster came when a power company put a dam across the gorge in the Ottertail River, flooding their land. "We moved that spring. Father, all his roots dug loose, wilted in the new place. . . ." His mother persuaded Krause to return to school. At a considerable economic sacrifice for her and by his working during every vacation, he was able to study for his B.A. at St. Olaf College and his M.A. and Ph.D. at the University of Iowa. For some time he was chairman of the English department of Augustana College in Sioux Falls, South Dakota. This selection from his novel The Thresher conveys his knowledge of farm life in the early part of the century and his recognition that that life was a mixture of great joy and sorrow. Krause died in 1976.

T HE OATS WERE READY TO CUT, ripely heavy, when Uncle Herm opened the door and said at lunchtime, "Well, they've done it. Dunkel and Geppert—they're going to have a cradling match. Two swaths across and two back in Dunkel's wheat field. Best man wins and the loser pays for the beer."

Johnny and Snoose chattered like red squirrels disturbed by a cat. The strife between the two neighbors, crackling like fat pine wood all spring, had exploded into raw flame that was to roar through their memories like fire through brush. Up and down the ridges folks tossed words from lip to lip about the match. Some were on Dunkel's side but more on Geppert's, seeing that he was bone-breed to the hills (as the saying went), while Dunkel was all but new-come and sproutful of notions. Kurt decided that Old Geppert had a good swing to his arm. He was called "old" because he had a son everybody called "young." The designation "old" had nothing to do with his age or his cradling abilities. It was a way the folks had of separating the father from the son in their minds. Johnny, anxious for Mr. Dunkel, said you had to have more than swing.

Alb Hukelpoke drove over to the Barewolfs' with a heifer in heat struggling at the gate of his wagon. He brought his opinion. "I've seen Dunkel cradle. Sheetin' Judas, Old Geppert better take a back seat 'fore he starts!"

But Mr. Nussbaum said at the store, "You ought to see Geppert. He goes through wheat like a greased pig."

Old Mr. Buckholtz, shaky with his more than eighty years, was glad. "Didn't think to see a cradlin' match before I went to the graveyard."

Folks who had cradled and seen cradling for years, common as ragweed, suddenly discovered art and science in the job and discoursed learnedly on the subject, although most of them regarded the work as irksome and old-fashioned, now that reapers and harvesters were being used and binders talked about.

Johnny, pestered by doubt, made up his mind that Mr. Dunkel must win the match. He tugged at the brass-wire band which Snoose had got from Old Man Fleischer to keep off the warts. He wondered whether its magic would put limberness in Mr. Dunkel's arms.

Aunt Phrena was sharp over the talk. "Them two, Dunkel and Geppert. Mad about an ox trade. It serves that old fool of a Geppert right he got beat in the deal. But to even it up with a cradling match——" She had no patience with the idea.

"Well," Uncle Herm tried to explain, "Old Geppert got mouthy. He figures Dunkel's bull is no good and says so; rubs it in. Dunkel, he got sore and said Geppert's talk was like his cradlin', a lot of swing and little to show. Well, the kitten led to the cat and before you knew it, they set a match."

"It's a spite match, all right." Aunt Phrena had dolor in her voice.

"'Tain't that exactly. It's—well, it's——" Uncle Herm tried to scratch the right word out of his mustache. "It's like two bulls in a pasture. They beller at each other a spell, they're that full of zip and peppermint. Then they're at it. That's when dirt and the bull wheels of Moses flies around."

"No." Aunt Phrena was firm. "No, the Pastor says it right. It's a spite match and it wasn't made yesterday. It has long roots and that's a mighty good poker to stir up trouble." But she decided to make pans of *Apful Kuchen* squares just the same and frizz her hair for the coming-together.

The harvest that year was lightened by the quick flame of anticipation running under the sweat and the exertion. And in Old Geppert's stall the red bull grunted. He was less ill now. One discomfort waned while another waxed.

Johnny felt the prod of excitement. Sleepy as he usually was in the morning, he crowded into his shoes with haste these days. Between wearing the path to Snoose's house a little deeper and fretting over Mr. Dunkel he almost broke into a rash. Once he thought, "If *he* loses, I won't get the silver-handled knife." He slapped his thigh quickly, ashamed of himself.

He raked cut grass one afternoon—a job Uncle Herm set him to do. But when he saw Mr. Dunkel lay the sickle of his cradle against a stand of oats and Mrs. Dunkel binding, he left the rake and walked over as if to assure himself that Mr. Dunkel still swung with a clean stroke. By the time he climbed the popple-rail fence into the field, Mr. Dunkel was resting over his cradle. On the acres beyond he could see Mr. Nussbaum beside his reaper, the vanes glinting in the sun.

Mr. Dunkel lifted a leg in welcome. They talked about nothing, neither speaking of that which lay heavy on their tongues, Johnny out of respect, Mr. Dunkel out of a kind of modesty. A quarter of an acre of oats lay in swaths behind him, still fresh from the stem and green-yellow in the stalk though washed-out-lemon color in the head.

With one eye on the little Gretel mixing sleep with shadows on the cool side of a shock, Mrs. Dunkel bound the oats close by. Her back curved like a spring to the ground. She picked a fistful of stalks, pushed and pulled them straight. With a supple twist that Johnny never could master, try as he would, she knotted the heads together and shook out a long string—a rope of oats. Seeing Johnny she waved it and said, "In a minute you can have a swallow, so hot it is. We got plenty water." The callus on her thumb knuckle was not yet thick. It was red from the rasp of straw, sharp-edged and brittle. In one hand she held the band; with the other she gathered the grain in the angle of an elbow, heaping it against the fulness of her breast, fruit against fruit, the heads sweeping like curls over her arm—curls like her little Gretel's. She pressed the bundle tightly about the middle so that butt and drooping heads spread out circlewise, the one as empty as the other was skinful of life.

Johnny saw kernels stuck in the sweat of her neck and felt shy when she put her hand inside her dress and pulled out a head of oats. "Scratchy old thing," she said. She bound the straw firmly with the cord of grain, slipping the free ends under the band. She let the firmly packed and tied stalks slide to her knees. With a rustle that was like a sigh, the bundle expanded against the band and was securely held.

He wished he could bind like that. He had wasted more than one handful of oats in trying. Time and again Uncle Herm stopped the reaper to show him how the thumb was a kind of knotter around which you wound the cord of grain to make a knot. Kurt learned easily and would repeat, scorn in his slow words, "No, this way. Can't you do it?"

"No, I can't," Johnny'd squeal. "It slips, and besides, it's so slow." All he got for his trouble was blisters on the knuckles of his thumbs. Neither of them bound much, for Mr. Marchen usually came, or Uncle Herm would exchange a day's binding with Mr. Dunkel. Aunt Phrena seldom put her foot on the field. She had a backful to carry in the garden, she said; it was enough that she sent coffee and bread to the fields for them. And so the grain was bound with neighbor muscle, Johnny watching while he gathered stray and scattered stalks, envious of hands that twisted deftly the straw into cord.

Mrs. Dunkel brought the jug. Johnny looked on warmly. The brown of her sunburned neck shading to white below the edge of her dress was good to see, he decided suddenly, although he couldn't have told why, unless it had something to do with his mother and her arms holding him from hurt. For all that sweat fell and a drop splashed on her bare foot, drawing the dust on her skin raggedly to its edges, no one could twinkle a heel lighter than Mrs. Dunkel, in polkas or schottisches at the barn dances.

"Here is water, Wilhelm." She put the jug in his hands. "I should go home soon now with Gretel. She crawled into the bushes again yesterday and went to sleep."

Mr. Dunkel took a long pull of a drink, his throat gurgling. Then he sighed, complaining, "It gets me here—cricks in the legs and in front of the shoulders, cradling does." He handed over the stone jug, cool with water beads. "Take a good one, Johnny." He brought the whetstone, spat on it and began moving it slither-slather across the blade. A grasshopper nibbled at a handle of the cradle, greedy for the salt where Mr. Dunkel's sweaty hands had darkened the wood. He snapped his finger at it. "Go away, you long-legged bastard, you! Wonder if we'll have those devils back again. They cleaned me and Pa in '77, slick as a whistle down in Nicollet County. We didn't have enough green stuff left on the place to fill a shovel."

He sharpened awhile, s'mira, s'mira, stone over iron. There was gentleness in his stroke, Johnny saw. Mr. Dunkel said, "Good many bundles I've laid in a row with this old cradle. It was my pa's. Old Geppert thinks he can *really* handle the sickle." It was out, what Johnny wanted to hear. He wriggled hopefully. Mr. Dunkel went on, "I'll mow him ten paces while he's still spittin' on the handle." He passed a hand like a caress along the top of the bow, which was curved like a finger with the sickle, as were the three other bows. Johnny saw how smooth the tips were, rounded like a cow's horns with the rub of stems. "You wait till the cradlin' shindandy next Sunday," promised Mr. Dunkel. "I'll shorten that tongue of his."

"Geppert is an old hand at it, Marchen says." Johnny was hesitant with the information.

"Oh, he can handle a brush hook, all right; but cradling——" Mr. Dunkel let it pass.

Mrs. Dunkel shook her head at Johnny. "It's been itchin' long in him, this wanting to cradle against Geppert; since young Nussbaum backed down, I guess, three or four years ago." She reached for the jug. "Now he can try. If he gets beat, I hope he's satisfied."

Mr. Dunkel waved his hand over this woman truck. Then he asked Johnny: "You coming, ain't you?"

"You betcha britches," Johnny answered sturdily as man to man with Mr. Dunkel, now that he was nearly thirteen and would be confirmed before many years. "There's going to be a whopper of a crowd, I hear."

"Ya." Mr. Dunkel wasn't complaining. "My house ain't big, but it'll hold 'em, or we'll put 'em in the outhouse. Ma, there—she's been bakin' stuff all week."

"I got the m'lasses cake yet to make. And not half enough to go around." Mrs. Dunkel was heavy with doubt. "And now there's this binding to do. Of course, if we had the money——"

Mrs. Dunkel was careful with her words, but Mr. Dunkel finished, as if he knew what she had in mind. "Not as fast as a reaper, maybe, this cradlin'. But a reaper now—does it always work?" He pointed with a whetstone. "Look, there. There's Nussbaum, stopping again. He spends half the day fixing the damn critter. Digs oat straw out of the gears, or has to run to the woods for a willow stick for teeth in the fans. Heavy grain comes along or there's a bush oak he don't see and, whoop-Jinny-and-fall-down, his reaper is out of teeth, that's all." He wiped the blade free of spittle. "Couple days ago the horses ran away for him and smashed a wheel. Na, na, I don't have to hitch up a team to make my cradle go. I ain't in no hurry to throw money after the dog." He rose and lifted the cradle. Afterward Johnny remembered how the whetted sickle was an arch of brightness in the sun.

He left the Dunkels to wade through the uncut meadow, grass shoulder-high, like swimming, he thought. After a while, he saw Mr. Nussbaum and the reaper. He put hands before him to bend the heavy growth apart. Once he sprawled to the ground over a hummock and was lost in rank meadow stalks. The minty smell of crushed motherwort was like balm in his nose. Looking up the green well of grass, he saw a cloud like a tower white against the blue. A song sparrow fluttered away and after a moment of poking, he found the nest in the lee of a budding sneezeweed, the youngsters feathered and hopping over the edge the moment he reached down. And there was a butterfly he chased from an early joe-pye weed nodding its dull pink head. A butterfly wing of brick-red brown with whitish spots pinned to his Sunday cap would make the kids in church open their eyes. But it escaped him.

He sat on a rock, resting and watching Mr. Nussbaum drive down a reaper-width of grain. The five vanes made a circle that was tilted like a windmill wheel on a slant. They swooped low over the sickle, forcing the oats against the blades. The fifth vane, setting its teeth, raked a bundle heap off the platform to the stubbles. Round and round went the vanes, teeth dribbling oat stems and trailing wild morning-glory vines. Armfuls of grain fell, left for the binders. Johnny saw the Nussbaum boys, tall and angular as their father, catching up straws for oat strings to bind the grain as Mrs. Dunkel did. But he ventured no closer, for Mr. Nussbaum was sharp with talk, and he didn't spare names on his horses.

Just then there came the sound of crashing wood, and he saw Mr. Nussbaum dancing in the oat swath, hopping mad, and heard cuss words bouncing over the stubble. Something broke again. Johnny slid off the rock, a fork of uneasiness prodding him. There was the sloo grass, he remembered, and in the west a cloud of rain. He legged it back and crawled over the popple-rail fence. Furiously he worked in the hay till sun laid sweat like oil on his arms. But there were more winnows than cocks of hay when Kurt shouted at him to come home.

Uncle Herm, folding his lips, only looked at the sky and the rain threatening and said nothing. He shamed Johnny by going out after dark and cocking hay by moonlight. Aunt Phrena shook her head, eyes running. "That poor sister of mine! Poor thing! Think of her looking down from heaven and seeing you run around like this. Like a yearling. Worse than thrashers." She blinked a tear, in sympathy with her thought. "Never at home. It runs in the blood." He was glad to be rid of her sticky tongue; left his barley coffee half drunk, and followed Uncle Herm to the sloo. Kurt stayed home. "He should read his Precious Comfort chapter tonight," Aunt Phrena ordered, pointed as a scissor.

Silently they raked under a watery moon. The sweat ran. Johnny piled hay until, slouching on a cock for a moment of labored breath, his sight fogged. The sweat of day and the wear of muscles slid over him. He fell into sleep like a dropped stone. He woke to find Uncle Herm lifting him to his unsteady legs and sighed, drowsiness like salt under his lids, "Mother, are the raisins in the pudding?" He grabbed Uncle Herm's hand as if it were Sport's brown ear and lagged home, too sleepy to notice how fast Uncle Herm's bony fingers closed over his sweaty palm.

They started for the Dunkels' the Sunday of the match late as usual, for Aunt Phrena discovered a rip in her flounces at the moment when Johnny drove the spring wagon past the door. She wouldn't move until she had threaded a needle and repaired it. They were no later than others. Uncle Herm remarked on the way, "His wheat's heavy, Dunkel's."

Johnny and Kurt were stiff-backed with loftiness at wearing new button shoes, though their toes ached. Aunt Phrena sighed, solemn over their vanity: "Ach, the harvest is great but where are the laborers, as the Bible says?" Her look was so brimful of meaning that Johnny felt "preacher school" in the air again. But stubbornness set his jaw. He sealed his ears in a plan to make Mosey Fritz ride the Dunkels' mad sheep buck.

The Dunkels' yard crawled with people—the Nussbaums, the Schadels, the Hukelpokes, the Marchens. Snoose ran to help Johnny unhook the team and whispered, "They got the beer keg by the machine shed."

Folks from over Jenny's Peak way and others to the north, ten miles over ridges, were there, and folks unknown in the hills, strange as a new waltz tune. There were the Habers, just come from Wisconsin, with most of their chairs and the baby's cradle and the boxes still piled in the wagon in which they came, now staying with the Fleischers until Mr. Haber cleared a patch and dug a cellar for a house. ("Not that we mind, I'm sure," Mrs. Fleischer told Aunt Phrena; "but eleven people usin' five spoons, and your buttonhooks gettin' mixed up with theirs—well, when the shoe gets crowded, the toe comes out, that's all.") And there was Mr. Krumlich, whose family stayed in Fergus while he hewed black oak for a log house up in section three, that place, wild and rock-scattered, where, Alb Hukelpoke said, God kicked together stone and brush for a place to spit and called it section three. They were all there, most of them already chewing food.

Geppert with a plate of pumpernickel and rye bread was bragging, "Yep, laid me down three acres of oats the other day; went at it so hard, the old cradle nearly got me hot on the stones." His tongue came out in a laugh. He was lean and tough with hardly a gray hair on his head.

Mr. Dunkel, disbelief in the hunch of his shoulders, pushed his fork tinnily against his plate. "That will be something to see." He was definite but polite; he didn't want to cast stones at a neighbor, even at a match.

Carrying their plates, Johnny and Kurt with Snoose drifted to a spot behind Mr. Mercer, who was grumbling, "I need a new grain cultivator the worst way. Getting tired of chopping down a dry oak to drag my grain under the ground. I can't buy, though. Elevator man beat me out of most of my wheat last fall."

"Just like them," Mr. Peiser said, hitching his belt. "But what can you do? I'd like to build me a house for once. Ma sure needs it. Old shack of ours, wind blows in, winters, so's her skirts flap. It was all right for a homestead shanty but now, with the kids——" He sighed through his whiskers. "My youngest died two winters ago; caught cold——Well!" He shrugged a suspender. "But what can you do?"

Folks talked. With side glances they appraised now Geppert, now Dunkel, those two who appeared so calm under their blue shirts and were so full of seething under their skins. "Had a letter lately from my sister in Olmstead County." Mr. Schadel rubbed his buttock exasperatedly. "The prices they pay there! Cream's selling twenty cents the inch, she says."

Kurt listened, forgetting his potatoes, ears wide as cupboard doors, but Johnny, only half paying attention, put a dandelion tube in Snoose's cup and sucked coffee when Snoose wasn't looking.

Mr. Nussbaum, coddling his whiskery jaw, said, "By jippers, we oughta have farmers in the wagon seat, that's what, and tell those pants warmers in St. Paul a thing or two. Oughta own the elevators and stores. From what I learn, they're going to start a Farmers' Elevator in Mary's Hill next year."

"Aw, hell! They tried that before." Mr. Schadel wasn't hopeful. "Always go broke. Big fellers laugh when a farmer puts on Sunday pants."

Old Geppert hefted his cradle and bellowed, "Feel fine—like a yearling with his first heifer," when somebody asked. He roared over his teeth at the joke. Johnny, refusing a third helping of cabbage and sour cream, overheard Mrs. Dunkel: "You find Gretel, Mrs. Beerwagon. She's had her meal; time for her after-dinner sleep, company or no company. Otherwise she'll be snippy as a crab tonight."

Leaning against the popple fence, a bunch of older boys, seventeen and after and dangerously close to dark fuzziness on their upper lips, guffawed over slippery tongues, their mouths puffed with stories of last night's barn dance. From the way Jack and Bill Marchen grabbed at their belt buckles and threw back heads in mirth, Johnny knew that the telling must be good, full of girl stuff. He ached to run and hear but didn't, knowing how they'd chase him off with scorn: "Can't hold it in, can you, you peashooter, you? Gotta get your ears full." One of these days he'd be with them; wait till he was confirmed.

Half hidden by lilacs, a Peiser girl let young Kory Mercer hold her plate and look at her ankle, plain in sight below the heavy hem of her skirt. Once he caught her hand (Johnny saw this with a start of blood), making sheep's lips at her, and she struggled but not more than would encourage him. Johnny nudged Snoose.

"Them two—rabbiting in the bushes and don't care who sees." He speared a crinkle of cabbage leaf, feeling that he wouldn't mind sitting in the bushes with a girl, some way, but was half uncomfortable at the thought.

Then he noticed Sophie Marchen swinging past on long legs. She cornered Clymy Humber before he knew, secure in the angle where the rail fence met the granary wall. Clymy hunched his shoulders as if somehow trapped. She had her fingers on his trouser belt now, folks said; they'd be married before many snows. Johnny regarded them, ruffled at such behavior. That a man should run away from a girl——He speared a cabbage strip that had crawled over the pate and was getting away.

Talk spread after eating, but here was the beginning of expectancy. Mrs. Nussbaum told Mrs. Beerwagon, gathering the plates, "Well, I take leftovers from pigs' heads and livers and such; stiffen it with buckwheat stirred in, and bake it. That makes the best scrapple. Cut it cold and use plenty of mustard."

Young Matt Dornhover, pleased with his new wife and his new twenty acres cleared of stumps, ventured: "Next year, I'm going to buy me a self-binder; one with wire to bind the bundles. It's secondhanded but my pocketbook's too flabby for a new one." He added, "Cradles and reapers—pretty well played out."

Mr. Dunkel answered him, "Don't know about that. You always have to have sickles. I got a piece up there, full of brush and all. You couldn't get around those stones with a reaper, nohow." He arose quickly without waiting for reply. Jumpy as a chipmunk's nose, the neighbors thought but said nothing, watching him sit alone on a box and grope in a pocket for his pipe.

Over near the woodpile, Mr. Lorimer let it be known, "Brine, that'll kill smut—dries it up. Old Willis says his fertilizin' salt is just the thing. You sow it with the wheat, maybe three bushels to the acre."

Almost shyly Johnny approached Mr. Dunkel. For Mr. Dunkel had his eyes on Old Geppert whetting his scythe and on the wheat field bordered by lilacs near the house. Thoughtfully he tamped his pipe. His fingers shook when he lifted the sulphur match. It was a kind of sign, that match; a sign of his newness and of his dipping a finger in tomorrow. Some of the men there, steeped in accustomed ways, still held a bit of stone beside the pipe in the round of their curved fingers and thumb. They struck the stone with steel grasped in the other fist, catching the sparks in the bowl to start the tobacco. Johnny often watched the spark in Old Geppert's pipe spread to a scab of red ember.

Then Mr. Dunkel saw him. "Na, Johnny. You here to see me

get licked? If I lose, maybe I'll feel so bad I'll have to take back what I promised you. And we won't go to Fergus after all. That would be a high price." He laughed at his own seriousness.

"I made a cross in the dust and spit on it," Johnny told him.

"That should settle it." Mr. Dunkel arose, a hand on Johnny's shoulder.

Around the beer keg men smacked their lips in the foam. Waves of gibble-gabble washed now against the straw barn, now against the tarpaper-roofed house, voices heard brightly for a moment and fading the next. Dishes clinked against pans in the house.

Clots of kids gathered in a game and broke to pieces; collected in another. Johnny and Snoose joined the circle for "needle's eye," marching under the upraised bridge of hands:

> "There's many a lass
> That I let pass . . ."

He felt prickles of delight on his skin when Gatha Blumen, shrilling,

> "Because I wanted you,"

pulled the bridge down on his shoulders and made him her partner.

She was tall with legs skinny as a deer's but with a boyish swing to her body and a smile as clean-cut as if whittled. She burst out to him boldly today, "Just look at my cold sore," holding Johnny's hand tightly. "They tease me. They say it's where you kissed me." She giggled until her eyes closed.

He went hot and cold as an April day, flushed over being her partner, chilled at her chatter there before Snoose and the rest. "Gee-god, Gatha—" he began but at once Mosey Fritz, short-legged and pudgy of belly and shoulder, squealed,

> "Here comes that stinking Johnny——"

Johnny tore away, half his forehead wrinkled, arms out to grab. But Aunt Phrena's throaty "John-ee! Johnny Schwartz! I've been watching you" slowed him to a walk, sullenly, for he knew how Mosey was making faces at him and how Gatha was looking at his back with brightness in her eyes. Snoose at his heels, he went back to Kurt.

Old Geppert put the whetstone into his pocket and arose. Now it's coming, Johnny thought, excitement in him. Now the tussle begins. But Geppert only took a plug of twist, looked at it, and then joined the others around the keg, saying to Mrs. Dunkel, "No, I don't," when she came by scolding, "If that ain't the beatenest. That Gretel—wonder where she's gone this time?"

"When they going to start cradling?" Johnny asked Uncle Herm, humping in impatience.

"Keep your brichin's up. No hurry. Afternoon's that young yet, it's hardly got a whisker on."

Johnny went with a string of boys, noticing how Gatha Blumen peeped at him over a sister's head. He put a strut in his heels. They passed the horseshoe game where Alb Hukelpoke had just made a ringer. They stopped by the barn and patted Mr. Dunkel's oxen. At the last minute, Lornas Tetzell, grabbing a fork, poked the handle between one bull's legs—"to see it wrinkle up," he said.

Snoose twisted the fork away quickly. "Want me to do that to you? You'd be sore, too, guess." And Johnny agreed, soberly.

They strung out to the pasture where on a level place the circle worn by last year's horse power was not yet erased by this year's grass. Like the round for fox and geese which the kids made in winter snow at school the circle lay, a scar marked in shorter grass, where the teams had followed one the tails of the other, round and round, in last season's threshing. Near by was the straw butt where ragweed flourished and where Mr. Dunkel forked up white grubworms for fishing.

Johnny was ready for a game of circle tag but the rest were too afraid of missing the start of the cradling match and soon they returned to the yard, restive as a brood of wood ducklings.

They passed the horseshoe players and saw Alb stepping back from the peg, his eyes on the iron whirling its own revolutions while it arced through the air and fell in an explosion of dust. "Sheets! Only a leaner." They paused to hear him say in the while between throws, "Yep, he was a feeder, that Carlie Homberg. Couldn't beat him in the hull of Nicollet County. The more dust he could eat, the harder he'd shove in the straw. Once he wore out six pair of bandcutters in a day. Then he walked ten miles to a shindandy and square-danced to near sunup. Back he come and he was waiting for bundles when the bandcutters finished sharpenin' their knives. Oh, he was a feeder——"

They moved on, Johnny wrinkle-browed over thinking that Carlie was a feller, all right; a feeder always was. Someday he'd be up there, between the bandcutters, face in the dust that rolled from the whirl of the cylinders, his shoulders swaying as he reached now to this side, now to that for the bundles spreading out under his hand. . . . He jerked up, stumbling over his own feet and out of his thought.

"What's the trouble?" Kurt wanted to know. "Gettin' duck-footed? That Hukelpoke lies so fast, it's a wonder he don't snag himself."

A boy among the men clogging the machine-shed door yelled, "By cripes, she's runnin' dry." They turned. The beer keg sputtered in the faucet and gurgled in its bowels. "She's empty; empty as a sucked egg."

Old Geppert had his last tin cup full and hoisted his suspenders a notch, flexing his muscles boastfully. He nodded. "I see Dunkel's sharpening his sickle. Well, let him." Once somebody in an alcoholic tenor lagged over the last verse of "Old Man's Drunk Again."

In a quickening moment, Johnny said, "Betcha ten dollars, Snoose, Dunkel wins first time around," though his pocket rattled with only six pennies. Mr. Nussbaum was saying, "Soapsuds—that's pretty good for hog sickness. I use——" but he broke off and got up when the others did. And Mrs. Beerwagon didn't get an answer when she questioned, "How do you make macaroni, Mrs. Hohmeyer? My old dunce of a man brought home a box, and now it sets in the cupboard, for I don't know how——"

Folks moved faster, the men slapping grass stems from their pants, the women uncreasing their skirts, leaving the dishes clean in the house, the neighbor tasks finished. The group around the keg thinned to nobody but the Haber twins sucking the last drops from the faucet and a rooster getting tipsy on a cob of corn that had got soaked in beer.

Mr. Dunkel wiped the blade and tested the edge with a critical thumb. He answered Johnny, "Sure, boy, I'll watch him at the end of the field. He'll not beat me at crossing over and exchanging sides, not me."

Old Geppert flung the cradle to his shoulders. Excitement

began running like a current among the crowd, catching them and drawing them together like a drawstring.

Then the Pastor was among them. His black team and his black buggy plowed a ditch through the crowd. The kids scrouged from the darkness of his black coat, stepping high and careful as roosters in a strange pen. Talk in the yard hushed a little so that the horseshoe players, coming from the barn, were noisy. "Why didn't you stick a ringer on 'er, Alb?" asked one.

Hukelpoke's loud, "Aw, sheets, can't lay an egg all the time, fellers," was clear on the air. He continued: "Put them shoes by the shed careful. Dunkel brought 'em clear from Nicollet County and he'd be madder'n hell if——" He stopped red-faced at Jake Peiser's nudge.

The Pastor's long legs stalked past the players and toward Mr. Dunkel. His voice boomed so that Old Geppert paused. *"Brüder,* what is this that you are doing? An abomination before the Lord, that's what it is. Neighbors' jealousies—they cannot be settled by a spite contest. Beware that you do not tempt the anger of the Lord." He dived into a sermon on profaning the Sabbath. "Like threshers." He glared at Uncle Herm and Hukelpoke. "And those godless men in the cities who befoul the Lord's day like cattle. For them is prepared a fiery doom, my brethren."

With a lowered pointing finger he tried to stop them. But Mr. Dunkel set his jaw and Old Geppert merely shifted his cradle, both deaf, as was the excited crowd, awed by the minister's stern gaze but heedless of his chapter and verse. His beard ends shook with wrath. Like handwritings on a wall there appeared in his mind blazing texts for a month of sermons, illustrated by neighborly stubbornness.

The crowd swirled away from him (let him follow), Mr. Dunkel and Geppert in the lead. They swarmed out to the field, Mrs. Dunkel pulling Johnny's arm and asking, "Did you see Gretel anywhere? I can't find her," he shaking his head, impatient to be with Kurt and Snoose, who were just in front of him.

Afterward Johnny would run this day through the runways of his mind with a sugar-and-salt feeling for the crusty sweetness of neighbors and with a kind of acridness which slow horror pricked in him, blotting out some things, leaving others scissor-cut and sharp: the field of wheat stretching its length of golden heads from the lilacs near the house to the wall of pine trees . . . the two men plunging forward like unbroken colts . . . the wide rhythmic swing of the scythes, whetted keen as knives for butchering, shearing stem and stalk with dull, thudding, thunking sounds . . . the wheat heads shaking for a trembling space under the wind of death as the iron struck . . . the grain gathering for a swift moment above the blade and leaning against the bows before it fell with the outward pull at the end of the sweep, dropping in rows, heads away from standing grain . . . the two men swaying in the wheat, harvesting this grain for more than money in a pocket or shoes for the family . . . across the field and back they must go, across and back again. A bird darted away and Johnny, stumbling in the morning-glory vines, wondered about a nest and the young.

There was Mr. Dunkel with his shirt off, his underwear, new for Sunday, white against the yellow of grain at the start but turning dark with sweat that stained it, chest and shoulders and underarms, before he finished half a length of mowing. Old Geppert was ahead of him, practice in each swing of the blade. The neighbors were noisy. Snoose jumped over a stone, Kurt near him. Johnny shouted, "He's gaining, Mr. Dunkel; hit yourself on the tail."

Once fire flew as Mr. Dunkel's blade met a hidden rock, sparks winking in the wheat. Folks gasped and a sound like a storm troubling a ridge of oaks rose from the lines straggling alongside the cradlers. Johnny felt his heart go to rags and heard Snoose say between steps, "Wonder he didn't break the sickle." But Mr. Dunkel tore the whetstone from his pocket and swiftly edged his iron with sharpness, though Geppert wasted his breath in a croupy laugh of triumph.

Folks pitched courage and hope to the cradlers. Johnny, caught in a knot of people, bumped against Mr. Nussbaum and bounced away, elbowing Kurt and grabbing Snoose by the shoulder: "Wait for me, can't you?"

The cradlers came back to the lilacs where they had started, completing the first round. Geppert was more than two wagon-lengths ahead of Mr. Dunkel. Behind them unrolled a double width of swaths and cleared spaces. They pointed their flaring nostrils at the pine wall. This was the second, the last round.

The crowd bunched and stretched along again. Little by precious little Mr. Dunkel regained the steps he had lost. Though Old Geppert had custom to show him where to lay the sickle and that certainty which comes to those who speak with authority among the tongues of neighbors, nevertheless Dunkel gained, for he had the lesser drag of fewer years and the confidence of one not yet old enough to be fearful of established neighbor ways—those ways unchangeable by anything except the ruthless smashing and the patient reassembling of the parts.

A flash of gray and a rabbit, confused by trampling feet, zigzagged among the treading shoes until, terrified and lost, it froze to the ground and let a Schadel boy pick it up before it screamed the fear of the dying. Then Johnny saw Mr. Dunkel step ahead and noticed that Old Geppert was tiring, rage paring his nose to pointedness. The shadows of these two, monstrous and black, struck at the ground ahead of them futilely. The pine wall towered just before them. Their breaths were getting thin now, their shoulders pushed ahead with the pumping of belly and chest muscles, their clothes soaked with sweat. They reached the pines. Half a round left.

They turned at the pines, the last turn. In front lay the stretch for home and the lilacs there. They swung into the wheat. Sickles flew faster. Mr. Dunkel crawled ahead now and Geppert, his breath hoarse and choked, teeth biting lip till the blood came, knew the bitter tears of those who see their honored place forgotten and their words flung to a common level.

Something like a glow came to Mr. Dunkel's eyes as he gathered his steps ahead, though his face was blotched red, and the white of tiredness grew about his mouth. His ribs, sharply marked on his wet underclothes, pulled at air that rushed through his throat in ragged, gulpy gurgles. His sickle was like lightning in the grain. His eyes became blind—blind to all but the wheat before him and the steel in his swinging arms. He lunged forward with steadiness in his arches though aches wrenched sinew and bone. He was going forward, going home, coming to his lilac bushes at the end of the piece. Geppert was behind him now, the loser, and he was the victor. There were the lilacs, there the end of the piece, the last of exertion, two rods ahead. Sway with the sickle, faster, faster; wield the bright edge, faster, faster, faster. . . .

Then a dreadful croaking shout dragged over his lips as if he were one who looked unexpectedly upon the toothy grin of death. He seemed to put shoulders back with all his strength like a brake against a forward lunge, the urgency of despair in his arms, desperately—and failed.

The scythe leaped forward blithely into a sickle-width of grain, into a small willow with shade. . . . A scream, high and childish and in agony, tore through the wheat and twisted itself corkscrew fashion into Johnny's ears. The folks stood in a hush, lips sewed with the needle and thread of unbelievingness—this couldn't be true; this couldn't happen in Pockerbrush, not to them. The Pastor shoved forward, all his anger gone, a shepherd of his sheep in mercy for this moment once again, praying "Father in Heaven."

Night after night Johnny, mulling over that awful hour, would squirm on the pillow as if the edge of the scythe with thrust and glitter were driving into his brain. He'd draw breath deeply as now he drew breath, horror like a vine crawling up his legs and holding him stiff and hardly moving, his eyes wide. He didn't know whether he cried aloud, though his head racketed with the words: "Oh, Mr. Dunkel, Mr. Dunkel, take your promise back, take it back. I don't want to go to Fergus. I don't want the silver-handled knife."

There was Mr. Dunkel, cradle thrown wide, hands clawing into the stalks. And there was Mrs. Dunkel running, a cry white on her lips but remaining unuttered. She paused, as if held back, and stood beside Old Geppert who sank panting to the stubbles. And then Mr. Dunkel came toward them, Gretel in his arms. He swayed to staggering—swayed as an oak does, hammered with thunder; his face broke, tears mixing with his rattly puffing, "Gretel, Gretel, my Gretel!"

Martha Ostenso

from O RIVER, REMEMBER!

Martha Ostenso was born in 1900 in the village of Haukeland, not far from Bergen, Norway, and was brought to the United States at the age of two. "The story of my childhood is the tale of seven little towns in Minnesota and South Dakota." She did not learn English until she attended school, and ironically, this may have led to her interest in writing. "I can remember how beautifully certain words rang in my ears—quite regardless of their meaning. Pail—cyclone—funeral—potato!" Her first novel, Wild Geese, *published in 1925, grew out of her experiences as a teacher in a log cabin school in Manitoba. She continued to write novels with rural settings, many of them set in Minnesota, but found time to write poetry and short stories too.* O River Remember, *from which the following selection is taken, is a panoramic story of two families over three generations. That the riches of America were a mixed blessing, with their temptation to a life devoid of humanity and to a too great devotion to work, is a theme that recurs in a number of her novels. But Ostenso was always aware of the evils as well as the largesse of nature. For a number of years she lived with her husband, Douglas Durkin, in Brainerd, Minnesota, until her death in 1963.*

IT WAS A SUNDAY, and everybody came, bringing hampers of food, dishes and coffeepots and tablecloths. They came in their ox-drawn wagons across the grassy trails from the north and the east and the south, and seated themselves in the solemn shade of the tall elms to listen to the sermon preached by the Reverend Clegg, the ardent young Presbyterian minister from Moorhead. Then, while the men sat about in their shirt sleeves and discussed their crops and livestock, and the children were occupied with their shrill games, the women spread the tablecloths on the ground, boiled coffee over the crackling fire, and set out the pickles and wild-fruit jellies, the molasses bread and the sugar cookies that were so rare a luxury.

Magdali Vinge had not come willingly. During the past eight months, since the birth of her son—yes, God had given her another son!—she had assumed the responsibility of having the minister at her house for divine service once a month, and the foregathering under her roof was a pleasure she jealously guarded. That he was not a Lutheran minister had troubled her at first, but the young man was earnest and deeply devout, and Magdali had taken him to her heart at last. He had in a sense become her special agent for the spread of righteousness among the settlers in the district, who had gone too long without the spiritual guidance they needed. She had admitted to Ivar that the idea of a picnic was an excellent one, but during the week of preparation she could scarcely conceal her resentment that it had not originated with her instead of with Kate Shaleen.

When the jollity of the meal had subsided and the men sat back to smoke their pipes while the women cleared away the leavings, Ivar overheard Magdali pay Jensine Engebrigt an extravagant compliment on the new arrangement of her hair, which even a man could see was hideous. Kate Shaleen's hair, too, was dressed in the new mode, with a loose lock on the forehead; but on her it was carelessly becoming. Yet Magdali had not deigned to notice it. Ah, well, there was no reckoning with the minds of women!

A hot, high wind had risen from the west.

"We could do with a little rain," Steve Shaleen said, stretching himself on the ground beside Ivar, who sat with his back to a tree, smoking his pipe. "That garden truck of mne is burnin' up."

"Maybe rain would be good for your garden," Ivar said, smiling into the distance, "but this is pretty good for my wheat. Two weeks more, and it will be ready to cut. It will be a good crop, too."

"That's the hell of farmin'!" Steve observed. "One man wants one thing, and another wants something else."

"We make it work, just the same," Ivar said contentedly. "In the end we both have a little."

"We ought to get together more, though," Steve went on. "I was readin' in the paper yesterday about a book that tells how to test soil for what there ought to be in it for growin' this and that. Take your wheat, for instance. Wheat needs one thing, but my onions need something else. It'd be a good book for the likes of us to have around the house. We could read it on winter nights when we sit warmin' our rear ends for the want of something better to do."

"I'd like to see a book like that," Ivar said.

"If I send for it, we could look it over and do a little experimentin' together, like, if you could get away from your family now and again."

"Ho, my family grows itself now," Ivar boasted.

Steve laughed. "That's one crop we don't have to worry about, rain or shine, eh, Ivar?"

"They come along—yours and mine," Ivar said, and glanced away to where Steve's wife Selma held her little Loren in her arms as she rocked back and forth to her own low crooning. A little beyond, Roald Bratland was standing over Magdali's strong eight-months-old Arne, who was on all fours, gazing raptly at the river.

"I keep tellin' Kate she ought to get herself a man and have a kid of her own," Steve said.

For a moment, Ivar could find no reply to that. What Steve had said was true, no doubt, even if his way of putting it was not altogether to Ivar's liking. He looked now to where Kate Shaleen was sitting in the shade of an elm, half a dozen children romping about her. He heard her call to little Rose Brazell, whom they called Rose Shaleen now, saw the child toddle on her plump two-year-old legs to fling herself across Kate's lap. Somehow, he had never imagined Kate Shaleen as married to anyone. He could think of no one who would be a fit mate to a girl so far removed in spirit from the very practical business of marriage.

Not that Ivar himself had always looked upon marriage as the merely useful expedient it had come to be in the last few years. There had been that moonlit night on the snow-covered mountainside in Norway—and many nights and days afterward, when he had gone about in a dream world all his own. There had been those storm-tossed nights on the Atlantic when he had awakened to the incredible reality that Magdali was beside him. There had been other days and nights, some of them not so long ago, when the familiar heart-hunger had struck him like an obscure pain that would not be stilled. But Magdali had brought him to see the foolishness of that. Well, he had seen the purposes of Nature fulfilled, he had begotten sons and daughters, he would leave to them the heritage of flaming desire and its aftermath of bleak discovery.

But what of Kate Shaleen? Was she never to know either? All Ivar's strength of mind and body rose in protest.

"Find the man for her, then," he said sharply, and looked at Steve as he spoke. "It would be better so. We would lose a teacher but we—"

Steve jerked himself erect. "Let them look for another teacher, and the hell with it!" he exclaimed. His eyes widened suddenly as he stared toward the river road where a tall, lean individual with a long, melancholy face came shuffling toward the picnickers, mopping his brow with a huge bandanna. "Jee-rusalem! if there ain't old Fiddler Luke!"

Ivar saw Kate Shaleen get up and run to meet Luke Nisselbaum, who had halted, his fiddle under one arm, to survey the group before venturing closer. He saw the young minister leave his place beside Ole Sondstrom and his wife and walk toward the newcomer, his hand outstretched to welcome him. Then he saw Magdali snatch the baby Arne into her arms and retreat to the moving leaf shadows on the river bank.

"Your wife looks scared," Steve observed with a grin. "And little wonder! Luke is the nearest thing to a scarecrow in these parts. But the preacher don't scare easy. He likes music—out of hell or heaven. You can trust a man that likes music, Ivar, even if he is a preacher."

Kate had led Luke to a knoll where the baskets were piled and was already plying him with sandwiches and coffee. Ivar was too busy with his own thoughts to give much heed to what Steve was saying, but when Luke Nisselbaum finally stood up and placed his violin beneath his chin, he leaned forward and touched Steve on the shoulder, a signal for silence.

"He is going to play," Ivar said.

Luke drew his bow, and it seemed that the trees above him paused in their rustling. It seemed that the hot wind died, and a cool, deep-sea greenness flowed over this glade in the woods where even the children sat large-eyed and still. Ivar had little knowledge of fine music, but he felt an aching fullness in his heart, a longing for something he had somewhere known and had forgotten—and yet had never known, would never know.

Luke played familiar tunes after that, hymns to which everybody sang, and comforting old pieces they all knew. Then, without warning, he burst into a wild cascade of music, a tumultuous rhythm that rocked and swayed and laughed in a kind of mad glory. It leaped upward and joined with the abandon of the wind in the trees. It sank and whispered shamelessly to the underbrush.

Magdali's face was shocked, and about Kate's mouth there was a troubled, withheld smile. But in the next instant, Steve and Selma, Pete Sondstrom and his sister-in-law Helga, the Featherstones and the four eldest Engebrigts were whirling about upon the grass in a hilarious and formless dance that brought shrieks of laughter from the participants and most of the onlookers.

The young minister, standing beside Ivar, leaned and said, "'Man does not live by bread alone,' Mr. Vinge. We work too hard—all of us, every day of the week. This is the Sabbath, but the good Lord will find no fault with what we do here today. I think—" He paused, startled. "Your wife, over there—she is beckoning to you. Something appears to—"

Ivar hurried to Magdali's side and looked up to where she was pointing at the sky beyond the river. A darkly moving cloud bore toward them above the trees on the opposite shore. In a moment it became a solid mass of churning lead with ragged edges from which fragments shot downward, while from overhead came a sinister drone that smote beyond hearing to the very heart.

Luke's violin had fallen silent now, the dancers were rushing toward the river, their eyes fixed in terror upon the oncoming tide.

"That's grasshoppers!" Steve Shaleen bellowed. "Holy Judas, my vegetables! Let's get out of here. Kate—Selma!"

In the scrambling panic toward the wagons, the young minister was jostled aside, and Luke Nisselbaum came to stand beside him. He looked in mild wonderment, first up at the confused and crackling air, then down at the violin in his hands. A dozen insects had already settled upon the strings. He brushed them off, removed his coat and wrapped the violin securely within it.

The minister stared upward while the olive-green flight of death struck him in the face. "Dear Lord," he said softly, "give us now the strength we need!" Then he spoke to Luke. "I hope I may have the pleasure of your company back to town. My horse and cart are just over there beside the Vinges'."

Already in the wagon seat, Magdali was cowering as she drew her children about her. "It's God's judgment on a wicked people!" she murmured as Ivar got up beside her.

Leaving Magdali to take the children into the house, Ivar drove his frantic team into the stable and closed the doors. The cows and the oxen were running blindly about in the pasture, but he had no time to fetch them in. The sheep were huddled under the lee of a haystack beside the stable. In the farmyard, hogs and chickens were gorging themselves on the grasshoppers that had come down to devour everything in sight.

Magdali had already fastened the doors and the windows of the house. Leaving Karsten to look after the younger children, she gathered bed clothes, floor mats, cast-off garments, and piled them outside the door. There Ivar met her and together they staggered through the fiercely whirring drift of hideous brown and green that came endlessly on and on. Every square inch of earth was a crawling tapestry of small, savagely intent bodies. The vegetable garden was already flattened under their weight, and here and there the ground was pitted where the insects had ravaged carrots and turnips to their roots' ends.

They had thrown only a few covers over the vegetables when Ivar gave up in despair. The ravenous creatures were champing their way through the thick woolen blankets and the heavy mats. He ran his hand through his hair, and grasshoppers sprang out between his fingers.

"It is no good, Magdali!" he cried. "They're eating the blankets, too. Take them away. We must pull up everything we can."

They snatched the covers off and ran with them to the stable that was only a few yards away. When they came back, Ivar seized a fork that had been standing in the ground at the edge of the garden. Its handle had been gnawed so that it was rough to the touch.

"Bring a basket from the house," Ivar said, and began digging the carrots and turnips from the ground in a sightless rage.

Magdali went pale. Then she turned and hurried toward the house, barely able to keep her footing over the mass of dead and living insects.

Not once had Ivar dared to glance southward, beyond the stable, to where his ten acres of wheat stood ripening in the sunlight. On the trail homeward, he had seen what was happening to his oats and barley—those fields looked as if an enormous filthy paw had clapped down upon them. Scarcely a leaf had been visible in the stanch grove of the tree claim, but it had been hung from root to uttermost twig by a ghastly, crawling fruit.

Magdali came back and set the basket on the ground. "Do you know what's happening to your wheat—your good wheat, Ivar?" Her lips were a chalk line.

"Fill the basket!" Ivar ordered.

With a kind of low whimpering, Magdali went to work. When the basket was full, Ivar carried it to the stable, dumped the vegetables in a corner, closed the door securely and hurried back to the garden patch. When they had taken everything of worth from the ground, the sun was low, a soiled and vaguely distinguishable glow in the west. Ivar lifted the last basket of vegetables and paused to look at Magdali. Her face was streaked with dirt and perspiration, her blue gingham dress smeared and tattered.

"Get back to the house, Magdali!" His voice came harshly from his parched throat. "Wash your face and lie down for a while."

He went to the stable then, set his basket on the ground, and sank down, from sheer weariness of spirit, upon a pile of new hay that Louie Spragg had carried in that morning before going to Moorhead to spend the day. It was peaceful here at least, with the door closed, and the comforting sound of horses nuzzling the sweet smelling hay in their mangers. Presently he got up and went to the small window that looked southward to his field of wheat. It was easier, somehow, to face that total destruction of his dreams with no one beside him. He could do nothing about it now. There was no way he could save a single golden head. Strangely enough, it was not so much of his own wheat he was thinking as he stood there at the small square of window. He was thinking of the tiny plot in one corner of the field which he had given Karsten to plant as his very own.

"Never mind, my son," he muttered aloud. "There will be another spring, and another planting. And you will help your father, because he needs you now."

When he first saw what looked like a plume of smoke rising from the edge of the field, he thought his eyes were deceiving him in the strange light shed from the setting sun. But a moment later he saw the solitary figure of Magdali darting about, half hidden in the weirdly tinted smoke clouds. He flung himself out of the stable and ran toward her, waving his arms and shouting, though he knew she could not hear him.

The wind was still coming strongly from the raddled sunset, heavy with an oddly acrid smell. Suddenly a flame leaped from the edge of the field and licked eastward over the swaying stalks of ripening wheat. Before it, the grasshoppers rose in sluggish clouds only to settle again a few yards farther on.

Ivar was gasping for breath when he overtook Magdali running with an armful of straw to where a kerosene can lay overturned on the ground.

"*Helvete*, Magdali! What madness is this?" he cried, seizing her arm.

She swung toward him in fierce scorn. "If *we* aren't going to have it, neither are *they!*"

Her foot shot out toward the kerosene can and sent it rolling toward the flaming straw. Ivar jerked her away from it, but she set her teeth as she fought to free herself.

"Let me go! Let me go!"

It was then that he saw the burn on the back of her left hand. "Come away, Magdali," he pleaded. "There is nothing we can do here now."

She sprang at him, but he caught her by the shoulders and held her helpless. Struggling and stumbling, he dragged her by main force away from the burning field, back along the pasture, and into the yard in front of the stable. In all their years together nothing like this had ever happened between them. Ivar was aghast at the thought of the children witnessing any such violence. He opened the door of the stable and all but threw her inside.

The Norwegian epithet he hurled at her would have made Roald Bratland's hair stand on end, had he been within hearing, but Magdali smiled and said gently, "You might better pray, my Ivar!"

The soft uttering of his name only angered him the more. He lifted his hand threateningly as he stepped toward her. "Pray— on a day like this? I might better get drunk!"

Her eyes were bright with tears as she looked at him. "Sometimes, Ivar," she said haltingly, "you seem strange to me—as if we had never known each other. Don't you care for me now the way you did—at first? Or have you forgotten?"

He saw that her dress had been torn from her shoulder, exposing the soft curve of one breast. He felt the old thickening of his blood as she stood before him in the half-light of the closed stable. His body had known her many, many times, but there was a look in her eyes now such as he had never seen there before, the bold, unbridled look of a—yes, of a wanton, he thought suddenly, and was afraid. Had some madness smitten her during those hours of fighting against hopeless odds? He had read of such things happening to women who were forced to live on the nation's frontiers. Men, too, had lost their reason when the battle had turned against them.

"Magdali!" He put his arm about her, drew her toward him, and hid his eyes against her hair. "You must not talk so. It isn't that I don't feel the same. And I haven't forgotten. It's just that you're different from me. You're the smart one, and I haven't always got the sense to see it."

She sighed in his embrace. "You are the strong one, my Ivar!" She gave a tender little laugh, reached up and kissed his mouth.

She held him so until she had drawn him down beside her on the new, sweet-smelling hay.

Peggy Harding Love

THE BETRAYAL

Peggy Harding Love was born in Chicago in 1920 and moved with her family to Minneapolis three years later. She attended local schools, graduating from the University of Minnesota High School in 1936. In 1940 she received her B.A. from Swarthmore College, and subsequently she studied with Joseph Warren Beach and Robert Penn Warren at the University of Minnesota. From 1942 to 1947 she and her husband, John Love, were pacifists and worked on cooperative farms in New Jersey and Pennsylvania. They returned to Minneapolis in 1948 for ten years and then moved to northern Minnesota where they lived until her death in 1976. A number of Love's short stories were published in literary and mass circulation periodicals during the forties and fifties. Her story "Jersey Heifer" was included in the O. Henry Prize Stores *for 1951. In addition to writing fiction Love was active in the Democratic-Farmer-Labor Party and did editorial work and collaborative writing of books on animals for children. Her intense interest in the North and in its symbolic meaning for a sensitive person is conveyed in the story "Betrayal," included here.*

W HEN SHE GOT ON THE BUS at Bemidji there was only one place empty, on the long seat at the back of the bus. A young Indian boy sat next to the window, then the empty place, then two GI's in wrinkled suntans, and an old lady with a basket in the other corner. Mary climbed over the soldiers' feet and knees, smiling apologetically, and squeezed into the empty seat. The Indian boy moved over as far as he could; he looked about seventeen, small and thin, and he held himself rigidly in his corner. It was a hot day in late July but he wore dark wool trousers, spotted and frayed at the cuffs, and a red and black checked wool shirt over a dirty white cotton shirt. He looked steadily out of the window, his profile dark and somber.

The soldier next to Mary turned to her and said, "You almost didn't get a seat. It's a good thing Gus and me were here to save one for you." He was blond and tanned, with dark eyes that were child-like in spite of their red rims and bloodshot margins. His whole face looked half-asleep and very young. He and the other soldier were pleasantly drunk. Mary laughed and said, "Thanks," and looked away. She was still hot and flustered from her run for the bus and making sure her suitcase got on, and now this soldier talking to her made her feel both friendly and con- fused. She didn't mind particularly that he was drunk, but she had to be quiet for a while to collect herself and prepare for this transition—the bus ride that would take her back from the silent lake country into the city and her job and the long waiting ahead.

The bus rumbled beneath them and they moved out of the dusty northern resort town onto the empty highway. With an almost mystical feeling of love and renunciation Mary watched the countryside that she was leaving. She had come to it and left it summer after summer ever since she was a little girl, and now the sight and smell of it was woven inextricably into all her memories of the joyous and innocent periods of her childhood. They passed through the sandy wilderness, grown over with scrub pine and sumac, past pine forests impenetrably dark even in the noontime heat and light, and always beyond, somewhere, lay the still lakes, sometimes only glimpsed secretly below a bluff and sometimes lying candid and open under the sky. The cabins of the summer people and the garish little resort towns that shriveled and faded with the first cold weather had made no real mark on this coun- try. It was too big, too full of its own secret life to be defiled by men. Even the cutover land where monolithic pines had once grown in a thick gigantic turf seemed not so much despoiled as reborn, beginning again its steady implacable growth under the sun and wind and snow.

Looking through the windows, Mary saw outlined against the brilliant light outside the dark profile of the Indian boy beside her. He was watching the land pass, too, and in his face and body there was something of its own vital and fierce dignity. Once they passed a group of three Indian huts, pressed back far under the trees, hovels of bark and tin surrounded by blankets and old rags on a sagging clothesline and birchbark baskets hung out for sale. The boy looked at them as he looked at the trees and sand, as impassively as he might look at his own face in a mirror. This country is his, not mine, Mary thought with a pang of envy. Why is he leaving it? From somewhere hidden a cool lake breeze full of the smell of fresh water blew through the window on her face. I would live in any hovel, I could stand the bitter cold and the loneliness, if only I could wait here for David to come home, she thought fiercely. I could wait here, I could be strong here. But the bus went on, southward; they were due in Minneapolis at eight o'clock.

The young blond soldier said to her, "You going far?"

Mary turned from the window and looked at him. His eyes were bland but his voice was friendly and persistent. He knew that it was his right to talk to her and to make her talk to him, and Mary knew it too. She did not mind now; there was no point any longer in cataloging the landmarks of this inevitable, irreversible journey. She smiled at him and said, "I'm going to Minneapolis."

"You hear that Gus?" the blond boy said to the soldier beside him. "She says she's going to Minneapolis."

Gus leaned forward and stared at her with bright, filmy eyes. He was older than the other, tall and lanky, with a long beaky nose and dusty brown hair that fell limply over his forehead. "Well, is that right, going to Minneapolis?" He continued to stare at her owlishly. "We've got some mighty fine company now, haven't we, Bennett? A nice pretty girl to talk to for three hundred miles."

"Two hundred," Bennett said. "Closer to two hundred."

"All right, for Chrissakes, two hundred," Gus said amiably. "Let's not get piggish about this. Maybe if this goddamn bus gets any more crowded she'll have to sit on our laps."

Mary looked away from them to hide the tenderness and pity in her eyes. Ever since the war had started she had never been able to look at soldiers, on the street, on busses or streetcars, alone or in noisy groups, drunk or sober, without feeling this terrible pity and sorrow and under it a pervasive, irrational sense of guilt. There was no soldier who was not too young to die, too innocent to be forced to kill. She could never bring herself to stand on feminine dignity to ward off the advances and attempted pickups that any girl alone was bound to run into from time to time. She could only smile and say, "I'm sorry," and go on her way alone, wrapping the thought of David about her loneliness and sad compassion. In her feeling for David there could be no pity. Even though he had been in the army for three years and in

Europe for fourteen months she never thought of David as a soldier. He was David and she loved him, and when you loved someone the way she did there was no room for pity.

Bennett was saying, "I was drinking sherry the past three days and I don't remember one damn thing about it. I always said when I got back in the States I wasn't going to drink nothing but real Scotch and I get up in Grand Forks and get blind on sherry."

"That's all right, you save a lot of money that way," Gus said. "Sherry now, that's a nice refined way to drink, isn't it, miss? Say, what's your name if you don't mind my asking? We got two hundred miles yet; we don't want to be formal."

"Mary," Mary said, smiling at him. "Are you boys going out to Fort Snelling?"

"Yeah," Bennett said, "we both gotta report back tomorrow. I landed back here the day before Fourth of July. I been in the country twenty-two days and I gotta report back tomorrow. Drinking sherry the last three days, too. Hell, I get the lousy deal every time," and his face looked like a petulant little boy's.

"That's tough," Mary said. "Were you in Germany?"

"I was there two months, all over the place. Signal corps. Gus here, he never got any farther than Cologne."

"Oh," Mary said. "My husband's in Germany. He was in Paris before, but now he's stationed at Nuremberg. He's in the medical corps." She was glad for the chance to say it, just to get everything straight. She hoped that saying it would make everything clear, would confirm from the beginning the pattern of just a friendly meeting on a bus trip; and she felt reassured and happy when she saw it made no difference to them and when Bennett, grinning, only said, "Wouldn't you know it? All the good-looking girls turn out to be married these days."

At Walker three more passengers got on the bus. They stood or sat on suitcases in the aisle, and now as the bus went on and the afternoon air grew hotter and heavier the bus began to fill with casual talk and a relaxed feeling of the community of their journey. Bennett and Gus lolled on the hard plush seats with their legs stretched into the aisle, while Mary, cramped behind the seat ahead of her, listened to their stories, asked the required questions, and laughed at their wisecracks. She found herself watching Bennett's face, so boyish and open, trying to find there some sign of the things he had been through, some revelation of what war and the eternal presence of death had meant to him. But it

seemed a mask of complete innocence, untouched and untoucha-
ble, reflecting nothing either from without or within.

The two soldiers seemed utterly at ease with each other and
with her, and once, wondering about it idly, she asked how long
they had been in the same outfit. Bennett looked at her in surprise. "Who? Him and me? We weren't ever in the same outfit. I
never saw this guy before we got on that bus at Grand Forks this
morning," and he and Gus looked at each other and laughed.
Mary felt unreasonably taken aback, as if she had been somehow
cheated, and she realized that she had unconsciously been fitting
Bennett and Gus into a stereotyped picture—the inseparable
buddies, sharing pleasure and sorrow, facing death together and
loyal to each other beyond any possibility of betrayal. She saw
now that there was really no way to know their relationship; it
was even conceivable that tonight in some dark downtown alley,
after the last, roaring drunk that they were planning, Gus, with
his bright, owlish eyes, might roll this naïve boy and leave him
lying there, unconscious, for the police or the MP's.

Immediately she knew that this suspicion was unreasonable
and idiotic and she was astonished that it had occurred to her; but
for a few moments she did not want to join again in their friendly
banter. She fumbled in her purse for her cigarettes—the No
Smoking sign had long ago been disregarded—and as she drew
out the pack she became aware again of the Indian boy beside
her. She felt him watching her and on an impulse she turned to
him and offered him a cigarette. His eyes flicked away immediately, but as she held the pack out to him he hesitantly took
one and nodded gravely. She lit his for him, then her own, and
silently they both looked out the window. It was a different landscape now—farmland and occasional hardwood woodlots with
fewer pines, and although this land too looked bleak it had an
appearance of being under control, domesticated in its meager-
ness. Soon even the bleakness and poverty would be past and
they would come to the rich, treeless fields of corn and the lush
pastureland that never had been forest. With a spasm of nostalgia
and almost physical longing she turned back to the soldiers beside her, and when Bennett put a casual arm across her shoulders
she was almost glad.

At Brainerd they stopped for half an hour and Mary, avoiding
the crowded station cafe, went down the street to a diner to eat.
She finished quickly and walking back through the hot, late-

afternoon sunlight climbed into the stuffy, silent bus several minutes early. The Indian boy sat alone on the back seat, still and watchful in the green-plush gloom, eating an egg sandwich. Mary took her place beside him, smiling at him shyly as she stretched her cramped legs into the aisle for a brief respite. With a sudden gesture the boy held out half his sandwich. "You want some?" he asked her in a hoarse soft voice, and his eyes looked into her face, dark and candid like lakes at twilight. But the bread was grimy from his curled, brown hand, and Mary wasn't hungry. She smiled apologetically and shook her head. "Thanks, but I ate in the diner," she said, and she couldn't understand why she felt so wounded when he turned away and went on eating, looking out the window and not speaking again.

When the other passengers got on, talking confidentially and settling like clucking chickens on their roosts, she saw them in a dream. She had not realized how tired she was, and when she saw Bennett and Gus stumbling tall and noisy down the aisle, waving a pint bottle of rye, she smiled at them from the bottom of a well.

"Hey, you going to sleep on us?" Gus protested, climbing over her. "You can't do that, we got some liquor for you."

She shook her head sleepily and started to move over to make room for Bennett, but he pushed her back. "You sit there and stretch your legs. I'll set behind the seat a while." He took her place beside the Indian boy and when the bus moved off again Mary sat between the two soldiers, relaxed and weary and unthinking. They talked across her, leaning heavily against her shoulders as they passed the bottle back and forth, and she found it comforting. She wouldn't share their liquor with them, refusing with a sleepy smile, but when they leaned their faces down to hers, saying insistently, "Isn't that right, Mary? Huh? Isn't that right?" she would open her eyes with an effort and smiling peacefully murmur, "That's right," although she had not heard a word they said.

She must have dozed off finally, for when she opened her eyes a little later, it was not a little later but already early evening, and the green-gold light outside was shining palely on the farms that lay outside the city. She turned her head and saw that in her sleep she had curled against Bennett's shoulder and that her crumpled cotton dress was twisted up above her knees. She felt as if she had not really woken but were still deep in some amorphous dream, and even when she stretched and sat up straight the buzzing and the ringing in her head went on. Gus and Bennett had not moved or changed. The bottle was empty but they still leaned across her, talking only a little more thickly and looking at her with eyes as bright as ever.

"I'm glad you woke up, Mary," Gus said, fumbling in his pocket, "I want to show you a picture of my wife. You didn't know I was married, did you? Got three kids, too." He brought a picture out of his wallet and, smoothing it tenderly, passed it to Mary, peering intently and breathing whiskey into her face. "Some shape, huh, Mary?"

It was a picture of a pretty blonde bursting out of a two-piece bathing suit, and it looked as if it had been cut from a magazine. Mary looked at it, smiling automatically as she said dully, "She's very pretty."

Bennett leaned heavily on her other side, looking at the picture in her hands. "That's Betty Grable," he said matter-of-factly. "A very nice dish," and he pulled out his own wallet. "I got something better than that, Mary. You want to read a poem?" he asked her, turning his wide young eyes on her and looking deep into her own.

Mary felt drugged with strangeness and confusion. Then the pretty blonde wasn't really Gus's wife? and he hadn't really three children as he had said? She didn't know what it meant, but she felt a frightened anger against Gus. She watched Bennett's clumsy, boyish hands unfolding a lined sheet of notepaper, and moved by the care with which he straightened the creases and by the painstaking, childish handwriting that covered the paper, she thought righteously, a poem means as much to this boy as a pin-up girl to Gus. Bennett gave the paper to her and turning to face her, watched her with a wide-eyed little smile as she began to read.

With the first words a shock of cold sickness went through Mary's body and for what seemed eternity she sat holding the poem in her hands, unable to move, her eyes stiff and her heart twisted in furious recoil. It was the first piece of real pornography that she had ever seen. Stanza after stanza covered the worn piece of paper, and the words, explicit and lovingly put together, were like red hot needles in her flesh. Her eyes had taken in the first two stanzas at a glance, before she knew what she was reading, and she knew that that was only the beginning, that even that was nothing to what was yet to come. She sat frozen, with unseeing eyes, unable to look at the childishly-written words and yet unable to move to get the filthy paper out of her hands, while a torrent of fury and terror such as she had never known raged within her. Finally with an effort of will that shook her whole being, she folded the paper with trembling hands and keeping her set, furious face straight ahead she thrust the poem at Bennett.

She saw nothing though her eyes were wide open, but she heard the paper being carefully returned to the wallet and Bennett's soft young voice saying sadly, "Guess she don't like my poem, huh, Gus?" and Gus's sharp, hoarse voice replying, "Why, that's a mighty fine poem, Bennett; maybe she just isn't the literary type."

For the last half-hour before they reached the city depot she sat rigidly between them, imprisoned between their heavy shoulders, staring with blind eyes straight before her. Bennett and Gus leaned and talked across her as if she were not there, unconcerned, untouched, with no change in their voices or in their bright, blank eyes. When they got to Minneapolis they pushed their way off the bus before the others, cursing cheerfully at the driver till he found their duffel bags; and by the time Mary descended, weak-kneed, to the platform, they had been swallowed up in the station crowd. As she waited to claim her bag she saw the Indian boy, carrying a cardboard suitcase, go out through the depot doors and stand hesitating, on the crowded sidewalk. But when she followed him out, her own suitcase in her hand, he was gone.

Walking along the downtown street in the early evening she felt as if she were in a strange city, a place she'd never been. The city noises were all around her in the hot twilight air, but they seemed to come to her across a great distance. In the half-empty yellow trolley the strangeness persisted; the hard straw seats, the indifferent conductor, the tired-looking people in their wrinkled summer clothes were all unreal. She looked at them but they did not look at her. It was as if either she or they were a dream and not really there, and she couldn't tell which was which. It was incredible to her that she had lived in this city all her life. She kept thinking, seven hours ago I was in Bemidji, and she could see again the flat sandy land stretching all about her and the blue lakes lying beyond. Was that land real or unreal now? In panic she opened her eyes wide, staring desperately at each blank face in the trolley, at each street, the same as every other, that passed outside. With a slow steady sense of horror she saw that time and space, moving with their implacable, terrible power, had somehow left her behind and she was lost.

When she got off the trolley at her corner her legs trembled beneath her. She saw no one as she climbed the stairs to her apartment, the suitcase hanging from her arm like a dead appendage. In the apartment she stood for a long time before she thought to put the suitcase down. Everything looked small, unfamiliar, impersonal. It was impossible that she had ever lived there with David. It was growing dark as she went about opening the windows, but she didn't turn on the lights. Black soot lay on the window sills and even when the windows were open the air was still and death-like.

In the bedroom she pulled back the bedclothes and took off her clothes. She lay in the middle of the hot, dry bed with the sheet kicked down and her nightgown pulled up over her knees, watching the sky darken into blackness. She tried to picture David's face, she willed it to come to her, but she saw instead only the dark, innocent eyes of Bennett, and his blank, expectant smile. She fought him furiously, digging her fingers into the mattress and turning her head sharply on the pillow, but he remained, and a wave of physical desire she could not stem swept over her. She lay still, seething with a helpless need, and the first few lines of the poem came into her head. She heard them repeated over and over by a grinning, boyish voice, and with despairing hatred and horror she found herself wishing, wishing desperately, to know the words of the rest of the poem.

Suddenly she knew, with certainty, something that had never occurred to her before. She knew that David had not been faithful to her during this year away, and she felt no protest. Just as she was betraying him tonight, so David had betrayed her, once or twice or oftener. She saw then that the circle of betrayal was endless—Bennett had betrayed her simple friendliness, she had betrayed the Indian boy's brave gesture of dignity and brotherhood, and he in turn had betrayed others, if only in the act of leaving his people and that secret, wasted country to come, self-seeking, to the city. She saw that Bennett himself, with all the millions like him, had been betrayed, helplessly and utterly, into war, into death, into the corruption of all that was young and simple in him. In wartime there could be nothing but betrayal. At every moment, all over the world, love and humanity were being betrayed by all mankind.

As she lay there hopelessly, her heart sick unto death, she felt again the presence of the vast north lake country, still lying there behind her as it had lain through centuries of war and exploitation. There only did betrayal end, and with the first transport of religious faith that she had ever felt she knew that some day, soon, both she and the Indian boy would go back.

John Milton

AN INNER DISQUIET

John Milton is poet, novelist, short story writer, biographer, and historian. Born in Anoka, Minnesota, he attended school in St. Paul. After receiving his B.A. and M.A. from the University of Minnesota, he completed his Ph.D. at the University of Denver. Milton's particular interest is Western American literature, which he has done much to foster as editor of the South Dakota Review. *"I think* The Great Gatsby *is the Great American Novel, which ties me even more closely to Minnesota, but otherwise my chief interest is in the Western American novel. Because I am a Gemini, it doesn't bother me a bit to remain loyal to Minnesota even while I create new homes in the West." Milton has been anthologized in* The Best American Short Stories *and has received various awards for his creative work, including a Wurlitzer Foundation Fellowship, a National Endowment for the Arts Fellowship for fiction, and the South Dakota Governor's Award for Creative Achievement. He is professor of English at the University of South Dakota.*

ONCE, WHEN HE STOOD IN THE HALL of a school building and looked down the length of the hall and out the door at the building across the street, the center bars of the door lined up exactly across the foundation of the other building so that he couldn't see where the building joined the ground. It floated, and it made him dizzy.

It happened again at a lake deep in the north woods, in a cabin, where the window frame covered the horizon line so that he could not see where the sky joined the water, and he felt very uncomfortable and walked away from the lake, into the woods, and found himself a place of peace, a holy place, where everything was united.

Or so it seemed.

They drove through the woods over a newly-constructed dirt road, and he knew at first that she was irritable and then guessed at when she became restless. He had to keep full attention on the curving, bumpy road, but he felt her moods beside him. She was not prepared for the crudities of the backwoods road, nor did she realize at first that trees crowded to both edges of the road and could have a smothering effect upon her. Then the constant turning and rising and dipping of the road made her dizzy. He was no help to her; he was too irritable himself from wrestling the car over twenty miles of twisting washboard, and he had quit talking an hour ago except to damn the road and assure her that it had to end sometime. His assurance faltered even as he gave it and so it did not mean anything to either of them.

She occupied herself with small disconnected thoughts of the trip: the dull but smooth highway from the city to the great lake; the beginning of impatience when they got lost while turning west away from the lake through its small port city; the increasing irritation as they left the paved road and plunged into the woods on what seemed to be a path rather than a road; the hubcap that rattled off and had to be retrieved from the ditch; and then the growing and unexplainable restlessness after they got deep into the trees. It was dark under the huge trees and she wanted to get out into the sunlight. She began to crave sun and air, although in the city she usually managed to avoid both.

When she first saw the cabin, as their car approached it through a narrow tunnel under the thick and lofty pines, she was shocked. It was almost hidden by the trees and it squatted so compactly on the green matting of the clearing that it appeared to be partly underground. She thought immediately of an animal's lair, a small and dirty hole in the ground.

After the car stopped, and they got out and stretched and sighed, she stood apart from the cabin while her husband carried the suitcases and boxes of food inside.

"It's not bad, Lee," he said. "Go in."

She waited as long as she could, until curiosity got the best of her, and she stepped carefully over the weatherbeaten door sill with a kind of excitement. Her arms and legs vibrated. She did not know what to expect.

The air in the cabin was musty, not just as though the windows had not been open for several weeks, but as though animals had occupied the shelter until a few minutes ago. She went cautiously into the darkened living room, bumped into the great castiron stove, used as a fireplace, and pulled aside the curtains. Dust settled possessively on her hands and she blew it off and then waved her hands out away from her body.

To her left was a door. She went through it into a small bedroom which lacked furniture except for the old-fashioned metal bed. She pulled the curtains aside from the two windows, disturbing more dust, and opened the windows. The crisp northern air revived her, stimulated her, drove her outside again. The cabin was too small, and she could not rid herself of the feeling that she would be just another animal holed up in its den. She instead of the bear, or whatever it was.

Outside she saw the endless forest of the north. The pine trees and lakes and cool shadowy retreats stretched away from her for hundreds of miles to the north and west. Here at least she could breathe again and, if she wanted to, could shout her restlessness to the empty blue skies. It was better than being shaken to dizzy pieces in the car.

Waiting for the car to be unloaded, she grew impatient. The restlessness teased her until she felt that her husband also was teasing her by being so slow with the luggage. The car could be unloaded at some other time, tomorrow or even another tomorrow, and she called to her husband but he only told her with a wave of his hand that he was not yet finished. She saw her new matched set of expensive leather cases, one for vanity, one for overnight, one for longer travels; they gave her a feeling of independence as well as possession.

The possessiveness extended to her husband.

She was restless, and night was coming on, coming rather early.

"Carey," she said, "aren't you almost through?"

"Almost," he said.

"It's getting dark."

"Don't be silly." He mumbled something else which she could not hear. His head was deep inside the trunk of the car and his voice sounded like dull thunder. He turned to look at her. "It isn't even late afternoon yet."

When he stopped talking the thunder continued. She looked at her watch. Three-thirty. She looked up into the sky. The bright blue of a few minutes ago had changed to deep blue and in some places to grey over blue. Then the unbelievable blackness came creeping over the jagged tops of the trees to the northwest, as she watched, and the dark clouds crawled bumpily through the low sky and the tops of the green pine trees hurt their undersides. They moved steadily forward until they formed a lid over the small clearing in the forest. As they came they were preceded by a sharp coolness which sent shivers through her. This country of the north was as contrary as a woman who couldn't make up her mind, and sometimes shockingly unpredictable. One day was numbing hot and full of sticky flies, and the only relief was the lake itself—jump into it and stay in; another day, and this was also a summer day, would send chills to the bone and demand a fire not just for pleasurable warmth or for daydreaming but for preservation of life. Anyone accustomed to a less tempestuous climate could go mad with the uncertainty of it all.

Her husband also saw the storm and quickly carried the rest of the suitcases into the cabin. He shoved one suitcase under the daybed in the main room and took the rest to the bedroom.

She found a coffee pot and a can of coffee and stood before the huge wood stove in dismay until she saw the little electric plate hiding behind a box on the shelf beside the stove. Thank God for the one dainty electric wire that pushed its way out of the village, hopped from pole to pole through the wilderness and allowed people deep in the woods to operate power tools and listen to the radio and cook coffee. She put the wood stove out of her mind.

When the coffee was ready she and her husband sat down on hard chairs by a large plank table on the porch. The coffee steamed between them, its odor tantalizing and civilized.

The storm broke.

Water hit heavily against the windows and drummed on the roof. Water formed a solid wall around the cabin, shutting it off from the forest as well as the distant city. There were no sounds except the splashing and drumming and running of the water. Like a furious wet cocoon the storm wrapped itself around the little clearing, the cabin, and the two people inside.

"I don't like it," she said.

"Are you afraid?" he asked.

"No, not that. It's a storm. But we're so cooped up here. It's almost stifling."

"That's one way of looking at it, Lee. But there's another."

"What?"

"Have you forgotten already? We came up here for a little privacy, get away from people, have time to think. I'd say we've got it now."

He pushed his chair back from the table, went around to his wife, tipped her head back and kissed her, long and hard, until she squirmed and tried to move away from him and he released her. She went to the window and stared out into the blackness and shuddered and went to the kitchen for more coffee and drank part of it before she returned to the table and sat down again. She was restless. Perhaps she was tired and it was nerves causing the little itchings on her skin and the sharp and unexpected movements in her muscles. She fidgeted on the chair.

"We're tired," he said, watching her as though she were a specimen under examination. She could read his eyes and wondered if he could read hers and what was in them. She worried about her restlessness and thought it might keep her awake, and then she remembered the storm and knew she would not sleep anyway. She felt trapped, the first time in her life that she had experienced such a strong sensation of being caught away from everything that gave her comfort and security.

"Let's go to bed," he said.

She stood up suddenly, as though a bond had been released, and went back to the window. She could not keep herself away from the storm even though she feared it for a reason that had no words.

"The storm is still bad."

"It will blow itself out by morning," he said.

By morning. The blackness outside, like the backing of a mirror, threw back her image from the glass. She could not see the lake, or the trees, only her own face, white within light brown hair that hung to her shoulders, full mouth drawn tight now. She was an attractive woman and both she and her husband knew it. He, especially, knew it. She saw in the window-reflection that he was looking at her intently.

"You're right. I'm tired." She didn't want to think, not about storms or cabins or animal dens or anything, just sleep. How odd, though, that the storm stimulated her and kept her nervously awake. And strange, that the small bedroom which had repulsed her when she first went in, now seemed the best place to be.

Carey was right. She needed sleep. But when she settled herself on the old bed and tried to turn into a comfortable position, he came to her side with a violence akin to that of the storm and swept her into the kind of passion she did not achieve, or want, very often. They burrowed into the center of their immediate universe with the outer layers of cabin and forest and storm sheltering them from all distraction except each other, and they fought and turned to fire and ceased to think rationally, and for a short time she flung herself about and like an animal in heat sought only her mate.

Later the rain turned to hail and beat thunderingly on the roof, lightning flashed earthward in searing streaks. Carey went to sleep, but she lay awake most of the night and marveled at the disappearance of her restlessness.

In the morning she found herself alone in bed. She could hear nothing. She slid her feet off the bed and was annoyed at the ache in her thighs. She dressed slowly and went through the main room to the back door of the cabin, promising herself that she would not wake every morning with such an ache.

Her thighs throbbed; she had gone a little crazy last night, but it was daylight now.

Carey sat on the chopping block by the woodpile, staring into the woods. It did not look as though he had done any work yet.

"Hey!"

He got up when he saw her and smiled sheepishly, then reached for her and kissed her roughly.

"Ouch!"

He pulled back. "What was that for?"

"Your face—it hurt me," she said.

"You didn't expect me to shave today, did you?" He rubbed his chin. "I love you—even with whiskers."

"I love you too."

"That's good. You should, you know. The storm really cleared the air last night. Just breathe. It's beautiful."

She stood back and arranged her hair, patting it into place with her hands. He reached for her again and touched the top button of her blouse, and she pushed at his hand and they wrestled until she got away from him and said, "Let's eat breakfast."

She turned back toward the cabin, toward the pile of logs painted brown and trimmed in green, just as she remembered it from the afternoon before, only now in the sharp light of morning the green trim looked bad against the fresher and lighter green of the birch leaves clustered on their bright white stalks around the cabin, and the brown paint looked artificial, not like real logs at all. The whole thing seemed terribly out of place in the woods. She reminded her husband that wood was needed for the stove and then she went in and looked with trepidation at the iron monster on which she would have to cook unless they wanted little hot plate lunches all summer. She felt her grandmother's presence there, daring her to be successful with the stove, taunting her with the softness of modern young wives who didn't know what life was all about. The cabin was all right, and even last night had been all right; nothing had really changed. But she felt presences that were even more dangerous than that of her grandmother.

A good breakfast and a lazy morning in the sun would remove her ache, and so she went into the cabin and buttered the frying pan and put four eggs and a pound of bacon on a plate and opened a can of orange juice. As she unwrapped a loaf of bread, Carey came in and started the fire. She forked the bacon into the pan and then went out to the front porch to see what the lake was doing this morning. She knew that her husband would tend to the bacon in his own special way, a way he insisted upon, always, and would fix the eggs while he was at it, and she was not surprised when he came to the porch carrying the two plates of food. They ate rapidly without speaking, looking out at the lake and seeing the sun shine on the tips of little waves so that the entire lake glittered yellow-silver on blue.

"You know," Carey said, "your trouble is just that you don't get outdoors enough."

As the summer days and nights gradually warmed and then reached a point beyond which they began to cool again, her husband found a new interest, one which he shared with her in conversation but not in actual experience. He took long walks alone in the woods, sometimes following two-rut roads which cut back into the forest, and often leaving the roads and plunging recklessly into the brush, struggling into back areas which seemed to recede without end into the wilderness depths of the very beautiful and yet somehow monotonous border country. He came back hot and dirty, tired and hungry, but always happy. He seemed to think that he was on the verge of discovering something back where no humans lived or, indeed, seemed ever to have lived. And one day he did in fact make a discovery which brought him back to the cabin elated although exhausted.

Behind the cabin, away from the lake, the land sloped sharply upward for less than half a mile, then leveled off for more than ten miles before it climbed steeply and abruptly to a ridge. From below the far side of the ridge an immense shallow bowl, like a flower bowl filled with miniature pines set solidly on the wide table of land which ended only at the great lake to the east, stretched northward until it reached a second ridge barely visible in the hazes of distance. On the other side of the second ridge were the hundreds of small lakes which formed a linked chain from east to west, at one time the watery back road of the fur trappers. It was on the first ridge, the southern edge of the bowl, that Carey made his discovery: evidence that primitive man had been there, although how primitive, how early, he would never know. He stared in amazement when he first broke through a dense cluster of stunted trees, berry bushes, and ferns, and saw the rock. He had come across many rocks in the forest, some of them large enough for him to climb up on, but he had never seen a rock like this one. It was an old rock, perhaps the oldest in his world. It was a beautiful rock with green and white and orange mosses clinging to its sides in waving and curving and scrolling patterns. Life marched up and down the sides of the rock, invisible except for the moss, and the presences were strong and demanding. The rock seemed to shimmer with an unknown magic in the dim forest. Old, long dead, yet never dead, it nourished the parasites while it lived its own existence over the centuries, waiting, watching. Life, pattern, death: it was all there. The answer to everything.

Carey was shaken with the sudden realization that he had been pulled, forcibly, mysteriously, into an eternal significance which he might never understand.

But he would try.

He told her about the rock as soon as he got back from that first encounter with it. Since he did not know exactly what he should think about it, or how he should feel about it, he had a difficult time in explaining and describing. She tried to seem interested, but she refused to accompany him to the rock. She was lying in the sun, resting, and she had no desire to undergo an all-day struggle through the woods. And so her husband went out alone, two or three times a week, and slowly he began to think that he understood the rock. He knew it. The camera helped. As he moved slowly around the tall and heavy rock, so big that it could have been a petrified house, as he sought new angles and new points of interest in his fascinating subject, he became acquainted with every lichen design, every scroll, every series of cracks in the rock, and every tree in the immediate background. One day, while peering through the viewfinder of his camera, he caught a glimpse of white in a crack near the top of the rock. He climbed up to it, his breath shortened by excitement as much as by exertion, and his imagination built possibilities before he reached it. His imagination was not necessary this time: it was a piece of bone, perhaps too large to be from an animal, perhaps left from some very ancient and long-forgotten sacrificial rite. His heart pounded as he examined the bone and then he set it back exactly as it had been for who knew how long—hundreds of years? thousands? The finding of the bone tempered his curiosity with reverence and he came back to the rock more often after that.

It was a dry summer until late in August.

They stood on the front porch of the brown log cabin trimmed in green. The insane laughing of a loon echoed shrilly over the lake, and the cry was answered from another corner of the lake.

"Lee," he said, "anything wrong?"

"Just a little chilly." She was tired and the witch-calls of the odd birds went deep into her and made her shiver.

The loon called again, shrieking because he couldn't find his family, then laughing because he sensed that rain was coming. Carey put his arm around his wife and they watched for the rain which had been on its way since morning. They had seen the clouds amass far beyond the lake and across the pine forest, and they had heard the thunder rumble. All day the clouds shifted and broke and regathered, and finally they darkened. The mumble of thunder sounded like heavy trucks struggling over the gravel road on the other side of the lake, but Carey and Lee knew by now that the loons made no mistakes about the weather.

By late afternoon the mumble had traveled slowly to the north and then moved quickly back to the west. Only a storm acted that way.

She opened her mouth to speak, but the small patch of blue sky that she had seen momentarily revealed by a break in the clouds disappeared, and she said nothing.

Now a gray haze swept across the sky and it was evening. The dark blue and black waters of the lake stirred restlessly. From somewhere came a disturbing sound, a rushing and drumming. She peered out into the darkness, trying to see the sound as it hurried toward the small cabin on the shore. Her husband listened intently with her. They looked into the dark sky and then at each other.

"Worried?" he asked.

"No."

"I wonder what it is."

"I don't know," she said.

The sound came nearer, rushing breathlessly and powerfully. Lee shivered again and drew closer to her husband. He touched her hand, beginning to forget the storm and the sound, and then the troubling sound swept in on their cabin and the rain fell in torrents, blotting out the high bank and the trees at the edge of the lake and beating on the roof.

"It was only the rain drumming on the water as it blew across the lake."

"I guess so," she said, "but it did frighten me after all."

He put his arm around her, although it seemed late for protection. He wanted his arm around her. "It was a weird sound, all right," he said, "but we should have known what it was."

"I guess so."

"It will just rain now."

"Yes."

"Want to go to bed?" he asked.

"No."

"Let's sit on the couch." He put a light pressure on her back with his hand and it was a physical suggestion that she go with him to the couch. It was a battered green couch with walnut-finish arms that were scratched and old-looking. It was not comfortable, but he had wanted for several weeks to make love to her there. She said it smelled old and she would not lie on it.

"I'll make some coffee," she said and left his hand dangling in the air and went to the kitchen.

"Lee?"

"What is it?" she answered from the next room.

"Are you all right?"

"Yes, I'm all right."

"You're sure?"

"Yes. Yes. I told you."

"Can I get you anything?" he asked.

"No. I'll bring the coffee in a minute."

"Shall I build a fire in the stove out here?"

"If you want to," she said. "I'm not cold any more. Just tired."

"I'll build one anyway. It may get cold later on."

She did not answer and he shrugged his shoulders and picked up old newspapers and wood and piled them neatly in the stove, three pages of crumpled newspaper on the bottom, then a slanted layer of small pieces of soft kindling, and two large chunks of birch, one in front at the base of the kindling and the other behind. He touched a match to the paper and a small flame ran quickly up into the first layer of wood. Soon it was reaching for the birch logs which would burn for several hours after they caught fire. He smiled. Building a fire was one of the things he did well, and he enjoyed it. He did not mind the impermanence. It was as though the craft became more important than the finished product.

He went into the kitchen, where Lee was standing in front of the stove, apparently absorbed in the coffee water which had not yet come to a boil. She had been almost morose for the past few weeks and he did not know why and he worried about her. She would not tell him anything.

"Where are you going now?" she asked.

He pointed to the woodbox. "The wood is almost gone. I'll get some now and it will be dry by the time we need it." He took his raincoat and hat off the peg on the back door and put them on.

"It won't take that long to dry," she said, but the words came out only as something to be said, not to be meaningful or even true.

"You know it will, Lee," he said. He smiled at her and went out. His voice came back, muffled by the rain and the closed door: "Have the coffee ready."

Of course, she thought, have the coffee ready, have the body ready, always have everything ready so that when the man returns he can be feted like a hero, catered to, soothed and stimulated. No, it wasn't that bad, but she was beginning to feel left out of an important part of her husband's life, his explorations, his picture-taking, and his note-making late in the evening, sometimes far into the night. She could not complain—did not want to complain—and she knew that he was disappointed as often as not when he suddenly wanted to make love, when he gave no consideration to time or place and only wanted it now, now, and now. It had never seemed right to her that love-making should occur on the spur of the moment, with no plans, no preparations.

It wasn't quite civilized. No, that wasn't right either, because she was no snob, and she had no lofty illusions about herself. It had something, rather, to do with the demands on a woman, that she should always be available for food, domestic duties, and love-making, while the man could be out adventuring on his own schedule, satisfying his variety of desires. She had heard this theory discussed in college, both in literature courses and in sociology and anthropology, but she could not wholly agree with it. It was too primitive, and therefore too animalistic. She had her passions, but they were not the passions of animals.

And this northern forest with its animal atmosphere was bothering her more than she had let her husband know.

She stared at the door through which her husband had gone only a moment ago, trying not to resent her presence in this place but knowing that she was tired of the vacation and that it had not done her the good that Carey wanted it to. She had loafed and slept in the sun and done little more than putter around the cabin for two months and now one rainy night made her feel cooped up again. She could no longer bear any kind of confinement, and the thought kept coming back that she was not a woman but an animal in the den, a subject, an object, an entertaining toy, a thing of beauty and a joy forever to everyone except herself. She hated self-pity, and as it overcame her she cried.

She was still crying when Carey returned. He shook the water from his coat and hung it on the hook and went to her. He shook her gently as though to dislodge her tears in the same way he had shed the rain from his coat.

"Lee, don't. What is it? What's the matter?"

And she was ashamed. "I'm sorry," she said. And as he held her she looked into his face, and he into hers, and her face was yellow in the weak lamp light and her cheeks were pulled tight from strain under shadowy eyes that blinked weakly against the tears. "It's the storm, and the tightness of the woods, and being holed up in this cabin, and no one to talk to—I'm sorry, I know we talk, it's not your fault."

"Please, Lee, this isn't any good."

"I know. But what is there? What?"

Outside the rain fell steadily.

Carson Lewis put some wood on the fire and stared into it moodily. His wife needed to go home, but he couldn't go yet. Not yet. There was more to do at the rock.

"It's getting warm in here now," he said. "You'll feel better."

"Carey, I want to go home."

"I know," he said. "It won't be long. Just relax and enjoy the fire and everything will look better. Try."

"I don't want to be warm. I can't stand it here any longer."

"Lee, please, please, try, just for a little while."

She stood up. She trembled. Her face was drained of blood, white, no longer yellow. She shouted at her husband: "I hate it here! Don't you understand that?" And she slapped him and crumpled into the chair.

A blinding flash of light illuminated the interior of the cabin and the beach in front, revealing for an instant the two white faces against a background of black and choppy waves rushing up to the shore and frothing in ghost-like splashes against the rocks and the beach. A sharp clap of thunder rattled the porch windows and trailed off in a long series of decreasing rolls and thumps until it was silent again except for the rain. Lightning flashed again, a long vertical streak in the stormy sky, reaching down toward the earth, toward her, into her, like punishment for a violation of some kind of natural law, a violation which displeased the forces of the earth and sky. The storm was terrible. She hated it and knew that it was aware of her hate and yet she felt the necessity of hating it even while she wished desperately that she might escape it. What was her sin? Could she not avoid the forest and the animals? She had not seen an animal the entire summer, but she could not throw off her awareness of them. They were out there. They hid in dark corners and they copulated and they ate and slept and they continually reminded her that there were other things to do with one's life than eat and sleep and make love; and Carey was kind to her now, asking nothing at all, only worried about her; and finally it was she who tumbled them onto the couch and pulled the blanket up over their heads until all was dizzy darkness.

When she woke up in the morning, Carey was gone. The sky had cleared and the water still dripping from the eaves of the cabin was touched by the sun and glittered.

He was not at the wood pile, and she wanted him. She had to talk to him; something was coming out of the grey mists of her mind and she had to talk about it and figure it out and she had to do it right away.

He was gone. She listened and heard nothing from the woods

except the small and bright chirping of birds. The forest seemed alive with sound, as though in celebration of the end of the storm. She went back to the bedroom and dressed quickly. Then she found the note, the short almost cruel note lying half-hidden under her moccasins: *I've gone to the rock.* The cry slipped out of her: "'No! Not today. Not today!" But only the birds responded to her cry.

She ran out to the wood pile. She ran again, out to the narrow dirt road and across it and into the woods. The underbrush was wet and she slipped and soon her clothes were wet. She (had they really started out like animals? and would it ever be different?) ran again, stumbled, ran, hardly noticing where she was going until she ran into a clump of thorny bushes and with a cry stopped short. She knew only that the rock was ten miles away from the lake (or five?) and that she had to find it. She was crazy to try when she was already bewildered, but she had to find her husband. She moved away from the bush, took a last backward look at the lake and, turning to the opposite direction, began to run as fast as her tired legs would take her through the forest. Her heart pounded and the sound echoed in her ears and she could hear nothing else and didn't care until a strange sound penetrated her numbness and she stopped quickly and skidded and fell down on the wet grass. She looked about wildly. "Carey!" But only a small brown and grey animal darted from the bushes and disappeared behind the trees. Only an animal. She felt that she too was little more than an animal now, a dirty and unthinking animal. She moved off again under the trees. There were no people in this forest world, only different kinds of creatures choosing mates, succumbing to unreasonable desires, reproducing, and dying. They all died. And was there any difference if you moved out of the forest into another world and discovered the only distinction in any world—that some animals were four-legged and others had only two legs? What kind of difference was that?

But there was one big difference: the four-leggeds had a clear advantage over the others—they were not troubled by the possibility of something better than the primitive.

She hit her head on a low-hanging branch and fell down again. Her brown hair was disheveled and wet and her face was dirty and scratched and brown. She was tired and her stomach hurt, but she got up and plodded through the woods.

She was on a path. Somehow she had wandered onto a path; it circled around a towering pine tree, circled it almost cautiously, as though the tree intimidated it. She leaned against the tree for a few minutes to catch her breath; it was a strong tree; she liked it; the reddish-brown trunk soared far into the sky above the other trees, and at the top a group of pointed and symmetrical and green arms reached out assuringly over the rest of the trees and the helpless woman in a benediction. The tree had lived, and survived, in the forest for a long time, longer by many years than the woman had possessed life. Time meant nothing to it. Only people worried about time. Even the animals lived only from day to day, from one season to the next, untroubled by questions of necessity or non-necessity. It was enough for them to survive, and their preoccupation with survival gave them another of those advantages over the woman: they were at ease where they were, in the forest; in matters of reproduction or food or shelter they accepted their place in the scheme of things. They were not cursed with the woman's inner disquiet.

She left the giant pine reluctantly and continued to waver through the forest. The first awareness of the stream came to her as she stepped into it. A remainder of her civilized life prompted her to remove her shoes and stockings although they were already wet. The finely-ground sands eased up between her toes and over her feet and for a moment she thought she was sinking—sinking deliciously into a rest which she had longed for and which she would accept willingly. The tender green ferns on the bank of the stream were turning yellow throughout their delicate laces; yellow maple leaves and birch leaves and brown oak leaves dropped lazily from above, landed in the stream, and floated away from her into an unknown distance. She tried to follow the leaves, hopping upon an outsized maple leaf so yellow that it glittered. It was almost dead but at least it would carry her around the bend in the stream and she could find the place where the leaves finally rested. But her leaf caught on a rock just short of the bend, and she turned sadly to look at herself standing disconsolately in the shallow water upstream.

She was alive and didn't know why.

It was getting dark in the dense forest where the tall trees shut out the light. She had climbed a ridge and now walked along it, her face brushed by spider webs, soft and clinging, and her feet cushioned by leaves. She was in a peaceful place where mature pines stood guard, where huge rocks testified to the established tradition, long undisturbed. She was almost willing now to be a creature of the forest; she felt at home on the timeless earth— perhaps because there was no longer any choice—contented though weary, unthinking except for the disquiet that still lingered in her mind.

She saw the rock. She walked to the rock as though she had been trained for hundreds of centuries to do so. All along she had somehow known it would be there, waiting for her. At first she was pleased, and then the disquiet rose again to the surface, up from the subconscious, and she was frightened.

Her husband was there. He stood on top of the rock, axe up-raised. He did not see her.

She ran, calling his name, "Carey! Carey!" She ran to the rock, her chest hurting from this final effort, her breath coming in hoarse gasps, but her feet miraculously carrying her closer and closer until she could see the heaviness and the strange beauty of the rock, and she climbed it, scratching and clawing for finger holds, desperate to reach the top, not knowing for sure what she would find there under the axe. She pulled herself over the last ledge and just before she fell against her husband and lost con-sciousness she saw a dead squirrel at her feet. Then stillness filled her and pushed out her insides and bloated her until she felt nothing, only a disappearing numbness that was white and orange and green and then no color at all.

Slowly she became aware again of the green, but the other colors did not come back, only green in both dark and light shades which jumped and assumed shapes resembling tree branches and pine needles. Then she saw her husband's face, white in the settling darkness, and she drew in as much air as she could and whispered "Carey . . . I wanted to . . . talk to you. Why did you leave?" She had been half-mad with fear and worry, had fought her way through the forest until the day was gone and her strength with it, and now she was not certain of what she wanted to say. It had something to do with being an animal, being treated like an animal, and yet not being an animal at all because of the fear of the woods and the gnawing restlessness. And then she remembered the squirrel. She sat up and looked fearfully around her. There was no squirrel.

"Carey," her voice faltered, "did you do it?"

"No," he said. "I didn't."

"Thank God," she said. "But why? Why were you going to?"

He could not tell her about the wilderness and the ancients and the traditions and the mosses growing not from water but from blood. He did not need to. She had her own growing awareness rising out of the questions she had wanted to ask and the confusions which were still confusions but which had finally taken shape. Both man and woman—all men and women—were a little mad and so they could not be animals even though they were.

The disquiet made the difference.

"Carey, were you mad too?" she asked.

"The squirrel?"

"Yes."

"Maybe I was. I had a wild notion that I should appease something, someone." He looked down at the age-hardened gray and green rock on which they sat. Some of the blotches and scrolls of lichen were blood-orange in color, and the last orange light from the setting sun brightened them and brought them life again. Life from blood. Life from sacrifice. "This may have been a sacrificial platform, a long time ago," he said. "At least, that's what I started to believe, after so many visits here."

"And you were using the squirrel to make a sacrifice?" she asked. "To what? Why?"

"I don't know. It seemed the thing to do. To cleanse my mind, or purify my soul, or something. I really don't know."

"And the squirrel?"

"I couldn't kill anything. I found out I couldn't kill anything. But the squirrel was already dead, and I thought that way I might be able to do it. Use it. Because it was already dead."

"I'm glad it was already dead," she said. "Very glad."

The sun had disappeared now, completely, and in the confines of the forest darkness came quickly, almost instantly. They were entirely alone, perched in the dark on the rock.

"Animals are lucky," she said.

"What do you mean?"

"They don't worry about anything."

"But they're just animals," he said.

Something akin to hate flared up in her. She tried to put it down, to avoid the memory of slapping him when she lost control at the cabin. Hate was not part of her, but it came in from somewhere outside and she had to push it away.

"That's all I was," she said. "In the storms, in the woods. And I didn't want to be."

"But you were never an animal, Lee. Just the opposite." He put his arm around her and she instinctively moved in closer to him. "You're a woman, and I loved you as a woman. Did you think I was an animal? Is that it? Because I wanted sex more than you did?"

"I don't know what I thought. And I'm still not sure," she said. "Sometimes everything is so primitive that it frightens me."

"The rock?"

"Yes."

"Pregnancy?"

"Yes." There had been no thought of a child in their relationship, but she conceded that the child lay unmentioned between them, as though conceived in the storm, perhaps destroyed on the sacrificial altar, confused or not by the disquiet which it would in turn carry within it. "Yes."

There was always the torment, and always the blessing, and the inner disquiet would not leave them alone; it would not leave anyone alone; it could only be softened a little now and then by man's limited understanding.

"I read once," she said, "that it is the juxtaposition in all of us of the primitive with something better that troubles us."

Sitting on the rock, knowing this, the man and the woman pondered the forest, the animals, and the rock itself.

Carey said, "It's too dark to find our way back tonight."

Lee said, "I almost didn't find it in daylight."

"We'll have to stay here tonight," he said. "It will be cold."

She felt the old terror coming back, but it was not as bad this time.

Robert Treuer

from THE TREE FARM

Writer/tree farmer Robert Treuer described his coming to Minnesota in
The Tree Farm, *an account of the restarting of his life on a derelict farm
near Bemidji, and the search for values inherent in the effort. His love of
the land emerges also in* Voyageur Country, *a book focusing on the
border lakes region which contains Voyageurs National Park: its natural
and human history, the political struggles as national values changed
from exploitation to conservation. He is a Jewish refugee from Hitler's
Vienna who came to America as a boy, served in the U.S. Army in World
War II, and became a union organizer and subsequently a school teacher,
Indian tribal employee, and writer. His wife is a Minnesota Indian from
Leech Lake, and he has been adopted by a Leech Lake community. His
most recent writings deal with the Ojibway experience as it relates to the
land and to spiritual values, consistent skeins in his writings.*

P AST EXPERIENCE should have warned me, but I am the eternal
optimist—a veritable Candide—in that each year I think that
tree planting will go smoothly. My notes to myself from previous
nights before planting should have prepared me for daylong disaster. When will I learn to accept this as a day when Murphy's
Law is automatically invoked? When "anything that can go
wrong will go wrong"?

There were no planting bars waiting for me at the forestry
station, they had been given to the Girl Scouts for a half-day
ceremony somewhere—the duty man didn't know where. But he
did know they wouldn't be back until Tuesday. I had visions of an
eight-man hand-planting crew next morning without planting
bars. There followed a complicated trade-off with Forestry: since I
had to drive to Badoura to pick up seedlings I would pass Guthrie
Forestry Station on my way; Guthrie happened to have extra

planting bars; Guthrie also happened to have some pinecones ready for delivery to Badoura for extraction of seeds. If I could save the Guthrie folks the trip to Badoura, they might let me have the bars. . . . The forestry radio network buzzed and crackled between Guthrie, Badoura, and Bemidji. Joe was out to lunch and Ned didn't know. . . . Two hours and several thimblefuls of adrenalin later, I'm on my way.

At Guthrie *thirty* planting bars are waiting for me. "But I only need ten!" "Well, Bemidji said to give you all I got and that's thirty, and I want you to sign for them." I sign, then load the bars and the sacks of cones. Badoura, next stop.

At Badoura the pace is frenetic. Forestry and private vehicles of every description are pulling in and out on tight schedules. By the time it is my turn as a "northerner," the crews are nearing the end of the spring pulling season, which lasts less than two months. The seasonal help is made up of farmers' wives, a few farmers, and some young men. Stress lines show around their eyes, and some of them have splotchy skin reflecting fatigue and work under constant pressure: pickups are tightly scheduled; some of the drivers come from far away. My own pickup distance is less than a hundred miles one way; all of us try to make the round trip in a day, so that the seedlings will not suffer damage in transit. They must not dry out or overheat.

In three days or so I'll probably look as tired as the Badoura workers, but I rarely have time to examine myself in the mirror at tree-planting time. My order is ready and waiting for me and I am in and out in fifteen minutes, sandwiched between a leased flatbed trailer hauling 100,000 pine for Forestry and a little pickup there for the first time getting two bundles. My order this year is small by Badoura standards: 5,000 Norway pine and 5,000 spruce. I leave the huge nursery, which is the solitary establishment in miles of lake and pinetree country. A few miles up the road are scattered fields, then the crossroads town of Akeley, which has a little coffee shop with the best homemade pies in seventeen counties. I stop there each time.

Murphy's Law blinks at my passing Badoura and Akeley, but is with me again in Bemidji when I try to pick up the planting machine. I find it parked next to the country garage Cyclone fence but can't budge it to hitch to my truck's bumper for the ten-mile haul to the farm. I finally lure some help from the garage and with considerable effort we clear the fence, jack and hook the machine.

The heavy weights are missing and we will have to jury-rig to-morrow or the planting mechanism won't ride deeply enough—the furrows would be too shallow to set the tree roots properly.

The last straw—when I go to pick up the tractor, neighbor Chuck says: "Oh, tomorrow the day? I'll have to see if it's running. Had some trouble with it a while back and haven't used it since."

Paul and Mary, and Derek, have arrived during my absence. Derek's wife, Elissa, was detained in the Cities at the last minute. I have help now in storing tree bundles in a moist, cool place, in greasing and checking the planter. The tractor comes chugging down the drive and we hook up, fasten the buckets that will carry seedlings, and check and double-check all details that, unattended, could cost critical time during planting: tools at hand for machine repair; extra oil, gas, and hydraulic fluid; water cans for seedlings and for seeders. It goes easier now.

We play whist and pop corn on the wood-burning range. Some of the tension is residual, but it is mixed now with anticipation of the morrow and the fellowship of family. Then Smith arrives, late in the evening; the little ones hear the racket and get up, and it's a little raucous and warm; the house glows and smells of woodsmoke, popcorn, and cocoa. Outside, the moon is big through the giant picture windows we made of salvaged plate glass.

It is overcast and heavy dew beads the grass blades, leaves, and pine needles. It is forty degrees and supposed to go to fifty degrees. The two bucket seats on the planter are sopping wet and everything is cold to touch. There is no sign of the hand-planting crew; we load spruce bundles, water, and extra fuel, start the tractor, and the caravan is off. All spruce will be machine-planted on the half-mile stretch along the fence; the pine will be hand-planted in the cutover if the hand-planting crew shows up.

The excitement of lining up the planter for the first run! The wonderful pungent smell of peat moss bursts forth when the first bundle is opened. The aroma curls up your nose and stays with you all day. The roots are moist, black and orange, about twenty-five trees in a sub-bundle, wrapped in moss; then another twenty-five, heading the other way; tops to the outside of the bundle, roots to the middle to retain moisture. We separate trees and set them upright in pails wired to the planting machine—one pail in front of each bucket seat—and the seedlings are wetted down again. By day's end we'll be less ceremonious but still careful about pulling apart the bundles. Mary is getting her first indoctrination, helping me separate trees. Paul fusses with the tractor, getting unsolicited advice from Derek, and Smith is admiring the older planting to our right; he had driven the rig for that early planting, now nearly twenty feet high, while Paul and I had sat on the planter. Derek had been too small that year. Now the older boys are taller than I am, and David and Tony are running around excitedly.

We've rigged the planter to ride nine inches into the ground. The huge coulter wheel cuts the sod and earth; behind it the shoe plow opens a furrow four inches wide and nine inches deep. I explain to Mary that she and I will be sitting alongside the opening furrow, setting in the seedlings. Underneath us the slanted packing wheels will push the loose earth back around the roots and pack it. That's why the weights are needed.

"As the rig moves, the packing wheels pull the trees out of your hand," I tell her. (She has the first dirt smudges on her face and is excited.) "I'll plant the first row and show you. You sit next to me and separate trees. Pull them apart and hand them to me. About fifteen at a time."

The machine starts with a jerk and nestles into the soil. The furrow opens up between us. I hold the seedlings by the stem, set them in the furrow at a slight angle—tops up and roots down—by feeding them into a metal guide chute that funnels them into the furrow. The packing wheels and the motion of the rig pull the trees out of my hand gently. I hold until I feel the set of the tree, until I can feel it anchoring into the ground, and for an instant there is physical bond between man, tree, and earth. First one tree, then the next, and the next; behind us the thin brown line stretches out, the tiny tree tufts peeking out and waving at the sky.

The earth is moist and dark, cold to the touch. I savor the little plants, the living roots, the open rich soil, and wish the plants well on their journey into time. I glance to our right at the first planting, now fifteen years old. It had not been futile, although sometimes we had wondered. On my left, some sixty feet away, is my neighbor's fence line: piles of stone labored out of the fields, then jack pine and willow planted by hand over the many years by the man and his father. The tractor putts along at a steady pace, the rhythm established. As my hands empty, Mary passes over another handful of seedlings, and we share the bond. Ritual. Thoughts of the Golden Bough.

"Am I doing this right?" I nod, because it's all right and I don't feel like talking. Already birds circle, following the furrow, feeding on grubs, coming closer to the rig: red-winged blackbirds, robins, cowbirds, bobolinks, crows.

The machine stopped. I looked up in annoyance, wishing to go on. We were at the end of the run, up against the fence line, and the rig had to turn around. We got off the bucket seats; I pumped up the hydraulic jack, lifting coulter wheel and shoe plow out of the ground. We stretched, brushed dirt and wet moss from our pants, looked at each other and smiled.

Mary planted the next run; I separated trees for her—my turn to get cold, wrinkled hands from handling the wet seedlings while she got the feel of the moist, gritty soil brushing against her hands. Where the land lay low the earth gave off cool breaths like puffs of icy winter winds as the furrows opened and closed, reminders of the great cold of winter that was and would be again. Something about the planting and nurture of trees evokes the pattern of the year, and of the years: of the growth of my children and now theirs; of the pattern of our lives and our loving. I looked over at my new daughter Mary, so intent and no longer worried whether she was doing it "right," involved now and following the train of her thoughts. The sun came out and made Mary's red hair glisten, highlighting the smudges on her face. I'm glad my son brought such a warm, loving woman into the family. The machine stopped again, to turn around where we had begun over half an hour ago (although it seemed but moments ago, with the earth and seedlings gliding through our hands). We had planted two rows, each half a mile long; and the earth had revolved a bit on its axis, and was a bit better for the hope of the trees. It was going too fast—we would be done in a day or two—and it seemed only moments ago that I had been a small child and had stood beside my father as he grafted fruit trees.

The youngest boys were waiting with a message, clamoring: "Come on, Daddy. The men are here to help plant the trees!" But we did part of another row, each of the little ones taking a turn on my lap, getting the first feel of this kind of bond with the earth. One more glance at the new furrows, six feet apart—at the tiny seedlings marching into the future in straight lines at seven-foot intervals. I knew they would lose that well-kempt look before long. Drought, disease, and the shock of transplanting would kill at least 10 percent—leaving gaps and open spaces.

I met the crew and passed out the steel planting bars, each sharpened to a good cutting edge at the four-inch base. We shouldered the heavy bundles for the quarter-mile hike to the planting site. "Plant them tight," I admonished. "Step them in. No air pockets around the roots." The crew consisted of the high school counselor, an old friend and planting partner; three students; and several men who work for Forestry on weekdays. We spread out in a line between the first windrows of slashings and began. Occasionally we could hear the machine in the distance; it can plant 1,000 an hour, if all goes well. One of us, in good condition, on clear, easy ground can hand-plant 800 a day. Today was not going to be an 800 day—that was plain from the start. The soil was hard, some of the men still soft, and the terrain was jumbled with branches, roots, and slashings.

I like to plant with a rhythm: Stride. Plunge bar in ground. Rock back and forth to make the wedgeshaped opening. Pull bar, slide seedling in hole, and pull up and down to seat hair roots. Plunge bar into ground two inches behind seedling, rock back and forth to pack. Step-in the newly planted seedling—left side, right side. Stride and plunge.

By late morning progress was slow. Peggy brought lunch and coffee and word that the tractor had broken down but was being fixed. Above us the sun was strong and hot, and I had a growing concern the trees might dry out: dry, dead hair roots mean a dead tree. We put the bundles in the little creek, sheltered by an overhanging tree.

I ate fast and headed back to the machine-planting, on the way tugging at the hand-planted tree tufts to check for firm packing. One day they would tower. . . . But the first one I checked would never tower over anything—it came out of the ground when I pulled it. So did the next one.

"Who planted this row?"

"Which one?"

"Second one up."

The planter was one of three high school students.

"Look, son, you're planting dead trees. The air pocket around the roots will kill that tree. Here's what you do to pack rightly.

This is how you step it in. Don't step over the tree, step right next to it. Both sides." We did a few trees together, retracing his steps. The other rows were better. A nice-looking, strong boy. But he didn't seem to care much about trees, though he was willing enough to work. Peggy didn't say anything, but after packing up lunch she took a planting bar and worked with the crew. Peggy's hair fell over her face in wisps which she brushed back in futile motions between plunges of the planting bar and setting of the seedlings. It wasn't strength so much as a quality of drive—of will and single-minded purpose—that she exuded.

The very qualities that made her an extraordinary supervisor and executive when she was a young woman in her twenties were apparent here. Her quiet example and thrust sparked the men better than any exhortation from me could have done. By midafternoon the planting quality improved and everyone was setting to with gusto, but we still wouldn't get done by day's end.

I hiked over to where the machine-planting was coming to an end. The machine-planters were doing stub runs—planting the short rows across the ends. There was much pumping-up of the mechanism and turn-around maneuvering during the short runs. They smiled. I knew the satisfaction of completing a seeding.

"We could use some more trees to plant the stub end of the old planting," Paul said. "We never did that and while we're here . . ."

I brought over a bundle from the hand-planters. As I left I heard debate about who would drive the tractor and who would plant.

The machine-planting was finished by late afternoon; by nightfall we had only 2,000 trees left for handplanting. I paid the crew. We'd plant the remainder on the morrow—just the family.

Best day of all. Weather same as yesterday, and morning started with a pair of loons flying over the little lake, splashing down for landing after much calling and crying. Good omen, loons. But that's silly; can't think of an animal or growing thing that isn't a good omen. It's just I'm fond of loons, and when I'm away from the land I miss their call.

We gathered around the remaining bundles after breakfast, leaning on our planting bars. We could have gone into the cutover area; there were some patches left to go. But I felt like spot-planting the earlier plantations, where there were open swaths. "I'll go between the two creeks. Always meant to do that and never have."

"I'll go on the hill over there," Paul said. "That's bothered me, that open space. We had tractor trouble and missed it a few years ago." And so we each went to our own place and put in the trees in privacy and with some leisure, taking a little extra care in the planting and for once not feeling that there was so much to be done we couldn't take the time to dally. Somehow, suddenly, there were no seedlings left and we gathered up the bars with regret. Off somewhere an American bittern was pumping— "swamp pump," the folks call them.

We held the family Memorial Day picnic under the big white pine atop the ridge, where we could see both lakes. We were all together—all five sons, grandchildren, wives—and the campfire smoke wafted by each of us, driven by a changeling wind. Then came the smells of pancakes and warming blueberry sauce and of sausage. The weather was damp and overcast at first, like yesterday's, but it warmed and the sun broke through as I took all the younger children to inspect the beaver dam at the outlet of the second lake. But someone had come during late winter and had trapped the animals out; no new ones had moved in yet. I wish we could stop the trapping—there are few beavers left.

We went to the township cemetery and gathered around Dad's grave. He'd asked to be buried there, in the place overlooking the river, a granite boulder from the fields marking his grave. It is flanked by two spruce—trees he liked nearly as much as the tamaracks. My sons and I had buried him as he had wished, without undertaker or folderol; just a family giving honor to its own with love, simplicity, and our own hands. Now we stood in a circle holding hands as we had that day eight years before. I wanted to say something now about him and his life, but Smith said, "He was a good man." There was nothing else to say and we went home, back to the farm.

Then it began to rain—a good, strong, steady downpour that will settle the seedlings into the ground.

Edward Eggleston

from THE MYSTERY OF METROPOLISVILLE

Edward Eggleston was born in 1837 in Indiana, where he attended coun-try schools and later became a circuit-riding Methodist minister. He drew on his Indiana experience in his novel The Hoosier Schoolmaster. *In 1856 he came to Minnesota hoping to restore his health. Eggleston's career in Minnesota is a microcosm of life on the frontier, where he alternated his preaching with selling soap, books, and insurance, organized the St. Paul Library Association, and gave stereopticon exhibitions. Pastor of the Jackson Street Church in St. Paul for a time, Eggleston was a force-ful and scholarly preacher. During his ten years in Minnesota he published poetry, short stories, and articles in national magazines as well as in the St. Paul newspapers.*

The Mystery of Metropolisville *was published in 1873, after Eggleston had left Minnesota, but it reflects his early days here. He had lived in Cannon City in 1856 in the period of the real estate booms, and although* Mystery *is marred by a certain sentimentality, it is an authen-tic picture of life in a new settlement.*

M R. PLAUSABY was one of those men who speak upon a level pitch, in a gentle and winsome monotony. His voice was never broken by impulse, never shaken by feeling. He was courteous without ostentation, treating everybody kindly without exactly seeming to intend it. He let fall pleasant remarks inciden-tally or accidentally, so that one was always fortuitously overhear-ing his good opinion of one's self. He did not have any conscious intent to flatter each person with some ulterior design in view, but only a general disposition to keep everybody cheerful, and an impression that it was quite profitable as a rule to stand well with one's neighbors.

The morning after Charlton's arrival the fat passenger called, eager as usual to buy lots. To his lively imagination, every piece of ground staked off into town lots had infinite possibilities. It seemed that the law of probabilities had been no part of the sanguine gentleman's education, but the gloriousness of possibilities was a thing that he appreciated naturally; hopefulness was in his very fiber.

Mr. Plausaby spread his "Map of Metropolisville" on the table, let his hand slip gently down past the "Depôt Ground," so that the fat gentleman saw it without seeming to have had his attention called to it; then Plausaby, Esq., looked meditatively at the ground set apart for "College," and seemed to be making a mental calculation. Then Plausaby proceeded to unfold the many advantages of the place, and Albert was a pleased listener; he had never before suspected that Metropolisville had prospects so entirely dazzling. He could not doubt the statements of the bland Plausaby, who said these things in a confidential and reserved way to the fat gentleman. Charlton did not understand, but Plausaby did, that what is told in a corner to a fat gentleman with curly hair and a hopeful nose is sure to be repeated from the house-tops.

"You are an Episcopalian, I believe?" said Plausaby, Esq. The fat gentleman replied that he was a Baptist.

"Oh! well, I might have known it from your cordial way of talking. Baptist myself, in principle. In principle, at least. Not a member of any church, sorry to say. Very sorry. My mother and my first wife were both Baptists. Both of them. I have a very warm side for the good old Baptist church. Very warm side. And a warm side for every Baptist. Every Baptist. To say nothing of the feeling I have always had for you—well, well, let us not pass compliments. Business is business in this country. In this country, you know. But I will tell *you* one thing. The lot there marked 'College' I am just about transferring to trustees for a Baptist university. There are two or three parties, members of Dr. Armitage's church in New York City, that are going to give us a hundred thousand dollars endowment. A hundred thousand dollars. Don't say anything about it. There are people who—well, who would spoil the thing if they could. We have neighbors, you know. Not very friendly ones. Not very friendly. Perritaut, for instance. It isn't best to tell one's neighbor all one's good luck. Not all one's good luck," and Plausaby, Esq., smiled knowingly at the fat man, who did his best to screw his very transparent face into a crafty smile in return. "Besides," continued Squire Plausaby, "once let it get out that the Baptist University is going to occupy that block, and there'll be a great demand—"

"For all the blocks around," said the eager fat gentleman, growing impatient at Plausaby's long-windedness.

"Precisely. For all the blocks around," went on Plausaby. "And I want to hold on to as much of the property in this quarter as—"

"As you can, of course," said the other.

"As I can, of course. As much as I can, of course. But I'd like to have you interested. You are a man of influence. A man of weight. Of weight of character. You will bring other Baptists. And the more Baptists, the better for—the better for—"

"For the college, of course."

"Exactly. Precisely. For the college, of course. The more, the better. And I should like your name on the board of trustees of—of—"

"The college?"

"The university, of course. I should like your name."

The fat gentleman was pleased at the prospect of owning land near the Baptist University, and doubly pleased at the prospect of seeing his name in print as one of the guardians of the destiny of the infant institution. He thought he would like to buy half of block 26.

"Well, no. I couldn't sell in 26 to you or any man. Couldn't sell to any man. I want to hold that block because of its slope. I'll sell in 28 *to you*, and the lots there are just about as good. Quite as good, indeed. But I want to build on 26."

The fat gentleman declared that he wouldn't have anything but lots in 26. That block suited his fancy, and he didn't care to buy if he could not have a pick.

"Well, you're an experienced buyer, I see," said Plausaby, Esq. "An experienced buyer. Any other man would have preferred 28 to 26. But you're a little hard to insist on that particular block. I want you here, and I'll *give* half of 28 rather than sell you out of 26."

"Well, now, my friend, I am sorry to seem hard. But I fastened my eye on 26. I have a fine eye for direction and distance. One, two, three, four blocks from the public square. That's the block with the solitary oak-tree in it, if I'm right. Yes? Well, I must have lots in that very block. When I take a whim of that kind, heaven and earth can't turn me, Mr. Plausaby. So you'd just as well let me have them."

Plausaby, Esq., at last concluded that he would sell to the plump gentleman any part of block 26 except the two lots on the south-east corner. But that gentleman said that those were the very two he had fixed his eyes upon. He would not buy if there were any reserves. He always took his very pick out of each town.

"Well," said Mr. Plausaby coaxingly, "you see I have selected those two lots for my step-daughter. For little Katy. She is going to get married next spring, I suppose, and I have promised her the two best in the town, and I had marked off these two. Marked them off for her. I'll sell you lots alongside, nearly as good, for half-price. Just half-price."

But the fat gentleman was inexorable. Mr. Plausaby complained that the fat gentleman was hard, and the fat gentleman was pleased with the compliment. Having been frequently lectured by his wife for being so easy and gullible, he was now eager to believe himself a very Shylock. Did not like to rob little Kate of her marriage portion, he said, but he must have the best or none. He wanted the whole south half of 26.

And so Mr. Plausaby sold him the corner-lot and the one next to it for ever so much more than their value, pathetically remarking that he'd have to hunt up some other lots for Kate. And then Mr. Plausaby took the fat gentleman out and showed him the identical corner, with the little oak and the slope to the south.

"Mother," said Albert, when they were gone, "is Katy going to be married in the spring?"

"Why, how should I know?" queried Mrs. Plausaby, as she adjusted her collar, the wide collar of that day, and set her breastpin before the glass. "How should I know? Katy has never told me. There's a young man hangs round here Sundays, and goes boating and riding with her, and makes her presents, and walks with her of evenings, and calls her his pet and his darling and all that kind of nonsense, and I half-suspect"—here she took out her breastpin entirely and began over again—"I half-suspect he's in earnest. But what have I got to do with it? Kate must marry for herself. I did twice, and done pretty well both times. But I can't see to Kate's beaux. Marrying, my son, is a thing everybody must attend to personally for themselves. At least, so it seems to me." And having succeeded in getting her ribbon adjusted as she wanted it, Mrs. Plausaby looked at herself in the glass with an approving conscience.

"But is Kate going to be married in the spring?" asked Albert.

"I don't know whether she will have her wedding in the spring or summer. I can't bother myself about Kate's affairs. Marrying is a thing that everybody must attend to personally for themselves, Albert. If Kate gets married, I can't help it; and I don't know as there's any great sin in it. You'll get married yourself some day."

"Did fa—did Mr. Plausaby promise Katy some lots?"

"Law, no! Every lot he sells 'most is sold for Kate's lot. It's a way he has. He knows how to deal with these sharks. If you want any trading done, Albert, you let Mr. Plausaby do it for you."

"But, mother, that isn't right."

"You've got queer notions, Albert. You'll want us all to quit eating meat, I suppose. Mr. Plausaby said last night you'd be cheated out of your eyes before you'd been here a month, if you stuck to your ideas of things. You see, you don't understand sharks. Plausaby does. But then that is not my lookout. I have all I can do to attend to myself. But Mr. Plausaby *does* know how to manage sharks."

The more Albert thought the matter over, the more he was convinced that Mr. Plausaby did know how to manage sharks. He went out and examined the stakes, and found that block 26 did not contain the oak, but was much farther down in the slough, and that the corner lots that were to have been Katy's wedding portion stretched quite into the peat bog, and further that if the Baptist University should stand on block 27, it would have a baptistery all around it.

122

Jon Hassler

from STAGGERFORD

Jon Hassler brings to his novel Staggerford *ample credentials for writing about small town life. Born in 1933, he graduated from Plainview (Minnesota) High School in 1951, received his B.A. from St. John's University in Collegeville, Minnesota, and his M.A. from the University of North Dakota. He has taught English literature at high schools in Melrose, Fosston and Park Rapids, and at Bemidji State University. Currently he teaches at Brainerd Community College. His short stories have appeared in the* Prairie Schooner, *the* North American Review, Four Quarters, *and the* South Dakota Review. *A second novel,* Simon's Night, *has been published by Atheneum, and he has also written for young adults. Hassler has received the Minnesota State Arts Board Creative Writing Award, a Minnesota State Arts Board Fellowship for 1972, and for* Staggerford *he received the Friends of American Writers Novel of the Year Award.*

F EW COULD REMEMBER a time when Miss McGee—slight and splay-footed and quick as a bird—was not teaching at St. Isidore's. This was her forty-first year in the same classroom, her forty-first year of flitting and hovering up and down the aisles in the morning when she felt fresh, and perching behind her walnut desk in the afternoon when fatigue set in. In the minds of her former students, many of whom were now grandparents, she occupied a place somewhere between Moses and Emily Post, and when they met her on the street they guarded not only their speech but also their thoughts.

They knew of course—for she had been telling the story for over half a century—that when she was a girl she had met Joyce Kilmer, but who would have guessed the connection between that meeting many years ago and the fire alarm this afternoon?

From *Staggerford*, © 1974, 1977 by Jon Hassler. Reprinted by permission of Atheneum Publishers.

Standing in the garden among her cabbages, she decided that she would never tell a soul—not even Miles—about the cause of the fire alarm. She could not lie, but she could keep a secret.

Agatha McGee met Joyce Kilmer when she was six. She was a first grader at St. Isidore's. The year was 1916 and her teacher, Sister Rose of Lima, primed the first grade for months, leading them in a recitation of "Trees" every morning between the Apostles' Creed and the Pledge of Allegiance; and then on the last day of school before Christmas break, Joyce Kilmer stepped through the classroom door at the appointed hour, casting Sister Rose of Lima into a state of stuttering foolishness and her students into ecstasy. Miss McGee remembered it like yesterday. Mr. Kilmer was handsome, cheery, and a bit plump. He wore a black suit and a red tie. With a playful sparkle in his eye he bowed to Sister Rose of Lima, saying he was delighted to meet her, and then he walked among her students, asking their names. The children's voices were suddenly undependable, and they told their names in tense whispers and unexpected shouts. Jesse Farnham momentarily forgot who he was, and the silence was thick while he thought. When he finally said, "Jesse," Mr. Kilmer told him that he had known a girl by that name, and the first grade exploded with more laughter than Sister Rose of Lima permitted on ordinary days. (Priests and poets melted her severity.) The laughter, ending as suddenly as it began, was followed by a comfortable chat, the poet telling stories, some without lessons. Before Mr. Kilmer left, his admirers recited "Trees" for him. For Agatha McGee his visit was, like Christmas in those years, a joy undiminished by anticipation.

But that was long ago. Nowadays poetry, among other things, wasn't what it used to be. Yesterday at St. Isidore's as Miss McGee sat at the faculty lunch table she overheard Sister Rosie tell Sister Judy in an excited whisper that Herschel Mancrief was coming to town. He was touring the Midwest on a federal grant, and would arrive at St. Isidore's at ten the next morning. The two sisters were huddled low over the Spanish rice, trying to keep the news from Miss McGee. She wasn't surprised. She was well aware that the new nuns, although pranked out in permanents and skirts up to their knees, were still a clandestine sorority. How like them to plan an interruption in the schoolday and not let her know.

"About whom are you speaking?" she asked.

"Oh, Miss McGee," said Sister Rosie, the lighthearted (and in Miss McGee's opinion, light-headed) principal of St. Isidore's. "We were discussing Herschel Mancrief, and we were not at all sure you would be interested." Sister Rosie was twenty-six and she had pierced earlobes.

"I will be the judge of my interests, if you please. Who is Herschel Mancrief?"

"He's a poet the younger generation is reading," said Sister Judy, blushing behind her acne. "We studied him in the novitiate."

"His credentials are super," said Sister Rosie.

"And he's coming to St. Isidore's? I might have been told. Will he visit classes or speak to an assembly?"

"He will visit classes. But of course no one is obliged to have him in. I know what a nuisance interruptions can be."

"Poets are important to children. I was visited by Mr. Joyce Kilmer when I was a girl, and I treasure the memory. Please show Mr. What's-his-name to my classroom when the time comes. What's his name?"

"Herschel Mancrief. He can give you twenty minutes at quarter to twelve."

So this morning Miss McGee announced to her sixth graders that they were about to meet Herschel Mancrief. They looked up from their reading assignment, a page headed "Goths and Visigoths," and as a sign of their undivided attention they closed their books. Divided attention was among the things Miss McGee did not permit. Slang and eye shadow were others.

"Meeting a poet is a memorable experience," she said. "When I was a girl, my class was visited by Mr. Joyce Kilmer, who wrote 'Trees,' the poem every child carries in his heart from the primary grades, and to this day I can recall what Mr. Kilmer said to us. He came to Staggerford a mere two years before giving his life for his country in World War One." She tilted her head back, in order to read her twenty-four sixth graders through her bifocals—difficult reading these days, for they lurked, boys and girls alike, behind veils of hair.

"The poet, you understand, is a man with a message. His mission is to remind us of the beauty God has made. He writes of the good and lasting things of life. His business is beauty. Are there any questions?"

There was one, and several students raised their hands to ask it: "How does 'Trees' go?"

"Heavens, surely you remember."

But it was discovered that no one in the class had heard it. As Miss McGee began reciting, "'I think that I shall never see,'" a frightening sensation crept up her spine and gripped her heart—an invisible tremor like the one she had felt in 1918 when her third-grade teacher said that Joyce Kilmer was dead in France. An imperceptible shudder that moved out along her nervous system and left her nauseous. Her name for it was the Dark Age dyspepsia, because it struck whenever she came upon a new piece of alarming evidence that pointed to the return of the Dark Ages.

Dark Age evidence had been accumulating. Last month at Parents' Night, Barbara Betka's father and mother told Miss McGee they would see her fired if she did not lift her prohibition against the wearing of nylons by sixth-grade girls. They were standing in the assembly room where coffee was to be served. Mr. Betka, fidgeting and averting his eyes, did most of the talking while Mrs. Betka, having called the tune, stood at his side and fingered his arm like a musical instrument. "Fired indeed!" said Miss McGee, turning on her heel and snatching up her purse in a single motion of amazing agility, like a move in hopscotch, and she flew from the assembly room before coffee was served. She was followed home by the Dark Age dyspepsia and scarcely slept that night, haunted by the specter of a man in his fifties sent out by his wife to do battle for nylons. "The craven ninny," she said to herself at dawn, rising to prepare the day's lessons.

And that was the day Dr. Murphy from the State Department of Education came to town to address a joint meeting of public and parochial school faculties. Both Miles and Miss McGee attended his lecture. "Never," Dr. Murphy said at the end of a tedious address on language arts, "never burden a child with a book written earlier than the child's date of birth. That way you can be confident that you and your students are in tune with each other, that you are moving with them on a contemporary plane." This harebrained proposal proved to Miss McGee that not even the State Department of Education was immune from the spreading plague of dark and crippling ignorance.

Nor were the sisters immune. More than once, for their spring picnic, Sister Judy had taken her fourth graders to a hippie farm. When Miss McGee first heard about that, she went to the pastor, Father Finn, and warned him about the return of the Dark Ages.

Father Finn, ordinarily a man of understanding, did not understand Miss McGee's anxiety. If the Dark Ages were coming back, he had not yet caught sight of them. He told Miss McGee that she was an alarmist.

This morning as she concluded with the line, "But only God can make a tree," the door opened and Herschel Mancrief appeared. He was led into the classroom by Sister Rosie. He was untidy. That was Miss McGee's first impression of him. Under his wrinkled suitcoat he wore a T-shirt and under his nose a thicket of hair that curled around the corners of his mouth and ended in a stringy gray beard.

Miss McGee said, "I am pleased to meet you," and she gracefully offered her hand.

"Groovy," said the poet, tapping her palm with the tip of one finger. Up close she saw that his neck and his T-shirt were unmistakably unwashed. His asymmetrical sideburns held lint. She hopped silently backward and slipped into an empty desk halfway down an aisle, and Sister Rosie introduced the visitor, training a spit curl as she spoke.

"Mr. Mancrief has already been to three rooms and he has another one to visit after yours, class, and he has to leave by twelve thirty, so when his time is up please don't bug him to stay." On her way out the door, Sister Rosie added, "Room 102 is next, Herschel. It's just across the hall."

The sixth grade regarded the poet.

"I am here to make you childlike," he began, blinking as he spoke, as though his words gave off too much light. "I am here to save you from growing up." His voice was deep and wheezy, and his frown was fixed. "You see, grownups aren't sensitive. They get covered over with a kind of crust. They don't *feel*. It is only through constant effort that I am able to maintain the wonder, the joy, the capacity for feeling that I had as a child." He quit blinking and inserted a hand under his suitcoat to give his ribs a general and thoughtful scratching. "Do you understand what I am saying?"

The class looked at Miss McGee. She nodded and so did they.

"Good. Now here's a poem of mine called 'What I Envied.' It's an example of what I'm saying." He closed his eyes and spoke in an altered voice, a chant:

"I envied as a child
the clean manikins in store windows

because their underwear fit
their toes were buried in thick carpet
their happy smiles immutable,
until my father driving us home
past midnight after a day in the country
passed a window full of manikins
and then I knew
the trouble it must be
to smile all night!"

After a silent moment the poet opened his eyes signaling the end of the poem.

Miss McGee had heard worse. Except for the reference to underwear, it came as close to poetry as most of the verse she had read lately, and she set the class to nodding its approval.

Herschel Mancrief shed his suitcoat and revealed that his pants were held up by a knotted rope. It was not the white, carefully braided rope of the Franciscans, who were Miss McGee's teachers in college, but a dirty length of frazzled twine.

"Good," said the poet, laying his suitcoat across Miss McGee's walnut desk. "You remember how heroic those manikins used to seem when you were small and they were larger than life. You would see one in a store window and it was enough to make you salute. The pity is that you gradually lose your sense of wonder for things like that. Take toilets, for example. My poem 'So Tall' is about a toilet."

He recited with his eyes shut. Miss McGee shut hers as well.

"How tall I seem to be these days
and how much I am missing,
things at ground level escape my notice
wall plugs wastebaskets heat registers,
what do I care for them now I am so tall?
I was once acquainted with a toilet
when it and I were eye to eye,
it would roar and swallow and scare me half to death.
What do I care for that toilet now,
now I am so tall?"

There was the sound of a giggle, stifled.

"You are surprised I got a toilet into a poem?" He was asking Miss McGee, who had not giggled. "But poetry takes all of life for

128

her domain. The beautiful and the unbeautiful. Roses and toilets. Today's poet seeks to represent the proportions of life. You don't very often pick a rose, but you go to the bathroom several times a day."

Certain now that he had taken the measure of Miss McGee's tolerance for the unbeautiful (color was rising in her face) the poet announced his third selection, "In My End of Town."

> "In my end of town
> like a cathedral against the sky
> stands the city sewage plant,
> the direction of the wind
> is important to us,
> in my end of town
> man disposes."

He opened his eyes to study Miss McGee's reaction, but the desk she had been sitting in was empty. She was at his side, facing the class.

"Students, you will thank Mr. Mancrief."

"Thank you, Mr. Mancrief." They spoke the way they prayed, in unison and without enthusiasm.

She handed the poet his coat and, not wishing to touch his hairy arms, she steered him to the door as if by remote control. "There"—she pointed—"is Room 102."

Nothing in his government-sponsored travels had prepared Herschel Mancrief for the brush-off. "Actually," he said, blinking as he backed into the corridor, "I hadn't finished."

"I regret we can spare you no more time. We recite the Angelus at twelve."

Looking more surprised than offended, he raised a hand as though to speak, but then thought better of it and stepped across the corridor and knocked on the door of 102. It opened instantly and Sister Judy put her head out.

Miss McGee, afraid now that her treatment of the man had been too delicate, said, "Another thing, Mr. Mancrief. Your poetry is . . ." She searched for the word. The poet and Sister Judy listened for it.

"Your poetry is undistinguished."

Sister Judy rolled her eyes and the poet chuckled into his hand. Miss McGee turned back to her class, pulling the door shut behind her. "Entirely undistinguished, class. You will rise now for the Angelus."

Later, entering the lunchroom, Miss McGee saw at the far end of the faculty table Herschel Mancrief and Sister Judy ignoring their beans and tuna and laughing like ninnies.

"I thought he was to have been on his way by this time."

"We asked him to stay for lunch," said Sister Rosie. "He has agreed to stay a while longer. Isn't he super?"

"He's horribly dated. He said 'groovy.' I haven't heard anyone say 'groovy' for at least three years."

"Oh, Miss McGee, he's super. Admit it."

"Pass the relish, if you please."

Two hours later, after putting her class to work on equilateral triangles, Miss McGee opened her door for a change of air. From behind the closed door of 102 she heard raucous laughter alternating with the excited voice of Herschel Mancrief. The man evidently could not bring himself to leave St. Isidore's. She stepped closer and listened through the door.

"Acquainted with a toilet," said the poet.

The fourth grade laughed.

"It would roar and swallow and scare me half to death."

More laughter.

"There, now you've caught the spirit of the poem. Now repeat it after me."

They did so, briskly, line by line.

"Now let's try another one—a poem I wrote just the other day called 'Be Careful Where You Grab Me.'"

Fierce laughter.

Miss McGee hurried to the nearest fire alarm and with a trembling hand she broke the seal and set off an ear-splitting jangle of horns and bells that emptied the building in forty-five seconds. Two ladder trucks pulled up to the front door and while the fire chief, a former student of Miss McGee's, gave the building a thorough inspection, Herschel Mancrief drove off in his rented car, the fourth grade throwing him kisses from the curb.

"A false alarm," declared the fire chief, emerging from the front door of the school in his yellow rubber coat.

"Someone set off the alarm near your room," he said to Miss McGee as she led her sixth grade up the steps and back into the building. "Did you notice anything suspicious, Miss McGee?"

"Goths and Visigoths," she said.

Mabel Seeley

from WOMAN OF PROPERTY

Mabel Seeley was born in Herman, Minnesota in 1903 and spent her first six years in Minnesota. After a sojourn in other middlewestern states she returned to Minnesota as a high school senior and lived in the state until 1949. Her father, a librarian, had a scholarly love for books and language, and her mother came from a large Norwegian-American family who provided Seeley with an ample repertoire of pioneer stories. At the University of Minnesota she was inspired by Mary Ellen Chase, at that time a member of the English Department. Seeley wrote advertising copy in Chicago and Minneapolis, an occupation she gave up in 1935 "to see . . . if I could write other kinds of fiction." A number of Seeley's tautly constructed mystery stories, including Listening House *and* Whispering Cup, *are set in Minnesota. In* Woman of Property, *from which the following selection is taken, Seeley departs from the mystery genre in favor of a character study of Frieda Schlempke from her girlhood in the 1880's until her middle age. The town of Amiot is a thinly disguised Northfield, Minnesota.*

S HE HAD LONG KNOWN she bore two stigmas: foreignness and poverty.

The Middle Western valley town in which she lived was one to which her family had moved when she was nine; they had no roots in it, little standing, few countrymen, no real friends. Of West Haven's four thousand inhabitants, half had come—or were descended from people who had come—from New England and New York, who had laid out wide tree-shaded streets, who had built porched and fretted white New England houses, who had founded Amiot College, and who called their town, nostalgically and blindly, "New England in the West." Of the rest, by far the greater portion was Norwegian, a compact close community which stood rigorously on its worth, and so was half accepted. The Norwegians had their rival college, St. Ansgar's, the fathers taught there or the children went there; together with the New Englanders they joined in scorning all "aliens"—the few German families, the Irish, Balik, the Hungarian photographer, and Pallini, the Italian in whose tonsorial parlor Otto Schlempke worked.

West Haven schools, as the *Independent* boasted, "opened their doors to rich and poor alike," but in them the children of these foreign families were alternately baited and ignored; teachers who, because the immigrants spoke a clumsy English, suspected their bodies of smelling and their minds of being turgid, seated them in rear corners and considered a righteous duty well done when they were allowed to listen while the fortunates were taught. At work they found open only such jobs as were socially unacceptable—house drudgery, rail laying, ditching, milling. Even before God they were separate—Catholic in a town which otherwise was solidly Protestant.

That the Schlempkes belonged to this outcast fringe they themselves did not question more inside the family than outside. All five children were American born, but both Otto and Ilse had emigrated from Bavaria; Otto, for all his quickness, could not manage a *th* sound; Ilse, under stress, lost her English entirely. And if the family's foreignness was thus fixed and immutable, so was its poverty. True, Otto Schlempke sometimes boasted he made twenty dollars a week in tips and wages—more than many a professor in the colleges—but this made no difference; it made no difference that Frieda and her brothers worked. Of Otto's income, almost the whole was spent on, or at least by, himself, squandered on drinks, gambling, cigars and those Benson House dinners to which he stormed out when he found the household fare uneatable. *He* was no peasant, as he frequently reminded himself and the rest of his family; his mother had been an officer's widow, the gayest and prettiest of Nuremburg; as a boy he had had everything he wanted; he had been raised (this was vague) to be banker, financier or diplomat; he had come to America to enter on a life of flowers, ease, wine, servants, rich clothes, admiration, perfume and the opera. It was only because of an incomprehensible and bewildering blindness among Americans, only because he had been dogged by bad luck, only because while still so young he had burdened himself with a wife and family, that he had been held from his birthright.

He might, as he did, grandiloquently order home the newest in ropework settees and rockers, and in ornate cupid-supported lamps; in the parlor these incongruous luxuries, together with the marble-top table, the Brussels carpet, the fringe-heavy scarlet curtains, sat tended and aloof, awaiting those few occasions when they were on display. But even these carried no weight against the humbling, shameful sparsity at every angle of their lives. Often there were no pennies for the collection plate at Mass, Lotte and Ernst filched paper and pencils from their mates at school, Viktor and Gottfried, at seventeen and sixteen, wore shirts and trousers rebuilt from Otto's. It was Ilse who held the family together, she who had induced Otto to learn barbering, she who maneuvered with limitless fierce patience until they had a cow and chickens, she who cleared weed-tangled wastes for gardens, she who sewed and preserved, she who bargained with the mill foreman for discolored flour, she who sold eggs, milk and vegetables to get the quarters and half dollars which bought staples and their meager clothing. Chickens could be eaten only when they got too old for laying; if they had other meat it was only because, perhaps once in a fortnight, Otto picked a butcher shop as the scene of his spending.

"Beef roast for my family—the best," he would say richly, hunching his shoulders to indicate his plight as the provider for so exigent a crew. "Nothing will do them but the best." At table afterward, reserving for himself the choicer portions of his purchase, he would continue to eulogize his provisioning, but even while his family ravenously ate, it kept the memory of all the evenings it had fared, and knew it yet would fare, on milk mush, on radishes with bread, or on a single egg for each.

This was the background with which Frieda was permeated; the background she knew as her own. And, looking about her at eight o'clock Mass, on the morning following the incident of the balcony, she had to feel—though this again was not in words— that here too, in what, except for her existence at the store, had been almost her only social contact, she was held within what was low, beggarly and alien.

The church structure enclosing her had been built for a scant twenty years, but already wall plaster was falling, revealing the rough laths and chinking; the ceiling above the rickety ash-gray stove was deeply grimed; the altar, though hung with an elaborate cloth, was unmistakably a pine kitchen table; the picture above it, of the Holy Family, was a rude lithograph in blues and reds; the benches were unvarnished and unpainted pine; the rough plank floor uncarpeted.

And of the congregation that jerkily creaked to stand, sit, kneel and genuflect within this edifice, most of the older generation, like her parents, wore the harsh stamp of Europe. Of the men, by far the greater number were farmers who had arrived in mud-caked lumber wagons and buckboards from a settlement near by, farmers who displayed the round bristled heads, thick necks, barrel chests and stumpy legs of peasants. Usually these men were thriftier than Frieda's father, most of them lived spartanly, working ten, twelve, fourteen hours a day, that in the future they might be rich, but there was something of Otto Schlempke in them nevertheless. No matter how humbly they might walk before the world, at home they were often overbearing and oppressive. Sentiment for a wife did not keep them from thinking of her as a servant; pride in a son did not prevent that son's being used as a source of labor and revenue through his minority.

This cult of the dominant male was one that had been brought from Europe, intact; it was one that in their lifetimes would never be broken. And if the men were like Frieda's father, then the women were even more like her mother: publicly silent, kerchiefed, wide-cheeked and cow-hipped, staring out with a blank passionate bleakness at a world in which they were given so little importance.

Between these parents and their children existed little but incongruity—and a lack of sympathy as deep as the oceans. The generation born on American soil might at home breathe the smog of Europe, might eat European cooking, might go almost as ill nourished as its parents had on those starved handkerchief plots that in Europe were called farms, might in addition bear through its impressionable youth the hated obloquy of being foreign. But still the newer generation was American, the young boys breathing and glancing like colts brought only resistantly and rebelliously to harness; the girls, even those as sullen and repressed as Frieda, carrying under their surfaces the gathering forces of ferment. Fathers were determined to press this young life into an old mold; mothers were frightened, before it came, by the inevitable separation; while the children spent themselves in loathing the parental language, the parental culture, the parental way of life—everything that seemed to make them inferior before their fellows.

When Father Doern, desisting from his Latin mumble, turned before the altar to deliver, in alternately shrieking and cajoling German, his usual sermon—a vivid portrayal of the postlife torments awaiting those who did not furnish the Church with one tenth of their gains—Frieda, who knew every facet of this group and her position in it with a dimmer but just as certain perception as that of sight, abruptly reached an overmastering necessity.

All her life she had kept away from those Other People of the town—the Americans, the people who Had Things, the people who made the judgments, the people who set the form. Now, however, she wanted to go where she could see, feel and know what made them different from herself.

She knew, too, exactly where she could go to do so. Between ten-fifteen and ten-thirty, on Sundays, the Best People of West Haven filtered themselves out from the Norwegians and the late-Mass Catholics, also church-bound at that hour, to move by carriage or on foot down Front Street toward the First Congregational Church. She would no more have thought of entering that chaste white-spired edifice than she would have thought of knocking at the gates of heaven, dressed as she was in her ignoble flesh. But across Front Street, under the low-hanging maples, anyone, even a foreigner, could linger and look on.

The thought of doing even so much was paralyzing, but there was a push in her muscles which almost violently propelled her toward it. So far in her life she had usually been alone in her activities: trudging alone to school, withdrawing suspiciously from any friendliness (Ilse taught her children to trust no one) offered by those of her own low caste, drudging by herself at the store. Now, however, she shrank from the thought of appearing under those maples unaccompanied. Yet with her on the short pine bench were only Lotte and Ernst, infants of five and seven, and not only would Ernst and Lotte be no support, but they might also reveal her new blind groping at home.

As uncertain in its quest as a bee, her glance skipped over the heads of girls she knew by name among the worshipers—Miss Klaumeister, the butcher's daughter, who, whatever she might have been christened, was known among her mates as Schatz, or Schatzi; Lise Hetweit; Maria Pallini; twelve-year-old Rozzie Balik.

135

Approaching any one of them was an act of such hardihood that it alone, at any preceding time, would have been incredible. Yet when Father Doern at last rose from his prayers, coifing himself and striding from the altar as a signal that the service was over, she found herself moving with puppet-stiff jerks toward Rozzie Balik.

"I don't suppose you'd want to—go by the Congregational." The hoarse words cut torturously at her throat and burst from her lips, seeming, the moment they were said, to be outrageous and indecent. At once she would have recalled them if she could, but Rozzie's head with its two long red-brown braids had already jerked about, Rozzie's brown eyes had sparkled and her whole angular face leaped to responsiveness.

"You mean stop by there and see the people? I *luff* to go by there; I often go by there." In the hushed words was the exact assurance Frieda cried for—Of course you have a right to see those people, that assurance said, I understand in every way. But even while Frieda was sending Lotte and Ernst—dumfounded by the freedom—home alone, even while she was stepping woodenly with Rozzie from the church steps to the tree-lined walk where in the sun the gum was oozing from the boards, she knew another hot discomfort. Rozzie limped terribly, without repression or concealment, her head rising and falling in a bobbing abandon at the level of Frieda's shoulder, her misshapen body twisting, her shorter leg flirting its foot to the side. At school—Frieda had left the year before, but Rozzie still attended—boys ran past Rozzie, catching with suddenly outshot feet at her good ankle, bringing her crashing to the ground. From these falls Rozzie always rose laughing and good-natured, as if she thought the boys were friendly—Rozzie expected friendliness in everyone. Not that she found much of it. In school the Germans and Irish at least had a few compatriots, but of Hungarians there was only Rozzie. Just as, of Italians, there was only Maria. Maria, cast on Rozzie as an only resource, fitfully accepted and rejected Rozzie's amity.

"Maybe Maria could come too," Rozzie now hinted, but when Frieda silently clopped on she accepted the rejection without argument. "What I luff *most* about First Congregational is the clothes," Rozzie immediately said, slipping into an easy confidence. Rozzie, apparently, could describe every Empire-green ostrich plume, every brocaded polonaise, every embroidered cashmere in West Haven.

While they went up one street and down another (Mass had been over shortly after nine) Frieda had good time to regret what she had started. Mutely and unseeingly, thinking only of her purpose, she followed wherever Rozzie led, past wide white houses set well back behind lawns studded with star and crescent flower beds, with flowers in kettles swung from iron tripods— sign that that family no longer rendered its own lard or made its soap; past cheaper houses set up near the walk, their narrow porches lumbered with rockers, kitchen chairs and dirt-smeared children; down into the business section of the town, past livery stables smelling acridly of ammonia, manure and dusty hay, past the sour-sweet smell of the lumberyard.

West Haven had been settled for a quarter century; it had two banks, a city hall, a Y.M.C.A., a power company; it thrived and bustled, vying with larger cities to the north for the eminence of being a metropolis; it lay pleasantly upon the flood plain of a river, the Cannon; it was surrounded by an undulant rich farm country of clear fields, substantial farmsteads, hardwood patches. Upon a low hill to the south, beyond the river, stood Amiot College, with its six buildings, its thirty acres of grounds, its tended trees and flowers and paths; on another hill to the north were St. Ansgar's fifty-seven acres, its path-threaded woodland, its two tall brick buildings from which the Gothic windows looked over the treetops at the town like brow-arched eyes.

Of this town through which she now passed, however, Frieda knew only what impinged directly upon her: the street where she lived, the Hake Grocery and Dry Goods Emporium where she worked, the river where occasionally she had gone with Ernst and Lotte to wade in the cold, red, bubbling, iron-smelling water.

"You'd look nicer than Nettie Orcutt if you had Nettie's fawn merino; it has stays." Rozzie, as they progressed, continued to babble. Schatz Klaumeister and Lise Hetwiet, seeing them walk off together, had glanced meaningfully at each other and giggled; no one else had seemed to notice, but Frieda felt intolerably that she had demeaned herself. Yet she could not break away, either. The necessity to look on at those Other People had now become a fever in her blood.

"Calico is nice, but it goes *slimp*." With shy fingers Rozzie touched the sleeve of Frieda's green calico, put on that morning for the week. "Someday," she confided, "when I get to sew better, I will make you a dress really *beautiful*."

At the stare which met this, Rozzie flushed darkly, red rising slowly over her wide high cheekbones; when next she spoke it was almost fiercely.

"I don't care. Someday I will do good sewing. See, I make my own dress now. Maybe it is not good, but it makes me look better than I *am*."

The dress of which she spoke was a sheer wool in dark rose, which fitted her smoothly but not closely, the basque rounding at the waistline, the skirt draped in slight U-folds across the front and caught into a puff in back.

"Someday," she went on belligerently, when Frieda's silence continued, "I will be the best dressmaker in this *country*." But then, lightly, she exploded her temerity with laughter. "No, but I will make pretty dresses to wear on Sunday in West Haven, and maybe *you* will get the prettiest."

Be friends with me, the words coaxed, and maybe you need not be sorry.

Deaf to anyone else's purposes, Frieda would have said she did not hear. The two girls were again, for a third or fourth time, across from the narrow, neat New England meeting house, complete with white clapboards, porch and spire, which was the First Congregational. This time it was not untenanted: the two big carved oak doors had been thrown open, revealing a dim interior which even across the street smelled richly of decorum, varnish, carpet, paint and plush; about the steps a group of half-grown boys had gathered, indulging in those swipes at hats, those jerks at coattails, those subdued knee-kicks in the pants, which were appropriate to that time and place.

Heart thickly beating, unconscious fingers clamping convulsively on Rozzie's arm, Frieda moved forward until she stood half under a concealing maple, her whole body becoming a medium for absorption and reception. This was the time she had awaited, now.

Halfway down the block a family was approaching, first a father and grown son, each with derby, short cutaway buttoned just below the breastbone, tight striped trousers. Next came four girls in ruffled white, and last the mother with a younger son, the mother toqued and parasoled in pink lilac, rustling in a dove-gray satin polonaise drawn back to reveal its pink-lilac underskirt.

"That's the Leveretts," murmured Rozzie. "Louise has her summer white on. Mrs. Leverett's parasol is nice; it makes her face and dress all rosy." But again Frieda only vaguely heard. It was not—or was it?—for lessons on fashion she had come.

As the parental Leveretts filed into the church, the six children, caught by suddenly imperative conversation, stayed out on the boardwalk. New groups, meanwhile, like the Leveretts but different, came in view—fathers leading small boys with prominent pearl buttons on their prominent anteriors, mothers fussing about little girls in full white lawns or muslins, with bright cascading hair and small round hats held to the backs of the necks by vivid ribbons, or swung swaggeringly from the hand. A young couple came alone, the man with his bowler in hand, bent toward a pert girl who twirled a black lace parasol and laughed up at him. Quickly now the street was full, families driving up in fringe-top surreys from which the men descended gravely to tie horses to the hitching posts, and from which stout women in black silk, some still wearing bustles, with great fuss and flurry got themselves to earth. Bachelors and more young couples dashed up in single buggies, the girls uttering subdued shrieks and giggles as, in the approved manner—hand to the shoulder of the gentleman, gentleman's hand under their elbows—they were helped down, their dainty slippered feet groping helplessly within a foamy sea of petticoats to find the small elusive steps.

"Those are the Cantrells," Rozzie whispered. "That's Mr. and Mrs. Page and their little boy. That's Mrs. Simon and Mrs. Langesley. That's the Coburn family. Those are the Wattses." Some of these figures, dimly, Frieda recognized; the Widow Noble, for instance, was a regular customer of Hake's, and so were the Bacons. When Rozzie, nudging, whispered the name "Amiot," however, her lips opened and all other cognizance faded out. The Amiots were people of such high importance that she scarcely dared look.

On foot they advanced down Front Street—West Haven's first citizen and his daughter. Two terms in Congress had affixed an "Honorable" to Thomas Amiot's name; he owned the mill where Viktor and Gottfried worked, he also owned the bank, the college honored by its name his generous donations. It was incredible to think that she, Frieda Schlempke, could thus stand to look on at his solid nearing bulk, his high silk hat, his tailed Prince Albert, his gold-tipped cane, his eyeglasses. And as for Cecilia—.

Everything about Cecilia Amiot, as Frieda had to see at once, was perfect. Cecilia was dark-eyed and waxen, Cecilia had pale, fringed, ash-blond hair on which rode the tiniest of green-and-pink-plumed hats; Cecilia was dressed in silk of palest green, the basque revealing an incredible slenderness, the skirt a miracle of drapery, panniers and ruffles.

Like other people of his advanced age, Thomas Amiot ascended at once into church, pausing only for a few grave, dignified greetings to those who clustered about the door, perhaps for this privilege. But Cecilia, like the other young people, slipped aside to join one of those chattering and merry-glancing sidewalk groups which, just then, seemed to be suffering an apprehension and a waiting.

"I don't think they'll get here at all!" one feminine voice could be heard, pouting. "They've gone off somehwere, that's what they've done!" But this plaint was broken by a flutter almost of applause.

From the direction of Amiot College appeared a dozen bicyclers, first discernible in the distance as a moving blot of flaming color, later resolving itself into the gay bloods of the town, young men in striped blazers, boaters, forelocks, slender trousers, who wheeled with incredible verve and dash the fashionable contraptions—mostly high-wheelers, but there were a few even of the brand-new safeties—which they bestrode, sitting back with arms folded to let their machines steer themselves, coming to split-second stops and turns, weaving in and out in convoluted patterns, performing miracles of balance as they made their descents.

Forthrightly, in the sun of their self-confidence, these audacious spirits invaded the waiting groups, setting bonnets on the bounce, drawing the chosen up into the church. After them, in a swiftly disappearing ebb tide, went the others. The double doors closed, the porch was empty, the church, to all senses but one, was deserted. From the interior came the sound of voices in a hymn. It was ten-thirty.

On the walk opposite Frieda stood awhile without moving, stood so long Rozzie made an uncertain offer.

"We could stay to see them come out."

"No," Frieda answered without inflection. "I don't want to see them come out." She began to move, taking leave of Rozzie with no more than an abrupt "Good-bye now." She had no more immediate need of Rozzie.

What seemed to remain in her mind most blindingly, as an apex and symbol of all she had just seen, was a mental picture of the stocky young man in an orange-and-blue-striped blazer who, skimmer in hand, had stopped to nod his head familiarly and easily at Cecilia Amiot before escorting her into the church. Once a week, at least, that same young man burst into Hake's to do what he called "knocking the old man for a rap." He was Palmer Hake, Junius B. Hake's only son. Mr. Hake didn't go to churches; Mr. Hake said so, with his tired indifferent insolence, even to ministers. But his son did. She had seen him. With Cecilia Amiot.

Her father, as she soon found, was home alone; Lotte and Ernst had chosen a lesser evil by trotting off with Ilse and the grown boys to second Mass. From a bitterly vituperative hangover, when she appeared, her father spat at her her latest sins: she had dared to send Lotte and Ernst home alone while she went off no one knew where, for no one knew what vicious purpose, but obviously to annoy him; she thought she was a clever Fräulein to defy her father and all decency, but she would find out.

As insensitive to his words, since he didn't actually ask where she had been, as to the slaps which punctuated them, Frieda waited until, infuriated by her passive lack of resistance, he at last screamed at her to go. Taking then the steep, curving, triangular-stepped stairway to her room, she dropped upon the patchwork-quilted bed.

She was, still, almost unconscious of herself, filled only by the people she had seen. Cecilia Amiot and Palmer Hake, as they walked up those church steps, had almost visibly exuded that golden haze of richness, self-confidence and impregnability, in which, for her, Those Others lived and had their being. They were the people who knew everything, enjoyed everything, owned everything, were at home in everything. They were the people who Had.

"Someday it might be yours." If she had money, as much money as Mr. Hake had thrown about the balcony, then she too—wouldn't she?—would be one of Those Others. Somehow, in getting money, she must be transformed out of her poverty,

141

out of her foreignness, out of her inconsiderableness, out of this room, in which one small square window looked in at the low sloped ceiling, the rickety short scratched wooden bed, the washstand. She would be transported to an unimagined realm of friends, admiration, Things.

Or perhaps, perhaps—

Heart beating out against her ribs in swelling, thudding bumps, she glimpsed a possible other way.

Perhaps it was by getting to look like those Other People, by walking like them, talking like them, that you got the money. Perhaps it was becoming one of those Other People that *came first*. Somehow you got accepted by them, taken into them, and then you *got the money*.

Into her small, round, scallop-edge mirror she gazed dispassionately. Between herself and the flecked and wavy glass hovered an image of Cecilia Amiot, of Cecilia's fringe, her palely gleaming coils of hair, her pallid skin, her fairy's dress. Through Cecilia she looked upon her own thick, dark, kinked mop—hair which, in spite of Ilse's tired chiding, seldom got much more than a few impatient tugs from the comb. She looked, too, upon the crudity of her color, and then, far beyond the mirror's confines, upon the shapeless ugliness of her unfitted bodice, the shortness of her skirt, the clumsiness of her shoes, the entire sodden nothingness of her person.

Impossible, one part of her mind cried fiercely, while another as fiercely answered, Sometime it might be yours. For a moment she saw another vision of herself—her hair changed not so much in color as in smoothness and luster, her color lessened, her figure tightened and lifted. That vision left, but after it was gone some difference seemed to remain—perhaps a steadiness of regard.

Vaguely she recalled a time when her mother had still brushed and dressed her, and when her father had occasionally called her *"Mein Herzchen mit Lochigem Haar."* After its infrequent washings, her hair still rippled.

Quietly stealing down to her mother's bedroom, as quietly returning, she stood again before the mirror, this time with scissors in her hand.

Margaret Culkin Banning

THE PERFECT JUROR

Margaret Culkin Banning was born in Buffalo, Minnesota in 1891, and grew up in the Duluth suburb of Hunter's Park. She has lived in Duluth intermittently ever since. Of her writing she has said, "I am, I think, less interested in projecting actual physical scenes than . . . in reflecting manners and ideas that seem to me to be significant either because they are typical or because they depart from the current type." After studying at Vassar College and working in a settlement house for a year, Banning married and had two children. Her novels and stories have continued to reflect her involvement in problems of religious bigotry, politics, and women at work. Much of her fiction is an index to the social and economic clashes in her native region, with its wealth based on iron mining, its recognition that the mines were wearing out, and the dichotomy between the mine owner and the worker in the range towns.

T HE DISTRICT ATTORNEY, Mr. Harvey Porter, passed his hand back over the sleek, oiled curve of his hair and ran through the formula.

"Now, Miss Monroe," he concluded, "do you know of any reason why, if chosen as a juror in this case, you should not be able to judge the matter fairly on the evidence as presented?"

"No, sir," said the girl.

"We accept the juror."

"The following will be the jurors in this case. The other members of the panel may report in courtroom number three," called the clerk of court, in his even, waveless voice.

He read the list off pompously, and the men and women who had been rejected as jurors rose to go to the other courtroom, a slight expression of chagrin on some of their faces.

"That Miss Monroe was chosen again. She never is scratched,"

First published in *Harper's Magazine*, volume 152, January 1926, copyright 1925 by Harper & Brothers. Reprinted by permission of the author.

said one woman to another as they went out. "She goes from one case to another. Of course, personally, I am very glad to be excused, especially from a bootlegging case; but I wonder why they always select such a young girl who can know so little of the world."

"Those lawyers are pretty clever. That's the kind they like, Mrs. Dowling. Someone told me they call her the perfect juror. I heard she's been on ten cases this term."

"Well," said the lady in blue foulard charitably, "she's very ignorant. She doesn't know anyone and she hasn't any opinion on anything. Personally, when I have an opinion I cannot keep it hid. I was glad to tell that Finn's attorney exactly where I stood on prohibition!"

Mrs. Dowling bridled with pride and remembered oratory. She had been scratched on all the bootlegging cases and had been retained on very few of any sort; but still at four dollars a day it was interesting to spend most of the day about the courthouse and pick up bits of news and sort out the women of the panel to gossip with. Courtroom number three swallowed her up temporarily.

Elsa Monroe put her soft felt hat in the locker in the jury room and took the high-backed chair which the bailiff indicated in the jury box. It was in the front row, and she was discovering after five weeks of jury duty that she did not like the front row. One had to stand the direct address of the attorneys who fixed their eyes so devastatingly upon the faces of members of the jury. It was too close to the action which was going on. Any movement seemed exaggerated into restlessness, any whisper seemed commotion.

She was a pretty, red-haired girl with a smooth, white face that told little and yet did not seem secretive, a face in which intelligence was pleasantly adequate without being raised to attack or intensity. The red hair lay in loose waves on the sides of her head and was caught into a knot at the back. She was neat in the manner of an expert stenographer and her dark-blue crêpe dress was firmly built and unwrinkled. From her place in the jury box she looked across at the profile of the accused bootlegger, a Finn, with an inscrutable, triangular face, sloping away from high cheekbones. He was still, still as those who do not comprehend can be sometimes in a kind of self-protection. Beside him sat his lawyer, a fat, heavy man, who made a business of defending such cases. The rest was usual: The tables, the court reporter, blinking under his green shade, the judge wearing the expression of routine and, back in the courtroom, shielded by rows of empty seats, a half dozen peering faces and slouching bodies, ill at ease, whispering now and then to one another and quickly stiffening when the eye of the judge rambled in their direction. There was a gnomelike little man with a queerly shriveled body, several uncouth, tow-headed younger ones, and two women, one of them young, cheaply dressed in country clothes.

It was one more bootlegging case on a crowded calendar. The courtroom was empty of spectators, and the members of the jury settled down in their chairs to positions of as much comfort as was conformable with their dignity. In the back row, as Elsa Monroe knew, some of them would let their minds doze behind their empty eyes.

The prosecuting attorney, rising and moving to the rail of the jury box, began quietly and informally:

"This, ladies and gentlemen, is a very simple case, a clear-cut violation of the laws enacted against the manufacture and sale of intoxicating beverages. The defendant was apprehended in the sale of what is known as moonshine whiskey on certain definite occasions. We shall put the case before you without many words and by calling few witnesses. I only ask you, ladies and gentlemen, to remember that the prosecution of these cases by this office is not a matter of routine. This is a criminal offense!" His voice rang sharply for a minute and the strange green-blue of the Finn defendant's eyes blazed apprehensively. "A criminal offense cannot be regarded lightly. You men and women have been chosen to sit upon this case because we feel that you think this offense as serious as any other criminal case. I ask you to regard this as a matter of upholding the constitution of the United States to which you, I, and every citizen is personally pledged. I will show you that on certain occasions . . ."

He was brief as he had promised and Mr. Carson, the Finn's lawyer, almost equally so. He appealed to the members of the jury not to forget that a man was innocent until he was proved guilty, not to have or hold prejudice against a man because he could not speak the English language, to consider this case as exactly what it was—not a test of the prohibition amendment, but a question as to whether this man was innocent or guilty of selling liquor.

Both lawyers spoke rapidly, easily. Their words rolled out as if they had been used in the same places before, and their minds might have been on their dinners, salaries, or loves, so glib were the formulæ. The judge paid no attention to them. He looked over some papers on his desk and called the bailiff to him.

"We will call Gilbert Sorenson," announced the prosecution.

From his corner seat a tall shambling man rose and went to the witness chair. He moistened his lips and, finding himself too long for the chair, leaned forward, his hands pressed together between his knees. He was part of the formula too and as he acknowledged his name and his vague occupation, "employed by the county," his eyes roamed over the jury and settled appreciatively on Elsa Monroe's white skin until she stirred as if to shake him off.

"You know the defendant, Pikkanen?"

"Yes."

"When did you first see him?"

"Wednesday, August fourteenth, near Redwood."

"Tell the jury under what conditions you saw him."

"We heard," said the stool-pigeon, "that there was liquor sold at Lahti's store, so we went up there that day and went in. This fellow was behind the counter there."

"What kind of a store?"

"Soft drinks—on the sign." The stool-pigeon grinned faintly.

"We object to the witness' interpolation," said the other attorney; "was it a soft drink parlor or not?"

"Is Lahti's a soft drink parlor?"

The witness lost his grin and said that it was.

"What did you buy there?"

"We asked him if we could get some moonshine. He said to wait a minute. Then he took us out to the shed and poured us two drinks."

"Drinks of what?"

"Moonshine whiskey."

"A liquid potable as a beverage and, if taken in sufficient quantities, likely to produce an intoxicating effect?"

"Yes, sir."

The answers knew the questions and the questions knew the answers. They almost met each other coming.

"Did you buy any liquor in bottles?"

"Not that day."

"Did you buy any later?"

"Yes, sir."

"When?"

"We went back the next day and Pikkanen sold us two bottles."

The district attorney leaned forward and lifted a bottle from the table after his exhibits had been formally identified. It was a plain glass bottle labeled heavily and the contents had no color.

"Is this one of the bottles?"

"One of them."

"Is this the other?"

"Yes, sir."

He questioned the witness as to the labels, the time they were written, the identification.

"The state offers these exhibits in evidence."

As the attorney walked up to the court reporter to record the entry the Finn's blue eyes again lighted with the flame of interest. But his lawyer paid no attention. The huddled figures in the back of the courtroom might have been carved of stone by some great sculptor of peasantry, so still were they.

Gilbert Sorenson sat shiftily through the cross-examination, peppered with objections from the district attorney. He'd lived in the county a long time. Yes, he admitted he had been a bartender at one time. Well, for maybe seven, eight years.

"How do you know this is moonshine liquor? Did you taste it?"

"Yes, sir."

"Know the taste of moonshine, all right, don't you?"

"Yes, sir," Sorenson grinned sheepishly, his eyes wandering again to Elsa Monroe, who lifted a scornful chin.

"Just how drunk were you that night you say you went back to buy the liquor?" asked Mr. Carson abruptly.

"Object to the question as irrelevant and prejudicial to the witness and move it be stricken from the record."

Stricken it might be and was. But in the minds of the jurors worked doubt, as the attorney for the defense had known it would work.

Sorenson was followed by a still more unattractive person who had been with him that day, a pimply man with a complexion that looked as if it had sprouted in a cellar, dead white under his pimples. He too recognized the white liquid as intoxicating as a beverage, under the sneers of the attorney for the defense. His story was merely one of corroboration. It all sounded rehearsed to

Elsa Monroe. One could see that the two men had been set on the Finn like a couple of hounds, and sniffing at their heels was another witness, the farmer's boy who had helped them, a shifty boy, less of the field than of the crossroads store, the strange product which is half rotten though it has always been exposed to sun and air. He said the Finns out there made liquor. Sure, everybody knew it. The judge turned sharply on him at that careless answer and the boy's words began to stiffen. When they released him from the witness chair he was purplish red from anger and embarrassment and went to sit beside Sorenson and his friend and seemed to be muttering under his breath. The judge announced adjournment.

The district attorney, resuming the case at two o'clock, remarked briefly that his case was closed. The jury shifted in their seats. It was half over now and they'd finish the case possibly by mid-afternoon and have the rest of the day off.

"We call Oscar Pikkanen in his own defense," said Mr. Carson.

The Finn was taller than Elsa had thought. There was a litheness to his body, a kind of spring in his step that indicated health. He took the witness chair awkwardly and his shining blue eyes were fearful. Elsa felt a strange desire to say something to him, to say that nothing was decided yet, not to be so frightened.

"The witness will need an interpreter," said his attorney.

"If the court please," said the prosecution, "we prefer to see how much English this man can muster up if he tries."

The court frowned but he recognized the right of the county attorney.

"Try him on a few questions, Mr. Carson, and if he doesn't understand we can get the interpreter then. Have you one ready?"

"Just outside."

"Very good."

"What is your name?"

It was different on his own tongue from what it had been on the others. Pikkanen became a used, familiar word, not a harsh thing of quarreling consonants.

"You live where?"

"Near Redwood."

"How long have you been in this country?"

"Three years."

"What do you work at?"

"Farm."

"You own your farm?"

The witness rubbed the chair with his hands in dismay. His English was failing him. He fumbled through a question or two more.

"If the court please," suggested the attorney for the defense, in irritation, "it is quite clear that we need the interpreter."

"Call him," said the court.

But the interpreter was not a man. She was a woman, or possibly a girl, grave and blonde and with the grace of acquired education which comes sometimes to those who regard it seriously. The Finn stayed in the witness chair and she sat beside him, her intent face mindful of his answers and her repetition of them was in an English so pure and careful that it was a pleasure to hear her. The girl on the end of the jury box, whom the lawyers called the perfect juror, leaned forward. She liked to watch Miss Aklan and she was curiously grateful for the ease and friendliness which had come into the testimony through the interpreter.

Through Miss Aklan the Finn said that he had been working on a farm. It was the farm of his friend, who had written him to come to this country. He lived there with his friend. Moonshine, no they did not make it. The word moonshine came out of his own speech, a curious incongruous word in the middle of the Finnish, and the interpreter repeated it gravely though on her lips also it hardly seemed suitable. Sometimes he worked in Lahti's store, behind the counter. Lahti too had been a friend in Finland. He helped him. He was there on the fourteenth of August. On the fifteenth he had not been there. He had not sold liquor to the men who claimed that he had done so. No. He had been making hay on the farm. One must make hay on the farm. The extra help had all been needed. He had worked all day. It was three miles to the store. He drove the Ford of his employer sometimes and went in to help Lahti in the store when his work was done. Not that day. No.

The cross-examination of the witness through the interpreter was difficult. That was why the prosecuting attorney objected to interpreters. The shock of his swift questions was broken as it came through the suavity of the girl interpreter. He let Pikkanen go after establishing the fact that, even after he had made hay all day, there would still be time to get into town with the Ford and be at the Lahti store at the time the stool-pigeons had said they bought the liquor from him.

There was a brief low-voiced consultation of the lawyers on

some admissible testimony and Elsa Monroe could hear the whisper of the man behind her to his neighbor.

"That bottle make you thirsty, Murphy?"

Murphy gave a half-hushed guffaw.

"Damned tantalizing," he answered.

The old man who owned the farm, Pikkanen's employer, was called to the stand. He was a gnarled old man whose body had been twisted by weather and ill-tended disease. His English was meager but he had enough to corroborate the story of the defendant and his eyes twisted around as he did it, not so much furtively as like the eyes of an animal in unfamiliar surroundings, fearful of danger.

Two other men, their faces black-brown from exposure, their English halting, testified that no moonshine was made near the place where they lived, and that Pikkanen had been at home on that day.

"Was he home the day before?" asked the district attorney.

They blundered. They did not know.

"Was he home the day after?"

That, too, they did not know.

"Yet you remember distinctly that on the fifteenth of August he was there?"

"Yes."

"You marked that special day off on your calendars, I suppose?"

They could not understand the reason for that query.

"Let it go," said the prosecution. It had been for the benefit of the jury anyway. Their testimony was too smooth, too organized. The old woman gave the same story.

"How do you remember the fifteenth of August?" the district attorney asked her.

"Yes," she said.

"Do you remember it because you and your husband and these other friends talked it over and decided all together to tell the same story to save Pikkanen?"

"Object," roared the defense's attorney.

The judge grew serious. He meditated.

"Objection overruled. She may answer."

A faint quiver went over the face of the interpreter as she repeated the question and the quiver was in Elsa's mind also. The old woman wouldn't know what the question meant.

"Yes," said the old woman in Finnish. She was a dull old woman and wanted to please and did her best.

The attorney for the prosecution grinned.

"That's all," he said cheerfully, and the jury members seemed to be tempted to smile with him. All but Elsa. She had been on motor-accident cases, trials involving money and bankruptcies, and even uglier things during this term, and none of them had hit deep in her mind like this one. She had an odd feeling that the thing was not quite clear, that someone should clearly bring out the fact that the Finns did not know the language, that from their whole manner they did not understand.

The defense called its last witness. She was the younger woman of the two and she had been in the country just a year. Yet the year had given her time enough to learn a little English. She had a Finnish face too, with a strange touch of Slav, smooth and withdrawn, and her blond braided hair twisted about her head. And she was frightened.

The questions were as they had been to the others and the answers the same. The stories of the Finns held together almost too well. If they had differed a little it would have been better for them.

"You too remember the fifteenth of August?"

She nodded with a quick monosyllable.

"Was Pikkanen there on the fourteenth? During the whole evening?"

"I think so. I cannot be sure."

"How about the sixteenth?"

"I do not know."

"Yet the fifteenth of August is clear to you?"

"Yes."

"Will you explain to the jury your remarkable memory, which picks days out of the month and remembers them accurately after a lapse of three months and quite forgets what happened on days which preceded or followed?"

She looked at him helplessly. He looked back cruelly authoritative.

"I don't understand."

"Get the interpreter," said the prosecuting attorney.

The two young women sat side by side and into the interpreter's tone had come an unconscious gentleness as she repeated with little limited expressions of her hands what the lawyer had

said. Into the face of the Finnish girl came a strange look of com-
prehension. She swallowed some emotion and her eyes went
straight to the face of the defendant, whose blue eyes were fixed
on her always.

"She says she remembers because it was a feast day."

"What feast day?"

"The feast of the Assumption of the Blessed Virgin."

"A Catholic feast?"

"Yes."

"Isn't it strange for a Finn to be a Catholic?"

The girl talked rapidly, bewilderingly and yet with a certain
reluctance and at last the interpreter took up the drama.

"She comes from the south of Finland and there are a few Finns
there close to Russia who are still Catholics. She says that the
Finns at the farm laughed at her, that she never went to mass but
she prayed secretly on these days which are feast days. She says
she remembers that day because she was asking the Blessed Virgin for a special favor."

"May we ask the favor?"

They were all intent, listening now. There was a pause. The
defendant's lawyer, seeing sympathy wake for his witness, did
not interfere.

The witness did not speak. The interpreter pressed her. Then
the words came slowly as the red spread over the Finn girl's
cheeks.

"She asked that the defendant might be able to marry her
soon."

"That's all."

Elsa watched the girl go back to her place without a glance at
Pikkanen. But she had caught too that glorious look of love which
swept his face as he heard her testimony and half rose from his
seat. She turned her eyes from him.

"After this little romance," said the prosecution, standing before the jury box and beginning his talk, "we will proceed with
the summary of facts. I assume the matter is clear to all of you as it
certainly is clear to me. These people, at least old Niemi, owns a
farm. They are clannish, these Finnish people. They come to this
country eager for its privileges and without regard for its laws.
They have taken up land. They are allowed the freedom of the
greatest republic on the face of the earth. Yet how do they repay
us? Four of these witnesses cannot speak the English language.

152

Four of them have not been naturalized. They have such contempt for the laws of the country that they manufacture and sell liquor. These men who found them out are agents, if you will. We must have agents to maintain this law of ours. But our agents have no grudges. They have nothing to gain by incriminating the innocent. As the farmer's lad said, it is known well that the Finns around Redwood make liquor and that these little country stores market it. Pikkanen did farm. Well and good. He also took the moonshine into Lahti's store and sold it. Ole Niemi, the farmer, knew that. Back of these farms on waste acres we have discovered stills before. We have tried in the interest of the law-abiding public to break up this notorious traffic and we are succeeding. They oppose us. They have given you this rehearsed cock and bull story about remembering where Pikkanen was every hour on the fifteenth of August. Search your memories, ladies and gentlemen! Where was each of you on August fifteenth? Can you remember? I don't question the honesty of some of these boys. They may be hypnotized into believing that they do remember what happened on that day. But I say it is unlikely, improbable that all of them could. I go far enough to say it is impossible. As for this poor girl, her testimony is that of a man's sweetheart. One must not credit it unduly. Even if she thinks she speaks the truth, do you yourself think it credible that a girl could tell exactly where a man is every hour? Perhaps he went to town for two hours while she was washing dishes, just long enough to help out Lahti while he went home to supper, just to sell this liquor. Ladies and gentlemen, I am not prosecuting the Finnish nation. I have nothing to gain from this case. I am in a measure yourselves, the American people, demanding that the laws enacted shall be respected by foreigners who come to make this their home. The bottles do not lie. They are labeled circumstantial evidence. When you take them with you to the jury room you will personally read the labels affixed by disinterested agents last August and instantly remanded to this office. I ask your support in teaching these people law abiding and law enforcement, and for the sake of a salutary and absolutely necessary lesson let there be no error in your verdict of guilty."

He talked well. The district attorney was noted for his good talks. He was often toastmaster at banquets, orator at the opening or dedication of some building. He retired with a smile as if he smacked his lips over his own speech, and the judge again adjourned court. It was five o'clock and the afternoon had slipped by so quickly that Elsa Monroe had not dreamed it was so late.

Some of the others felt differently as they went down in the elevator with her.

"Dragged it out, didn't they?" asked a man of Elsa. "Well, we'll get the case before noon to-morrow anyway. And maybe we'll get the afternoon off. Ever see anything like the way those Finns hold together?"

Elsa only looked at him. She couldn't think of anything to say. Her words never came easily. She only knew that she was disturbed and worried and would be glad to see Fred.

Outside the courthouse on the steps she saw the Finns. The men were talking but the girl stood a little apart. Her eyes were turned toward the building across the way where the windows were barred and a look of horror was on her face. In the late afternoon the sun made her hair golden where it showed beneath the lace shawl she wore over it and there was something virginal and enduring about her.

Elsa's friend took her out to dinner. Fred was good-looking in his city way. He wore the clothes one saw in the windows of big clothing stores in the manner the wax figures wore them and he smiled with a cigarette-advertisement smile of pleasure.

"Getting your money easy these days, aren't you, Elsa?" he asked, "pretty soft to pull down four berries a day for sitting and deciding who'll go to jail and who won't."

"It's not always jail and it's not always easy."

"The way I feel about it is that birds who get in courtroom deserve just about what's coming to them."

"But that doesn't mean anything, Fred. There are two sides."

Fred cut his steak masterfully.

"You can pretty nearly always tell who's right," he said largely; "anyway, as I say, people who get that far deserve to take a chance. People ought to keep the law and keep out of court."

Elsa's plate was neglected. She sat staring at the wall of the little booth in which they were eating.

"Say, you haven't any appetite at all, girlie. You mustn't worry about that stuff. How about a little snort of something to put some pep into you?"

"What?"

Fred tapped his pocket.

"I got some pretty good stuff to-day." He pulled out a little silver-plated flask.

"This will put the ginger in you."

"No, thanks," said Elsa.

"Better have some."

"No. Where'd you get it, Fred?"

"Oh, from a fellow. It's not so hard. Prices are coming down too, do you know that? I think before long we'll be getting this stuff at pretty near before prohibition prices. Fact." He poured himself a drink in his glass. "Of course the quality isn't what it used to be but it's pretty darn good at that."

She watched him curiously as he swallowed the drink and breathed hard in his satisfaction.

"Who makes it?" she asked.

"You don't really know. The fellow who made that knows his business. Some of these foreigners who made it in the old country have a pretty good knack. Sure you won't?"

"I wish you wouldn't, either."

"Say, girlie, I don't drink enough to hurt me. Ever see me drunk?"

"No."

"And you never will, believe me. I haven't got any patience with these souses. A fellow's got to have control, that's all. A drink now and then is different from steady drinking, Elsa."

"It's the principle, isn't it? Don't the people who make it get in trouble?"

Fred grinned. "That's their problem," he said, "precious few of them get caught and they get their money out of it. Say, dearie, you do look tired. What's the case to-day?"

She shook her head.

"We're under orders not to talk about them, Fred. Not until the cases are over. You know."

"Well, you mustn't let them wear you out or I'll have to go beat up that judge, that's all." He put his hand across the table and patted hers and she felt the little usual thrill run through her. "Come, we'll go see the best movie in town."

When the case of the State against Oscar Pikkanen was resumed in the morning it was as if they had all held their poses. Elsa Monroe in a yellow flannel dress on the end of the jury box was like a serene daffodil. The man beside her, a disgruntled manufacturer, serving his time to be done with it, slouched in his seat and on the other side a keen-faced matron lifted an aging chin out of her collar. The judge wore the same tie. The stool-pigeons lounged together in case of redirect examination or question of any sort. The attorneys held their places, the same papers spread out before them, and on the table two bottles, full of a colorless liquid, were standing. In the same places in the courtroom sat the Finns. Elsa wondered where they had spent the night, in what cheaply rented bed somewhere that Finnish girl had lain, perhaps whispering a prayer to the saints she did not worship publicly.

Her eyes were hollowed to-day and the look of patience in her face overcast by fear. Elsa saw the defendant's eyes meet those of the Finn girl and hold them for a minute. How still their emotion was.

There was an air of wanting to get through with it. The defendant's lawyer rose on call of the court and sauntered to the jury box, loose fat hands thrust in his pockets.

"Ladies and gentlemen of the jury, I appeal to you in behalf of an unhappy foreigner, a childlike ward of this country, who is misjudged."

He was inadequate. He was sentimental and trite. He might have used the same talk dozens of times at fifty dollars a recital, thought Elsa in irritation. The Finn's eyes were on his lawyer, eagerly, devotedly. In the back of the room the other foreigners strained to catch what words they might, sculptured now in the idea of hope. And Elsa could feel with that jury sense of hers, which had developed in the past weeks, how Mr. Carson was failing to convince the men and women who listened to him. She was glad when he was done and the judge, turning formally to the jury, addressed them in short curt sentences.

"You must judge this on the evidence. If you are convinced that this man sold the liquor no sympathy must sway you. This is a serious offense, as serious as any other criminal offense. You must judge of the credibility of the witnesses as best you can. You will retire to the jury room and elect one of your number to be your foreman and deliberate on your verdict."

The jury room, council and judgment room, was warm and bright. Around the long polished oak table were the chairs, comfortable and broad armed. The jury, left to itself, relaxed into that intimacy and amusement which was inevitable, everyone avoid-

156

ing the chair at the head of the table which might be the fore-man's.

"Shall we lunch on the county—that's the question," chuckled someone, half jocosely.

The bailiff, entering, brought in the two glass bottles.

"Here's lunch," said someone and there was a roar of laughter. Elsa did not laugh. One reason she could not was because she had turned to see the girl again as she went out of the courtroom and caught her tragic look of fear, helpless fear. There was noth-ing she could do, that was what the look meant.

"Miss Monroe would make a charming foreman," said one of the gallant gentlemen.

"No, I couldn't," said Elsa, sharply, "no, I won't."

A pudgy gentleman said he thought the fairest way was to draw lots.

"Takes too much time. You be foreman."

That was the pudgy gentleman's secret notion. It took little urging to get him seated at the head of the table where an omi-nous air of importance came over him. The others settled into places here and there.

"Well, the first thing to do is to take an informal ballot."

"Look at these bottles. That's the way they do them up." A man lifted and shook them. "Looks like good stuff."

His wink was knowing and furtive.

"Maybe it's just water. Been in the district attorney's office a long while."

"Are we supposed to open them?"

"Sure, we're supposed to open them."

"Say, Mr. Foreman, how about it? Do we open these bottles and decide for ourselves?"

There were three women and nine men on the jury. The two women beside Elsa were the matron with the high collar and a gay, rouged plump young woman who had been on several juries with Elsa.

"I'll bet you men are pretty good judges of whether it's good or not," she said coyly.

"The women are getting to be good judges too," said one of the men, and that brought on another laugh.

"Let's get to business, Mr. Foreman," said the impatient manu-facturer, eager to be back at his office.

The informal ballot was taken and Elsa, one of the tellers,

counted it. Ten for conviction, two for acquittal. She wondered who the other one was.

"Well, ladies and gentlemen, in the minds of the majority the case seems to be pretty clear. I wonder if these two who believe in acquittal would just tell us why they feel as they do," said the foreman with a large air of being ready to hear all sides.

No one spoke at first. Then the high-collared matron broke silence.

"I didn't like the look of those stool-pigeons," she said; "seems to me they're the worst of the lot. Everyone knows what kind of people they are. That man admitted that he had been bartender in Morrison's saloon. I know all about Morrison's saloon. It was two blocks from my home. I didn't like the look of that man from the first, and that Morrison's saloon was an open scandal!"

"Still, Mrs. Dallas, he'd have no reason for framing the Finn."

"I think the district attorney ought not to hire men of that character," said Mrs. Dallas obstinately.

"But we've got the evidence."

That reopened the question of whether the bottles should be tested and a rather heated argument ensued ending by one of the men producing a small bottle opener on a keychain.

"Say the word, gentlemen," he suggested.

"Go ahead," said the foreman.

The top of the bottle was nipped off and the man who did it smelled appreciatively.

"That's not water, believe me. Gosh, that stuff has a kick!"

Elsa saw three men lean toward it interestedly.

"Those Finns know how all right," said someone smelling it.

"Try it."

"Well, in the interest of justice."

"That's real stuff."

"No poison that. There was a fellow down street who had some liquor and it was like dynamite."

The smacking of lips, the air of knowledge, of camaraderie seemed to blend all the men in Elsa's eyes. They did not drink the liquor. It was only a touch of the tongue, a few drops.

"Powerful stuff. That ought to be good for a jail term all right, all right."

"Well, gentlemen, suppose we get to business. I appreciate that Mrs. Dallas' feeling may in a measure be right. But at the same time, it isn't a question of whether we like the stool-pigeon or not.

It's a question of evidence. These bottles were bought and dated. The Finns told too smooth a story for anyone to credit. Don't you feel that yourself, Mrs. Dallas? How could they remember every minute of the fifteenth? Did you notice how the Finn's attorney slid over that point in his final talk? In my mind there's no doubt. Pikkanen sold the liquor and is liable for the penalty."

"The thing I object to," said Mrs. Dallas in a weakening voice, "is the man's character!"

"Waiving that—"

Elsa sat rigid. Her feet were cold and her hands hot. In all the other cases she had been on it had been so clear, so easy to be reasonable. But now—she looked back in her mind desperately. Where had she been on the fifteenth of August? She didn't know except that it was the week before her vacation. The old Finnish woman had said they all got together and talked it over. Yet for these men, sniffing at their liquor, for Fred with his flask, to sit in judgment on this trapped Finn whose girl had prayed and looked at the bars in horror was somehow hideous. It was confused and topsy-turvy.

"Who else felt the Finn was not guilty?"

No one spoke.

"Let's take another ballot and see if the minds have changed after this discussion."

They had. It was eleven to one. Elsa stood alone.

"Now, if this gentleman or lady will discuss their feeling in the case," said the foreman.

Elsa spoke. Her tongue seemed to stick as she did so.

"I can't discuss it. I was the other person who voted for acquittal. I feel it isn't fair."

"Fair?"

"You all buy the liquor, use it—you all break the law—why doesn't everyone go to jail? He doesn't even understand English—he's just learned that prohibition is one law no one obeys. It isn't fair to send him to jail for following the spirit of law breaking that he feels everywhere. It's not fair to him or that girl to brand them!"

"We mustn't be sentimental, Miss Monroe, you know. You mustn't let your pity for the man's sweetheart sway you."

"Those Finns are pretty tough stuff."

"It's we who are tough!" said Elsa, "it's we who are creating the whole situation."

A man sighed heavily.

"We're not here to discuss the liquor laws, as I see it, young lady. We're sent here to decide whether this Finn sold liquor on the fifteenth of August or not. Personally, I believe he did."

Elsa turned a flaming face on him.

"So do I!" she said, "but I feel more criminal in sending him to jail than he did when he sold it. And so should you!"

There was an embarrassed hush.

"Suppose we take another ballot," said someone smoothly, "if Miss Monroe feels he is guilty, I hardly see how her other opinions affect the issue. I hardly see how she can possibly vote any way except for a conviction."

"You see that, don't you, Miss Monroe?"

Elsa did not answer. She saw. She saw the futility of her protest, trapped in the immediate situation.

"She was a damned good juror on other cases I've been on with her," whispered one man to another, "aren't women funny when it comes to liquor? They don't see straight at all."

"I move we have another ballot."

Elsa's fingers were stiff. The letters she wrote did not seem like her own. There was no use.

"Guilty," she wrote.

"Well, I guess we buy our own lunches. Wish we could take the exhibits along," said a jovial relieved gentleman.

The foreman nudged him to be silent, looking at Elsa, whose head was bent. When they moved back into the courtroom she tried not to look at Pikkanen but she was driven to do it by some force within her. His eyes dilated a little but he did not move. Only the Finn girl's hand rose in a kind of maddened protest and then her head dropped on them. The bailiff led Pikkanen away.

"You want to be excused, do you?" said the judge who had charge of the jury panel a half hour later. "Well, you've served very faithfully, Miss Monroe. I understand you've been an excellent juror. Tired out or what?" He looked at her quizzically and kindly because she was so pretty. "Don't you like administering justice?"

"I haven't been administering justice," said Elsa, "it was the law—not justice."

"Why, my dear young lady, that's a strange statement!"

"Oh, let me go," cried Elsa, "I'm tired. I'm tired!"

The judge, recounting the breakdown of the perfect juror, said that was the trouble with women, on juries especially. They couldn't stand the strain of a full term.

Fred said indignantly that they had worn her out. He said that when she was his wife she never would be allowed to serve on a jury, on all those dirty cases, listening to things a woman shouldn't hear. He asked her if she would like a little bracer, that he had some real good stuff, and could not understand it when she burst into tears.

But Mrs. Dowling, drifting from courtroom to courtroom, whispered the news that Miss Monroe had been dropped from the jury and that she understood that the judge had refused to let her serve any longer. What could you expect of a girl like that anyway, a girl with no experience of life, she asked.

Grace H. Flandrau

from BEING RESPECTABLE

Grace Hodgson Flandrau believed that writing was "life seen through a temperament," and in her case it was a temperament compounded of a sharp eye and ear for the foolishness, frailty, strength, cupidity, and kindness that make up the average human being. She was born in St. Paul in 1889, and at the age of eleven was sent to a school in Paris "whose only distinction was the fact that it was housed in one of the oldest buildings in France. We could have done with less antiquity and more instruction!" After nearly five years out of her own country at a formative period, she felt isolated when she returned to St. Paul. But the experience may well have provided her with a certain distance, so that eventually she developed into a fine social commentator. She married Blair Flandrau and in 1909 went with him to his coffee plantation near Jalapa in Mexico, so remote a place that it took two days by horseback to reach it from the rail line. Her first stories were written there. When the revolutions of subsequent years erupted the Flandraus returned to St. Paul, where she continued to write. Being Respectable, published in 1923, is a quietly satirical picture of the upper crust of St. Paul that was shocking at the time of its publication. "I was supposed to have cruelly exposed private lives, not only those of people in St. Paul, but in Kansas City, Houston, Texas, and Baltimore." In 1927 Flandrau went on a six-month safari through Central Africa with her husband and three friends, a trip that resulted in a travel book, Then I Saw the Congo. *St. Paul was her home for many years, but she continued to travel widely and died in Farmington, Connecticut in 1971.*

"I'M NOTHING on God's green earth but a funny-paper husband." This surprising statement burst as it were unexpectedly from Philip Denby. He actually spoke the words and then looked around shamefacedly to see if any one had noticed him, talking that way to himself. He had just left his office and come out into the street. This was one of the days he walked home from down town.

Denby had fallen into routine ways of doing things. Two afternoons a week during the season, when they were in town, he played golf, motoring to the club directly after lunch. The other days he worked in the afternoon, and walked home for exercise. He might have golfed oftener, but he made a point of working very hard, harder than was necessary. It seemed essential, in some way, that he do this. Louisa was so rich.

He had nothing to do with her money. It was true that the business he ran had originally been a Carpenter interest and he had got into it through his marriage with Louisa. But that was a long time before and the business was now practically his own. Sometimes, he did not know quite why, he wished it had been a different business—one which had never at any time been connected with the Carpenter activities.

Denby, marching home in his good, expensive clothes, was not an elegant figure. He walked as he read in the medical column of the daily paper it was beneficial to walk—chin high, shoulders back, holding his insides up as much as possible. Just then the daily column was belaboring its readers with the prevalency of sagging organs, and the sinister, even fatal consequences of this condition. A few years before it had been bran, at which time Denby had sprinkled it in spoonfuls on his rolled oats. But bran was out now and splanchnic anhedonia in. So he was mindful of how he walked and took exercises in the morning with his hands over his head.

A funny-paper husband—Although the emotion which called forth this statement was not new, its crystallization into speech was. Something of which he had been only formlessly aware, confronted him now as a complete and recognizable fact.

It had begun on the telephone. He had, that afternoon, experienced a certain restlessness—a disinclination to return to his house and eat dinner with Louisa and Millicent. He was granted, to be sure, one evening every two weeks to do with as he wished. He devoted this occasion, as a rule, to playing backgammon with a few cronies he had outside the connubial acquaintance. Middle-aged persons they were, not belonging to Louisa's smart young—or, rather, youngish—"set"; not belonging to any set. Visualized by Louisa, for some reason, as dubious, heavy drinkers, with hard faces like political bosses. A fancy quite unrelated to fact. Like the wives in the funny papers she objected violently to these friends. But it was in vain that she pointed out to Denby that there were plenty of people "one knew" with whom he could play backgammon. In this matter she was powerless.

To-night was not Denby's official night of carnival. He merely, as he phrased it, took a chance on getting away with it. He did not get away with it.

Was it possible he had forgotten the Clarks' dinner dance that night? Yes, he had. "But, dear, they won't care a rap whether I'm there or not—"

She did not deny this. But she said: "We can't begin to drop out of things, Phil. The first thing you know they won't invite us."

"I wish to God they wouldn't," he was bold enough to declare.

"Phil, you just don't help me at all. You're so selfish."

"But I thought you didn't like the Clarks. Two years ago you were doing your best to get out of their invitations."

"Why, what on earth do you mean? Everybody goes to the Clarks'."

Denby relinquished his project sadly. He knew who was meant by everybody. He knew that so long as Louisa wished, one obscure unit of that distinctly not all inclusive designation would be himself. He was suddenly aghast at the vulgarity of it all.

Striding forward, mindful of the position of his abdomen, he foresaw the evening; dressing; sitting beside Louisa in the car— Louisa in a superb, brocaded cloak, trimmed with fur—smelling of furs and of Foolish Virgin sachet. At table he would be placed between the two oldest, no, the two ugliest women there—or the two dullest. And even they, with restless eyes and straining ears, would be looking and listening away from him, up and down the table. He did not blame them. What he would be able to think of to say would not be worth listening to. They never gave him soft, pretty Mrs. Marty Davidson or Valeria Winship, who knew how to put men at their ease. No, he got the ones who made up for their lack of looks by being terribly vivacious, or who did not make up for it by anything.

Then, when every one at the table was dancing but Louisa— Louisa sitting alone, such of the men as repaid dinner invitations by asking their one-time hostess to dance, having already asked her— sitting alone in her gorgeous attire, a wide, uneasy smile on her lips—Denby would go and ask her to dance. She would say, for the benefit of ears that were not there—"Why, Phil, you scamp—

rushing your own wife—" and, still with a smile, give herself to his grim, unpractised embrace.

And as slender nymphs in wisps of tulle undulated past them in eccentric, graceful, unimaginable postures, his solid *one* and, *two* and, interpretation of an already archaic fox trot, would convey him and Louisa back and forth, back and forth, until the endless cutting in, romping, jazzing, slowed up and one more dance was over with.

He was sorry, too, for Louisa. Since that was what she cared for, he was not, to be sure, much help. She should have married some one who was good at it. He was not; and it was just plain hell to him.

He looked down the years. No respite discernible until Millicent came out. Perhaps not then. Did all women cling to boarding-school pleasures till they were old women? Or was Columbia unique? He did not know.

He knew that a good many of the men relied on drink to carry them through Columbia's unceasing pleasures. But Denby could not do that. If he drank at all, he wanted to drink more than enough. Far more. He wanted all the respite, the Nirvana, it could bring. He wanted to go with it as far as it could take him—to oblivion. To do so often was obviously out of the question. He thought of those other men—They work hard all day to make money enough to be able to do in the evening what they can only endure or at least enjoy if they are drunk. . . . Sometimes the life of Louisa's world seemed very strange to Denby.

But, as he walked, the immanence of these painful things diminished. The rhythmic motion assuaged him, and the impersonality of the streets. He liked walking this way in the early twilight. He liked these gray city streets, where life passed by him like scenes in a play.

Men and women—men and women—each so curiously rapt in his own destiny. Hidden in it. Revolving in it—a circle, round and round. People—millions, countless. Little circles, touching or not touching. Never touching in a way that mattered—really. Or did they, sometimes?

Past court house, post office, drug stores, tobacco stands. Across street car tracks—street cars, bewildering loud things, rushing; noise, movement, some meaning but without a key. And a beautiful grayness over everything. He felt the play of lights and shadows on ugly buildings and ugly people, giving them beauty. Significance descended on what he saw—the significance not of actuality, but of something more poignant.

He took the hill slowly. People once more whom he knew. Men in the back seats of huge touring cars, asking with a gesture whether they might give him a lift. Old ladies with snow-white hair, benignant, inside electric broughams—plate glass boxes, incredibly silent, creeping backwards up the hill propelled by long black pokers in respectable, gloved hands. His world once more, where people had names and had lost the exquisite reality of those others—unknown—back there in the rush and the gray twilight.

He toiled up, lifting his chin, aware once more of the splanchnic pool. The sky was gray-blue above the cathedral—a fine lump of granite, affronted by little carven wreaths, but holding its gold cross up into the clouds. At the top he paused to get his breath, looking down over the mass of city buildings. Pebble colored the picture was; soft grays, pinkish, brownish, yellowish grays and the pure slate gray of the twin towers of the German Catholic church. He had noticed just these soft pebble colors in pigeons.

The roofs and towers made him think of other cities, foreign cities and of railway trains. He did not know why, but the blue towers and smoky horizon made him think of these things. An impression came to him of a life of his own in some remote, gray city—London, perhaps. It came to him, not clearly as in a dream, but with the vagueness of things long past, with the poignant and wistful sweetness of things that are long past. It even peopled itself with shapes, dim shapes, one or perhaps two. At any rate they would be few, unknown to him at present.

He passed Darius's house and reached his own. Bright red geraniums, later, would stare at him through the expensive, wrought iron fence. He seemed to see them now. They were always the same, as though they were made of tin and painted fresh each summer.

A heavy sense of inferiority invaded Denby. He felt as he did when he sat at a large dinner party unable to think of anything to say.

That day marked, or effected, a sort of turning point for Denby. Something was subtly, inexplicably different. The following week when Louisa asked him, not without apprehension, to forego his privileged Thursday, he acquiesced indifferently. It did not seem to matter. He had come, quite irrationally, to have about it all a temporary feeling.

Louisa had invited the Clarks and their guests to dinner and, as she put it, a few other "couples." Habitually Louisa referred to human beings as couples. A result, perhaps, of so much thinking in terms of dinners and cotillions.

She had just been waved. She sat at her dressing table giving forth an odor of hot hair, engulfed in a robe of watermelon pink. Unbecoming. Denby, in trousers and dress shirt, stood in the doorway. He was stouter without a coat. His glasses had just been polished, and, in the peace of self-sacrifice, he looked benevolent. He had keys in his hand.

"Not many cocktails, Philip. You know Lily and Helen don't take any. And they always watch to see what other people take and talk just *frightfully*." She laughed an irrelevant and harassed laugh. Denby found for this quite true statement nothing but silence.

"And only a little champagne with dinner. If Billy takes too much Judy will blame us—and you know how he likes it."

The matter of drinking bore, in Columbia, an odd and tedious importance. There were in what Louisa called society, people who drank and people who did not. People who drank formerly but who did not drink now. People who drank now and formerly did not. A certain number who pretended that they did not and secretly did. And almost everybody disapproved of somebody.

Louisa, of course, did not know what to do. In her father's day, wine was a part of all fashionable entertaining and Louisa inherited the tradition. She liked it, too, herself. But she would have forsworn it gladly if she had been convinced it was no longer the thing. As respectable opinion, however, was divided, she compromised by drinking with those who drank and disapproving with those who disapproved. It was part of the many terrible complexities of being respectable.

Still in his shirt sleeves, Denby descended to the cellar; Katy, with her round, red cheeks, went with him, to help carry up bottles. When they were alone in the cellar she suddenly became human. Upstairs she was never human—Louisa was too good a housekeeper to permit that.

"I wouldn't be drinking any of the stuff."

"I suppose not, Katy."

"Though it's many a barrel of it I've seen drunk up at home. At my grandmother's wake there was never a sober man in the county."

"Well, that was a tribute all right."

"My grandmother made plenty of it, too, in her day. And they'd be sending me off to help her. Right up to the hills where she lived. Ye had to be like that, right away off, because of the smell it have."

Katy, holding the bottles carefully, went up stairs. Denby sat down on a stool in his wine cellar, looking about him. There was pale light from the slightly swaying electric bulb which depended from the ceiling by a long wire. The bottles lay in rows, snouts sticking out; Burgundies and champagnes evenly wrapped in gold foil; dusty claret bottles with corks rammed in; whiskey bottles spick and span with white enamel stopper coverings.

He seemed to see Katy, a little girl in a wool skirt; the quiet hill road; blowing grasses; swift shadows of clouds; a shanty and women making poteen, far away from the officers of the English law—"because of the smell it have." In Galway.

A terrible disinclination to go upstairs and put on his white waistcoat and black coat. What would he say to them when they came?

Louisa was acutely aware of and afflicted by this social inadequacy. Denby, she knew, came of "nice" people—American stock of sound, even superior ancestry. There had been an unbelievably plain sister who had come out from Providence once or twice to visit. Louisa apologized for her clothes and dropped wide, smiling hints as to her prominence in the society of the Colonial Dames. Now she was dead and Louisa had almost forgotten the Colonial Dames. Denby's deficiencies she could not forget.

She could not understand why he so desperately lacked the social elegance, as it seemed to her, of Peter Clark or Ted Hermann. Peter Clark's grandfather, as Louisa well knew, and frequently mentioned to common acquaintances, had been a cobbler mending shoes in a small street stall on River Street. And the Hermann grandmother was a sturdy German wench who efficiently and beautifully washed the soiled clothes of the pioneer bourgeoisie at seventy-five cents a day. Yet Ted and Peter were the grace and ornament of ballroom and dinner table. It was puzzling to Louisa and sadly disappointing.

Alvin Greenberg

FOOTNOTES TO A THEORY OF PLACE

Poet, novelist and short story writer Alvin Greenberg was born in Cincinnati, Ohio in 1932. He received his B.A. and M.A. from the University of Cincinnati and his Ph.D. from the University of Washington in Seattle. Before coming to Minnesota, Greenberg taught at the University of Kentucky. He has been on the staff of Macalester College in St. Paul, teaching in the English department, since 1965. Greenberg's novels, Going Nowhere *and* The Invention of the West, *were published in the 1970's. He has had several volumes of poetry published and his short stories have appeared in literary periodicals such as the* Antioch Review, Antaeus, *and the* American Review.

MANY YEARS AGO I swore I would never be a participant in an academic fiction, and yet here I am, all the same, a voting member of the Committee on Committees. So much for oaths. For what I want to ask myself is, what am I doing here? What? In the silence that follows, I am moved to start out from this point (precisely at the opposite end of the table from the Chairman, and at the furthest corner of the room from the doorway) in several directions at once, but where would I go? As an old friend of mine used to say, "Which of us, if he received a telegram reading FLEE ALL IS DISCOVERED, would not pack up and be on his way at once?" Not me, that's who. I don't want to go anywhere at all.

For a long time, I pondered this curious phenomenon of my immobility in the stillness of my office, where even the cigar smoke hung motionless in the stale air. On the other side of the door, of course, my colleagues scurried away with briefcase in one hand and baggage in the other to regional conferences in nearby cities, national meetings in New York or San Francisco, international congresses in London or Vienna, Fulbrights, Fords,

First published in *Antioch Review*, Volume 32, number 31, 1973. © 1973 by *Antioch Review*. Reprinted by permission of the author.

Rockefellers, Guggenheims, all those great names that give scholars wings. Then one day the door opened. I must have given a startled little jump; I had been seated at my desk reading Gide. It was only a student turning in a late paper, but there was something in the way he said, as he poked his head into the room, "Aha, I knew I'd find you in there," that made it difficult for me to go back to my book. The phone rang, the Chairman of the Department calling to say good-bye, he was off to the Folger, the Library of Congress, the annual meeting of the Modern Language Association. Somewhere. They knew him in all those places. And suddenly I recognized the source of my own inertia: What sense was there in fleeing, when whatever was discovered about one was already known everywhere? I need someone to address all this to.

Let us hypothesize, then, a small man, dressed primarily in browns, who is on his way to deliver a lecture before the annual spring meeting of a literary and philanthropical society in a large American city. Fairly large. He didn't really want to go. On the other hand, he didn't really not want to go, in spite of his wife's amused response. It is the first time he has ever been *invited* anywhere to do anything remotely connected with his profession. In spite of her relentless teasing, he has excused himself from classroom and committee and accepted. And she, having likewise excused herself from office and patients, is now sleeping soundly in the window seat next to him, having fallen asleep before the plane left the runway.

He, on the other hand, is wide awake, contemplating a well-before-lunch bourbon which, when it arrives, will be placed next to the stack of note cards on the little metal tray in front of him, and thinking about the future. He has been asked to lecture on "The Literature of the Midwest." That is what prompted his wife's hilarity. But when the bourbon arrives, the future he holds in his mind contains such non-Midwesterners as Conrad, Borges, Nabokov, and Robbe-Grillet. And the note cards, which he flips slowly between sips at his drink, are sparsely populated and say such things as:

only three dimensions: space, time, and presence

and

in some cultures it has always been the custom to put something

alive—a potted plant, a goat, a child—into the foundation or walls
of every new structure (not a principle to be taken lightly)

and

the discovery of a new word for

and

"in a first-rate work of Fiction the real clash is not between the
characters but between the author and the world"

and

in the structure of art not this ⌒
    but this ∿∿∿∿∿∿∿

= *the ripples of real time*

and

the earthbound ethics of airplanes: landing the sole good

and

back to school in a narrative suit of olive drab time

and also

stay loose, swing level, and follow through

He thinks that even for committee meetings he has generally
been better prepared than this.

He also thinks people would be surprised if they were aware,
as he presumes he is, having recently read something on the
subject in a national news magazine, of the vast numbers of
travelers who change flights at the last minute, in the hope of
frustrating death. Not to go by car, for the accident rate there is
higher still, but only to take a later plane. Perhaps to be able to say
to their friends, "Remember that American Airlines jet that
crashed on the approach to O'Hare last fall, killing everyone
aboard? Well, I was supposed to be on that plane, but I had a
sudden premonition. . . ." Perhaps they really do have premo-
nitions, really don't want to die. Perhaps they believe that no matter how ill-prepared you are, if you just keep shuffling the cards
something safe will turn up.

Except for the river running through it, he recognizes nothing
of the city on the approach, though once he lived there for eight

years. Below him, it is white, still snow-covered. He pockets his cards and folds the tray into the back of the seat in front of him. His wife shuffles about in her seat, half waking. The plane touches down. The runway flashes by, the motors roar, I wish they wouldn't do that.

II

He is in the center of his hotel room, between the bed and the TV set, squatting naked before a pile of scrambled note cards, when it is pointed out to him how much he looks like some pale, scrawny savage praying for divine ignition of his wretched pile of kindling. Spare me, darling, that's not a kind thing to say to a man whose frail spark of intellect has been damped out by a hopeless subject, a sleepless night, an airplane, and an afternoon nap. I was going to leap out of bed and head for the shower, but didn't. You got there first. We should have stayed in bed and made love.

He shuffles the cards together, taps them into a thin, neat pile, looks for a pocket to stow them in, then places them on the night table, and prepares to make himself presentable for an appearance in the lobby at 6:30 sharp. Even committee work is better than this. He is appalled to uncover such a thought in his mind, like someone else's note card slipped into his pack. A title in red ink: The Real-Life Drama of Public Appearance. This, he suddenly realizes, is what I meant by an academic fiction.

Nonetheless, though a fiction should be more pliable, more amenable to his desires, both he and his wife descend, at 6:25, to a lobby where they are met by a distinguished member of the Foundation. In an equally distinguished vehicle, a fawn-colored Mercedes, with the Foundation member at the wheel, they rise effortlessly up the hills from downtown into the residential area. A new form of flight, he considers: he is seriously considering flight. He holds his note cards in his hands, on his lap. He had hoped to have a last chance to look through them, in search of something useful, on this drive, but what with the early dark of the season, the idle conversation between his wife and the Foundation member, and the major distractions of his own mind— already in rapid flight—he can see that this was a futile notion. The card on the top, which he can just manage to make out from the intermittent glow of street lights, reads:

I've learned that the most important thing for an actor is
honesty. And when you learn how to fake that, you're in.

A quote from a TV star, but as he can no longer remember the star's name, he gives up on it and looks out the window.

They are moving through streets that are, to his surprise, only vaguely familiar to him, where all the trees are elms. It is, he presumes, their integrity they demonstrate, standing up as they do, black and leafless, through the interminable winters of this latitude, out of the grimy snowdrifts banked against them, staunch and motionless. Perhaps hundreds of miles to the south, where a truer spring is underway, the elm bark beetles, carriers of the deadly and incurable dutch elm disease, are already on the march against them. So much for integrity. The University Club looms up ahead, at a bend in the street, surrounded by the tallest elms of all. The Mercedes swings sharply into its circular drive. The note cards go sliding to the floor.

III

Never before has he attempted to lecture on such a full stomach. He has always been careful not to schedule his classes for the hour right after lunch, while the very idea of a luncheon committee meeting has always been enough to ruin his appetite, thereby leaving him the lone lightly-fed, clear-headed member among his soporific colleagues. That has been extremely helpful at times. He also regrets the vulnerability of his position at the head of the table, actually at the bottom of an expansive U-shaped arrangement. He remembers a former undergraduate classmate, a German exchange student, who once told him how his uncle, a low-ranking member of the World War II high command, had gone hungry at many of Hitler's banquets, because though he sat well down the table, and was therefore served first, no one was permitted to touch his food until Hitler, who, as host, was served last, had begun to eat, so that by the time Hitler was lifting the first spoonful of soup to his mouth, the waiters at the lower end of the table, in order to have the next course laid out by the time the Fuehrer was ready for it, were already clearing away the now cold, but still full, bowls of soup from in front of all those hungry uncles. A little avuncular hunger is just what he thinks he needs at the moment.

During the course of a lengthy introduction, which appears to be less concerned with him than with the occasion upon which he is to speak, some sort of noteworthy local literary date, the precise nature of which he has missed—most likely, he supposes, the birthday of the only important writer ever to have emerged from this region—he sits with bowed head, shuffling the deck of note cards on the table before him and eyeing, fondly, the cigar container, still sealed, that lies beside his coffee cup. Between the heavy, sweet dessert and that thick rich coffee, he has been called aside by a tall, grey-haired gentleman, none other than the Secretary of the Foundation, who has proffered that expensive cigar and, as he accepted it, also passed him an envelope, sealed and demure. Slipping the envelope into his inside jacket pocket as he returned to his seat, he has laid the cigar gently on the table, planning on giving it the attention it clearly deserves when the inevitable question and answer period arrives, and he finds himself in need of something to fill the gap between the question and the answer. And there, for all I know, it may be lying still, unless some sneaky bus boy made off with it, in the midst of the confusion, and tried to smoke it in the pantry, too fast of course, and so had to go out and stand coatless and shivering in the snow beside the garbage cans, taking in deep breaths of painfully cold air until the dizziness passed.

He presumes, quite reasonably, that he could get away with reciting passages from his book, for it is not likely that anybody in this room, aside from the Director of the Foundation, to whom he sent a complimentary copy when it was published several years ago, since it was a small research grant from the Foundation which helped initiate the project, has even seen it. All he would have to do would be to toss in the names of a few Midwestern novelists to accompany those—mostly continental—with whom the book had dealt. But it is futile to think that he could recall any complete passages from a book written that long ago, not read again since it was in the proof stage. He is not even certain that he can explain, without actually going back into the text to dredge up the very words he had used—and then forgotten—just what it was he had been trying to say there. A sense of where, in what, a character was, in modern fiction, and where, into what, he was going. What does that mean? Who is Midwestern, anyway? Everybody? Or is that only a flighty fiction of his own recent reading experience? And what has he been doing all these weeks when, instead of looking over the same old random collection of note cards, in search of something, perhaps their true order (unshuffled at last!), or any design that might have proved useful to him this evening, he could have been putting together something sensible to say. Adding a few more note cards, is all he can remember doing. And what do they have to do with what he is doing here? Nothing, so far as he can remember, rising.

While beginning in upon what a pleasure it is, to speak to this gathered body of patrons of the arts, he cuts, without looking, his stack of note cards, lying on the table in front of him, in the middle, placing the bottom half on top. Now, looking down, he sees both the unopened cigar container which, aside from his empty coffee cup and recently refilled water glass, is all that remains of the meal, and the new top card, which reads:

> *the curiously ignored fact of the self-ingestion*
> *of certain mammalian organs once their purely*
> *formal function has been completed*

He remembers writing that on his last birthday, recalls that his next is not now far off, wonders just what sort of annual container he is in, and stumbles into and out of a clumsy sentence on the sense, that is, the essence, of belonging, in modern literature. Belongingness-in-the-context-given: a German word for it. He notes, in passing, that the Midwest is only a very small part of a much larger organism, the whole of modern literature. But somehow that fails to come out the way it was intended. Faces bent over coffee cups arch upward to look at him. Great white exhalations of cigar smoke billow upward. He shuffles his note cards rapidly as he plunges ahead. O modern literature, where are you? I mean, who is in there, wherever you are? says the voice of this native Midwesterner. Or rather, how is it, that one is in there, in the midst of whatever it is? What a world! In it, or in one like it, looks grow more querulous around the table, necks and backs more arched and strained, coffee cups move about with greater frequency, until a pause is achieved.

Look, he tries to explain, in the gap that has been opened up just for explanation, the Midwest, to tell the truth, is not exactly my—he fishes around for a comforting sort of expression—cup of tea, he says, disappointed. I am not even sure there is such a subject as the Midwest. I mean, of course, the literature of the Midwest. He looks over at his wife, midway down the left arm of the U, and sees, to his surprise that she has a solemn, almost adoring expression on her face. Either that, he adds, haltingly, or there is no other subject except the Midwest. No, that can't be real; underneath she is either chuckling at these verbal absurdities or about to give in to total hilarity at the absurdity of the entire situation. It's all the same. The real academic fiction, he is in the process of discovering, is right where he lives. Is. When it comes to that, he says, I am a committee of one. Then, not having meant to report that discovery aloud, he adds lamely, so far as the Midwest is concerned. That does it.

IV

He has been, so to speak, in another country, thanks to the miracle of communication, in its many forms. He has had a phone call (to determine his interest in a speaking engagement, in that city of previous residency, where he was not, in a small way, totally unknown), a letter (on fine embossed stationery, comprising a formal invitation) and, not least, a telegram (confirmation of date, time, arrangements). He has also had a round trip plane flight, not alone. So far as he can remember, that was the only real telegram he has ever received. He does not presume to expect any further communication (a note of thanks), from the same source, by any means. He does not assume he ought to let today's, now yesterday's, activities creep into the conversation of tomorrow's, now today's, lunch, at the Faculty Club. Much is discovered, perhaps, but much more is already known. He is not even sure that the check, which sits now on his dresser top, weighted down by a lovely, fist-sized hunk of polished agate, is still cashable. But it is.

Now it is his wife who is naked in the middle of the room, sitting cross-legged in the center of their double bed. Not a scrawny savage at all, but more like his solid idol, breasts and belly a little overripe and the smile on her face, whatever else it may mean, the same one that usually accompanies her yoga breathing exercises. At this hour of the night! For, of course, it was quite a late flight that they caught in that flight of their own which carried them swiftly beyond any possibility of staying overnight in that city, in that modern hotel room so carefully reserved for them. So that it was well past midnight when they arrived in a more familiar airport, and now, in their bedroom, it is a good bit later yet, though neither of them feels much like sleeping. And why should they rush to sleep. He has, come to think of it, already cancelled his classes, she her patients, for tomorrow. Today. Now, perhaps, is the time to make up for the time that they slept away in that useless hotel room. He turns from where he is standing by the dresser and looks at her there on the bed, breath held deep and full, chest expanded, raised, then, with the long, slow exhalation, breasts easing downward, and says to her, "All is discovered."

More is known, that's the truth. And yet here we are. Sooner or later the telegram arrives. Almost before the word is out, one is in flight—probably from an academic fiction. Midway between bed and closet you pause to reread it. This time your gaze includes the signature. "*I* sent this?" you exclaim, dropping the empty suitcase to the floor. What a question! But only on such a flightless and unmusical note as that can we, at last, turn out the lights and climb into bed together, comfortably.

Norman Katkov

from A LITTLE SLEEP, A LITTLE SLUMBER

Norman Katkov was born July 26, 1918 near Kiev in the Ukraine. He came to Minnesota with his parents in 1921 and grew up in St. Paul, attending Crowley Elementary School, Roosevelt Junior High, and Humboldt High School, and received his B.A. from the University of Minnesota in 1940. From his childhood Katkov wanted to write, and he achieved his first break into print when he won a prize from a department-store-sponsored essay contest in the seventh grade. In April 1944 he sold a story to Collier's Magazine *while he was a reporter on the* St. Paul Pioneer Press *and before the year was out he was a reporter on the* New York World Telegram. *More short stories were published in* Collier's, *the* Saturday Evening Post, *and a wide variety of other national magazines. His first novel,* Eagle at My Eyes, *was published in 1948. In 1949* A Little Sleep, a Little Slumber, *from which the following excerpt was taken, appeared. Other novels are* Eric Mattson *and* With these Hands. *Katkov has lived in Los Angeles for the past twenty years, writing for movies and television.*

B EN BARATZ had been after him for years to bootleg. Back there on Winifred Street when they lived under the eaves, Ben Baratz wanted Lev to set up a still in the barn, cook the mash there, and let him, Baratz, sell the stuff.

Baratz said he could sell it through the state, among the farmers; said he *was* selling it, wanted Lev Simon to get some of the easy money.

"If they catch me," Lev Simon said.

"Catch you! Who will catch you?"

"If they catch, Ben. What then, Ben? Back to Russia?"

"They don't catch," Ben said.

"Then *you* cook," Lev Simon said. "You cook and you sell. I don't come to America for this crooked business. I'm not a stealer, Ben. Not in Russia, and not here."

"You're a pautz," Ben Baratz said.

"Certain. That's me."

"Pautz."

"All right, Ben. I'm a pautz. Don't talk with me more from this business, Ben. This crooked business."

Until that morning in March when Sarah sent him to the drugstore for the eczema salve. She gave him the prescription and he walked to Michaelson's there on Robert Street.

And Michaelson said no.

"I can't," he told Lev Simon. "I can't keep charging this stuff," he said. "Jesus and Christ, Simon," he said, "I can't afford it."

"Suppose not."

"You know I can't." He held the prescription out to Lev Simon.

"Mike," Lev Simon said. His arms were at his sides. "You know, is not for me. My kid there, for him."

"Jesus—I can't. I promised myself. I can't afford it."

Lev Simon looked at the display tray attached to the counter. He looked carefully at the red cross on the adhesive tape. He watched it very carefully.

"Mike, please," he said.

"Simon, I can't."

Looking at the red cross, he said: "Please . . . Please," and wanted his tongue cut off so he could never beg again.

Michaelson dropped the prescription on the counter and almost ran to the back room. He could not blame Mike. He owed Mike over a hundred dollars. Mike was a poor man, how could he blame Mike, or be mad with Mike? He reached for the paper.

On Robert Street the snow was packed up against the gutter, black and gray and dirty and manure on it. The street was glassy and the wind came down from Cherokee Heights and slammed against Lev's leather jacket, stole inside the jacket and inside the sweater, and Lev Simon could feel it against his skin. Today he could feel it inside of him and there against him between his legs.

He came down toward Colorado Street and he stopped at the theater, asked the manager if he needed sweeping or ashes hauled or something.

He stopped at the undertaking parlor there on Delos and asked if they had ashes. He knew what he was going to do, all right, but he wanted to postpone it, lay it over, and everybody's ashes were contracted for.

Lev Simon had the prescription and another six weeks before there was a nickel to be made. He had the horse and wagon and customers on Cherokee Heights and nothing to sell them, and now he needed merchandise.

His kid had eczema and asthma.

There was a Jewish relief agency and there was the Community Chest and the visiting nurse, the city doctors, and Ancker Hospital, but he hadn't come to America for charity. Not ten borders for handouts.

He walked into the yard of the four-family building and back to the stable. The wagon was in the stable, unused since October, and he got axle grease for the wheels. He put the harness on the horse and hitched him up and took a dozen bushels from the mound against the wall and filled each half full with hay.

He took the heavy blanket off the horse and spread it over the bushels on the floor of the wagon.

She didn't see him until he was sitting up there on the seat with the reins on his hand. She came out on the back porch with a sweater over her and she said: "The medicine, Lev."

"Takes couple hours."

"Where are you going? In this cold. You'll catch cold. Do I need you sick, Lev?"

He couldn't talk to her. In his mind you could not put such things to a woman. In his head there was a woman's world and a man's world, and he could not tell her.

He urged the horse forward and out of the yard, toward Robert Street and the West Side. The horse had not been shod for six months and Lev Simon drove very carefully and slowly, keeping the horse up against the curb so the animal could get footing in the snow.

The wind invaded the wagon and Lev Simon stopped the horse once, climbed back into the wagon to push the blanket under the bushels. The wind came in under his trousers and against the long underwear. He could see the steam from the horse's nostrils and the steam from his nose when he breathed.

He could see Marty with his face swollen with eczema.

He turned off into the West Side and here the going was easier; the plows had not been through regularly. He came down Fairfield, turned, and went into the alley behind the synagogue on Mendota Street. He backed the wagon up against the synagogue's rear door and he braked the vehicle. He dropped the tail gate and then for an instant he felt his leg going, but he pulled up on his trousers and he spit and ran the cotton glove over his chin, feeling the hay smell in his nose, and took a bushel under his arm and went into the synagogue.

He found Shmul Goodkind in the basement, in the morning prayer room.

A handsome man, Goodkind, the sexton. A big man of about sixty years who wore black suits, alpaca coats, always white shirts. A man with a gray, full beard and thin, blue lips and white, amazingly white, puffy hands below the French cuffs. A handy man with a knife, Sexton Goodkind, enjoying an odd monopoly in St. Paul, untouched by the Securities and Exchange Commission.

Sexton Goodkind, the *mal*, the circumciser, handy man with a knife. He had cut Hub and he had cut Marty, and always, at the High Holidays or at Jewish picnics, he would smile at the women, point at a boy or a youth, or now, after so many years, even a man, and say: "I cut you, yes?"

A very religious man, the sexton. All his days in the synagogue, except when he was called to city hall for good government committees, for he spoke English and *wrote* English. Except when he'd have a special summons from an isolated Jew in North Dakota or northern Minnesota, in which case the fee jumped from ten dollars to a hundred, and he had been known to demand and get two hundred.

In cash. No credit for the sexton. And a round-trip railroad ticket. Pullman.

Leader in the community, with a son in medical school and another, the oldest, a rising young man in the county attorney's office.

"Landsman," said Goodkind. "Another one?" he asked jokingly. He had a full head of hair below the skullcap.

Samuel Goodkind crossed his arms, pushing his hands up his sleeves in mandarin fashion. "Brought something for the *shul*, synagogue?" he asked.

"Need something," Lev Simon said.

"Sure." Shmul Goodkind smiled and his eyebrows raised and he disengaged his hands. "Why not? You're also a *mentsch*, person. Why not? A pint, landsman, or a quart?"

"Maybe a quart." Lev Simon wanted him with the merchandise. "Let me see first."

"A pleasure," said the sexton. "Why not? You're a customer," he said, and he led Lev Simon from the prayer room, through the basement, and up the stairs to the synagogue proper, musty and dank. He led him down the main aisle, the podium and the ark up on the platform, and he led Simon up to the ark.

The sexton moved one of the high-backed velvet chairs in which the president sat at services and he sat down. He pushed against a panel at the base of the ark and removed a handful of prayer books.

The whisky was stacked behind, in pints and in quarts, corn and colored, as neat as a medicine cabinet. The sexton was a meticulous man.

"All right," Lev Simon said. "A dozen quarts," and he set down the bushel. "A quart in a bushel."

Shmul Goodkind turned in his chair, bent over, his elbows on his knees, and he smiled at Lev Simon with new respect. "Landsman," he said. "Mazeltov," he said to the new ally against the stupid laws. "Mazeltov."

"All right." Lev Simon had felt violence within him for few men.

"*Gelt*," Sexton Goodkind reminded him.

"Come on," Lev said. "Quick."

The thin-lipped smile. "*Gelt.*"

All right, then. "When I sell."

Sexton Goodkind closed the panel and turned to look up at Lev Simon, smiling and shaking his head.

There was no arguing with the sexton.

Lev Simon took his gloves off and he said to the gloves in his hand: "My horse. There outside. From here to the government." He meant the Federal Building. "Not to the police, Shmul; with the police you are partners. To the government."

Sexton Goodkind gestured with his hand, showing the way, as a headwaiter.

Lev Simon picked up the bushel and put it under his arm. "*Mein kind*," he said. "You think I'm here if not for him?" He went down the stairs to the main level and started up the aisle, and he was at the rear near the women's section when the sexton stopped him.

Lev Simon came in twelve times, and in each bushel the sexton dropped a quart of whisky, the good merchandise that had been colored.

The sexton walked to the rear door with Lev and he said: "Twenty-five dollars. This is wholesale."

"Tonight."

"Better," the sexton said. "You better come, landsman," he said. "Come and stay for evening prayers," he said.

"I don't pray."

"Twenty-five dollars. God ride with you," he said, and clapped Lev's shoulder and then hurried inside to the warm prayer room in the basement. There was a passage in the Talmud which had been bothering him.

Lev Simon sold eight quarts for five dollars each. His customers in Cherokee Heights were delighted; one woman bought three quarts. They were very pleased on Cherokee Heights, although three customers haggled, and to them he sold quarts for four dollars each.

And the big, handsome woman, Mrs. Lord, she who had bought the first hand of bananas and had never given up trying to have Lev Simon sample her wares, she paid ten dollars for her quart.

Coming down the George Street hill at noon, he walked before the horse, leading the animal slowly, the hoofs slipping and sliding on the ice. He had sixty-two dollars in his pocket and he was very careful coming down the hill, for he could not afford a lame horse or even a set of shoes for the animal.

The wind almost felled him there on the hill, but he came down slowly, the blanket over the empty bushels in the wagon, the money in his pocket, and the horse breathing steam around Lev Simon's head.

He climbed onto the wagon on Concord Street and rode down to the Y in the street where it became Robert after the turn. He left the horse standing in front of the drugstore, the near wheels four inches deep in the soiled snow.

He got Michaelson in the back room and gave him thirty-seven dollars on account—and the prescription.

He would not use the money for food, for coal, for rent, for hay.

For medicine, all right.

He could not control the sickness. If Marty had eczema, he could not fight that. He had it in his head that for the other things—food, rent, coal—he was to blame, this was at his feet, but he could use the money for medicine.

He waited for the prescription, and when Michaelson had wrapped the small bottle of salve he beckoned the druggist to the cigar counter.

"Pack Lokies," he said.

Michaelson reached in under the glass and put his hand over the box of Bull Durham sacks. "No makings?" he asked, looking up at Lev.

"Lokies."

"Splurging, eh?" Michaelson never asked how Lev had gotten the money, nor did he ever again worry about being paid.

"Yeah, splurge," he said. He gave Michaelson a dollar and waited for the change.

He'd get fifteen cents from Sarah this afternoon. She could take it from Joe's penny bank. He wanted nothing from the good circumciser.

Standing outside, leaning back against the door, the sexton's money in his pocket and the small jar of salve against his hip, Lev Simon opened the pack of cigarettes, lit himself a smoke.

He took one long, deep drag, and then he looked at the wagon, the blanket covering the bushels, remembered the wares he'd carried, remembered the other wagon and the Canadian moon that night, and let the cigarette fall from his fingers onto the icy walk.

Lev Simon moved to the wagon and let the pack of cigarettes fall into the dirty snow. Standing against the wagon, his feet deep in the snow, holding onto the tail gate, his legs spread and his forehead touching the cold, cold wood, he threw up for five minutes.

Garrison Keillor

WLT (THE EDGAR ERA)

Garrison Keillor was born in Anoka, Minnesota in 1942, attended public schools there, and graduated from Anoka High School in 1960. He received his B.A. from the University of Minnesota in 1966. In 1970 his satirical pieces began appearing in the New Yorker. Keillor's work uses the Minnesota scene to comment on universal foibles, and the gentle but accurate rapier that he wields in his writing is given a different form in his live broadcasts under the name of "A Prairie Home Companion," whose home base is the mythical Lake Wobegon, Minnesota, "where all the women are strong, all the men are handsome, and all the children above average." Keillor has one son and lives in Marine-on-St. Croix.

I T WAS THEIR SANDWICHES and their magnificent sandwich palace on Nicollet Avenue, not radio broadcasting, that brought the Elmore brothers, Edgar and Roy, to wealth and prominence in Minneapolis. In 1919, a few years before electric refrigerators became general, the brothers sold their ice company at a fine profit, purchased the former Sons of Knute Temple, and opened Elmore's Court restaurant, with six sandwiches on the menu: egg salad, onion and cucumber, toasted cheese, ham, ham and cheese, and the Hamburg. All were delicious, but the egg salad was tops. Three inches thick at the middle and served on wheat bread with a hard crust, the Elmore egg salad was a Minneapolis landmark, a lunch beloved by thousands, and, because the sandwich craze was then sweeping the Midwest, a gold mine for Edgar and Roy. Among the better families, however, the sandwich was still scorned as an inferior food, served free in taverns and eaten by mechanics, and they did not patronize the Court. Roy, who managed the kitchen and who was something of a free-thinker, didn't give a darn for them, the Peaveys and the Heffelfingers and the Pillsburys—all cake eaters, to him—but it was Edgar's weakness to covet their patronage, and once the Court was on its feet he set out to improve its quality and tone.

Edgar was a fine old gentleman, a devout Presbyterian and a natty dresser (red polka-dot tie with a navy-blue suit, navy-blue bow tie with a white linen suit), and in the majesty of the Court—with its oak tables beneath a blue-and-gold stained-glass skylight, its neo-Norwegian columns supporting the marble mezzanine, and, upstairs, its walnut-panelled Throne Room, with oil portraits of Past Knutes and their lovely Elses—Edgar was more the admiral than a sandwich-palace proprietor. His glance could straighten a man in his chair and quicken the step of a waiter, but as to quality and tone, he was nervous, indirect, and uncertain.

He invested in a string quartet to play at lunchtime—Schubert mostly, and some Mozart and Beethoven (the slow movements)—but he wasn't sure he liked the music, so he hid the musicians in a forest of ferns. He labored at writing advertisements extolling the beauties of the Court, its music, its architecture, its civility ("The establishment to which gentlemen repair with no fear of embarrassment"). "People will take us for a French whorehouse," said Roy, for Edgar never wrote a word about *sandwiches*. The radio station was Roy's idea. Radio, Roy said, would take Elmore's right *to* the Pillsburys in their own homes; they could hear for themselves what a fine place it was. (Also, it would give Roy Jr. something to do with himself; he was unhappy in his job as egg buyer, and he talked of nothing but radio.)

Edgar was sixty-two. He had misgivings about assuming a new headache like a radio station at his age. He worried about the expense, the danger of electrocution, and the possible influence of radio waves on the mental processes, but he also saw the Pillsburys seated around a radio receiver in their mansion, enjoying the fine music from Elmore's Court. And so on April 6, 1925, patrons came to lunch to find the Throne Room draped with velvet, the tables arranged in a semicircle, and in the center a bastion of broad-leaved plants from which rose a black iron stand adorned with a golden eagle, the Stars and Stripes, and a microphone.

Of the six sandwiches, the one most in need of association with fine music was the Hamburg, which many people still shunned out of leftover patriotism, and it was this sandwich, a simple beef patty in a bun, that Station WLT (With Lettuce and Tomato) was

186

intended particularly to assist. The first broadcast featured the Hamburg Tuxedo Trio (formerly the Three Nicolleteons) and Miss Lily Dale, the Hamburg Soprano, who sang that day—and every day thereafter for eight years—the Hamburg Song (to the tune of "Over There"): "It's the one, it's the one, it's the one with the fun in the bun. When you eat a Hamburg, you always clamor for just another one, one, one." Dedication Day also included two spirituals and an original song, "The Laughing Water of Minnehaha," by the Trio, and selections by Schubert, Mozart, and Beethoven, played by the Court Orchestra (the string quartet plus a piano). Finally, Edgar was brought up for a few words. He set his feet firmly, grasped the microphone with both hands, pressed it to his lips, and prayed in a loud voice that all of this might turn out for the best and be found pleasing in the eyes of God. His prayer practically deafened Roy Jr., who was at the controls in the linen closet, but, all in all, everyone judged the day a complete success. After the broadcast, there was a reception.

Oh the days when radio was strange and dazzling! Even the WLT performers could not quite believe it. To think that their voices flew out as far as Anoka, Stillwater, and Hastings! And yet it seemed to be true. Roy Jr. had friends in those towns who had promised to listen, and they said WLT came in loud and clear, so the proof was there, but some didn't accept it for years—not entirely. For years, Clarence Peters, the Tuxedo tenor, would remark to his wife in the evening about a particularly good number he had sung on the radio that day, "You should have heard it!" "I *did* hear it, as clear as a bell," she always would say. Of course, Clarence knew this, and yet, never having heard it himself, he wasn't ready to believe it.

One day, unable to bear the mystery, Clarence backed away from the microphone during the last chorus of "Cowboy's Farewell," edged toward the door to the linen closet, opened it, and, still singing ("I am gone away to a home in the sky, where love never fades and hopes never die"), recognized his own voice on the receiving set nearby, and cried out, "I have heard it!" Sensing immediately that the home audience might not grasp the meaning of his remark, he quickly added, "I am on the radio!"

Because of his good enunciation and presence of mind, Clarence Peters soon became WLT's first announcer, and as such he performed the first broadcast interview in Minnesota. Miss Dale was ill that day, the Trio was strapped for new songs, and Clarence, needing to fill a few minutes, took the microphone to the nearest table and invited those present to make a talk. A tall man in a white suit (his name has been forgotten) stood up and nervously donned his straw hat as the microphone was put before him. "It is an honor to be given this opportunity," he said gravely, "and I sincerely thank you for it."

This speech, though brief, was a real innovation at the time—the voice of an ordinary person, a person such as the listener himself or herself, carried to countless unseen homes, the same as if he or she were the Governor, or the Archbishop, or a Pillsbury—and soon the whole city knew that Elmore's was the place to go to "get on the air." Hundreds vied for the choice tables in the Throne Room; families from distant towns journeyed to Minneapolis to visit Elmore's, having alerted neighbors and friends to listen to their broadcast. Many were prepared to pay money for the privilege. Some demanded it as a right. Edgar had to hire two ushers to handle the crowds. The Throne Room became a regular auditorium—people were too excited to eat anyway, and Edgar had to hire two ushers to shush them. The tables were hauled downstairs to the main dining room and replaced by pews from the Knute chapel.

It was wonderful to be on the radio, and awful. Many a man who had rehearsed words in his mind found himself tongue-tied at the crucial moment, and sat down in shame and wept. Many a man who had thought to tell a joke chucked it at the last moment in favor of a religious or patriotic sentiment befitting the importance of the occasion. ("This is Albert M., of Waseca. Hello. For all have sinned and come short of the glory of God.") Some requested prayers for sick friends. Respect for the flag was expressed, and the need for vigilance; also the superiority of Minnesota cheese and butter, the beauty of her lakes and rivers, the belief in democracy, the hope for a better future.

Through that first summer and winter and into the next summer, Edgar pondered what he had wrought—the once lovely restaurant now crowded and noisy, waiters quitting every week, and, thanks to WLT, the Hamburg now the hot item on the menu. This was a bitter pill for Roy and the cooks, Dorothy and Inga, who resented the hard assembly-line work of frying Hamburgs by the hundreds and got sick from the grease. What was worse, Edgar had to contend with hundreds of patrons who demanded radio time and old regulars who expected special consideration, and soon he was hounded by musicians, singers, actors, poets, comedians, and entertainers of every stripe, who saw radio as their chance to be presented at last to the Minnesota audience. These included some good ones who later became famous: Whistling Jim Wheeler and His All-Boy Band, Elsie and Johnny, "Ice Cream" Cohen, Norma Neilsen and Fargo Bill, the Orphan Girls Quartet, and many more. But most of them were the others—the child elocutionists, yodellers, mandolin bands, gospel-singing families, people who did barnyard sounds and train imitations, and dozens of Autoharp players, all of whom had to be refused, some of them repeatedly. "We have opened a Pandora's box," Edgar said, "and now everyone and his brother is trying to get into it."

At first, Edgar was puzzled by the performers' ambition, and then, as he brooded on it, he became wary, and at last a fear took hold of him that never let go for the rest of his life. He decided that, while most people were harmless, some ("and it only takes one") were not. He imagined that they were driven by a desire to ruin him by doing something awful on his radio station—a vulgar remark shouted by a stranger in the audience, an off-color story, perhaps filth in a foreign language. He saw someone latching onto the microphone, wresting it away from Clarence, and saying *something*—something so repulsive, crude, and vile as to make his name Mud in thousands of homes, including the Pillsburys'. They would never be seen in a place where things like that were allowed. "We are helpless," he told Roy. "We work ourselves sick to make a good restaurant, and now the kitchen is a hellhole, and the sandwiches I wouldn't feed to a dog, and now anyone who wants to could walk in and put us out of business in a minute."

Edgar swung into action. He hired a young English teacher, Miss Phelps, to observe the audience for any who appeared agitated. The public-speaking time was limited strictly to fifteen minutes in the morning and a half hour in the afternoon, and Roy Jr. was instructed to keep a hand on the switch at those periods and be ready to throw it instantly. Edgar hired two announcers, big sturdy fellows, and showed them how to keep both feet planted during interviews and how to place one hand on the person's shoulder so as to have good leverage if push came to shove. He wrote up a WLT code covering all aspects of broadcasting ("The Principles of Radiation"), and he made all performers agree to it.

It included a dress code, "Subjects To Be Avoided," and "Regulations Concerning Music." " 'By the grace of God, it is given to us to cast our bread on distant waters,'" he wrote in the code. " 'See then that ye walk circumspectly, not as fools, but as wise.' Eph. 5:15." And he drew up a program schedule and ordered that it be followed, no exceptions:

10:30 *Piano Prelude.*
10:45 *The Homemakers Hour.*
11:00 *Morning Musicale.*
11:45 *Meet Your Neighbors.*
12:00 *Let's Sing!*
12:30 *Orchestral Interlude.*
12:45 *The Hamburg Tuxedo Trio Hour.*
 1:00 *Let's Get Together.*
 1:30 *Orchestral Interlude.*
 1:45 *Scripture Nugget.*
 2:05 *Miss Lily Dale.*
 2:20 *Up in a Balloon.*
 2:35 *The Classroom of the Air.*
 3:00 *Obituaries and Notices.*
 3:10 *The Story Hour.*
 3:25 *Piano Postlude.*

Gone forever were the days when Clarence might reminisce about his Wisconsin boyhood for ten minutes until the missing sheet music was found, or the Trio repeat the verses of "The Lost Chord," or Evelyn Wills Duvalier carry on endless impromptu piano variations because nobody knew what was supposed to happen next, or when a person in the audience might rise to give a demonstration of cow-calling.

As WLT neared the end of its first decade, Edgar turned over the management to Roy Jr. He was tired of listening to the radio for five hours every day and worrying that someone (the same old *someone*, who hadn't turned up yet but was only prolonging the suspense) would go over the edge and give him a good solid heart attack. He didn't care much for WLT. The Trio mumbled words, and Miss Lily Dale sounded like a goat, and nobody sang the songs that he wanted to hear. And it was more tiresome to listen now that he was getting hard of hearing. Roy Jr. had built him a receiver so powerful that it rattled windows, and another one was installed in his Buick (the first car radio in Minneapolis) which

190

could be heard for blocks. People complained to the police. Edgar was always switching the darned thing off, but he was uneasy with it off, and he was always turning it back on. To give him a rest, Roy Jr. scheduled a fifteen-minute newscast at one o'clock, Edgar's naptime; Edgar appreciated the gesture, but every day he expected *someone* to put in an appearance.

One show that always lifted his spirits (and that he himself sponsored) was "Up in a Balloon," with Vince Upton and his wife, Sheridan Thomas, playing the parts of Bud and Bessie, a wealthy Minneapolis couple who roam the earth in a luxurious balloon, seeking adventure. Edgar loved the show less for the dialogue, which was quite ordinary, than for the sound effects, which Vince spent days and weeks perfecting. The balloon format was well suited to Vince's perfectionism, for it allowed the couple to spend long periods in the stratosphere, which required only the creaking of the gondola (a horse halter) and the sighing wind (one of the Tuxedo Trio, or anyone handy), along with a spoken description of the scenery below, while Vince planned the effects for their next descent. WLT's modest budget did not permit the balloon to visit cities (there weren't enough staff members on hand to provide hubbub), and so its descents tended to be emergency landings in isolated regions. Even at that, Bud and Bessie crashed several times in the Arctic Circle before Vince was satisfied with his glacier effect, which was first an aluminum cookie tin (plied by Clarence) and then a bag of rock salt that was put through a meat grinder; finally, he hit on the idea of rolling a basketball containing a microphone along a bed of gravel. Likewise, he experimented for weeks to produce dripping rain on the leaves of a tropical forest, the shifting sands of the Sahara, and the pounding surf at Waikiki (fifty pounds of oats and a wheelbarrow).

Hundreds of new effects were subsequently created, many of them submitted by listeners, who strove to surpass each other with stranger and more exotic adventures: a wave of molten lava destroying a grain elevator, an army marching across thin ice, Bud and Bessie climbing the Eiffel Tower using suction cups, and (Edgar's invention) Bud and Bessie throwing their radio into the Grand Canyon during a broadcast of "Carmen" (the Court Orchestra seated on a freight cart, a portable tile wall, and an alarm clock). It was the invention of a disillusioned man with a great deal of leisure time.

The Depression years, in fact, were unhappy ones for Edgar.

His doctors ordered him to stay away from the Court and to avoid those WLT programs that made him anxious (he was more anxious, though, when he couldn't hear them). Denied even the egg salad sandwich, his favorite, he took to his bed in the big house on Lake Calhoun, and sulked at nurses. Once, he tried to return the WLT license to the government, and, failing at that, changed his will to make the Pillsbury Company his beneficiary. He was not, as Roy Jr. later proved in court, a man of sound mind.

On October 12, 1940, his birthday, Edgar lay in bed and listened to "A Salute to Edgar Elmore" on WLT—all five hours of it. Beginning with "Piano Prelude," all of the music programs featured his favorite songs, and Lucille Larson gave the original egg salad recipe on "The Homemakers Hour." The neighbors on "Meet Your Neighbors" were his friends; the "Scripture Nugget," read by the Rev. Irving James Knox, was Edgar's beloved I Corinthians 10; the story on "The Story Hour" was his own life story. But the highlight surely was "Up in a Balloon," for Vince had gone all out. The episode, entitled "Bud and Bessie Visit the Old Testament," included the Creation, the destruction of Sodom and Gomorrah, and the parting of the Red Sea (ten quarts of motor oil and an upright vacuum cleaner).

The five hours were an eternity to Edgar. He was positive that *someone* had chosen this day, his day, to pull a fast one. As the last notes of "Piano Postlude" died out ("Lead, Kindly Light"), he turned to Roy and said, "I can't go through this again." He passed away exactly one month later.

The dread event that Edgar waited fifteen years for occurred finally on August 7, 1942. It happened to Vince Upton, during "The Story Hour." On that day, Vince, as "Grandpa Sam," sat down in "the old easy chair," invited his young listeners to gather close round their radios, and picked up the script and began to read. It didn't take him long to realize that *someone* had slipped him a wrong story, a story that began, "I was born twenty-seven years ago in a place called Northfield, Minnesota, the dullest little burg in the dullest state in the Union, and as soon as I was old enough to earn the train fare, I set out to see what life was all about."

Vince swallowed hard and continued. The story was the "confession" of a young man named Frank who gains wealth in Chicago and takes up with a dark Paraguayan beauty named Pabletta, whose breasts are pale and small and shiver at the thrill of his touch. Slowly, his voice shaking with the effort, Vince picked his way through the story, glancing ahead as he read and skirting the obvious outrages, but some things escaped his eye until he was right on top of them. These he read quickly, adding, "Of course, I knew I should not have done this," or "Something told me that someday I would be punished." The writer of the story had certainly tied it together tightly—you had to give him credit for that.

Finally, with ten minutes left, Vince arrived at an episode that seemed to lead the story in a direction that could not be pursued any further. Now, Vince was a script man through and through, and hated to speak impromptu, but he put the story aside and rose to the occasion. In a sad and weary voice, he confessed his sinful pride and sensual nature, and begged the forgiveness of his family. He denounced the evil influence of movies and modern novels. He announced that the beautiful Pabletta had died beneath the wheels of a truck. "Today, doctors tell me that I have but weeks to live, my body ravaged by a disease without a name," he added, and concluded with an appeal to all within the sound of his voice to consider prayerfully what would be the outcome of their ways. "Repent! Repent!" he cried, and collapsed in tears just as the sweep hand approached twelve. "That's all for today. Be sure to join Grandpa Sam tomorrow at the same time for another exciting story," the announcer said, and Evelyn Wills Duvalier played "Just As I Am" from memory, for "Piano Postlude."

After that, the scripts were guarded closely by Miss Phelps, who kept them hidden on her person and proofread each one at the last moment before broadcast. As an extra precaution for his own peace of mind, Vince wrote an emergency "Story Hour" script, which he kept in an inside coat pocket and could switch to at any point, and which began, "But enough about that. Let's get on to today's main story, which concerns a young boy named Jim and his dog Buster." This script, never used, lies today, yellow and stained, in the back of the loose-leaf copybook in the main WLT studio. Two generations of WLT announcers have revised the story in their spare time, polishing the dialogue, fleshing out the plot, introducing new characters, including Pabletta and her friend Ramón, and it is said to be quite good—though not, of course, suitable for broadcast.

Meridel Le Sueur

A HUNGRY INTELLECTUAL

Meridel Le Sueur was born in Murray, Iowa in 1900 and grew up in many parts of the Middle West, including Minnesota. During her childhood Le Sueur's mother, Marion, and her stepfather, Arthur Le Sueur, were involved in the Non-Partisan League and other progressive movements. As prominent members of the Industrial Workers of the World the family was persecuted for its stand against America's entry into the First World War. Its home on Dayton Avenue in St. Paul was shot at, rocks with obscene messages were hurled through windows, and books were rifled and burned in the front yard. But the idealism and optimism implicit in her family's fights and the visits of the members of the IWW to the home in St. Paul nourished young Meridel. For years she was accustomed to such outstanding men as Eugene Debs and Joe Hill meeting at their house. The material that these experiences provided for her fiction is evident in the recurrence of several noteworthy threads running through her work: an abiding faith in the common people, particularly when they work together; a deep belief in the strength of women; an unromantic awareness of the intrinsic violence in life and of the closeness of death and birth; and a belief in the proximity of human life to external nature.

ANDREW HOBBS was an intellectual. He continually said he was an intellectual, an idealist. Before the depression he had had a job as an advertising writer, and had a stenographer of his own, that's what he said. He was always telling us what a good position he had had and how he was getting on in the world. Of course he was just going into advertising until he got started with his writing, he said, but he seemed to get farther and farther into debt, so he never could stop his job. That was before the depression scooped him out, with not so much as a by-your-leave, and left him without any of the gadgets he had bought, and dumped him on the streets.

The first time I saw him he was talking against God down at Gateway Park, standing very tall, his narrow head showing above the crowd of workmen. The old gospel-monger was holding forth across the street, and Hobbs was talking Ingersoll atheism on the opposite corner, and he would take up a collection afterwards which would sometimes amount to even fifty cents. Anyhow he could eat off it. But he said he didn't really care for the collection, it was just the principle of the thing, if a person didn't pay for a thing they didn't appreciate it, even a few dimes like that.

I always had an awful time keeping the children quiet, waiting for the speaking to be over and the boys to come home to dinner. Karen was only two and Sybil just nine months. There was fifteen months between them. Somebody brought him over and introduced him and he stood back very modestly and tried to keep his shoes in the dark. He looked like he was trying to step back through a door that wasn't there. He seemed to be stepping back away from something, away from any one touching him so that his face and even his body seemed to have a receding look about them as if he would presently disappear into something behind him. For all that, he was well-meaning anyone could see that. And he had his own pride.

When Karl introduced him, he took off his hat and bowed a little, like a Southern gentleman, and sure enough I found out he had been raised in Georgia, the lower middle class, always trying to get up further, always thinking themselves ascending a little on the social ladder and really descending frightfully from generation to generation. This continual lowering and defeat gave him a sad gentility. He took off his hat and bowed a little and seemed to recede.

Karl went back to the corner with the boys to distribute some leaflets about the mass meeting the next night, and Hobbs sat down in the car with me and politely asked about the children, but he was ignoring them. The pigeons walked around the feet of the unemployed men sitting in the park, getting the last breath of summer air before going to their flops. "You know," Hobbs said, "I don't have to do this."

"Listen!" I shouted at Karen, "sit still just a minute and I'll get you a cone. What?" I said.

"I graduated from the University of Georgia," he said delicately.

"Yeah? Listen!" I shouted between my teeth. "I'll get you a tooth brush with Mickey Mouse on it." I couldn't keep them quiet. Hobbs looked offended as if he had smelled something bad. He jerked up his pants over his knee and I could see his awfully white shanks and he had no socks on. He jerked down his pants again and I felt sorry because I could see his poor feet, in somebody else's shoes and one shoe had a big place like a carbuncle where the guy who had had them before kept his bunion.

"I don't know what I am going to do," I said. "I can't wait around at these meetings all the time because the milk gets sour."

He smiled abstractedly, and looked out past the tattered top of the Ford at the sky. He had a thin face. He looked hungry. I remember the way I had seen his pants bag down over his rumps as if he had filled them more at some time.

"Why don't you come along and have supper with us?" I said. "We're going to have a swell stew."

"Well," he said, vaguely, so very delicate and evasive, "I don't know, I was supposed to meet a fellow over here." He waved his long white hand. "I don't know. I might. . . . Wait a minute . . . I'll see if I can find him."

He swung his long thin shanks out the door. "O.K." I said, swatting Sybil's hands so they wouldn't catch in the door. I watched him take a walk behind the statue of the unknown soldier, duck a few seconds on the other side and come back. He didn't have to meet anybody. He didn't have anybody to meet.

He came to our house often just about supper time. He never came right in and had something to eat like others. He always stood vaguely in the door, and bowing a little, and my lord he got thinner and thinner until he seemed like a wraith and his pants hung on his poor shanks like an old sack. "Well, well," he would say, politely, "You're just having supper. No . . . No, I don't want to spoil your evening meal."

"We're just having supper," I would say. "Come on in and have supper."

"No. No," he would say, flapping his white hands. "I just ate." And he would brush his face off with his hands as if he had walked through cobwebs. He would sit on the step and we would whisper inside about it.

"I know he hasn't had any supper."

"The poor guy," Karl would say.

"Why doesn't he say . . . just SAY he's hungry and come in and eat."

"It's pride."

"My God, everyone is hungry."

"I know, but he's an intellectual."

"Ohhhhh!"

Then all who were eating would fall against each other sniggering.

"Shut up," I'd say. "He'll hear."

Afterwards, when the boys went out to the meeting, he'd come in sometimes and help me with the children. If I went out of the room for something, I could see that he took things off the table, and when I would come back, he wouldn't chew a bit but sit there smiling vaguely, with his mouth full of food, so I would have to go out again so he could chew it up.

He never once said he was hungry. He always had mysterious places where he said he slept and ate. Yet we all knew that he slept at the mission and ate that slop. Lots of the boys saw him there, but he never said a word about it, never said that he did, as if not saying so made it not so.

He seemed to like better to be with me than with the boys. He was raised by women I guess and felt easier with them, and the boys made fun of his high-falutin' ideas. He would say all sorts of great high-sounding phrases he must have remembered from school. "We must all struggle," he would say, "life is progress." And yet he seemed neither to struggle nor to make any progress. You could see he felt fine when he was talking. I would feed the babies or change them for the night, and you could see in a few minutes he made the world a place it was easy for him to be in. He kept saying that change must come without violence, that it must be intellectual.

I said, "When you have a baby, birth is violent."

"No. No," he said. "Change must come from the intellect with understanding and non-violence, non-resistance."

"I don't think it's that way," I said. "From having a baby I think it's different. It comes out violently."

I could see him eyeing the last chop left on the plate. "Why don't you eat that chop?" I said. I wanted to give the bone to the baby to chew anyway; besides, one chop is nothing to fix another meal with.

He said, "Oh, I had plenty, plenty," and he went on talking, telling about how you must educate everyone and then they would understand.

"Understanding comes in the stomach," I said, turning the baby up for powder.

When I went out to put the baby to bed he ate the chop. Then he cleared the table so I wouldn't notice and washed all the dishes. I didn't say anything about it until later when I talked it over with Karl. "Why wouldn't he eat the chop?" I asked Karl.

"Damned if I know," Karl said.

"I guess it was too simple a way to do it," I said.

"If your belly's empty, it's empty," Karl said. "That's all there is to it to me."

"But it's different with him," I said. "It must be something more to him, something subtle."

"Well, the point is," Karl said, "he did eat the chop. He did actually eat the chop, that's the point."

"But he didn't say so."

"No, the say is worth something to that guy."

"Sure, the say is everything. . . ."

"What the hell's the say worth? The point is he ate the chop," and Karl went off into a huge howl of laughter. I had to make him promise he wouldn't tell anyone so they wouldn't guy Hobbs about it.

"Yeah, he ate the chop," Karl howled.

Sometimes Hobbs would look like he had some mysterious grievance and wouldn't speak for days. He would come to the meetings or do some typing, but he wouldn't say a word and acted very polite and mysterious as if he had some great secret tragedy connected with him that he couldn't speak of. He would hardly speak to the boys, but he would come and take care of the babies while I did some work. It got awful hot and he would roll the babies out to the park.

He was always awfully clean. Once his collar was torn a little and he tried to mend it but he couldn't do anything with his hands. They didn't seem to have any life in them. We used to talk about it sometimes, how that fellow always had a clean shirt and his feet never stank. It's something to be able to do that when you never have a place to wash or a bed alone but he always looked scrubbed. I don't know how he did it, but no one ever asked him outright because he wouldn't have told anything, he would have had something mysterious to say, as if he had been washed in the blood of the lamb or something. Nothing natural and outright seemed to happen to him. Once I asked him if he ever had a woman.

"Didn't you ever have a woman?" I asked him because I couldn't imagine it, everything seemed so ideal and delicate to him. The boys always laughed at the way he came and sat with me like another woman. Once he helped me move and even if I did most of the work I felt delicate and precious. I had to laugh. The boys said, "Well, I suppose Sir Walter Raleigh helped you move." I had to laugh.

When I asked him if he ever had a woman, he blushed and spread out his long thin hands, "Well, if you mean have I ever been in love?"

"Well, all right, have you ever been in love?"

He looked at his hands a long time. I felt it as plain as your face that he was having a struggle between what had really happened when he was in love and what he wished to tell me had happened. I felt an awful disgust and pity for him, like shouting out at him, "Go on tell, tell me all the dirt, don't fix it up into the ideal, get it all out of your poor lean body, spit it out, vile and awful." But I knew he wouldn't tell me what had happened. There was something vague all over him. I saw the shanks of the poor guy, his shoes a little hard from being damp so much, turned up at the toes and hardened in the leather, living for the glorious mind and sitting, pawing webs over his own face.

He told me a long tale about his wife. I couldn't look at him, at all. He said he had made five hundred dollars a month and had a pretty wife, and it seems she had fallen in love, he said, with a racetrack man, a driver of a fast car, and she had gone off with him, and then he said, and I was astonished, I couldn't believe it, that they had been killed, both of them, together. He seemed to like that almost and licked his thin lips over something. Yes, they had gone around the track together, driving very, very fast, he wasn't sure how fast, and they had both been killed.

About this time they were organizing a Hunger March to the State Capitol of all the farmers and unemployed to demand bread and milk for their children. Karl had been telling me that Hobbs never seemed to be there when anything actual was happening.

199

He would talk or write plenty but somehow or other he never seemed to be at a meeting, where there was danger. I said to Karl, I couldn't believe it.

"That's the way it turns out," he said. "I don't believe it," I told him. "He's trying. He feels timid. He's sore from being alone."

"Just the same you'll see," Karl said. "Wait till the Hunger March and you'll see what I say is so, all right."

Before that we had a picnic down at the grove along the Mississippi. It was a fine summer afternoon in harvest, a good summer day with the wind blowing the heavy trees and the water like the sky and the little curl of beach golden in the bright sun. A day when you like to see your fat children running naked in the sun and water. Rose was there with her baby one month off and we all felt happy sitting on the beach with the tiny waves curling up and the sound of summer wind and the sun beating down into our pores like golden fire and the rosy naked children. Rose said, "Gee, I can't wait to see mine. I feel all the time like taking it out to look at it." Karl laughed and we all looked, laughing at each other through the sunlight.

Hobbs was sitting by himself and had taken off his awful shoes showing his long white toes but he wouldn't go in the water. We all put on our suits in the bushes and went into the river, but Hobbs wouldn't go in. He sat on the beach and that day somehow his eyes looked so cunning and dead I could hardly speak to him. And he somehow made Rose being so heavy with child seem out of place although we all liked it. "A woman," he said, "shouldn't come out like that." It made me kind of mad.

After we had lunch and Sybil and Karen were lying under a spotted beach tree sleeping with the shadows splotched on them, he said, "I don't see why people have children. We have no right to bring children into the world until we know more about it. Perpetuating the race," he called it. He got quite excited talking to me about it until I went to sleep too. I sort of dozed off, but I could hear Karl and Rose's husband talking very earnestly planning the Hunger March where they squatted down on their heels at the edge of the water as if they didn't quite have time to sit down even. Somehow the drone of their voices, earnest, real, coming through the heat and the wind, filled me with assurance. I wasn't afraid. The sun seemed to pour down on us expanding over and in and through the water, and sky, sand and bodies and the lovely full mound of Rose sitting in the sand over her beautiful stomach.

"The masses won't stand together," Hobbs was saying, writing words with a stick in the sand. "They'll betray one another," he said. "They won't stick together . . . You can't make a silk purse out of a sow's ear."

I could hear the lovely drone of the men's voices and the life and dream singing in the heat, and our bodies intertwined together. . . . "Look what the masses read . . ." I heard his dry voice going on and on.

A long time later I heard him say, "My wife and I might have had a child once but we got rid of it."

The afternoon of the Hunger March, Hobbs came over and stuck pretty close to me. He seemed silent and then he would talk very fast and loud. I kept thinking he would go but he helped me put on Karen's sun-hat and said he would carry Sybil. It was a hot day but I was going to push the carriage up to the Capitol. I thought we could sit across in the park anyway and see what happened. The walks were sizzling, but Hobbs helped me push up the steepest hills. I was used to pushing them until I felt like a dray horse. We sat down on the grass on the mound across from the Capitol. We sat where we could see the marchers coming down University Avenue. The heat was like a falling curtain you couldn't look through. Hobbs had been telling me about a girl he saw at the Busy Bee cafeteria and what a pure face she had. It got to be past time for the marchers who were coming from the heart of the city. Hobbs got nervous and stopped talking and wrung his hands together in his lap. A dog lifted its leg right on the bench he was sitting on, but he didn't pay any attention. I let the children out of the buggy to play on the fine freshly mowed green grass. They don't get to see green grass too often.

Hobbs said, "What time is it?"

I said, "It's three o'clock."

After a while I said, "You keep yourself pretty safe all right." A slow color mounted his neck and half up his cheeks. He didn't say a word.

"Listen," I said, but then I could see the dark clot of men down the highway like a mass of angry bees moving swiftly towards the Capitol. "There they are," I cried, trying to see Karl, but they all looked like the same man, loose dirty clothes, angry pressing-forward faces, and all lean as a soup bone, but they came in a thick swift cloud, black and angry, bearing banners saying, "WE WANT BREAD. WE WANT MILK. OUR CHILDREN ARE HUNGRY."

I began jumping up and down with a cry in my throat and my children climbing up my thighs. "Listen," I said. "You can still go. You can still join them. . . . Look . . . Run . . ." But he never moved.

He didn't come around for a long time after that. I felt sorry for the poor guy after all. I knew it hit him pretty hard, in a way, not being able to go that day.

We got kicked out of where we were living and moved into a kind of shack down the river. And one day there was Hobbs in the doorway making a bow, clean as ever, with his hair plastered down on his head as if he had been ducked in the river. He said that he had swum four miles down the river and walked back, but looking at him I thought he hadn't done it at all, that he had just wet his hair and then come up and told me a tale. It would be a daring, clean thing to do, to take off your clothes and go down a swift river. . . .

Then he says that he got a boat for twelve dollars and that he expects to hear from his old advertising company in Detroit any day now and they will have a place for him in January, so he thinks he will go down the river alone for a spell and have an adventure until then. He sat very delicately in the room keeping his pants legs down so as not to show his bare shanks.

But, my lord, I even thought that maybe he would go down the river. A woman has always got faith and hope certainly. I felt glad and thought now maybe he will do it, maybe he will go down that river.

He sat on the couch telling about the books he had been reading. Pretty soon he got up and said he was going down to the river now and see about that scow he was dickering for and he stooped over and drew a diagram on the back of a leaflet, how he would fix it up for himself. It was all quite clear, there on paper.

Then he made a little bow, backed off into that space that would never protect him and went down to the river.

I didn't tell Karl anything about his having been there, but the very next day we got back from trying to get an extra quart of milk from the relief which they wouldn't give us, and we felt pretty discouraged because many that were demonstrating needed it worse than us and it didn't seem we got very far with all our organizing—and there was a note on the table, held down by the butcher knife stuck into it very dramatic, and scrawled on it with an elegant hand, it said:

Am going down the river. Save all my letters. Will write my adventures and we will publish them. It will be the only record of the trip. Save all.

We never heard of him again.

Frederick Manfred

from BOY ALMIGHTY

*Born Frederick Feikema in 1912 near Doon in Rock Township, Iowa,
Frederick Manfred was educated at Calvin College in Grand Rapids,
Michigan, and Nettleton Commercial College, Sioux Falls, South
Dakota. Subsequently he worked as filling station attendant, harvest and
factory hand, salesman, and newspaper reporter for the* Minneapolis
Journal. *This nomadic life during the thirties has informed many of his
works. He is perhaps best known for his literary Siouxland, located in the
center of the Upper Midlands and including southwestern Minnesota.
Many of his novels recreate the lives of legendary figures of that area, the
most famous of them Hugh Glass, the hero of Manfred's novel* Lord
Grizzly. *But he has been interested in less heroic lives too. The following
selection from* Boy Almighty *is a rendering of a young man in the grip of
tuberculosis and has the immediacy of some of his epic tales. His most
recent novel is* Green Earth.

T HE BULKY AMBULANCE-DRIVER pushed a thin pillow beneath
Eric's head and covered his long body with a clean white
sheet.

The bulky man gestured. His stubby assistant hurried. And together the two men lifted the stretcher and carried him from the
narrow room.

As Eric passed through the door, he turned his blue eyes side-
ways to look at his books and manuscript for the last time, turning his eyes so far they hurt in their sockets.

Gravely the two gray-clad men carried him down the winding
stairs. For heavy men they were surprisingly gentle. Only when
they reached the last turn in the stairwell did they bump his
long-toed feet dangling from the edge of the stretcher. The bump
stirred the fierce little animal in his left side and it gnawed at him

and he held it stiffly against his naked body. The bulky man swore considerately, and drew in his breath.

As they emerged from the tenant-aged frame house on Hickory street, the late afternoon sun filtering through the just-leafing trees splashed sprinkles of light on Eric. He blinked and hesitated and then jerked his joint-knobby limbs a little, like a gray-bellied bug discovered beneath old bark.

Faintly he heard a car drive up and heard the fall of the engine murmur. The car door opened and he heard a woman draw in her breath and exclaim, "Why, it's Eric!"

He recognized the woman. She was the sturdy wife of Bud, a friend, who had given him his only good meals during the hungry months. He remembered she liked to cook.

Vaguely he heard her rush across the sidewalk and the lawn, and ask the men, "What's wrong? Where's he going?"

The bulky man did not answer. He had taken a deep breath to lift his end of the stretcher into the ambulance.

"Tell me, what's wrong?"

The big man set his end on the edge of the ambulance floor and said, "Nothin's really wrong with him, Ma'am. Just sick, is all. Got a bad cold, maybe."

"Where's he going?"

The big man hesitated, and then blurted, "Well, Ma'am, he's goin' to a sanatorium."

"What? Eric going . . . not our Eric! Why, he always looked so strong and healthy."

Eric stirred again and blinked. "I was hungry," he mumbled.

"What was wrong, Eric?"

"Hungry."

"Hungry? Didn't you have any money? Why didn't you tell me? Or Bud?"

"Hungry."

They shoved him into the ambulance. The doors began to close.

The warm-hearted woman, crying, turned to the men. "Tell me, tell me what happened? I want to know. Please tell me."

"Lady, he's full of bugs. TB bugs. An' we're haulin' him off to the Phoenix Sanatorium."

"Hungry," Eric mumbled.

The doors clanged to and the motor started.

The driver of the ambulance was a gentle man. He had some

concern for the patient. Eric could feel the tenderness of him in the way he drove around corners, the way he eased the machine over rough streets and slipped it effortlessly between grumbling cars.

They went along slowly. Every now and then the driver's assistant opened the panel behind the seat to ask Eric if he felt all right.

Eric nodded. His left side pained him too much to make an effort at speech. He held the side of his body as a separate entity in his arms. All the muscles of his neck and his back on the left side, the muscles over his abdomen and in his thighs, were taut and frightened. A few quivered involuntarily at the strain. He lay stiffly, holding his pain closely in his arms. If the evil beast got away, he thought, it might attack again. He held it closely.

The light in his braincase was dim. It wasn't a flame anymore; it was barely a glow; it was hardly light enough to help him find his way from moment to moment. Only when the ambulance jarred him did the coals in his body's grate flare up.

The brake-drums groaned and the ambulance hesitated. Eric poked at the glow in his brain. He caused it to light up and he worked at lifting his head so he could look through the two small panes in the rear door. He looked, and grayly, dimly, saw they were rounding Lake Calhoun. There was a sharp wind out and the waters of the small, oval lake were full of bared teeth. Some of the waves were caught with fierce white splashes. There were a few boats on the surface, and, far beyond, out where a row of bolleana poplars curved slenderly and accurately like a row of trees in ancient Attica, he saw a car moving slowly. He wondered who was driving it. It might be himself. He found it difficult to sense just where he was. His head fell back on the finger-thin pillow and the glow faded and the walls of his braincase receded so far into the distance that his skull seemed miles wide and the ceiling of it a lofty, vaulted dome.

The glow came up again and reached at the edges of his skull and seeped out through its apertures. He was surprised to find himself covered with a thin sheet and still lying stiffly on the stretcher within the ambulance. He could not understand his situation. He had a notion that an eternity of living had slipped between himself and the car he had driven on the other side of the lake.

The ambulance twisted beneath him and he heard the heavy

tires rumbling over rough brick-paving. He tried to force himself backward, far enough to get at some storehouse where he had put away volumes of memory. He got there eventually and took them down and spread them out. He opened the pages. He found recorded that southwest of the city a way lay paved with bricks. This road led out towards Lake Minnetonka, out over the mauve, biscuit hills. And near the lake was the sanatorium.

The glow faded again and he lay deep within himself like a raced-out hound, panting, resting, deep in the recesses of his temple. He could see his brain lying on its side, its head resting on its forepaws and panting, tongue out and gaunt. Could even see the saliva running from its mouth, dripping upon its forepaws. It was very tired and sweaty.

The ambulance shook. It was trying to shake him off its back. The jarring awakened the glow. It brightened suddenly. Once more his braincase was filled to over-flowing with light. He raised his head and looked out of the panes of the door.

They were out on rolling land. He studied it with care. The green he saw, a yellow-green, was spring's first grass, and the ruffles on the tree branches were the first bursts of leaves, curled and opening like just-born babies' fists.

A lift in the road tumbled the ambulance a little and his regard went swiftly to his side. The muscles stood stiffly at pain's attention, tightly holding the clawing little beast against his ribs. He faintly remembered the fox gnawing away at the Spartan boy's vitals, and was pleased that he could still remember stories, pleased that he could still lift himself, feet and all, above the monotonous drift of one moment becoming another.

The ambulance turned and slowed and then sped up and then slowed again and turned, circling, turning, until he was sure he had fallen onto a phonograph turntable. He held his side stiffly, fearing the pain that would spring up when the speed of the turntable slackened.

There were voices about. The glow brightened and he lifted his eyelids and looked at the world. The ambulance doors were opening. He saw two men, a burly man and a stubby man. They seemed vaguely familiar. He saw two other faces, women's faces, as white as the nurses' caps they wore. The stretcher moved and he felt himself moving with it, and he felt the brush of the world's breath upon him, the wonderful touch of spring's breath and spring's crisp coolness upon his face.

The nurses were rough. The stretcher disturbed the beast in his side and the beast ate at him and he stiffened his muscles against it and tried to smother it by hugging it close.

He forced his eyes open again. The sky was too blue to be sky at all. It was an immense blue eye, staring so sharply he blinked.

People seemed stilt-tall as they moved past him. There were too many of them.

Two huge doors opened and a stench of carbolic acid hit him. It was fearful, the stench was, and he almost retched. But he fought it and kept the animal quiet. It would eat no more of him if he could help it.

The two doors closed behind him, like two huge lips of a whale lying on its side, and he was inside the stinking body.

He felt eyes brushing his face. Some of the eyes were square with pity. Some were slitted as if the owners of them were afraid to look out of them. Some were bold and cruel, staring at his nakedness.

He was rolled down a hallway and into an intensely dark room where the glow of his brain, instead of sharpening like a lantern does when night's darkness presses upon it, almost went out. There was a smell of burnt air. He had no feeling of anything about him. There was no sky nor depth, no grass nor stars, no sun, no walls nor floor nor ceiling, no white, but black and black and nothing. He was lonesome here.

A voice, a calm voice spoke, softly, "Can you roll on your side?"

He rolled against the little animal. He tried to smother it. He held himself stiffly.

"Take a deep breath. Hold it."

He heard a click, a buzzing. A strange glow, an X-ray's glow, lighted outside his braincase. It was so like his own glow that he was sure it was the open skull of another man, accidentally revealed.

"Good. That's it."

Hands lifted him upright, held him against a machine.

He heard a murmur of voices. A kind voice was exclaiming, "Bad? Hah! Look. There's a major lesion. There's some more trouble. And that's pleurisy, maybe pneumonia. Or, it could be still another lesion."

"What's a lesion?" Eric suddenly asked, opening a lucid moment.

"It's a . . . trouble."

"A trouble?" Eric looked and saw four white faces peering at him and nodding. The faces were masked. "A trouble?"

"Yes. It's a hole. TB bugs ate a hole in your lung about the size of an egg."

"A hole!" Eric exclaimed. Without moving a muscle, he laughed a little. The glow rose and he laughed still more, still restraining his muscles from mirth. "The little rascals. So they ate a hole in me. A hole. Holy Moses."

The faces quivered. Hands laid him on his side. The door opened. The stretcher began to roll again and he with it. The stretcher rolled down the hall, a high gray hall with an uneventful ceiling.

He saw many faces and smelled much foul air. He heard many people coughing; sometimes so hard he had to restrain an impulse to imitate them.

He was in an elevator. He could feel it ascending. He wondered if God were taking him up to place him on His right hand to sit for a pitiless eternity.

He forced his wick to glow. He forced his eyes to open. He saw a kind face near him. Beneath it stood the body of a man with hands on the controls of the elevator. His face smiled down at him. Eric looked at the face carefully. It was a mirror. On this mirror he saw countless other faces, an endless procession of faded white faces that had come into the San just as he had come this day. It was a kind face, a gentle face, a gentle mirror. Its reflection improved one's looks.

They were pushed into the hall, he and the stretcher and the little beast in his side.

A pusher rolled him quietly down the hall, and through a door.

He heard women whispering. They were nurses.

One was saying, "Out in the hall."

"All right, all right!" The voice was harsh.

He was out in the hallway. He heard some scraping and, when he opened his eyes again, he found himself on a stretcher with white screens around him. There were windows on his left.

The house must be full of visitors, he thought idly; so full I have to sleep in the hall tonight. There is no room at the inn.

He drifted off. The ember fell, fell, fell, and flickered and went out. He fell asleep.

Food was moving in his mouth when the tiny flame came up again.

He waited a moment. Yes, it was food, and it was rolling around in his mouth and his mouth was moving too. He pushed at the glow and awakened it and then lifted up his eyelids again, pushing them up as if they were heavy sliding doors, and saw a white woman feeding him.

The food had no taste, and he took his tongue and scooped it toward the front of his mouth-cavern. The cavern was very wide and high and it took him some time to sweep the food forward to the door. But soon he had it all swept up in a pile and thrust it out.

"Oh, but you must eat," said the white woman's voice. "You've got to eat. You must eat or you won't get well."

That was a thought. Get well.

He held his tongue quiet. Maybe he had better let them store some food in his mouth after all. He took up his tongue and set it over to one side to make room for the food.

The white woman loaded in a few shovelsful.

"Chew it," she said. "You better chew it."

He considered this. How could a granary chew its own contents? Of course. The white woman was squirrelly. A corncrib . . . who ever heard of a crib chewing its own corn?

"Chew it," she said. "Chew it. Chew it hard."

Slowly, though he thought it foolish, he opened the sides of the corncrib and began to chew on the corn.

He smiled. This was funny. No one had ever seen what this white woman was seeing. She was actually watching a corncrib chewing its own corn.

The smile widened. He could feel it cracking open the sides of the crib. He would really give her a run for her money. He would give her a treat. He hurried the movements of the crib sides, chewing the corn inside it.

"Swallow it," she said. "Swallow it. Please swallow it. I've got a lot more for you."

He considered her talk. She had more? Holy Moses, Pa must have quite a corn crop this year! Quite a corn crop that he could refill the cribs again and again.

"Swallow it," the white woman said insistently. "Swallow it, swallow it."

What did "swallow" mean? He considered it. He tried to turn up the wick. "Swallow it." Now what did that mean? Did the corncrib have a belly? A sort of cellar-belly?

A cellar-belly.

He would try it. He took his tongue again and swept the huge piles of corn together into one lump and pushed it back toward his cellar and down it went. He waited to hear it fall. He waited.

"Now eat some more," the white woman said.

"Wait," he said. "Wait. It didn't go down yet."

"What?"

"Shhh . . ." he cautioned. "Wait." He waited, listening.

But there was no sound.

"Stuff must've landed on some hay down there," he confided. "Cellar must be full of hay. That's why we didn't hear it."

"Sure, sure," the white woman said. "Sure it did. And now, here, eat some more."

He opened his cribs again.

But then the little animal started to eat at him again. And swiftly the glow went up and, pfft, out.

Two file-rough voices were talking.

"Ain't you the new head orderly on Third West now?"

"That's what the super says."

"Nice going. You must be a pet of his."

"What?"

"Yeh."

"Honest-to-God, Joe, I've never played up to him. Just went along. Then all of a sudden he called me and gave it to me. Really."

"Skip it."

"But . . ."

There was a silence. Eric hoped they would talk some more. It had been beautiful.

"Oh nuts! Skip it."

The protesting orderly asked, "This stiff just come?"

"About five minutes ago."

"Did he look bad?"

"Gray as a dead man."

"Are they gonna leave him here in the hall?"

"Guess so."

"Wonder why they don't give him a room?"

"I dunno. The floor doc says he won't last the night. He'll croak. No use making up a room for him then, is there?"

"No, I suppose not. Christ, them docs are hard-boiled. No feelings at all."

"You can say that again."

They stood breathing together.

Eric stirred. Tomorrow morning, there would be no sun tomorrow morning?
No sun?

Ole Rölvaag

from THE BOAT OF LONGING

Ole Rölvaag came to America in 1896 when he was twenty years old. He had been born on Dönna Island, just below the Arctic Circle in northern Norway, in a cottage occupied by his family for six generations. Rölvaag attended school for seven years, but it was the beauty of the sea and the mountains of his homeland and the spirits that peopled this world that fired his imagination. After working as a fisherman for several years, he came to South Dakota to work on his uncle's farm. Determined to acquire a formal education, he attended Augustana Academy in Canton, South Dakota and then St. Olaf College in Northfield, Minnesota. Following his graduation with honors, he spent a year at the University of Christiania (now Oslo) where he steeped himself in Norwegian culture. Ultimately he was made head of the Department of Norwegian at St. Olaf. Threading his novels is his pessimism about the effects of immigration— his doubts about any true transplantation taking place, and his disgust with fellow Norwegians who abandoned their spiritual lives in the great rush for affluence in America. In his most famous novel, Giants in the Earth, *the highly sensitive Beret Holm is at times driven to madness in her attempt to adjust to an alien world. In this selection from an earlier work,* The Boat of Longing, *we see a simple fisherman, Nils Vaag, in the confusions and rootlessness of Minneapolis in the early twentieth century. Rölvaag died in 1931.*

IT WAS EARLY SUNDAY MORNING the second week of November. Day had come. Nils rolled away from the light and tried to steal another hour's sleep. Convinced after a couple of unsuccessful attempts that it was no use, he got up and dressed. Then he made himself a little breakfast. The Poet was still snoring peacefully over in his own quarter.

Breakfast finished and the food and dishes cleared away, Nils went first to one window to have a look at the weather, then to the other. The sky was cloudless and pale gold in colour, without any of the more vivid hues even this early in the morning. The sun hung stupid, shedding a feeble glow; today it sent forth no rays; only wan, yellowish light. By the air at least one could tell it was the Sabbath. The city, too, lay very still. Now and then one could, to be sure, hear a wagon rattling along on the pavement, its noise spreading wide, since there was nothing to hinder it; but soon it, too, would die away.

After a little Nils was standing on the street corner below, debating in what direction he had best strike out. From the Milwaukee Railway Station came the roar of rolling trains and the uncanny hoots of whistles. The everlasting whorls of black coal smoke were rising above the house-tops. Today they would not mingle with the still, yellow air, but slunk away in patches and heavy clouds.

In "Babel" it was fairly quiet yet. Nils had stopped in the hallway a moment on his way out. Up above he had heard the sound of a child whimpering, and the voice of a woman, also tearful, hushing it. The Söderbloms, he had reflected. Outside he saw little Ralph Pinsky perched at the top of the back stairs, holding a big piece of bread in his hand. Otherwise "Babel" lay as if altogether lifeless.

But despite its seeming so quiet and desolate now, there had been bedlam enough during the night, though perhaps it had not been greatly worse than usual of a Saturday night.

It had started in Otto Hansen's room a little after midnight. Otto and Söderblom had come home together, both on a merry pin. Nils, asleep by that time, had not been sufficiently disturbed at first to come wide awake; he had, instead, been roused into a half-doze, in which he lay dreaming about a cormorant which sang. The fact had puzzled him, for he had never, that he could remember, heard a cormorant sing. But was it actually a cormorant? In his half-doze he had concluded that it must be a sea gull. Yes, it was a sea gull, sure enough. Satisfied of it, he had been on the point of slipping over the borderline into a sound sleep again, when all of a sudden he had been startled by a terrible commotion in the hallway above. A barrage of curses from the Poet cracked the air like forked lightning. Nils, now thoroughly aroused, began comprehending, if only hazily, what was going on.

It had happened thus: When Otto and Söderblom came into

214

Otto's room, they had decided to have a last swig together—a parting drop, as it were. It and several more had made the two of them well-nigh as fuddled as it is possible for two men already drunk to become. But they were at the time fairly quiet.

Trouble had, however, finally arisen. The question was whether "Terje Viken" was not the greatest poem ever written, which Otto swore beyond all doubt that it was. The contention had at first met with no real objection from Söderblom. So eloquent was Otto in "Terje's" behalf that all the Swede could manage to say was:

"Sure—sure. "Terje" is a beautiful poem, all right—as you say, no doubt. But," he thundered, bringing his clenched fist down on the table with such a blow that it set the glasses clinking perilously, "can that poem be sung?"

Otto Hansen howled with laughter. "Terje Viken" be sung? Whoever heard of "Terje Viken" being sung? Had Söderblom gone crazy? Why, certainly not, "Terje" couldn't be sung!

—Well, sir, then it was not the greatest poem, Söderblom protested, much offended. Every Swedish poem could be sung, even "Goodman Noah"! The mere recollection of that convivial ditty being enough to set him going, he launched into it forthwith, singing at the top of his voice.

It was then matters had broken loose up there. Never had the greatness of "Terje Viken" been so manifest to Otto Hansen as it was at that moment; let no Swede even dare mention it in the same breath with such trash as "Goodman Noah."

Though no battle had been waged aboard the wreck,[1] there had been one in the hall of "Babel" that night, which ended in Söderblom's committing Otto to the foot of the back stairs. There Otto, on the bottommost step, had continued to ponder the singability of "Terje Viken." If it were possible, then that Swede would at last be treated to a song that was a song. Intent upon establishing the superiority of "Terje," Otto had begun trying all sorts of hymn tunes to it; but without success. He simply could not find one to fit. Overcome with grief, he had begun to cry. . . . What a shame that "Terje" couldn't be sung! Unthinkable that it couldn't. Everyone knew it was the greatest poem. Hence it must be possible to sing it! Again he tried, with exactly the same result. To think that he couldn't find the tune for "Terje"! Overcome by the thought, he had bawled like a baby.

[1] In the poem.

Before sleep overtook him, however, he had recovered his senses sufficiently to grovel his way up the stairs. In the dark he had unluckily mistaken the doorway and staggered into the room of Dagny and Marie. In that place he had encountered more persons than convention would, strictly speaking, permit at this hour of the night. For Otto, however, the circumstance had been fortunate, one of the number having come to his assistance, hushed him up, and helped him to bed in his own room. There he had lain sobbing and experimenting with tunes for "Terje" till he fell asleep.

Per Syv hadn't come home at all that night, which was the first time it had happened; as a consequence, Nils had spent the rest of the night awake, looking into those eyes of Ole Hansen's. It would be impossible for him to write home hereafter. No, he couldn't even write his own parents!

And so a melancholy lay upon Nils as he walked down Fourth Street that Sunday morning, which even the beautiful Indian-summer sun was powerless to dispel. He passed the Norwegian Evangelical Lutheran Church; read the name mechanically, as he had often done; and got a vague feeling back in his consciousness that he ought to go to church today. But it would be some time yet till services began; he'd better take a long walk first.

Having reached Cedar Avenue, he turned the corner and proceeded along that street as far as Seven Corners; thence down Washington to the bridge. Across the river lay the university, beautiful in the serenity of the Sabbath; most likely thither he was bound, though he had no distinct notion of it.

But he halted when he came to the bridge. Below, in the depths, a group of boys were playing in the trestles. They appeared to be having great sport, scaling the lattice-work in the trusses with the agility of cats, and then laughing and whooping high over the abyss. Instead of crossing the bridge Nils began descending the stairs leading to Bohemian Flats—mostly for the sake of watching the boys.

The houses in the pit, viewed from above, resembled black scorch flecks in the bottom of a huge kettle. Nils had often wondered how human beings could endure living down here.

He went clear to the bottom. Finding himself presently at the head of the narrow principal street, he followed it until it ran square into a perpendicular cliff wall; thus brought to a halt, he crossed to the opposite side and returned to his starting-point. There he stopped. He looked down the row of little houses, at the tiny front gardens enclosed with picket fences, and at the chickens and ducks, yes, even geese, poking about in them. So this is a place where folk and fowl live together, mused Nils. Now and then he would see some person moving quietly about. Not even children made noises here—except those boys up in the air. Nils's eye followed the long stair he had just come down. Obviously there were oceans and whole continents lying between this place and the one up above, even though only a bridge separated them.

On the corner where he stood, a low house squatted on its haunches. It looked as though it had come scooting down the cliffside, heading straight for the river; and then, having hooked itself fast just in the nick of time, had remained there. He could see that the curtains in the little windows were spotlessly white. He also thought he glimpsed a human form watching him from behind them. For that reason he moved on to the river.

Down there he almost fell into a fine humour; his gloom seemed to fall off by layers. He was a boy again—felt like a human being once more. An old Nordland melody began running through his head; his lips shaping themselves unconsciously, he commenced whistling it.

The closer he got to the river, the more powerfully it drew him. Taking the remaining distance in a couple of long leaps, he landed way down on a strip of flat sandy beach. "Sakes alive!" he exclaimed, "here's a sand beach just like ours at home!" Imagine having lived near this all these months without knowing it! He immediately started skipping stones, gaily whistling the Nordland melody as he did so. Like the youth he had been, he hunted flat pebbles and tried his skill at skipping them clear across the river. Now and then he glanced at the boys playing in the air, and was almost tempted to join them.

During the moments that Nils had stood on the corner surveying the place, a thin, elderly woman had been observing him from behind the curtains. Struck by something in his appearance, she had kept on watching him; and when he had walked down to the river she had gone out and continued to gaze after him. The tune he was whistling seemed likewise to be exerting some strange influence over her; for she was trembling so that she had to sit down. When she saw him begin to skip pebbles she rose and followed him.

Nils having skipped pebbles till he was tired, was squatting by the water's edge, washing his hands; upon rising to leave the river, he was confronted by the woman.

They stood face to face . . . Nils, his hat way back on his head and his hands dripping with water; the woman with her hands under her clean, threadbare apron.

She spoke first, in a voice so soft that it fell like a benediction upon his ears, filling him with a sense of peace, just as do the notes of a beautiful song; it was in the pure low dialect of Nordland.

"Aren't you from Nordland?" she began. Her pronunciation and inflection were as genuine as though the two of them had been standing on the beach in Norway.

With just as genuine open-heartedness Nils answered:

"Yes, I am. You are too, I hear."

Her haggard features distended, rounding out into a great childlike look; tears came into her eyes.

"Didn't I know it! I could tell by the tune you were whistling; to think I should hear that song again after eighteen years. And with you skipping those pebbles I knew I couldn't be mistaken. I had to follow and listen, I simply couldn't help it. You're the first Nordlænding I've met over here."

The expression on her face and the tone of her voice compelled Nils to turn away and dry his eyes. While his face was still averted, he answered,

"Reminds me of home here."

"That so?" she came back eagerly. "It really isn't bad right here by the river, is it? But in this country no one seems to care about such things," she added, as if to inform him.

"What sort of people live here?"

"Very kind people, for the most part."

Her answer made him laugh. "I was wondering where they came from."

"Oh, I understood you all right," she smiled. "They're Bohemians, mostly. They call this Bohemian Flats. But there are quite a few Scandinavians, too. A Swedish family in that little house over there; and one from Trondhjem on the street to the east of us. And they say there are a couple of other Norwegian families, though I haven't learned to know them yet."

"What do these people do?"

"Well, some do this, some that. . . . But you really must come in, so I can talk to you. My feet have sort o' played out on me lately," she added, as if by way of excuse for her invitation.

Nils went with her.

The room she ushered him into was a veritable doll parlour.

The ceiling, distressingly low, almost touched his head. All the objects seemed to be scaled to proportion: a cot did service for both bed and sofa; the stove was of the small oil-burner variety, such as young women frequently have in their rooms; the table was diminutive; and the chairs looked as though they were never intended for grown ups. But the room was as tidy and attractive as human hands well could make it.

Upon the walls hung many small pictures. Also a violin. Which struck Nils as being strange. He fell to looking at the instrument, curious to know the owner.

"Who plays that?" he enquired, pointing.

"That? Oh, that was Johan's violin."

—A memory was here being kept sacred; Nils asked no further questions.

"Karl Brakstad drops in occasionally and plays me a tune on it. He's the Trondhjemmer I mentioned. . . . Maybe you play?"

"Well—not to speak of."

"No, that's hardly to be expected; very few can. But Brakstad is really pretty fair—at times."

Nils vouchsafed no reply.

"From what part of Nordland do you come?" he asked.

"Ravnöy."

"In Helgeland?"

"Yes. What about you?"

"From Dönna."

"Dönna in Helgeland?"

"Yes."

"Did you ever!" she exclaimed, striking her hands together in amazement. An even deeper music and warmth came into her voice. "Then we two are neighbours, so to speak, from the old country!" Tears came into her eyes.

"So we are! How long have you been in America?"

"Just eighteen years in September since I came. When did you come?"

"The fifteenth of June this summer."

The reply touched her instantly.

"Then you have just come from there!" she cried.

"Oh no, I shouldn't say that exactly. It seems long since to me. . . . I suppose you've earned a good deal, when you've been here so many years?" laughed Nils.

She laughed, too. "I'd hardly say that; but it's a fine country for anyone who can work."

Gerald Vizenor

THE PSYCHOTAXIDERMIST

Gerald Vizenor, former editorial writer for the Minneapolis Tribune, *teaches Native American literature at the University of California in Berkeley. He has also taught at several colleges and as a Hill Visiting Professor at the University of Minnesota. Vizenor is a member of a Minnesota Chippewa Tribe and the author of six books about Native American experience, including a novel,* Darkness in Saint Louis Bearheart, *and* Wordarrows: Indians and Whites in the New Fur Trade (*University of Minnesota Press*). "The Psychotaxidermist" was *first published in the* Minneapolis Star Saturday Magazine.

C OLONEL CLEMENT BEAULIEU, the old mixedblood fur trader and teller of fine tales, leaned forward into the autumn wind as he walked down the hard earth trail to Saint Benedict Catholic Mission on the White Earth Reservation. His white hair wagged on the wind, and while he walked behind three tribal mongrels he turned over in his mind, like sunwarmed stones, the stories he could tell the old nuns and priests during their evening meal.

Colonel Clement smiles on his uncommon memories. The wrinkles on his slim face purl from interior humors. The mongrels pitch their heads back, tongues swerving to the side, when he clears his throat four times and gestures with his lips in the tribal manner—his ceremonial preparation in the oral tradition that stories are about to be told.

District Court Judge Silas Bandied snapped his ceramic teeth in the hollow downtown courtroom, Colonel Clement said in his mind, remembering the strange tale about a tribal shaman psychotaxidermist, and cleared his throat three times, his religious trine, like a cormorant, before reading the sentence:

"Shaman Newcrows, alias Random New Crows, alias The

First published in 1978 in the *Minneapolis Star Saturday Magazine*. Reprinted, slightly revised by the author, with his permission.

Crow, alias The Psychotaxidermist, we have reviewed the charges and evidence here and find you this fine morning full of guilt without a doubt . . . This court sentences you now and forever to serve ten years at hard labor for the crime of wild animule molestation, indecent liberties with dead animules in public places, to wit, a four hole golf course, the first in the state, might we add here, and then . . ."

"Evidence?" questioned Newcrows.

"Silence," commanded Bandied, "The evidence is clear that you were dressed in a bear animule mask, rapacious sight that it must have been that night, and . . ."

"Ceremonial bear," explained Newcrows, who was leaning back in his chair at a comfortable escape distance from the judge and the prosecutor, dressed in a red velvet suit with a bear claw necklace. He was smiling like a human, but his head shifted from side to side, the morning motion of the bear in him, and his distance, his powerful energies danced through the memories of oak and cedar and summer ponds in the courtroom.

"Nothing more than a circus bear mask, leaning over dead animules at the golf course, which you admitted stuffing . . ."

"Take care with what you tell here," warned Newcrows, "the animals and birds are listening."

"Rubbish," sneered the judge. "Dead is dead and no man, not to mention animules, has ever come back from the dead . . . No sane man that is . . ."

"What dead animals?"

"Indian evildoer," snapped the judge and his teeth, "savage, how dare you defile this courtroom with your word trickeries? You are beyond contempt, you are pitiable and must remain silent here."

"But Your Honor, please," pleaded the prosecutor whose face and neck was covered with brown tic bites. "Your Honor, consider this: we have dropped the charges on this man because we lost the dead evidence . . ."

"You lost dead animules?"

"Yes Your Honor," the tall prosecutor responded, scratching at his chest and arms. "We had the dead evidence on the fourth green, but it up and disappeared during a thunderstorm."

"Mister prosecutor," said Judge Bandied, stretching his thin cormorant neck over his dark bench, "let me warn you now, this crime took place on our new four hole course, and this is no time for you to misplace the evidence, dead or alive. We will recess a few minutes now for you to gather your wits and find the dead evidence."

Judge Bandied was a charter member of the new four hole golf course at the Town and Country Club of Saint Paul and he boasts that it was he who dropped the first official putt with a green ball through the snow and cold on February 11, 1888, when the course first opened. Now, during the first full season the fourth hole was fouled forever, so the judge reasoned, because "some strange dead animule exorcism by a damned circus clown in a bear mask."

Shaman Newcrows, born on the shores of Bad Medicine on the White Earth Reservation, was blessed with animal spirits and avian visions. He has traveled in magical flight through four levels of consciousness and the underworld. During the summer when he was twelve, lightning flashed from the eyes of seven crows in his dreams, from whom he took his spirit name, and from bears, ursine shivers from the darkness, and he took from the woods for the first time the languages of animals and birds and flowers and trees. He listened to the languages of the living earth.

Newcrows heard the wise crows curse the evil in men, which was traditional in most human minds, but unimaginative. His vision revealed that crows lust for attractive women, white women, their opposite in tone, and their raucous conversations, crow to crow between trees, is seldom more than prurient gossip.

Newcrows heard his own voice rumbling from the heart of a bear. Standing down at the treeline near the water, slow and certain in his movements, he laughed from his solitude and darkness, from the interior of his sacred maw. He listened to secret languages from the darkness, the bears spoke and he heard animal languages that humans once understood.

Newcrows saw in his vision, from the lightning flashing all around him, the auras and shadows of trees towering over their stumps. The cedar and white pine spirits spoke to him from their sacred places on the earth, from the places where trees were cut, and together each tree, cut but not dead, recited the names of the cutters and the places in the cities where their bodies were sold as beams and fence posts.

Newcrows listened to the animals and trees tell him that all who have died will return to the earth. Under a full moon, said an otter, his brothers and sisters will return in face and breath and spirit from the land of the dead. The trees told about the coming fires when their ashes will return to the earth together with their woodland auras.

Newcrows dreamed that strokes of lightning would resurrect all dead animals and those who praised and celebrated their lives. Whenever he passed beneath a tree, or watched a bird in flight, wolves on the run, beaver, insects turning in the morning sun, the crows when their stories were not prurient, he heard them all whisper: There is one who carries our dream to return to the living earth. His vision was to deliver the dead to the great spirit during a thunderstorm.

But on the outside Newcrows was neither tree nor otter, he was in his manner three parts fool with humans. His head rolled on the run and he dropped words in simple phrases, lost his references to time, and the colonial agents on the reservation solicited his signature, his precious mark, five times for federal treaties with the tired tribes because he could remember but one line at one place at one time. His memories were episodic, his form was his content, and he did not perceive his world in grammatical models, cumulatives, generalizations and plurals.

When he was three years old he walked into the woods alone while his mother was gathering wild rice. He was missing for three days when his mother feared the spirits had taken him to the underworld, but on the morning of the fourth day he walked out of the woods smiling, with bear hair on his face and clothes.

Newcrows did not speak the language of humans for several years, but when he did speak again, when he was twelve, he spoke from his vision with animals and trees returning to the earth. He tossed his head, followed bears into the woods, laughed and shivered with the trees, and never thought about possessions until he found a woman undressing.

"Stop drooling and open the door," said Sister Isolde to the peeping stranger she saw stuck between the logs. Her white breasts wambled in the light from the fire.

Newcrows blinked twice and turned to the darkness, but before he disappeared, she leaped through the door and stopped him at the dark treeline.

Sister Isolde lived with several mongrels and an affectionate fox, in a small cabin she had built from scraps, near Mallard on the White Earth Reservation, which was an abandoned sawmill town. Little remained of the town but her cabin and huge piles of sawdust. She was abandoned too, at age ten, the lone daughter of a skidder and a timber town prostitute.

Newcrows drooled and drank and laughed too much at the animal in him until his new woman and her animals were bored with his cabin weaknesses. It was the affectionate fox, snapping at his bare feet at night, who turned him back to the woods and his vision. Months later, when his blood was clean, he was reminded of his vision to return the animal dead to the earth.

Near his birth place at Bad Medicine, Newcrows collected the dead, from natural and unnatural causes, for the coming storm. He perched and poised thousands of birds and animals near the shore of the lake. But without the lightning he saw in his vision, the animals decomposed. Not one bird or animal came back to the living. The fetid smell burned in the nostrils of the tribe, but it was not his familial nonfluences which led to his banishment, not the tribe, but the white colonial officers who ordered him to leave the reservation, banished at last from his place on the earth for remembering the earth.

Newcrows traveled from reservation to reservation, but the word was out about his strange habits and he was asked to leave. He was seeking the secret of preserving the dead, not knowing how long the dead should wait for the coming lightning. He asked white people. A mortician taught him the art of taxidermy, but stuffing animals transformed their images and separated their bones and blood from their spirit without ceremonies. He listened to tribal prophets, the new ones, speak of the new gods and resurrection, but not until he listened to an old shaman woman who lived at La Pointe on Madeline Island in Lake Superior, did he understand the secret of holding the dead for the coming of the great spirit and the balance of the earth. The secret was imagination, imagining the spirit and shape of the earth in animals and birds and trees. She taught him to travel with the dead and it was the dead who told him how to hold the dead and their spirits in his imagination. Imagination, he was told, will hold the earth in balance, our bones have been separated and defiled and our languages are seldom spoken now in the hearts of humans. The spirits from the underworld told him to prepare for the storm and the fires to come.

"Your Honor," pleaded the prosecutor, scratching his neck and shoulders, "if it pleases the court, permit me to continue with this explanation . . ."

"Remember this, mister prosecutor, our fourth hole has been

defiled forever with these strange animules," Bandied warned, with his neck extended over his bench. "We must not permit this crime to pass without punishment, fitting punishment."

"Yes Your Honor. Now, permit me this review: We found the accused man, New Crows . . ."

"Newcrows."

"What?"

"Newcrows, one word, one consciousness, one time in all to live on the earth as a bird and animal," explained Newcrows.

"Newcrows, we found Newcrows on the fourth hole under a full moon dressed in a bear costume and dancing around hundreds of dead birds and animals which he explained were his friends . . . Now, we arrested him then and there, but because the evidence was so strange, we left it *in situ* and called the zoo. The animals were dead but somehow appeared to be still living, and, forgive the contradictions Your Honor, asleep, motionless, but with their eyes open, alert, awake and poised . . . More like creatures waiting to attack or be attacked. The experience was too strange to move, but before the zoo people could get there a thunder storm blew up from nowhere and when lightning struck all around the fourth green, the animals and birds let out this horrible primal scream, loud and clear, and then, sure as you see me here before you now, the dead evidence walked, some ran, loped and leaped, and flew with the storm. Not even a feather or a claw remained on the fourth hole as evidence."

"Damn your evidence," wailed Bandied. "There must be evidence, charge him with something as an evildoer then. Lock him up somehow."

"But we have no statute for evil."

"Psychotic and dangerous to the living then," demanded Bandied, clearing his cormorant throat three times and stacking his stout white fingers on his bench with pride.

"Dangerous to whom?"

"Not to whom."

"Dangerous to what then?"

"To the fourth green, to the human spirit," Bandied snapped, "dangerous to civilization, men and women who take pleasure in outdoor exercise and a good game."

"But Your Honor . . ."

"How did he do it," asked the judge. He seemed more calm. "How did he do it with all those animals, what was the trick?"

"Never a trick," said Newcrows.

"Close your evil mouth in this courtroom," snapped the judge, changing his mood. "The accused is not permitted to speak here to me . . . No telling what evil could come from your mouth."

"My words from the dead," said Newcrows.

"Silence," demanded Bandied.

"Silence," mocked Newcrows.

"Silence that evildoer."

"Silence that evildoer."

"Officer, remove him now."

"Officer, remove me now."

"Please continue, mister prosecutor."

"With what, Your Honor?"

"How does he do it, fool."

"Yes, yes Your Honor, if it pleases the court, we have a letter from Samuel Mitchell, a medical doctor, to one Samuel Burnside, which was published in a recent edition of a book entitled: *Study of Mortuary Customs among the North American Indians* by H. C. Yarrow. This letter bears on your question Your Honor, in that the letter and the female described in the letter are both held in the American Antiquarian Society.

"Mitchell writes, after examining a female corpse, that 'it is a human body found in one of the limestone caverns of Kentucky. It is a perfect exiccation; all the fluids are dried up. The skin, bones, and other firm parts are in a state of entire preservation . . . The heart was in situ.'"

"What does that mean?" asked the judge.

"In situ, Your Honor, means the pagans did not eat her heart out like they do the animals, bears for example," explained the prosecutor while he scratched harder at his chest and stomach.

"What is all this scratching?"

"Tribal tics . . ."

"What, if anything, can this evildoer know about bears or animules?" asked the judge. He leaned over behind his massive dark bench to scratch his ankles and did not hear the prosecutor read from *Bear Ceremonialism in the Northern Hemisphere*, a University of Pennsylvania dissertation written by A. Irving Hallowell:

"The categories of rational thought, by which we are accustomed to separate human life from animal life and the supernatural from the natural, are drawn upon lines which the facts of primitive cultures do not fit.

"Animals are believed to have essentially the same sort of animat-

226

ing agency which man possesses. They have a language of their own, can understand what human beings say and do, have forms of social or tribal organization, and live a life which is parallel in other respects to that of human societies."

"Magical or supernatural powers are also at the disposal of certain species; they may metamorphose themselves into other creatures or, upon occasion, into human form . . . Dreams may become a specialized means of communication between man and animals."

"Where did those tics come from?" the judge asked as he emerged from behind his bench. He pulled his black robe off and scratched at his thighs and crotch.

"From the bears," explained the prosecutor, scratching at his cheeks. "Bear tics trained to disrupt our system of justice . . ."

"That evildoer did this to us . . ."

"Drop the charges," wailed the prosecutor while he scratched. "Drop the goddamn charges and call the tics off Your Honor."

"Charges dismissed!" screamed the judge from the floor behind his bench where he was scratching and scratching like a reservation mongrel on a tic mound. In seconds the bear tics were gone and the prosecutor and the judge were back at their benches and chairs with their forms and robes and pencils and plurals.

Gathering his papers and charge sheets, the prosecutor looked up at the judge and said: "Hallowell was told by an old Indian that a bear . . ."

"Hollowill who?" asked Bandied.

"No, Your Honor, not Hollowill but Hallowell, the author of *Bear Cermonialism*, which we read into the record," explained the prosecutor. "Hallowell was told by an old Indian that a bear is wiser than a man because a man does not know how to live all winter without eating anything."

Judge Bandied stretched his cormorant neck over his dark bench one more time and said, in a patronizing tone of voice, "but bears suck their paws and masturbate."

Colonel Clement rounded the last curve down the hill to Saint Benedict Mission. He pulled back his white hair, gestured to the mongrels with his lips in the tribal manner, cleared his throat four times, pushed the door open and started his stories during the evening meal with the nuns and priests.

"This is a true tale from the reservation," Colonel Clement began, "about Sister Isolde, an old white shaman woman from Mallard who lived in an abandoned scapehouse that lightning struck four

227

times each summer. The crows gossiped about her because she loved a bear who had a vision that he was human. Sister Isolde learned from the bear how to preserve the dead and how to train tics to disrupt the evildoers in the white world.

"In Saint Paul one summer before the turn of the century, when the first golf course was opened there, Sister Isolde followed her bear to the fourth green for a bear ceremonial with the dead, with thousands of dead birds and animals dancing under the full moon and waiting for the lightning to return them to the earth . . ."

The mongrels pitched their heads back and waited outside for the stories to end on the inside. The mongrels waited for their master to lead them back through the dark before the storm. The animals were honored by his preparation.

F. Scott Fitzgerald

ABSOLUTION

F. Scott Fitzgerald was born in 1896 in St. Paul. A teacher at St. Paul Academy remembered him as an indifferent student, but one whose imagination surfaced in the stories which he wrote for the school magazine. At Princeton his scripts for the Triangle Club dramatic productions were highly successful, far more so than his studies. In 1917 he was commissioned a second lieutenant in the Army, and while he was stationed in Montgomery, Alabama, Fitzgerald met Zelda Sayre, who was to become his wife and the model for some of his heroines. His first published novel, This Side of Paradise, *was accepted by Scribner's when he was twenty-four, and on the strength of its success he and Zelda were married, beginning the peripatetic life—St. Paul, New York, Long Island, Paris, Antibes, Baltimore—that lasted until she was committed to mental institutions in the 1930's.*

Fitzgerald's first novel was followed by The Beautiful and the Damned *in 1922 and* The Great Gatsby *in 1925. In spite of a running battle with alcoholism, he worked hard at his writing and* Tender Is the Night *was shaped during some particularly bleak years of the 1930's. He died in Hollywood in 1940. Malcolm Cowley has said that Fitzgerald retained "a sense of living in history. Manners and morals were changing all through his life and he set himself the task of recording the changes. They were revealed to him, not by statistics or news reports, but in terms of living characters. . . ." "Absolution," the story which appears here, was originally intended as a prologue to* The Great Gatsby.

THERE WAS ONCE a priest with cold, watery eyes, who, in the still of the night, wept cold tears. He wept because the afternoons were warm and long, and he was unable to attain a complete mystical union with our Lord. Sometimes, near four o'clock, there was a rustle of Swede girls along the path by his window, and in their shrill laughter he found a terrible dissonance that made him pray aloud for the twilight to come. At twilight the laughter and the voices were quieter, but several times he had walked past Romberg's Drug Store when it was dusk and the yellow lights shone inside and the nickel taps of the soda-fountain were gleaming, and he had found the scent of cheap toilet soap desperately sweet on the air. He passed that way when he returned from hearing confessions on Saturday nights, and he grew careful to walk on the other side of the street so that the smell of the soap would float upward before it reached his nostrils as it drifted, rather like incense, towards the summer moon.

But there was no escape from the hot madness of four o'clock. From his window, as far as he could see, the Dakota wheat thronged the valley of the Red River. The wheat was terrible to look upon and the carpet pattern to which in agony he bent his eyes sent his thought brooding through grotesque labyrinths, open always to the unavoidable sun.

One afternoon when he had reached the point where the mind runs down like an old clock, his housekeeper brought into his study a beautiful, intense little boy of eleven named Rudolph Miller. The little boy sat down in a patch of sunshine, and the priest, at his walnut desk, pretended to be very busy. This was to conceal his relief that some one had come into his haunted room.

Presently he turned around and found himself staring into two enormous, staccato eyes, lit with gleaming points of cobalt light. For a moment their expression startled him—then he saw that his visitor was in a state of abject fear.

"Your mouth is trembling," said Father Schwartz, in a haggard voice.

The little boy covered his quivering mouth with his hand.

"Are you in trouble?" asked Father Schwartz, sharply. "Take your hand away from your mouth and tell me what's the matter."

The boy—Father Schwartz recognized him now as the son of a parishioner, Mr. Miller, the freight-agent—moved his hand reluctantly off his mouth and became articulate in a despairing whisper.

"Father Schwartz—I've committed a terrible sin."

"A sin against purity?"

"No, Father . . . worse."

Father Schwartz's body jerked sharply.

"Have you killed somebody?"

"No—but I'm afraid——" the voice rose to a shrill whimper.

"Do you want to go to confession?"

The little boy shook his head miserably. Father Schwartz cleared his throat so that he could make his voice soft and say some quiet, kind thing. In this moment he should forget his own agony, and try to act like God. He repeated to himself a devotional phrase, hoping that in return God would help him to act correctly.

"Tell me what you've done," said his new soft voice.

The little boy looked at him through his tears, and was reassured by the impression of moral resiliency which the distraught priest had created. Abandoning as much of himself as he was able to this man, Rudolph Miller began to tell his story.

"On Saturday, three days ago, my father he said I had to go to confession, because I hadn't been for a month, and the family they go every week, and I hadn't been. So I just as leave go, I didn't care. So I put it off till after supper because I was playing with a bunch of kids and father asked me if I went, and I said 'no,' and he took me by the neck and he said 'You go now,' so I said 'All right,' so I went over to church. And he yelled after me: 'Don't come back till you go.' . . . ."

II
"On Saturday, Three Days Ago"

The plush curtain of the confessional rearranged its dismal creases, leaving exposed only the bottom of an old man's shoe. Behind the curtain an immortal soul was alone with God and the Reverend Adolphus Schwartz, priest of the parish. Sound began, a laboured whispering, sibilant and discreet, broken at intervals by the voice of the priest in audible question.

Rudolph Miller knelt in the pew beside the confessional and waited, straining nervously to hear, and yet not to hear what was being said within. The fact that the priest was audible alarmed him. His own turn came next, and the three or four others who waited might listen unscrupulously while he admitted his violations of the Sixth and Ninth Commandments.

Rudolph had never committed adultery, nor even coveted his neighbour's wife—but it was the confession of the associate sins that was particularly hard to contemplate. In comparison he relished the less shameful fallings away—they formed a greyish background which relieved the ebony mark of sexual offences upon his soul.

He had been covering his ears with his hands, hoping that his refusal to hear would be noticed, and a like courtesy rendered to him in turn, when a sharp movement of the penitent in the confessional made him sink his face precipitately into the crook of his elbow. Fear assumed solid form, and pressed out a lodging between his heart and his lungs. He must try now with all his might to be sorry for his sins—not because he was afraid, but because he had offended God. He must convince God that he was sorry and to do so he must first convince himself. After a tense emotional struggle he achieved a tremulous self-pity, and decided that he was now ready. If, by allowing no other thought to enter his head, he could preserve this state of emotion unimpaired until he went into that large coffin set on end, he would have survived another crisis in his religious life.

For some time, however, a demoniac notion had partially possessed him. He could go home now, before his turn came, and tell his mother that he had arrived too late, and found the priest gone. This, unfortunately, involved the risk of being caught in a lie. As an alternative he could say that he *had* gone to confession, but this meant that he must avoid communion next day, for communion taken upon an uncleansed soul would turn to poison in his mouth, and he would crumple limp and damned from the altar-rail.

Again Father Schwartz's voice became audible.

"And for your——"

The words blurred to a husky mumble, and Rudolph got excitedly to his feet. He felt that it was impossible to go to confession this afternoon. He hesitated tensely. Then from the confessional came a tap, a creak, and a sustained rustle. The slide had fallen and the plush curtain trembled. Temptation had come to him too late. . . .

"Bless me, Father, for I have sinned. . . . I confess to Almighty God and to you, Father, that I have sinned. . . . Since my last confession it has been one month and three days. . . . I accuse myself of—taking the Name of the Lord in vain. . . ."

This was an easy sin. His curses had been but bravado—telling of them was little less than a brag.

". . . of being mean to an old lady."

The wan shadow moved a little on the latticed slat.

"How, my child?"

"Old lady Swenson," Rudolph's murmur soared jubilantly. "She got our baseball that we knocked in her window, and she wouldn't give it back, so we yelled 'Twenty-three, Skidoo,' at her all afternoon. Then about five o'clock she had a fit, and they had to have the doctor."

"Go on, my child."

"Of—of not believing I was the son of my parents."

"What?" The interrogation was distinctly startled.

"Of not believing that I was the son of my parents."

"Why not?"

"Oh, just pride," answered the penitent airily.

"You mean you thought yourself too good to be the son of your parents?"

"Yes, Father." On a less jubilant note.

"Go on."

"Of being disobedient and calling my mother names. Of slandering people behind their back. Of smoking——"

Rudolph had now exhausted the minor offences, and was approaching the sins it was agony to tell. He held his fingers against his face like bars as if to press out between them the shame in his heart.

"Of dirty words and immodest thoughts and desires," he whispered very low.

"How often?"

"I don't know."

"Once a week? Twice a week?"

"Twice a week."

"Did you yield to these desires?"

"No, Father."

"Were you alone when you had them?"

"No Father. I was with two boys and a girl."

"Don't you know, my child, that you should avoid the occasions of sin as well as the sin itself? Evil companionship leads to evil desires and evil desires to evil actions. Where were you when this happened?"

"In a barn back of——"

"I don't want to hear any names," interrupted the priest sharply.

"Well, it was up in the loft of the barn and this girl and—a fella, they were saying things—saying immodest things, and I stayed."

"You should have gone—you should have told the girl to go."

He should have gone! He could not tell Father Schwartz how his pulse had bumped in his wrist, how a strange, romantic excitement had possessed him when those curious things had been said. Perhaps, in the houses of delinquency among the dull and hard-eyed incorrigible girls can be found those for whom has burned the whitest fire.

"Have you anything else to tell me?"

"I don't think so, Father."

Rudolph felt a great relief. Perspiration had broken out under his tight-pressed fingers.

"Have you told any lies?"

The question startled him. Like all those who habitually and instinctively lie, he had an enormous respect and awe for the truth. Something almost exterior to himself dictated a quick, hurt answer. "Oh no, Father, I never tell lies."

For a moment, like the commoner in the king's chair, he tasted the pride of the situation. Then as the priest began to murmur conventional admonitions he realized that in heroically denying he had told lies, he had committed a terrible sin—he had told a lie in confession.

In automatic response to Father Schwartz's "Make an act of contrition," he began to repeat aloud meaninglessly:

"Oh, my God, I am heartily sorry for having offended Thee. . . ."

He must fix this now—it was a bad mistake—but as his teeth shut on the last words of his prayer there was a sharp sound, and the slat was closed.

A minute later when he emerged into the twilight the relief in coming from the muggy church into an open world of wheat and sky postponed the full realization of what he had done. Instead of worrying he took a deep breath of the crisp air and began to say over and over to himself the words "Blatchford Sarnemington, Blatchford Sarnemington!"

Blatchford Sarnemington was himself, and these words were in effect a lyric. When he became Blatchford Sarnemington a suave nobility flowed from him. Blatchford Sarnemington lived in great sweeping triumphs. When Rudolph half closed his eyes it meant that Blatchford had established dominance over him and, as he went by, there were envious mutters in the air: "Blatchford Sarnemington! There goes Blatchford Sarnemington."

He was Blatchford now for a while as he strutted homeward along the staggering road, but when the road braced itself in macadam in order to become the main street of Ludwig,

Rudolph's exhilaration faded out and his mind cooled, and he felt the horror of his lie. God, of course, already knew of it—but Rudolph reserved a corner of his mind where he was safe from God, where he prepared the subterfuges with which he often tricked God. Hiding now in this corner he considered how he could best avoid the consequences of his mis-statement.

At all costs he must avoid communion next day. The risk of angering God to such an extent was too great. He would have to drink water 'by accident' in the morning, and thus, in accordance with a church law, render himself unfit to receive communion that day. In spite of its flimsiness this subterfuge was the most feasible that occurred to him. He accepted its risks and was concentrating on how best to put it into effect, as he turned the corner by Romberg's Drug Store and came in sight of his father's house.

III

Rudolph's father, the local freight-agent, had floated with the second wave of German and Irish stock to the Minnesota-Dakota country. Theoretically, great opportunities lay ahead of a young man of energy in that day and place, but Carl Miller had been incapable of establishing either with his superiors or his subordinates the reputation for approximate immutability which is essential to success in a hierarchic industry. Somewhat gross, he was, nevertheless, insufficiently hard-headed and unable to take fundamental relationships for granted, and this inability made him suspicious, unrestful, and continually dismayed.

His two bonds with the colorful life were his faith in the Roman Catholic Church and his mystical worship of the Empire Builder, James J. Hill. Hill was the apotheosis of that quality in which Miller himself was deficient—the sense of things, the feel of things, the hint of rain in the wind on the cheek. Miller's mind worked late on the old decisions of other men, and he had never in his life felt the balance of any single thing in his hands. His weary, sprightly, undersized body was growing old in Hill's gigantic shadow. For twenty years he had lived alone with Hill's name and God.

On Sunday morning Carl Miller awoke in the dustless quiet of six o'clock. Kneeling by the side of the bed he bent his yellow-grey hair and the full dapple bangs of his moustache into the pillow, and prayed for several minutes. Then he drew off his night-shirt—like the rest of his generation he had never been able to endure pyjamas—and clothed his thin, white, hairless body in woollen underwear.

He shaved. Silence in the other bedroom where his wife lay nervously asleep. Silence from the screened-off corner of the hall where his son's cot stood, and his son slept among his Alger books, his collection of cigar-bands, his mothy pennants— "Cornell," "Hamline" and "Greetings from Pueblo, New Mexico" —and the other possessions of his private life. From outside Miller could hear the shrill birds and the whirring movement of the poultry, and, as an undertone, the low, swelling click-a-click of the six-fifteen through train for Montana and the green coast beyond. Then as the cold water dripped from the wash-rag in his hand he raised his head suddenly—he had heard a furtive sound from the kitchen below.

He dried his razor hastily, slipped his dangling suspenders to his shoulder, and listened. Some one was walking in the kitchen, and he knew by the light footfall that it was not his wife. With his mouth faintly ajar he ran quickly down the stairs and opened the kitchen door.

Standing by the sink, with one hand on the still dripping facuet and the other clutching a full glass of water, stood his son. The boy's eyes, still heavy with sleep, met his father's with a frightened, reproachful beauty. He was barefooted, and his pyjamas were rolled up at the knees and sleeves.

For a moment they both remained motionless—Carl Miller's brow went down and his son's went up, as though they were striking a balance between the extremes of emotion which filled them. Then the bangs of the parent's moustache descended portentously until they obscured his mouth, and he gave a short glance around to see if anything had been disturbed.

The kitchen was garnished with sunlight which beat on the pans and made the smooth boards of the floor and table yellow and clean as wheat. It was the centre of the house where the fire burned and the tins fitted into tins like toys, and the steam whistled all day on a thin pastel note. Nothing was moved, nothing touched—except the faucet where beads of water still formed and dripped with a white flash into the sink below.

"What are you doing?"

"I got awful thirsty, so I thought I'd just come down and get——"

"I thought you were going to communion."

A look of vehement astonishment spread over his son's face.

"I forgot all about it."

"Have you drunk any water?"

"No——"

As the word left his mouth Rudolph knew it was the wrong answer, but the faded indignant eyes facing him had signalled up the truth before the boy's will could act. He realized, too, that he should never have come downstairs; some vague necessity for verisimilitude had made him want to leave a wet glass as evidence by the sink; the honesty of his imagination had betrayed him.

"Pour it out," commanded his father, "that water!"

Rudolph despairingly inverted the tumbler.

"What's the matter with you, anyways?" demanded Miller angrily.

"Nothing."

"Did you go to confession yesterday?"

"Yes."

"Then why were you going to drink water?"

"I don't know—I forgot."

"Maybe you care more about being a little thirsty than you do about your religion."

"I forgot." Rudolph could feel the tears straining in his eyes.

"That's no answer."

"Well, I did."

"You better look out!" His father held to a high, persistent inquisitory note: "If you're so forgetful that you can't remember your religion something better be done about it."

Rudolph filled a sharp pause with:

"I can remember it all right."

"First you begin to neglect your religion," cried his father, fanning his own fierceness, "the next thing you'll begin to lie and steal, and the *next* thing is the *reform* school!"

Not even this familiar threat could deepen the abyss that Rudolph saw before him. He must either tell all now, offering his body for what he knew would be a ferocious beating or else tempt the thunderbolts by receiving the Body and Blood of Christ with sacrilege upon his soul. And of the two the former seemed more terrible—it was not so much the beating he dreaded as the savage ferocity, outlet of the ineffectual man, which would lie behind it.

"Put down that glass and go upstairs and dress!" his father ordered, "and when we get to church, before you go to communion, you better kneel down and ask God to forgive you for your carelessness."

Some accidental emphasis in the phrasing of this command acted like a catalytic agent on the confusion and terror of Rudolph's mind. A wild, proud anger rose in him, and he dashed the tumbler passionately into the sink.

His father uttered a strained, husky sound, and sprang for him. Rudolph dodged to the side, tipped over a chair, and tried to get beyond the kitchen table. He cried out sharply when a hand grasped his pyjama shoulder, then he felt the dull impact of a fist against the side of his head, and glancing blows on the upper part of his body. As he slipped here and there in his father's grasp, dragged or lifted when he clung instinctively to an arm, aware of sharp smarts and strains, he made no sound except that he laughed hysterically several times. Then in less than a minute the blows abruptly ceased. After a lull during which Rudolph was tightly held, and during which they both trembled violently and uttered strange, truncated words, Carl Miller half dragged, half threatened his son upstairs.

"Put on your clothes!"

Rudolph was now both hysterical and cold. His head hurt him, and there was a long, shallow scratch on his neck from his father's fingernail, and he sobbed and trembled as he dressed. He was aware of his mother standing at the doorway in a wrapper, her wrinkled face compressing and squeezing and opening out into new series of wrinkles which floated and eddied from neck to brow. Despising her nervous ineffectuality and avoiding her rudely when she tried to touch his neck with witch-hazel, be made a hasty, choking toilet. Then he followed his father out of the house and along the road towards the Catholic church.

IV

They walked without speaking except when Carl Miller acknowledged automatically the existence of passers-by. Rudolph's uneven breathing alone ruffled the hot Sunday silence.

His father stopped decisively at the door of the church.

"I've decided you'd better go to confession again. Go and tell Father Schwartz what you did and ask God's pardon."

"You lost your temper, too!" said Rudolph quickly.

Carl Miller took a step towards his son, who moved cautiously backward.

"All right, I'll go."

"Are you going to do what I say?" cried his father in a hoarse whisper.

"All right."

Rudolph walked into the church, and for the second time in two days entered the confessional and knelt down. The slat went up almost at once.

"I accuse myself of missing my morning prayers."

"Is that all?"

"That's all."

A maudlin exultation filled him. Not easily ever again would he be able to put an abstraction before the necessities of his ease and pride. An invisible line had been crossed, and he had become aware of his isolation—aware that it applied not only to those moments when he was Blatchford Sarnemington but that it applied to all his inner life. Hitherto such phenomena as "crazy" ambitions and petty shames and fears had been but private reservations, unacknowledged before the throne of his official soul. Now he realized unconsciously that his private reservations were himself—and all the rest a garnished front and a conventional flag. The pressure of his environment had driven him into the lonely secret road of adolescence.

He knelt in the pew beside his father. Mass began. Rudolph knelt up—when he was alone he slumped his posterior back against the seat—and tasted the consciousness of a sharp, subtle revenge. Beside him his father prayed that God would forgive Rudolph, and asked also that his own outbreak of temper would be pardoned. He glanced sidewise at this son, and was relieved to see that the strained, wild look had gone from his face and that he had ceased sobbing. The Grace of God, inherent in the Sacrament, would do the rest, and perhaps after Mass everything would be better. He was proud of Rudolph in his heart, and beginning to be truly as well as formally sorry for what he had done.

Usually, the passing of the collection box was the significant point for Rudolph in the services. If, as was often the case, he had no money to drop in he would be furiously ashamed and bow his head and pretend not to see the box, lest Jeanne Brady in the pew behind should take notice and suspect an acute family poverty. But to-day he glanced coldly into it as it skimmed under his eyes, noting with casual interest the large number of pennies it contained.

When the bell rang for communion, however, he quivered. There was no reason why God should not stop his heart. During the past twelve hours he had committed a series of mortal sins increasing in gravity, and he was now to crown them all with a blasphemous sacrilege.

"Domine, non sum dignus; ut intres sub tectum meum; sed tantum dic verbo, et sanabitur anima mea. . . ."

There was a rustle in the pews, and the communicants worked their ways into the aisle with downcast eyes and joined hands. Those of larger piety pressed together their finger-tips to form steeples. Among these latter was Carl Miller. Rudolph followed him towards the altar-rail and knelt down, automatically taking up the napkin under his chin. The bell rang sharply, and the priest turned from the altar with the white Host held above the chalice:

'Corpus Domini nostri Jesu Christi custodiat animam tuam in vitam æternam.'

A cold sweat broke out on Rudolph's forehead as the communion began. Along the line Father Schwartz moved, and with gathering nausea Rudolph felt his heart-valves weakening at the will of God. It seemed to him that the church was darker and that a great quiet had fallen, broken only by the inarticulate mumble which announced the approach of the Creator of Heaven and Earth. He dropped his head down between his shoulders and waited for the blow.

Then he felt a sharp nudge in his side. His father was poking him to sit up, not to slump against the rail; the priest was only two places away.

'Corpus Domini nostri Jesu Christi custodiat animam tuam in vitam æternam.'

Rudolph opened his mouth. He felt the sticky wax taste of the wafer on his tongue. He remained motionless for what seemed an interminable period of time, his head still raised, the wafer undissolved in his mouth. Then again he started at the pressure of his father's elbow, and saw that the people were falling away from the altar like leaves and turning with blind downcast eyes to their pews, alone with God.

Rudolph was alone with himself, drenched with perspiration and deep in mortal sin. As he walked back to his pew the sharp taps of his cloven hoofs were loud upon the floor, and he knew that it was a dark poison he carried in his heart.

V

"Sagitta Volante in Dei"

The beautiful little boy with eyes like blue stones, and lashes that sprayed open from them like flower-petals had finished telling his sin to Father Schwartz—and the square of sunshine in which he sat had moved forward an hour into the room. Rudolph had become less frightened now; once eased of the story a reaction had set in. He knew that as long as he was in the room with this priest God would not stop his heart, so he sighed and sat quietly, waiting for the priest to speak.

Father Schwartz's cold watery eyes were fixed upon the carpet pattern on which the sun had brought out the swastikas and the flat bloomless vines and the pale echoes of flowers. The hall-clock ticked insistently towards sunset, and from the ugly room and from the afternoon outside the window arose a stiff monotony, shattered now and then by the reverberate clapping of a far-away hammer on the dry air. The priest's nerves were strung thin and the beads of his rosary were crawling and squirming like snakes upon the green felt of his table top. He could not remember now what it was he should say.

Of all the things in this lost Swede town he was most aware of this little boy's eyes—the beautiful eyes, with lashes that left them reluctantly and curved back as though to meet them once more.

For a moment longer the silence persisted while Rudolph waited, and the priest struggled to remember something that was slipping farther and farther away from him, and the clock ticked in the broken house. Then Father Schwartz stared hard at the little boy and remarked in a peculiar voice:

"When a lot of people get together in the best places things go glimmering."

Rudolph started and looked quickly at Father Schwartz's face.

"I said——" began the priest, and paused, listening. "Do you hear the hammer and the clock ticking and the bees? Well, that's no good. The thing is to have a lot of people in the centre of the world, wherever that happens to be. Then"—his watery eyes widened knowingly—"things go glimmering."

"Yes, Father," agreed Rudolph, feeling a little frightened.

"What are you going to be when you grow up?"

"Well, I was going to be a baseball-player for a while," answered Rudolph nervously, "but I don't think that is a very good ambition, so I think I'll be an actor or a Navy officer."

Again the priest stared at him.

"I see *exactly* what you mean," he said, with a fierce air.

Rudolph had not meant anything in particular, and at the implication that he had, he became more uneasy.

"This man is crazy," he thought, "and I'm scared of him. He wants me to help him out some way, and I don't want to."

"You look as if things went glimmering," cried Father Schwartz wildly. "Did you ever go to a party?"

"Yes, Father."

"And did you notice that everybody was properly dressed? That's what I mean. Just as you went into the party there was a moment when everybody was properly dressed. Maybe two little girls were standing by the door and some boys were leaning over the banisters, and there were bowls around full of flowers."

"I've been to a lot of parties," said Rudolph, rather relieved that the conversation had taken this turn.

"Of course," continued Father Schwartz triumphantly, "I knew you'd agree with me. But my theory is that when a whole lot of people get together in the best places things go glimmering all the time."

Rudolph found himself thinking of Blatchford Sarnemington.

"Please listen to me!" commanded the priest impatiently. "Stop worrying about last Saturday. Apostasy implies an absolute damnation only on the supposition of a previous perfect faith. Does that fix it?"

Rudolph had not the faintest idea what Father Schwartz was talking about, but he nodded and the priest nodded back at him and returned to his mysterious preoccupation.

"Why," he cried, "they have lights now as big as stars—do you realize that? I heard of one light they had in Paris or somewhere that was as big as a star. A lot of people had it—a lot of gay people. They have all sorts of things now that you never dreamed of."

"Look here——" He came nearer to Rudolph, but the boy drew away, so Father Schwartz went back and sat down in his chair, his eyes dried out and hot. "Did you ever see an amusement park?"

"No, Father."

"Well, go and see an amusement park." The priest waved his hand vaguely. 'It's a thing like a fair, only much more glittering. Go to one at night and stand a little way off from it in a dark place—under dark trees. You'll see a big wheel made of lights turning in the air, and a long slide shooting boats down into the water. A band playing somewhere, and a smell of peanuts—and everything will twinkle. But it won't remind you of anything, you see. It will all just hang out there in the night like a colored balloon—like a big yellow lantern on a pole."

Father Schwartz frowned as he suddenly thought of something.

"But don't get up close," he warned Rudolph, "because if you do you'll only feel the heat and the sweat and the life."

All this talking seemed particularly strange and awful to Rudolph, because this man was a priest. He sat there, half terrified, his beautiful eyes open wide and staring at Father Schwartz. But underneath his terror he felt that his own inner convictions were confirmed. There was something ineffably gorgeous somewhere that had nothing to do with God. He no longer thought that God was angry at him about the original lie, because He must have understood that Rudolph had done it to make things finer in the confessional, brightening up the dinginess of his admissions by saying a thing radiant and proud. At the moment when he had affirmed immaculate honor a silver pennon had flapped out into the breeze somewhere and there had been the crunch of leather and the shine of silver spurs and a troop of horsemen waiting for dawn on a low green hill. The sun had made stars of light on their breastplates like the picture at home of the German cuirassiers at Sedan.

But now the priest was muttering inarticulate and heartbroken words, and the boy became wildly afraid. Horror entered suddenly in at the open window, and the atmosphere of the room changed. Father Schwartz collapsed precipitiously down on his knees, and let his body settle back against a chair.

"Oh, my God!" he cried out, in a strange voice, and wilted to the floor.

Then a human oppression rose from the priest's worn clothes, and mingled with the faint smell of old food in the corners. Rudolph gave a sharp cry and ran in panic from the house—while the collapsed man lay there quite still, filling his room, filling it with voices and faces until it was crowded with echolalia, and rang loud with a steady, shrill note of laughter.

Outside the window the blue sirocco trembled over the wheat, and girls with yellow hair walked sensuously along roads that bounded the fields, calling innocent, exciting things to the young men who were working in the lines between the grain. Legs were shaped under starchless gingham, and rims of the necks of dresses were warm and damp. For five hours now hot fertile life had burned in the afternoon. It would be night in three hours, and all along the land there would be these blonde Northern girls and the tall young men from the farms lying out beside the wheat, under the moon.

Charles Macomb Flandrau

MRS. WHITE'S

Charles Macomb Flandrau (1871–1938). This graceful, urbane essayist and short story writer was born in St. Paul, the son of Judge Charles E. Flandrau, who distinguished himself as the hero of New Ulm during the Sioux Uprising of 1862. As a child Flandrau was taken to Europe for an extensive trip, and this experience apparently created a desire for travel that was never appeased. He attended Harvard, graduating in 1895. Not long afterward his stories, subsequently gathered together under the title Harvard Episodes, *began to appear in magazines. In many ways, they anticipated F. Scott Fitzgerald's stories of misfits at prestigious Eastern colleges, and some critics have suggested that the younger writer was influenced by Flandrau's work. For several years, during the first decade of this century, Flandrau helped his brother run a coffee plantation near Jalapa, Mexico, and the literary result of this experience was the fine series of essays published as* Viva Mexico! *These pieces and other essays appeared originally in* The Bellman, *a Minneapolis-based magazine of some distinction, and in addition Flandrau wrote for St. Paul newspapers. He continued to travel widely in Europe, and, although he spent a part of each year at 385 Pleasant Avenue in St. Paul, he eventually bought a home in Normandy which he named Le Petit St. Paul. A Johnsonian suspicion of cant, an acute perception of the incongruities in human behavior, an eye for telling detail, and a bewitching sense of humor converge in his essays, some of them gathered together under the titles* Prejudices *(1911) and* Loquacities *(1932). The best of his fiction is marked by a quiet awareness of human frailty and hidden tragedies.*

THIS MORNING I READ in the paper of the death of Mrs. White and the short, inadequate paragraph startled me, not exactly because Mrs. White was dead but because until yesterday afternoon she was alive. I had assumed that the good lady (How I wish I could remember just when I left off hating her and began to

First published in *The Bellman*, volume 10, number 242, March 4, 1911.

think of her as a good lady!) had died years ago and there was something grotesque and uncanny in her suddenly up and dying again out of a blue sky, so to speak. It was very much as if some one should pop out of an old tomb in a cemetery, take a hasty look around and then pop in again. If I hadn't long ago ceased to feel bitterly about her I should have told myself that it was just like Mrs. White, that she was not a sincere woman, that she had never inspired me with confidence. But water has been flowing under the bridge for thirty-two years since my tears used to flow at Mrs. White's, and it so long ago eroded my bitterness that I cannot now recall when it was I last had any. Had I been asked yesterday how old Mrs. White would have been by this time, I should have answered very conservatively, for fear of seeming to exaggerate, "About a hundred and ninety-six," and the paper tells me she "passed away" in her seventy-first year. Good heavens!—then when I knew her and regarded her as a senile monster with a gizzard of granite, she must really have been a nice-looking young woman of thirty-eight. How very strange.

Whenever I begin to think of Mrs. White's I have a more than usually uncontrollable desire to write my memoirs. I'm sure I don't know why I have always so longed to write my memoirs. Perhaps it is because I know that memoirs, however inane, are the only form of literature that is absolutely sure of getting itself read. Then, too, they must be so easy to produce. They don't have to be by anybody in particular and they present no technical difficulties whatever. Of course they have to begin somewhere, but one need never be bothered by wondering how they ought to end. They don't end; they merely stop. Very often, indeed, they refuse to do even that. Madame de Genlis, for instance, after minutely covering the ground in her "Souvenirs," trimmed a new pen and without pausing to separate herself into chapters or to take breath, dashed off eight obese volumes of "Memoires." Like all works of this nature, they are "perfectly fascinating" and are still read, but there is no reason in the world why I shouldn't produce eight volumes just as twaddlesome. Mine would have to begin with Mrs. White's, for with the exception of the statue of a woman modeled in butter at the Centennial Exposition of 1876, Mrs. White's is the first thing I vividly remember.

Mrs. White's was a parental mistake. Some children are born without the kindergarten temperament, and when this happens the effort to develop it is usually futile. Not that my mother consciously attempted to do so. I asked her a short time ago why she had been guilty of sending me to Mrs. White's—of blighting, even in the bud, an originally fine mind, and she was obliged to confess she didn't know. There was in the act no high and definite concept of education. I suspect her of motives as mixed as they were worthy. By sending me to Mrs. White's she could relieve the household of my beloved but exhausting society for hours and hours and hours at a time, she could "help Mrs. White along" and she could give me the opportunity of learning "how to observe." Mrs. White's was the first of Froebel's infantile observatories to make its appearance in our town and strange things were expected of it.

The prospectus said that "the busy baby fingers" were "trained from the first to co-ordinate and keep pace with the germinating mentality," which later I was to find out was merely a polite paraphrase of the good, old-fashioned expression "unmitigated hell." Every morning a dire conveyance, locally known as the White Maria, drawn by two rusty, long-haired, bay ponies and driven by Mr. White, who was likewise long-haired, rusty and bay, careered up to our door at half-past eight, and afterwards,—depending on the length of time it had taken to extricate me from the bannisters among which I had entangled my arms and legs and between which I had thrust my head, in order to render my removal as difficult and painful as possible for all concerned,—my father would emerge from the house flushed, panting but triumphant with me, screaming, kicking but defeated, in his arms. He would then transport me, still howling, to the White Maria, thrust me in, slam the door (it opened at the back) and return to exclaim to my mother, "I really don't see how we can keep this up much longer."

Once inside the White Maria, the busy baby fingers began straightway to co-ordinate and keep pace with the germinating mentality by transforming the dusky interior into a veritable black hole of Calcutta. I slapped faces, pulled hair, kicked shins, threw lunch-baskets on the floor and stamped upon their contents, while the other children, goaded on to madness and piercing shrieks, ran amuck and did the same. Mr. White never interfered with this perambulating inferno, both because he was of an incorrigible cheerfulness—the result of a severe sunstroke—and because he couldn't see it. As one of Mrs. White's specialties was the observation of nature in all its various, ever-pleasing and instructive moods, the superstructure of the White Maria was a kind of square limousine of black oilcloth that at any season of the year effectually shut out air, light, the passing landscape and also Mr. White. The "precious freight" (as Mrs. White called us) within could therefore dismember one another undisturbed. After stopping at several more houses to recruit our spent legions, we finally arrived at the school, furious, tearful, disheveled, hating life as we have never hated it since, and proceeded at once to praise God in song and thank him for our manifold and inscrutable blessings.

> "Oh blessèd work,
> Oh blessèd play,
> We thank Thee for
> Another day!"

—was the mendacious refrain of every stanza. When sufficiently irritated by anything, I can still sometimes remember the tune. Later in the morning we were supplied with round, flat discs like paper chips and again burst reluctantly into melody, exclaiming this time, as we shied the discs into a basket on the floor,

> "Did you ever, ever play,
> Skipping pebbles on the bay,
> On the [something-or-other] water?"

Just what kind of water it was, I have never been able to remember. The missing adjective has worried me for years. All over the world I have lain awake at night skipping pebbles on the bay for hours and wondering whether the water was "shining," or "glassy" or "rippling" or "placid" or "deep blue." Metrical exigencies of course insist that the name be writ in water of two syllables and I have often cajoled myself into a troubled sleep by almost deciding that this particular water must have been "pretty." But even "pretty" lacks the certain completely vapid authenticity that ever eludes me.

The blessèd play was ghastly enough, but the blessèd work was torture. I was endowed with neither skill nor patience and at that time I could not lose my shyness before strangers except when I lost my temper. The public exhibition of my inability to coordinate was a daily anguish and I do not yet understand how I ever at last achieved the unspeakably hideous mat of magenta and yellow paper that after the death of my grandmother I found, spotlessly preserved, among some of her most cherished possessions. But I not only did, I furthermore succeeded, after days and days of agony, in constructing a useless, wobbly, altogether horrible little house out of wire and dried peas. It was characteristic of Mrs. White to select, from the comprehensive inventory of the world's possible building materials, wire and dried peas.

If dear Mrs. White had now and then betrayed the impatience, the annoyance, the despair she had every reason to experience over my stupidity and awkwardness, if at the "psychological moment" she had occasionally spoken sharply, blown me up as did the teachers later at the public school, the effect, I am convinced, would have been definite and salutary. But hers was the haggard benevolence of the child-gardener in its most indestructible form. All day long sweetness and light automatically glared from her eyes like pharos rays that faileth not, because they've been wound up. There was in the loving expression around her mouth something appallingly inanimate, objective, detachable; one felt that it hadn't grown there, it had been put. It bore about the same relation to reality as does the art of the confectioner. It lay against her teeth like the thin, white icing on a cake, and the hand that itched to box an ear, faltered half-way in its flight, pausing to caress a curl. It terrified me to realize that the perishable, narrow strips of glazed, colored paper we tried to weave into mats, and the dried peas with which I finally builded better than I knew, were, even as the hairs of our heads, all numbered. This was for the purpose of teaching us neatness and thrift, the husbanding of our resources. To crumple the former or scatter the latter was, we realize, a crime; but Mrs. White's method of calling our attention to it was merely an insult to the intelligence. The punishment was a deliberate misfit, an elaborately artificial evasion of the point at issue.

When, for instance, an evasive dried pea would slip through my clumsy fingers and rattle over the uncarpeted floor with what sounded to me like the detonations of artillery, Mrs. White never told me to wake up and be more careful of what I was doing. Instead, she would coo like a philandering pigeon and murmur, "Why, laddie—what would the hungry little birds say if they were to see *all* that nice food wasted?" When, panic-stricken at the number of my crumpled failures, I feloniously thrust them into my pocket, she would fish them out with sweet amaze, exclaiming, "Why, dearie—how did *these* get here? Does any little girl or boy know how *all* these poor little strips of paper got into the very bottom of Charlie's pocket?" When, as once in so often happened, I would "all alone beweep my outcast state, And trouble deaf heaven with my bootless cries, And look upon myself and curse my fate," she never told me to stop at once and behave myself or she'd know the reason why. She would open her eyes to their incredulous roundest, slightly drop her lower jaw, wonderingly scan every face and then purr, "Why, manny—what's become of *all* the smiles?"

There was invariably an answer to these inquiries and it was almost as invariably furnished by one Adelaide Winkle, a dreadful child, but one more sinned against, I now appreciate, than sinning. Forced to the limit in the hothouse of the home and deeply imbedded in the fertilizing approval of Mrs. White, Adelaide was in all our gay little parterre the most brilliant and the most noxious bloom. At the age of seven she already had the executive air of women who preside over the meetings of clubs. She also played the piano, danced fancy dances, sang, recited, wore three rings, a necklace and a red plush dress. I hated her even more, if possible, than I hated Mrs. White; for she not only kept an eye on my shortcomings, she formulated them into ready words and then, by request, smugly proclaimed them. But it was the manner in which Mrs. White exploited her before visitors that most enraged me. When visitors appeared, as they often did, for a kindergarten under cultivation was a decided novelty, Adelaide was called upon to execute her entire programme, from A to Izzard. She sang, she elocuted "Bobolink, spink, spank bobolink," she played her show piece ("Fairy Chimes") on the piano, she withdrew to an adjoining room and tripped coquettishly in again, strewing like the springtime an armful of tissue-paper roses and, last of all, she gave a short discourse, with experiments, on geography that brought tears to the eyes of the most criminal. The experiments were evolved in sight of the audience with the aid of a large wooden trayful of sand and a tin dipperful of water. Under Adelaide's precocious fingers these helpless elements gave a presumably correct rendering of the Book of Genesis in action, becoming, at her will, a continent, a river, a lake, an island, a peninsula, a mountain. One downward thrust of an unerring thumb upon a soggy peak and lo! the mountain was a volcano which, Adelaide always ended the lecture by informing us, "spouts, when in a state of act-iv-it-y, fire, smoke, glow-ing stones and mol-tennn law-vaw." Powerless to protest, and crushed beneath the weight of my own incompetence I have sat through the performance of this revolting rite as often as three times in a single morning.

Revenge came slowly. It took nineteen years to arrive; but it arrived. Unduly familiar in childhood with continents and dizzy heights, Adelaide, as she matured, reached out, expanded, longed to become a world-power. At the age of twenty-six, therefore, she eloped with a French "count" who not only failed to observe the convention of proving to be a waiter or a hair-dresser, he absolutely failed to be anything at all, and Adelaide ever since has had to support him.

At eleven o'clock we took a dejected, orphan asylum prom-enade about the suburban streets in two long lines, led by the older pupils of the more advanced school downstairs and fol-lowed by Mrs. White who, by constantly running back and forth in order to satisfy herself that no one was neglecting to "observe nature," must have covered miles to our blocks. How we all loathed Nature! I loved animals and flowers, clouds and rain, snow and sunshine then, as I do now, but "Nature" was some-thing quite different. I don't believe we ever knew just what it was and probably connected the term in our minds, not with the works of God themselves but with the inescapable obligation of perpetually fussing about them. Without doubt I should have ended by becoming very fond of the White Maria's shaggy old ponies if the labored pretense that we were all dying to bring them a handful of oats for their Thanksgiving dinner, and a dozen other pretenses concerning them, had not ended by preventing it. Birds were wonderful, heavenly creatures to watch and examine, but weeks of prattle about the Christmas present (seeds, bread-crumbs and more oats) of birds we had never seen merely re-sulted in a little band of ornithological cynics. This fictitious pas-sion for just birds—disembodied, abstract birds—that Mrs. White entirely imagined for us and widely advertised, was taken seri-ously by our families for years. My grandmother fondly believed in it to the last and nearly embittered my young life by bequeath-ing in her will three beautiful family portraits to my brothers, and to me, the "nature-lover," the unwilling product of Mrs. White's, a set of Audubon.

On our return from the walk Mrs. White inspected our lunch-baskets, confiscating what she considered injurious to our digestions and our teeth, and then allowed us to fortify ourselves against further blesséd work and blesséd play with the remains. I have often wondered what actually became of the cake and candy she daily took from us "for our own good." I shouldn't be surprised if she wantonly scattered it along the sidewalk, or threw it into passing carriages. It would have been a natural reaction from her incessant, official pother about "neatness and thrift," but at the time we all, of course, devoutly believed that she put the loot away in a pantry and that the entire White family lived on it for weeks.

Almost everything we learned at Mrs. White's was sure to be incorrect, to the point of imbecility. For I don't know how long after leaving there, I took it for granted that a thoughtful Creator had supplied dear Bossy with a "dewlap" in order that she could wipe dry each mouthful of wet grass before eating it.

"When Bossy goes out to the fields in the morning for her breakfast, this long, soft fold of skin you see here under her neck (pointing to the picture) swings from side to side, brushing away the damp and chilly dew," Mrs. White had told us, and I need scarcely dwell upon the disappointment, the sense of injury, I experienced when I subsequently sought Bossy in her graminaceous lair and watched her dewlap quite otherwise engaged. But even so—Mrs. White is no more, and anyhow, I always was a facile relenter. At times I have found myself actually grateful for Mrs. White's. There was, for instance, the mystery of Mary Blake, and the mystery of the White Maria. I have often felt grateful for them.

Mary Blake was an overgrown girl in the school downstairs. She was a pervasive lass—"a perfect romp." We all knew her well. She belonged to a family prominent in our growing town and, although my family and hers were not intimate, they no doubt would have thought they were had they unexpectedly met, for instance, on the spiral stairway of Rue Scribe. There were two sons and four daughters in Mary's family, and none of them was named Jane. This is important. Years elapsed. I had spent considerable time abroad, I had been occupied in growing up, in going to school, in preparing for college. There were still four Blake girls, but my interest in them was vague—collective. Then, one day, I heard of the marriage of Jane Blake, which surprised me somewhat, as there never had been a Jane Blake. This led, a short time later, to my expressing to Mrs. Blake a belated interest in Mary, at which Mrs. Blake looked mystified for an instant and then said, "I think you must mean Susan." I didn't mean Susan but refrained from saying so, and from then on I have been haunted by the mystery of Mary Blake. For apparently there is no Mary Blake and never was one, although, in answer to my feverish inquiries, several persons who went to Mrs. White's with her have assured me that they remember her perfectly. Every now and then I meet Jane Blake and talk to her, wondering the while if she can be Mary. The fact that Jane is dark and Mary was blond is perhaps negligible. Once I sat next to Jane at dinner and when, after a long pause in our conversation, I said, "Come now—aren't you really your sister who died?" she answered coldly that none of her sisters had ever died, and immediately afterward refused to let the servant help her to any more champagne.

The mystery of the White Maria I have never tried to solve. It is enough to know that it was, and to wonder if I shall ever again see anything so lovely. The White Maria, as has been mentioned, was a large, square box of black oilcloth. Its inner surface, however, was white, soiled to a neutral gray. On our outward journeys when I noticed this at all, it was only to feel the tragedy of life with a greater intensity. But on the return. . . . To state in words what we saw when returning gives but little idea of It. We were always tired and a trifle drowsy when we started for home, and we at once leaned back and quietly watched for It. It often appeared, but sometimes it refused to show for days, and I then used to wonder if I had ever really seen it. The perpetual fascination it had for us was a most complicated one, consisting as it did of the mystery, the beauty, the reality and the unreality of the thing itself, together with the fact that Mrs. White was somehow being thwarted. The black canopy, in a word, sought to imprison us, to impose an impenetrable barrier between us and the outside world, but as we jogged along, the houses, the trees, the horses, and the people we passed were all reproduced in miniature on one of the inside walls. The details were always clear enough to let us know where we were; frequently they were perfect. Moreover, the little panorama was without color, which gave it an additional, ghostly charm. I have never been hypnotized, but I think that in staring at this dreamlike, dissolving procession I used to be very near the hypnotic state. At times, when the White Maria drew up at our front door, I would be asleep and it would take me half an hour or more to get entirely back again into my own body—I can remember the sensation even if I can't describe it. The moving picture shows of today always seem to me like crude and vulgar attempts to recall and commercialize the age when we were mystics and had visions.

Borghild Dahl

from HOMECOMING

Borghild Dahl, born in Minneapolis in 1890 of Norwegian parents, learned to speak their language before she spoke English. From her early years she suffered from severely impaired vision, but she had tremendous will to participate in everyday life. She attended public schools in Minneapolis, received her B.A. from the University of Minnesota, and later studied at Columbia University and the University of Oslo. Dahl became the principal of high schools in western Minnesota and in North Dakota. Since 1943 she has lived in New York City, where for some time she tutored students in English and other languages. Her autobiography, I Wanted to See, *tells of her battle with failing vision, her nearly total blindness, and the surgery which brought her the vision she had managed without for so long. Since that time she has written a number of books—among them* Homecoming, *about a Norwegian-American family. The chapter included here is a moving day-to-day account of two cultures colliding.*

I T WAS LATE IN THE AFTERNOON of what Grandmother Skoglund called the Third Day of Christmas, and Tante Gunara and Tante Tallette had come from St. Paul for their annual Christmas visit.

Grandmother Skoglund was serving coffee and small cakes from Bernt Moe's night table, which had been moved into the center of the parlor. Bernt Moe had been their roomer going on three years now—ever since the fall after Nils Johnson had gone back to Norway to marry his sweetheart. And, since Bernt Moe was spending the Christmas holidays with his sister in Fargo, he had offered the use of his room to the family until his return the day after New Year's. Lyng's mother, who was having the day off to make up for the long hours of night work during the pre-

Christmas rush, was seated in the blue upholstered rocker. Lyng and Haakon and Kristian were being served coffee with the grown-ups.

Tante Gunara and Tante Tallette were dressed almost alike— long, full, black wool skirts and black satin blouses with stand-up collars whose white ruching came up well under their chins and ears. They both had gold watch chains that looped over their wide stiff belts, and inside the belts were large gold watches. But in the front of Tante Tallette's collar was a brooch with two mother-of-pearl hands clasped inside a gold heart. Instead of high black calfskin boots like Tante Gunara's she had patent leather shoes with high heels and pointed toes. Tante Tallette's head was one mass of gold-tinted curls, and her china-blue eyes were gentle and smiling. Tante Gunara combed her straight, graying hair severely back from her thin face, and her silver-rimmed glasses made her keen brown eyes seem even more penetrating.

The Christmas visits with Lyng's aunts from St. Paul were always an occasion in Lyng's life, and today everything had seemed especially enjoyable. For one thing, her mother had been in unusually good spirits all day. She had let Lyng and the boys take turns playing the mouth organ Tante Tallette had brought them without once complaining about the noise. And during dinner, when Kristian spilled gravy on the best white linen table cloth, she hadn't scolded him at all.

As Lyng sat sipping her afternoon coffee in the parlor, she wondered if she could get up courage enough to ask her mother the question she had been wanting to all day. Ever since the disappointment of having to stay home from the picnic at Minnehaha Falls, Lyng had never asked her mother for permission to go anywhere outside their circle of Norwegian friends. But Hattie was taking part in a Sunday School program at the Franklin Avenue Church this evening and had invited her especially to come.

"Reidun, don't you think the floor in here is cold?" Tante Gunara asked. She pulled up her feet and drew her black knitted shawl closer around her shoulders. "I feel a draft from the door leading into the hall."

"I don't feel any drafts," Lyng's mother said tartly.

"I wish you had served the coffee in the kitchen where it's warm," Tante Gunara went on. "While we were eating dinner in the dining room, I didn't notice the cold too much. But this parlor—ugh!"

256

"I am bringing up my children to become ladies and gentlemen," Lyng's mother said. "They will be able to look back with pride to their Christmases at home. People whose early vision has been limited to kitchens retain the outlook of servants and underlings all their lives."

Tante Tallette helped herself to several of the small cakes Grandmother Skoglund offered her. "How do you ever get your *fattigmand* so smooth and crisp, Mother?" she asked, turning the thin, diamond-shaped cake with its finely scalloped edges and regarding it admiringly. "Mine are always thick and lumpy, no matter how much pains I take with them. I've tried rolling the dough out thin, but then it either tears while I'm taking it off the board, or the *fattigmand* breaks when it's coming out of the hot lard."

"It's merely a matter of practice," Lyng's mother said shortly.

Oh, dear, Lyng thought. Now Mother's cross again. I should have asked her while we were eating dinner, but the meat balls and the mashed potatoes and creamed carrots and burnt sugar pudding were so good, I couldn't risk spoiling our enjoyment of all that. Now I'll simply have to ask her before things get worse.

Aloud she said, "Mother, Hattie Fleming is going to be in a Christmas program tonight in her church. They're going to give away presents to the children afterwards. Hattie got a cute little doll buggy last year and Bert got a game of dominoes. The grown-ups in the church pay for everything, so they're not even going to take up a collection. It's all free. And I'm already dressed up in my Christmas dress and new hair-ribbons. Can I go? Please, Mother."

"Where is it you want to go?" Tante Tallette asked.

"To the Franklin Avenue Church," Lyng said, trying to keep the eagerness out of her voice. "Hattie Fleming's Sunday School is having their Christmas program."

"You have already been at your own Christmas program," her mother said. "You got a lovely present there, too, a New Testament. I don't want you wandering from one church to another like a gypsy."

"I've never been inside any other church but our own," Lyng protested.

"Oh, let the child go," Grandmother Skoglund said gently.

Lyng's mother took a sip from her coffee cup. "That church is American. I know what happens when children start going around to these Yankee services. It was good-bye to the Norwegian after Gerd Jacobsen had been with that Baptist crowd on Twenty-third Avenue. And it was the same with Valborg Aanerud as soon as she got a taste of those Congregationalists. Both girls became Yankeefied right away. Now the parents of both girls have had to let them prepare for confirmation from books in the English language. Imagine repeating the Ten Commandments and the Lord's Prayer in a foreign tongue! It's the first time that any parents in our church have been guilty of allowing such a thing to come to pass. And once Valborg and Gerd are confirmed, you may be sure it will be the last their own church people will ever see of them."

"There can be no harm in allowing Lyng to go there once." Grandmother Skoglund looked pleadingly toward Tante Gunara and Tante Tallette.

"How do I know Lyng will be welcome there?" Lyng's mother went on. "I certainly wouldn't blame a church for not wanting to take in strangers. And I'm not sending my children where they're not wanted. Worse yet, begging for presents."

"I wouldn't be begging," Lyng managed to say. "Hattie invited me and she goes to that Sunday School. She's to be one of the angels tonight. She said for all of us to come and—"

"Who pays attention to what children say?" Lyng's mother interrupted.

"The people in the American churches are awfully friendly," Tante Tallette said. "There's a little Methodist Church near our place in St. Paul. I sometimes go there, if it's cold or I'm late. The minister always shakes hands with me and invites me to come again. And some ladies have asked me to join one of their societies. I'd kind of like to."

Grandmother Skoglund looked frightened. Lyng's mother frowned. "I've told Lyng she can't go and that settles it." Her voice sounded cold and hard. "She has company at home, and I'm bringing up my children to have good manners, even though people in America seem to pay little or no attention to such matters."

"My goodness, don't make her stay at home on our account," Tante Tallette said. "We'll have to be leaving soon anyway."

"That's right," Tante Gunara agreed. "I'm getting anxious about the fire in the furnace. Knute Bjork promised to look after it for me. But you know how it is, leaving things to others."

There was a painful silence. Then Grandmother Skoglund

picked up the tray of cakes and walked over to Lyng. "You aren't eating any cakes, *Vesla-mi*."

"She's mad because she can't go to the Sunday School program," Haakon said. He leaned over to reach the tray of cakes and helped himself to a handful. "I don't wander around to strange churches, do I, Mother?"

"No, thank God, I have one child I never have to worry about."

Grandmother Skoglund kept standing in front of Lyng. "Try a sand tart," she whispered. "A heart-shaped one. You know you like them so much."

Lyng shook her head. There was another painful silence. With a sinking heart, Lyng watched the fading daylight disappear behind the thickly frosted bay window. Grandmother Skoglund blew out the last candle on the Christmas tree. The room was left in total darkness.

"If they are giving away toys anyway," Tante Tallette said, breaking the silence, "Lyng might as well get one as anyone else."

"No," Lyng's mother snapped.

Tante Gunara cleared her throat. "You wouldn't stand in the way of your children's happiness, would you, Reidun?" she asked.

There was no sound from Lyng's mother.

"Haven't you had enough of your father's stubbornness to see where it leads to?" Tante Gunara went on. "You and Markus might have been sitting pretty on the Skoglund estate, if he had been willing to listen to reason. Instead, it went to that aristocratic brother of yours who had never learned the value of a day's work, and now the place is in the hands of strangers."

Grandmother Skoglund lighted the lamp on Bernt Moe's night table. The greenness from the shade made her face look unreal. "Gunara," she pleaded.

Tante Gunara's eyes were fixed on Lyng's mother. "I don't like to have to say this, Reidun, but it's for your own good as well as the children's. You had better face facts now before it's too late. You are not going to be able to keep Lyng bottled up inside the fence of that Norwegian pride of yours much longer. Nor the boys either. If you try, they'll climb over it, and then God help you."

"Gunara," Grandmother Skoglund repeated. "Not in front of the children."

"It can't be helped. With Markus gone, there isn't anyone else to tell her. I realize what a struggle it has been for her, and you, too, Mother, to supply the family with the barest necessities. But that is all the more reason for letting the children enjoy whatever pleasures and luxuries they can get free."

Lyng's mother stood up. "They have no sense of reverence for God over there, I tell you. Putting on a show in church. Having a sinful child like Hattie take the part of a heavenly angel. It is desecrating all that is holy."

"Hattie isn't a sinful child." Lyng was on the verge of tears.

Tante Tallette stood up, too. Her eyes met Lyng's mother's squarely, but there was no anger in them. "In the old days they acted out the life of Christ in the churches," she said calmly. "And other stories from the Bible. I've been reading all about it in a book one of our roomers let me borrow."

Lyng's mother's eyes blazed. "If you will wash the dishes now, Mother Skoglund, I'll wipe them for you." With that she swept from the room.

"Mother, you sit still. Tallette and I will clear up everything in the kitchen," Tante Gunara said, starting to follow Lyng's mother. "And then we really must be going."

But Grandmother Skoglund hurried after her and the boys tagged along. Lyng was left alone in the parlor. She walked over to the upholstered rocker and climbed into it. Her eyes rested on the picture of the Skoglund estate. The green light from the lamp shade had cast a spell of enchantment over the place. Lyng could imagine her grandfather, the Timber King, a crown on his head and a scepter in his hand, standing at the entrance of the great manor house.

I'm glad Mother married Father, even though she did have to be disobedient, Lyng thought.

She could hear the rattle of dishes out in the kitchen and the murmur of distant voices.

"If Mother thought it was all right to disobey her father, it can't be wrong for me to go to the Franklin Avenue Church tonight without Mother's permission. Mother just doesn't realize how much I want to see a Christmas program in an American church, especially with Hattie acting as a heavenly angel."

She listened. Everyone was in the kitchen.

Tante Gunara and Tante Tallette thought it was all right for her to go to the church tonight. And Grandmother Skoglund did, too, even though she didn't say so.

Lyng slipped down from the rocker and tiptoed across the room to the door leading into the front hall. As she opened the door, it squeaked. She stood breathless. No one had heard. She took a step into the hall and pulled the door behind her so slowly that only a soft click told her that the lock had caught. The hall was pitch dark, but Lyng had no trouble finding her coat and cap that she kept on a peg in the front closet during the holidays. The outside door stuck when she opened it and without stopping to close it, she dashed out on the porch. The chunks of hard snow that Haakon and Kristian had been unable to pry loose when they shoveled creaked under her feet as she tore down the steps and onto the main sidewalk.

As she ran through the snow, Lyng was seized with a feeling of guilt for not having tried to take Haakon and Kristian along. They would have been thrilled to have received a toy for their very own. But Lyng knew that it would have been impossible to smuggle them out of the house without their mother's knowledge. Oh well, if she received a toy they liked, she'd let them take turns at playing with it.

Lyng caught sight of the lighted windows of the Franklin Avenue Church when she was still a block away. It stood out against the deep blue evening sky and the paler blue snow covering the ground. The door was wide open and people were streaming in.

Inside the vestibule men, women, and children stood around talking.

You wouldn't believe they were in a church, Lyng thought.

Suddenly she felt lost. She didn't belong among these people. No one was glad to see her.

"Lyng!"

Hattie had her arms around her.

"Oh, Lyng, how wonderful that you could come! But didn't your family?" Hattie's green eyes were sparkling with excitement, and her cheeks were flushed. Her red hair hung in soft curls down her back. Over her arm she carried something long and white.

"I—I—we had company," Lyng stammered. "My aunts from St. Paul."

"I wish I'd known and I'd have invited them, too. But you could have brought them along without an invitation. I'm glad, though, that you're here." She gave Lyng another squeeze. "Mr. Morrow told us on no account to leave the Sunday School room downstairs. But I wanted to be sure that Fred Sterling kept his promise to give you a seat up front, so I sneaked out. There he is now. I'll send him over to you. I have to hurry back. Mr. Morrow said we had to be dressed and ready to go on the stage at least fifteen minutes before the program was to start."

Lyng's entire body tingled. "Be ready to go on the stage." It sounded like a real theater. A smiling young man came toward her. He must be at least sixteen or seventeen years old.

He bowed. "You are Lyng, I believe. Lyng Skoglund, Hattie Fleming's friend. I am Fred Sterling. May I have the pleasure of escorting you to a seat?" He took Lyng's arm and together they started down the aisle.

They treat you like a grown-up person here, Lyng thought. Soren Bruhjeld, our church janitor, shoos us around like chickens and scolds us if we talk. He ought to come here and take lessons in good manners.

The Franklin Avenue Church was smaller than hers and there was neither an altar nor a raised pulpit up front. The pews were painted gray without cushions, but on the back of each was a long rack full of books. After Lyng had been seated, she picked up one of the books and opened it. Across its two pages were bars of music under which were printed words. Lyng read, "Holy, holy, holy, Lord, God Almighty." In her church only the words of the hymns were given and these in very fine print and in Norwegian.

This church was well heated and brightly lighted. People soon filled the pews, and after they sat down, they greeted one another cordially. Almost everyone was smiling.

A woman with three small boys sat down in Lyng's pew.

"I believe you must be a visitor here," the woman said. "I'm glad you came. You will enjoy the program our young people have prepared for us, I'm sure."

Mother would be shocked at people who talked in church, Lyng thought.

Suddenly it became quiet and everyone looked toward the front of the church. A man in a gray suit came out of the door at the right of the platform and sat down on a small, straight-back chair. He smiled, and to Lyng it seemed he had singled her out and was giving her a silent but reassuring welcome.

"Let us sing hymn one hundred and five," he said.

Where could the minister be? Perhaps he didn't attend the Sunday School Christmas program. Did he, like Lyng's mother, disapprove of putting on a show in church? If he did, why would he allow it at all?

The singing was brisk, almost gay. Lyng caught herself tapping her foot in time with it. As soon as she realized what she was doing, she stopped. That was almost as bad as dancing. Much embarrassed, she glanced furtively at the woman standing beside her. To Lyng's great relief, the woman's head was turned the other way.

At the close of the singing, the man in gray walked over to the lectern. He read a passage from the Bible and folded his hands. "Let us pray," he said. The congregation rose from their seats once more. "Our Father Which art in heaven," he began. Lyng, alone, it seemed, was unable to repeat the words after him. She had never before heard people pray in English. Nor had she seen anyone but the minister stand up front to lead the congregation in prayer. Perhaps after all he was the minister, even though he didn't wear a black robe and a white ruff. At the close of the prayer he stepped down from the platform and sat in a pew across the aisle from Lyng.

From behind a door came soft music. At first it was barely an audible hum. Then it grew louder. "Silent night, holy night." Lyng recognized the tune which was identical with one of the Norwegian Christmas carols she had known as far back as she could remember. Two little girls, dressed alike in soft green, appeared through the side door and pulled back a curtain that had closed off a part of the platform. A woman was sitting on the floor, a huge doll in her arms. She laid the doll in the cradle close beside her and bent over it. Immediately she was surrounded by white-robed, young girls who sang, "Glory to God in the highest, peace on earth and good will toward men."

Hattie was one of the white-robed girls. She waved to Lyng. Lyng stood up and raised both arms as high as she could. Then she felt herself being drawn down into the pew.

"I'm sure you'll be able to see everything without standing up," the woman whispered.

Lyng was too much excited to mind. She gazed with all her eyes at what was taking place upon the platform. Bearded men wearing all the colors of the rainbow approached the cradle. They sank to their knees and placed packages around the cradle. "We have brought gifts to the Christ Child," one of them said.

The voices of the girls rose in a triumphant finale. "Hallelujah! Hallelujah! Hallelujah!"

Lyng sat without moving. She was roused by a gentle tap on her shoulder.

"Did you enjoy the program?" the woman beside her asked.

"It—it was wonderful," Lyng breathed.

Suddenly everyone was talking. "Santa Claus." His name was being repeated all around Lyng. She became frightened. Her mother had been careful to explain to her and Haakon and Kristian that it was sinful to identify Santa Claus with Christmas, which celebrated the birth of the Savior. She had firmly refused to allow the children to go to see him whenever he appeared at the department stores downtown, or to go with Hattie and Bert when he distributed presents to the poor on Christmas morning. Surely the people of the Franklin Avenue Church didn't believe in Santa Claus or intend to include him in this beautiful Christmas celebration.

Then Lyng almost lost her breath. There he was, dressed exactly as she had seen him in pictures. He was coming down the aisle toward her. Her first impulse was to flee. But before she could make up her mind, Santa Claus was standing at her pew.

"Here are some children who look as though they have been very good," he said in an extremely deep, yet gentle voice. "Let me see. How about you three boys over there?"

"They have been very good," the woman next to Lyng said pleasantly. The boys giggled.

"Then here is a little something for them." Santa Claus handed each boy a package. "And since all three of you have been so very good, my helpers will be around soon with some goodies." Then he turned to Lyng. "And this little girl—I'm sure she deserves a present."

For the life of her, Lyng couldn't make herself refuse the flat package he held out. Instead she grasped it with both hands and stammered, "Thank you, thank you, Santa Claus."

"Oh, you're welcome. You have fine manners, child. Not all boys and girls remember to thank Santa Claus for what he brings them." The boys in Lyng's pew regarded Santa Claus sheepishly. Santa Claus chuckled and went on down the aisle.

One of the boys opened his package. He had gotten a top. In no time he was spinning it on the seat. Lyng watched it admiringly. Haakon and Kristian would have loved a top like that. It was the one thing they had wanted for Christmas this year. But Grandmother Skoglund had knitted warm woolen stockings for them, and her mother had made Sunday suits out of remnants she had bought from customers at the shop. Tante Gunara and

Tante Tallette, who usually remembered the children with some toy for Christmas, had spent all they could afford this year on a pair of shoes for each of them. The battered mouth organ that Tante Tallette had salvaged from a roomer's wastebasket was all they had to play with at home.

"Aren't you going to open your package to find out what Santa Claus brought you?" the woman beside Lyng asked.

"Oh, yes," Lyng said.

Carefully she untied the knots of the string around the package and wound it into a tiny ball. Grandmother Skoglund would be glad to get it for the bedspread she was knitting. Lyng removed the paper wrapping and folded it. That could be used either to wrap up the sandwich that her mother took to the shop for lunch each day or to kindle the fire in the cook stove at home.

The gift was a book with bright red covers. On the front cover, Lyng read the title in gold letters, *A Christmas Carol* by Charles Dickens. She opened the book and turned its pages curiously. First the pictures caught her eye. One showed a man sitting at a desk with an ugly scowl on his face. Near him was another man on a high stool, bending over a table as though he was writing. Another picture showed a man carrying a tiny boy on his shoulder.

Then Lyng turned back to the first page and read, "Marley was dead; to begin with. There is no doubt whatever about that."

Lyng laid the book down in her lap and stroked it lovingly. She had never owned a book written in English before. Neither had anyone else in the family except Tante Tallette, who collected books left by roomers after they had moved away. These Tante Tallette kept locked behind glass doors in the combination folding bed, desk and bookcase, and Lyng had never been allowed to touch them. To be sure, she had studied out of books written in English at school. But the textbooks were usually old, without pictures, and bound in drab gray or brown covers, and they could only be used under the teacher's strict supervision. This brand-new, bright little book with shining gilt letters on its cover and interesting pictures inside was Lyng's very own to be read whenever and wherever she pleased. And it was in English.

In her own church, Lyng had, as her mother had reminded her that afternoon, received a copy of the New Testament. It was a tiny book with fine Norwegian print, and so far Lyng had done nothing with it since she had brought it home. Grandmother

Skoglund had promised that, as soon as she could spare the time, she would sit down and read parts of it aloud.

Lyng loved to hear Grandmother Skoglund read. Her voice was so soothing that listening to her made Lyng feel good all over. Grandmother Skoglund accompanied her reading with explanations of the difficult parts, and when she reached a dramatic climax she used gestures. At such moments, Lyng felt as though the action in the story was really taking place.

I'll ask Grandmother Skoglund to read aloud to me from this book, Lyng thought. Then she remembered that Grandmother Skoglund could read nothing but Norwegian.

"Here are some presents for you from Santa Claus." Fred Sterling and another boy came by, carrying a basket between them, and gave Lyng a bag of candy, an apple and an orange.

"It's nice of you to give me all this when I don't even belong," Lyng said.

"Everybody gets presents at Christmas time whether he belongs or not," Fred Sterling said.

Someone tugged at Lyng's arm. "Come on," Hattie said. "My folks are four rows behind you."

Hattie's mother put her arms around Hattie and kissed her. "Darling, you were wonderful!" she exclaimed. "I declare, you looked so much like a real angel that for a minute you had me scared."

"Did you hear, Hattie? You fooled Ma for only a minute."

"Bert Fleming, you—"

A scuffle followed.

"Didn't your mother and your grandmother come?" Hattie's mother asked. "Hattie said she had invited all of you. I did so want to meet them."

Lyng blushed furiously. "We—we had company," she stammered. "And—and they had to stay home—to wash dishes."

It seemed colder to Lyng on the way home. In spite of the woolen scarf Hattie's mother had insisted on lending her, her teeth chattered.

"I wonder if Tante Gunara and Tante Tallette have gone back to St. Paul. I hope not."

The closer she came to the house, the colder it grew. By the time she had reached the back stoop, Lyng was numb. But before trying the door, she stopped to pull off the scarf. She wound it around her presents and tucked the bundle inside her coat.

The door was not locked. She pushed it open and slipped into the kitchen. It was dark and there was not a sound anywhere in the house. Everyone must have gone to bed. If Lyng undressed in the kitchen and was very quiet, her mother might not hear her. By tomorrow—

"You ungrateful, disobedient child! What have I done that God visits such tribulations upon me?"

In the dark Lyng heard her mother strike a match and by its flickering flame, she lit the small night lamp she held in her hand.

Never in her mother's worst moods had she spoken like this. Speechless and horrified, Lyng gazed at her mother. Her face was outlined by a white, tight-fitting nightcap. Deep shadows streaked her cheeks from which all color was gone. Her eyes looked twice their natural size.

Lyng put her arms protectingly up to her face.

Her mother set the lamp down on the kitchen table. With slow, deliberate motion, she approached Lyng and took her arms in an iron grip. "I'll teach you to disobey me!"

Lyng screamed.

"Reidun!"

Lyng's mother, still keeping her grip on Lyng's arms, turned her head. "This is one time when I shall not tolerate any interference."

Grandmother Skoglund came over to them. "Reidun," she repeated. There was not the slightest trace of fear in her voice.

"Obedience is the first duty of a child toward its parents," Lyng's mother said. She was breathing hard.

"I know, Reidun. Only sometimes we elders forget that the problems of our children are different from our own. And we ask unreasonable things of them."

The pain in Lyng's arms made her tremble, but her mother did not let go of them.

"I want my children to grow up in their own church and to have respect for—"

"You must remember that they are Americans. You can't expect them to have the same feeling for Norway and the Norwegian language that we do. Nor for our Norwegian church. They don't understand the meaning of many of the words in the sermons."

"If they are made to, they will."

"You are too intelligent, Reidun, to believe that such an attitude will bring about good results. Surely you haven't forgotten how bitterly you cried when Markus, your playmate, was not allowed to join you in the schoolroom because he was a peasant. Your father, man of iron though he was, finally gave in. And until you were both confirmed in the village church, you and Markus sat side by side in the schoolroom of the manor house on the Skoglund estate and received instruction together."

"Sometimes I feel that the children are yours more than mine. All except Haakon." Lyng's mother let go her grip on Lyng's arms and backed away from Lyng and Grandmother Skoglund.

"Don't talk like that. Give your children a little more love and a little less—"

"I'm trying to bring them up as Christians."

"Of course, you are. And some day they will appreciate it. Only don't break your heart because the children want their own language in church. And now I think we should all go to bed. There's a draft from the floor and you and I, Reidun, can't afford to take cold."

For a long time after Lyng had crawled into bed, she lay shivering. She remained stiff and motionless, and even tried to control her breathing so her mother wouldn't hear her. When she thought her mother had finally fallen asleep, she dared to curl her legs up under the flannel nightgown. Soon she stopped shivering and she began to feel drowsy.

"Good morning, *Vesla-mi.*"

Grandmother Skoglund was standing at her bedside. Through the heavily frosted window, Lyng could see the weak daylight. Grandmother Skoglund stroked Lyng's tousled hair with one hand, and in the other she held a steaming bowl.

"I brought you some oatmeal *velling.* I thought you might be hungry this morning."

Lyng took the bowl. It was queer how Grandmother Skoglund knew, without being told, what a person needed.

She sat down on Lyng's bed, and after Lyng had eaten the last of the oatmeal *velling,* she took the bowl.

"About—about last night, Lyng," Grandmother Skoglund began.

Lyng pushed herself up against the bed board. Grandmother Skoglund had never called her "Lyng" before. It made her feel grown-up.

"About last night," Grandmother Skoglund repeated. "It would have been better, Lyng, if you had obeyed your mother."

"But I wanted to go, Grandmother Skoglund."

"I know—But maybe—if from now on, you talk things over with me beforehand—we can find some better way out of it."

Lyng's lower lip drooped. "But she always says no."

"Promise me that you will try first anyway," Grandmother Skoglund persisted.

"All right. I promise."

"That's my own Lyng Skoglund. Markus would have been proud of you now."

Lyng pushed away the bedclothes. "You ought to see the presents they gave me last night, Grandmother Skoglund."

Suppose her mother had—no! That would be too terrible. She ran out into the kitchen. Her coat and cap were still on the chair where she had left them, and underneath the coat she found the bundle. Hastily she unwound the scarf Hattie's mother had let her borrow, and inside of it were the orange and the apple and the small bag of candy. And yes, there was the red book with the gilt letters on the front cover.

"See, Grandmother Skoglund," she called out. "It's a real American book. They gave me a real American book at the Franklin Avenue Church last night. And I don't even belong."

Grandmother Skoglund had returned to the kitchen. She took the book out of Lyng's trembling hands.

"It's a very pretty book," she said, examining it curiously. "And such good big letters on the inside, too. If only it had been in Norwegian, I could have—"

"Oh, but Grandmother Skoglund," Lyng interrupted her, speaking eagerly, "I'm going to read it to you. And after I can read English a little better, I'm going to teach you the words."

Grandmother Skoglund put her arm around Lyng's shoulders. Together she and Lyng looked at the first picture: Scrooge and Bob Cratchit in the counting-house. Then from the opposite page Lyng started to read slowly and laboriously:

A CHRISTMAS CAROL
Stave 1
Marley's Ghost

Marley was dead: to begin with. There is no doubt whatever about that.

Charles A. Eastman

from INDIAN BOYHOOD

When Charles Eastman was born into a Santee Sioux tribe in Redwood Falls, Minnesota in 1858, he was named "the pitiful last" because his mother died in his birth, but he was renamed Ohiyesa or "winner" at the age of four. Blessed with an unusually strong and strong-minded grandmother who became his surrogate mother, Eastman survived the hardships of persecution when the Sioux were driven out of Minnesota after the uprising of 1862. At the age of fifteen the young Ohiyesa entered the white man's world and adopted the name Charles Alexander Eastman. He was educated at Dartmouth College and Boston University, receiving his M.D. at the age of thirty-two. He practiced medicine at the Pine Ridge Agency and later at Crow Creek, both in South Dakota. His varied career took him to Washington, where he worked for Indian rights, and during the Coolidge administration he was made United States Indian Inspector. As a child Eastman listened to the legends of his native tribe and when he was in his forties he wrote his recollections of his childhood for his own children. The following selection is from his book Indian Boyhood, *published in 1902. He died in 1939.*

IT IS COMMONLY SUPPOSED that there is no systematic education of their children among the aborigines of this country. Nothing could be farther from the truth. All the customs of this primitive people were held to be divinely instituted, and those in connection with the training of children were scrupulously adhered to and transmitted from one generation to another.

The expectant parents conjointly bent all their efforts to the task of giving the new-comer the best they could gather from a long line of ancestors. A pregnant Indian woman would often choose one of the greatest characters of her family and tribe as a model for her child. This hero was daily called to mind. She would gather from tradition all of his noted deeds and daring exploits, rehearsing them to herself when alone. In order that the impression might be more distinct, she avoided company. She isolated herself as much as possible, and wandered in solitude, not thoughtlessly, but with an eye to the impress given by grand and beautiful scenery.

The Indians believed, also, that certain kinds of animals would confer peculiar gifts upon the unborn, while others would leave so strong an adverse impression that the child might become a monstrosity. A case of hare-lip was commonly attributed to the rabbit. It was said that a rabbit had charmed the mother and given to the babe its own features. Even the meat of certain animals was denied the pregnant woman, because it was supposed to influence the disposition or features of the child.

Scarcely was the embryo warrior ushered into the world, when he was met by lullabies that speak of wonderful exploits in hunting and war. Those ideas which so fully occupied his mother's mind before his birth are now put into words by all about the child, who is as yet quite unresponsive to their appeals to his honor and ambition. He is called the future defender of his people, whose lives may depend upon his courage and skill. If the child is a girl, she is at once addressed as the future mother of a noble race.

In hunting songs, the leading animals are introduced; they come to the boy to offer their bodies for the sustenance of his tribe. The animals are regarded as his friends, and spoken of almost as tribes of people, or as his cousins, grandfathers and grandmothers. The songs of wooing, adapted as lullabies, were equally imaginative, and the suitors were often animals personified, while pretty maidens were represented by the mink and the doe.

Very early, the Indian boy assumed the task of preserving and transmitting the legends of his ancestors and his race. Almost every evening a myth, or a true story of some deed done in the past, was narrated by one of the parents or grandparents, while the boy listened with parted lips and glistening eyes. On the following evening, he was usually required to repeat it. If he was not an apt scholar, he struggled long with his task; but, as a rule, the Indian boy is a good listener and has a good memory, so that the stories were tolerably well mastered. The household became his audience, by which he was alternately criticized and applauded.

This sort of teaching at once enlightens the boy's mind and

stimulates his ambition. His conception of his own future career becomes a vivid and irresistible force. Whatever there is for him to learn must be learned; whatever qualifications are necessary to a truly great man he must seek at any expense of danger and hardship. Such was the feeling of the imaginative and brave young Indian. It became apparent to him in early life that he must accustom himself to rove alone and not to fear or dislike the impression of solitude.

It seems to be a popular idea that all the characteristic skill of the Indian is instinctive and hereditary. This is a mistake. All the stoicism and patience of the Indian are acquired traits, and continual practise alone makes him master of the art of wood-craft. Physical training and dieting were not neglected. I remember that I was not allowed to have beef soup or any warm drink. The soup was for the old men. General rules for the young were never to take their food very hot, nor to drink much water.

My uncle, who educated me up to the age of fifteen years, was a strict disciplinarian and a good teacher. When I left the teepee in the morning, he would say: "Hakadah, look closely to everything you see"; and at evening, on my return, he used often to catechize me for an hour.

"On which side of the trees is the lighter-colored bark? On which side do they have most regular branches?"

It was his custom to let me name all the new birds that I had seen during the day. I would name them according to the color or the shape of the bill or their song or the appearance and locality of the nest—in fact, anything about the bird that impressed me as characteristic. I made many ridiculous errors, I must admit. He then usually informed me of the correct name. Occasionally I made a hit and this he would warmly commend.

He went much deeper into this science when I was a little older, that is, about the age of eight or nine years. He would say, for instance:

"How do you know that there are fish in yonder lake?"

"Because they jump out of the water for flies at mid-day."

He would smile at my prompt but superficial reply.

"What do you think of the little pebbles grouped together under the shallow water? and what made the pretty curved marks in the sandy bottom and the little sand-banks? Where do you find the fish-eating birds? Have the inlet and the outlet of a lake anything to do with the question?"

He did not expect a correct reply at once to all the voluminous questions that he put to me on these occasions, but he meant to make me observant and a good student of nature.

"Hakadah," he would say to me, "you ought to follow the example of the shunktokecha (wolf). Even when he is surprised and runs for his life, he will pause to take one more look at you before he enters his final retreat. So you must take a second look at everything you see.

"It is better to view animals unobserved. I have been a witness to their courtships and their quarrels and have learned many of their secrets in this way. I was once the unseen spectator of a thrilling battle between a pair of grizzly bears and three buffaloes—a rash act for the bears, for it was in the moon of strawberries, when the buffaloes sharpen and polish their horns for bloody contests among themselves.

"I advise you, my boy, never to approach a grizzly's den from the front, but to steal up behind and throw your blanket or a stone in front of the hole. He does not usually rush for it, but first puts his head out and listens and then comes out very indifferently and sits on his haunches on the mound in front of the hold before he makes any attack. While he is exposing himself in this fashion, aim at his heart. Always be as cool as the animal himself." Thus he armed me against the cunning of savage beasts by teaching me how to outwit them.

"In hunting," he would resume, "you will be guided by the habits of the animal you seek. Remember that a moose stays in swampy or low land or between high mountains near a spring or lake, for thirty to sixty days at a time. Most large game moves about continually, except the doe in the spring; it is then a very easy matter to find her with the fawn. Conceal yourself in a convenient place as soon as you observe any signs of the presence of either, and then call with your birchen doe-caller.

"Whichever one hears you first will soon appear in your neighborhood. But you must be very watchful, or you may be made a fawn of by a large wild-cat. They understand the characteristic call of the doe perfectly well.

"When you have any difficulty with a bear or a wild-cat—that is, if the creature shows signs of attacking you—you must make him fully understand that you have seen him and are aware of his intentions. If you are not well equipped for a pitched battle, the only way to make him retreat is to take a long sharp-pointed pole for a spear and rush toward him. No wild beast will face this unless he is cornered and already wounded. These fierce beasts are generally afraid of the common weapon of the larger animals — the horns, and if these are very long and sharp, they dare not risk an open fight.

"There is one exception to this rule—the grey wolf will attack fiercely when very hungry. But their courage depends upon their numbers; in this they are like white men. One wolf or two will never attack a man. They will stampede a herd of buffaloes in order to get at the calves; they will rush upon a herd of antelopes, for these are helpless; but they are always careful about attacking man."

Of this nature were the instructions of my uncle, who was widely known at that time as among the greatest hunters of his tribe.

All boys were expected to endure hardship without complaint. In savage warfare, a young man must, of course, be an athlete and used to undergoing all sorts of privations. He must be able to go without food and water for two or three days without displaying any weakness, or to run for a day and a night without any rest. He must be able to traverse a pathless and wild country without losing his way either in the day or night time. He cannot refuse to do any of these things if he aspires to be a warrior.

Sometimes my uncle would waken me very early in the morning and challenge me to fast with him all day. I had to accept the challenge. We blackened our faces with charcoal, so that every boy in the village would know that I was fasting for the day. Then the little tempters would make my life a misery until the merciful sun hid behind the western hills.

I can scarcely recall the time when my stern teacher began to give sudden war-whoops over my head in the morning while I was sound asleep. He expected me to leap up with perfect presence of mind, always ready to grasp a weapon of some sort and to give a shrill whoop in reply. If I was sleepy or startled and hardly knew what I was about, he would ridicule me and say that I need never expect to sell my scalp dear. Often he would vary these tactics by shooting off his gun just outside of the lodge while I was yet asleep, at the same time giving blood-curdling yells. After a time I became used to this.

When Indians went upon the war-path, it was their custom to try the new warriors thoroughly before coming to an engagement. For instance, when they were near a hostile camp, they would select the novices to go after the water and make them do all sorts of things to prove their courage. In accordance with this idea, my uncle used to send me off after water when we camped after dark in a strange place. Perhaps the country was full of wild beasts, and, for aught I knew, there might be scouts from hostile bands of Indians lurking in that very neighborhood.

Yet I never objected, for that would show cowardice. I picked my way through the woods, dipped my pail in the water and hurried back, always careful to make as little noise as a cat. Being only a boy, my heart would leap at every crackling of a dry twig or distant hooting of an owl, until, at last, I reached our teepee. Then my uncle would perhaps say: "Ah, Hakadah, you are a thorough warrior," empty out the precious contents of the pail, and order me to go a second time.

Imagine how I felt! But I wished to be a brave man as much as a white boy desires to be a great lawyer or even President of the United States. Silently I would take the pail and endeavor to retrace my footsteps in the dark.

With all this, our manners and morals were not neglected. I was made to respect the adults and especially the aged. I was not allowed to join in their discussions, nor even to speak in their presence, unless requested to do so. Indian etiquette was very strict, and among the requirements was that of avoiding the direct address. A term of relationship or some title of courtesy was commonly used instead of the personal name by those who wished to show respect. We were taught generosity to the poor and reverence for the "Great Mystery." Religion was the basis of all Indian training.

I recall to the present day some of the kind warnings and re-proofs that my good grandmother was wont to give me. "Be strong of heart—be patient!" she used to say. She told me of a young chief who was noted for his uncontrollable temper. While in one of his rages he attempted to kill a woman, for which he was slain by his own band and left unburied as a mark of disgrace— his body was simply covered with green grass. If I ever lost my temper, she would say:

"Hakadah, control yourself, or you will be like that young man I told you of, and lie under a *green blanket!*"

In the old days, no young man was allowed to use tobacco in any form until he had become an acknowledged warrior and had achieved a record. If a youth should seek a wife before he had reached the age of twenty-two or twenty-three, and been recognized as a brave man, he was sneered at and considered an ill-bred Indian. He must also be a skillful hunter. An Indian cannot be a good husband unless he brings home plenty of game.

These precepts were in the line of our training for the wild life.

Shirley Schoonover

from MOUNTAIN OF WINTER

In "Route I, Box 111, Aurora" Shirley Schoonover says, "The snows of my childhood came shaking down the sky, mute thunderstorms that shawled the trees and capped the fence posts." Memories of a northern childhood in her community of Finns, in Biwabik on the Iron Range, permeate her novel Mountain of Winter. *Schoonover attended public schools there and later the University of Minnesota and the University of Nebraska. A number of her short stories have been published, and two of them have won O. Henry Awards. Her second novel,* Sam's Song, *was published in 1969. She has taught creative writing at the University of Rochester.*

T HE DAY WAS intensely clear, making Old Big look deceptively close and mild. They ran through the pasture, galloped up the sloping turf and slid under the barbed-wire fence. Free of the farm now, they entered the outlying fringes of the black woods, walking beneath the few silver poplars that stood just at the edge of the wood. They followed the old lumber trail, going in and out of the early sunlight that already burned the dew off the grass. Following the trail made the walking easy and they chattered back and forth, certain that they would climb to the top of Old Big by nightfall.

"How'll we come back down?" Piss-ant asked.

"Well, you nut. It'll be a lot easier coming downhill. We'll just run all the way back down." She was confident that she'd know the way down, for wouldn't it be easy to see the lights of the farm from the top of Old Big?

The trail ended in a patch of torn-up bushes and tree stumps that Ava's father had cut down. The children went past this place into the deeper shadows of the black wood. They walked in knee-deep moss that held sweet and jeweled water, the drops glittering in the half light. Ava stooped. "Hey, look at this." She touched a small plant that stood six inches high.

"What?"

"Pitcher plant. It catches flies and eats them." She demonstrated by running her finger down the slender green throat of the plant. True enough, the plant was shaped like a small pitcher with water inside. "It doesn't grab at bugs. See, it has water in here and the flies and bugs come to drink. But they can't get out again because these little hairs point down at them." Ava stuck her finger down into the pitcher's bottom, stroking the silver hairs that lined the green throat. "That's the flower part there," she said, holding her other hand out to a flat green blossom that had leathery, almost crisp petals.

"Why don't the flies just fly out?" Piss-ant asked.

"They can't. Dumbhead, they walk down on the hairs and slide into the water. Flies can't fly if their wings are wet, and these hairs point down so they can't get ahold with their feet."

"Mphm." Piss-ant wasn't impressed. "Rather see a real mean plant that grabs at things. This only sits around."

"Well, it gets its bugs that way."

"How'd you know? You a wizard or somep'n?"

"No. Mummu read about it to me in her Nature Book. You know. The one in the fancy glass-door cabinet. Know something else? She read me a long story-poem about the heroes of Kalevala. I bet they live up on Old Big. I seen their lights in the sky last winter, those Northern Lights." She whispered, "That's why we're going up Old Big. I wanta see them up close."

Piss-ant's eyes grew big and serious. "You mean it? Heroes? Like giants?"

"Yeah. Vainomoinen was the best one. Boy, he did all kinds of adventures."

"Did he fight any monsters?"

"Yeah. Kalma. He was a bugger that lived under the water of Lake Tuonela. He's always trying to kill Vainomoinen."

"Jeez. What'd he look like?"

"All black." Ava was inventing now, to keep Piss-ant interested in the long walk ahead of them. "All black with a gray face. And no eyes, just deep holes in his head. And he's cold. Clammy, you know, like a dead fish."

Piss-ant shuddered appreciatively. "He's up there, too?"

"I don't know. I guess."

"Oh." He regarded her with suspicion. "How'd you know that other guy lives up there?"

Ava curled her lip scornfully. "Where else would he live? In a house? He's ten feet tall, I bet."

Piss-ant scratched his head and looked around. "My feet are cold and wet. Ain't there no better way to go but through all this wet stuff?"

"Yeah. But I got a little lost. We'll find the dry part soon."

They set off again, looking for dry ground. A flock of crows flew up sharply, startling them until Ava waved an arm in recognition. "Noisy old crows," she scolded. The crows called to one another and flew off, their racket fading with distance. Ava found a rabbit trail and they turned onto it. "Rabbits know the fastest way around in these woods." They came to higher ground and left the moss, now walking amid the black-green shadows. The ground here was soft, ankle-deep with pine needles. Ava paused beneath a tree and picked up a small furry object, holding it out to Piss-ant.

"What's that?" he asked.

"Owls live around here. This is a kind of cud that owls spit up. When they eat a mouse or rabbit they almost eat it whole and then spit up the fur and bones. This must've been a mouse."

Piss-ant took the dry, fragile cluster of fur and tiny bones. "Jeez, that old owl must've had a big belly to gobble up a whole mouse in one bite."

"Oh, that's only a snack. You should see the rabbits a big owl can stuff away. Pa said he bets a big owl could take a fifteen-pound rabbit easy."

"Don't the rabbits scratch awful, though?" Piss-ant was remembering the large jackrabbit Ava had caught last summer, and how that rabbit had clawed her arms when she had picked it up by the ears.

"They don't get a chance to scratch. The owl flies down real quiet and just grabs them on the back and flies away. The rabbits scream so bad it hurts your ears."

Piss-ant urged her on. "What else do they do? Do they peck out the eyes?"

"Ah no, the owl takes the rabbit to its nest up in a tree and just kills it." Ava glanced upward, trying to find the sun. "Let's eat our lunch and get started. Don't wanta fool away any more time gabbing." They munched a sweet roll apiece and set out again. Ava saved two rolls for the afternoon, in case they might get hungry again. They jogtrotted along the firm ground, not talking, saving their breath to work up the side of the mountain. When they came to a clear place Ava went up a tree to see how much farther they had to go.

"Well?" Piss-ant asked when she came down.

"I don't think it's very far anymore. I couldn't see the top any from here. But that's because of the trees in the way." She paused for breath, eying the sun that was sliding over the western shoulder of the mountain. "Remember, when we started we knew the top was just on the other side of this woods? Well, I bet we only have a half mile to go and we'll be there."

But she was thinking that they could go straight up the mountain as a crow flies. She didn't realize that they could not go straight up but would have to work at an angle, turning back and forth to work up the side of the mountain. It would take an adult on horseback days to climb that side of the mountain. But she didn't know this, so they began walking again.

By the time the sky had turned a citron green of sundown the children were tired and cranky. They had eaten the last of the sweet rolls and had drunk from a lake they had found. They kept walking, although Piss-ant complained of blisters on his heels, for Ava was sure that once they came to the upper edge of the black woods they would be within reach of the summit of Old Big.

"Hell, Ava. When're we going to get out of this woods?"

"Any minute. Shut up and keep walking." She was impatient and beginning to wonder about the size of this old mountain. She didn't want to spend the night in these black woods, and she hurried Piss-ant along.

Night fell suddenly. All the light went out of the sky and the forest was truly black now, full of silence. Ava walked uneasily, wishing they would come out from this dark place. At least a clearing wouldn't be so full of blackness, she thought, biting her lip.

Piss-ant crept up behind her and grabbed the belt of her pants. She squalled and twitched around. "Don't grab at a person like that!"

"I got lonesome all of a sudden," Piss-ant explained.

"Oh. Well, I know." She let him hang on to her belt, relieved by his physical nearness. They walked along for some distance, skirting the darkest places in the woods. Piss-ant kept crowding up behind her and tripping her heels. She took his hand and they walked side by side, staring into the darkness, listening now for any sound. But it was all silence upon silence, for no bird sang, no crow shrieked imperiously from the treetops. Ava's hide began to prickle with apprehension. She had not wanted to be up here at night, not in these trees, she realized; and her chest shriveled so that breathing was hard. She hunched her shoulders and peered ahead, avoiding the darkest shadows.

Piss-ant said, "Wait a minute. What's that up there?"

"Where?" Ava looked around, upward.

They had come into a small clear place. As she looked, the moon flew up out of the treetops, thin as a curved needle but infinitely bright.

"Oh, it's the moon," Piss-ant said, disappointed. "I saw a light coming from those trees. I thought it was home."

"Couldn't be home," Ava said, a little scornfully. "Home's back down there."

"Well, why don't we go back? I ain't in the mood to climb this damn mountain anymore."

Ava, too, wanted to go home. She thought a minute. "I'll go up one of these trees and see where it is. Then we'll just run back downhill." She went up the tree in a hurry until she had come to the place where the tree swayed back and forth like a pendulum with her weight. She shimmied around to look down the side of the mountain and strained her eyes to see the lights from home. There were none. She caught her breath and looked harder. She scanned the entire horizon of black treetops and could see no glimmer of light. Only stars were there and they looked coldly back at her. She let herself cry a little up there in the tree so Piss-ant couldn't hear her, then she went slowly back down to the ground.

Piss-ant had cuddled up to the tree trunk, waiting for her. "Is it far?" he asked anxiously.

Ava was silent. She sat down next to him in the soft needle cover beneath the tree.

"Huh, Ava?"

"I couldn't find any lights."

"Did you look hard?" He searched her face to see if she was lying.

"Yeah. My eyes almost fell out of my head, I looked so hard."

They were quiet for a moment. The forest drew close to them and they could feel an immense breathing go through the trees. Piss-ant snuggled up to Ava, burrowing his head into her chest. "What'll we do?" he asked.

"Well, let's yell for Pa. He might be looking for us already. And he'd hear us." Ava put her hands to her mouth and yelled, "Pa-ah!"

The breath of the forest carried her voice out and down, spinning it along through the trees. An echo came back to them, Ah-Aah!

They took turns calling; calling and then listening. The echo always answered, eerily coming from some place deeper in the forest.

Then a sound came to them, the shrieking laughter of a loon, and it shattered the night around them. Both children flinched and grabbed each other. "What was that?" Piss-ant whispered.

"A loon, I think."

The echo laughed mockingly through the forest and Piss-ant said, "Let's don't yell anymore. It don't like it."

Ava agreed and they sat together under the tree, staring out at the dark around them. The moon made too many shadows and the forest breathed too chilly and close. Ava said, "Let's find another place to sit. Where it's lighter." Piss-ant followed her and they stepped into the small clearing. They walked a few small steps and paused while Ava squinted around for a place. From behind them a loud thrumming, beating sound started. Ava half turned and yelped. A huge, tall black something flew at them, was on top of them, clawing at Piss-ant's bald head, pummeling Ava's face with harsh wings. All Ava saw was a dark shape with glowing hollow eyes. She squawked and broke for the woods. Piss-ant, clutching her belt, ran blindly after her.

They fell down under a low-branched pine tree, huddling together, too scared to move. "It got me, Ava. I'm bloody." True enough, the owl, for that's what had attacked them, had scratched Piss-ant's head, leaving deep cuts. Now the blood trickled into his eyes. Ava wiped his face with pine needles. "Boy, that was a monster—*hey*, like you were telling about!"

"*Shh.* Let's sit quiet until it's gone for sure."

They sat motionless, staring out from their covert; silence had returned to the black woods. "I'm gonna yell for Pa again. Maybe it can't find us in here." She began calling in a soft, high voice,

"Pa-ah!" She made her voice stretch the sounds so that they would fall a little longer on the waiting air. She imagined that she could throw the words so lightly that they would cast a thread of sound through the darkness, and that that sound would loop and fall over her father (who was surely looking for them by now). She listened for the echo to come back before she called again, afraid if she broke the silence too often that from somewhere in the alleys of these black trees the loon would be aroused to shouting its vindictive laugh. Or that the dark shape would find them. But the loon was still. Ava called and called, listening always for the echo, and for some response from down the mountain.

Finally, as she began to fall into a half dream that held only her outgoing voice and the darkness, the night changed around her. A flickering, swinging light came along the floor of the forest. She called, loudly, to bring the light nearer. "Pa-ah!"

It was her father, carrying a lantern; the yellow circle of light advanced and stopped as he listened, then came straight toward her.

She flung herself at him, glad to hang on, smelling the warmly familiar tobacco-sweat scent of him. He put the lantern down and hugged her, then hugged Piss-ant. "You shouldn't of come up here so far," he began to scold.

"Boy, I'm glad you got here!" Piss-ant yelped. "That Kalma guy chased us. He got me all bloody!"

"You been telling him scarey stories, Ava."

"No, I never. Look at the cut on his head."

Juha lifted the lantern and looked at Piss-ant's skull. "Owl did that. Saw that fuzzy head 'n' thought you were a rabbit." He took Ava's hand. "Hold on to Ava, Joel. Get you home before any more owls grab you."

At home in the snug kitchen they were fed, washed, spanked and scolded. "And you don't set foot past those fences, understand?" But they were asleep at the table and Old Big was far away.

Mary Hedin

PLACES WE LOST

Mary Hedin was born in Minneapolis in 1924, attended Minneapolis public schools, and was graduated from Minnehaha Academy in 1941. In 1946 she received her B.S. from the University of Minnesota and subsequently a Masters of Language Arts degree from the State University of San Francisco in California. Hedin has written from her early years. The first poem that she remembers well was written when she was in second grade at Northrop Elementary School and her first published work appeared in the American Junior Scholar *when she was sixteen. Her prose has been included in the* Best American Short Stories of 1966 *and the* O. Henry Prize Stories of 1978 *and in literary and popular magazines. Her poetry has appeared in literary journals and anthologies. Hedin has been a member of the Humanities Department of the College of Marin in California for a number of years.*

T HAT HOUSE was more than ordinarily loved. My father had built and sold houses all over the south side of Minneapolis. Almost every year, we had moved into and out of one of them. Move in, fix it up, sell it. That was the pattern. But that house was built just for us. It was a high-gabled, English country-style house, and when we moved in, Mother announced that that was it. She had had her fill of moving, and she had things just the way she wanted them there, from the clever limed-oak phone niche in the hall to the breakfast nook with its trestle table and built-in benches.

Four years later, we were in the middle of the Depression. My father no longer built houses. He worked at intervals for a sash-and-door shop. Mostly he was home. In those days, shabby-looking men knocked on our door and asked for food, and abandoned cats howled in the alleys at night.

In spite of that, we children did not understand. Buddy was

still a baby, and Jenny and I were fed. We were clothed. We heard the words—Depression, breadlines, WPA, Mecklenburg scrip. They had a grand and mysterious sound, and we did not comprehend them. When Father announced, one day, that the sash-and-door shop had closed, it meant less to us than the quick change in weather that was moving March from winter into spring.

Then, on a Friday night in May, an evening warmer than the calendar allowed, Jenny and I grew keenly aware of the change and loss threatening us all. That it came then, on the same night that Jenny came to something else, launching the risk and deceit which harmed us all, was not, perhaps, entirely coincidental.

Usually, Jenny and I were among the first to be called home from the evening games. That night, no one called us. We marveled, at first, at our unexpected freedom. We played Kick the Can furiously as the evening turned dusky, crowding the last minutes with the greatest amount of pleasure. Even after most of the children had gone home and we were much too tired, we played on. At last, there were just three of us—Jenny and I and Carrie Bergman, whose parents had gone to church and didn't know she was out.

We huddled by the telephone pole that had been goal and watched the final excessive blooming of stars in the altogether darkened skies. Still no one called. Jenny looked at me, caught between wanting to be called and wanting to stay there in the dew-sharpened, strange night air. The trees were high black shadows against the lighted sky. Beneath them, fireflies scudded over an unseen earth. Down the avenue, the houses in formal rows were large and remote from us. At last, our sense of freedom grew so immense that we were strange in it, unsure of it, and wanted to escape before it swept us toward things we only sensed and did not wish to know.

"Let's go," Jenny whispered. "Let's go," Carrie agreed.

We turned and ran our separate ways. I clutched Jenny's hand and pulled her as fast as I could down the alley, across the grass, up the concrete walk to our back door. The house was still there. The kitchen windows facing the alley were dark, but the double windows of the dining room gave out an old light. Seeing that, I knew that part of the thumping of my chest, there in the enlarged darkness, was caused by the notion that house and parents might have disappeared into the great, dark night.

But I stopped when we reached the steps. We were out too late.

I knew that. "Jenny, did you hear Mother calling us?" I whispered.

"No, she didn't," Jenny warbled. "She never called us."

"Jenny, we're going to get spanked." I was gloomily sure of it.

Jenny stood still, considering. The crickets' warnings riddled the dark. Finally, she tugged like a fish at the hand in which I still held hers. "Come on," she said carelessly. "Let's go in."

"We'll get spanked," I repeated.

Jenny tossed her head. The fair hair moved like wind in the scant light. "Well, I don't care. I'm going in. Come on, Berit. Let's go." She started up the steps; but on the second one, she stopped. Her hand left mine. Her head leaned toward the night. "Shh," she whispered. "Listen."

I stopped. I waited. I heard nothing. "What? What do you hear?"

"Shh," Jenny whispered again.

Then I heard it, the faint, fine tissue of sound, a thin belling of woe, moving without source into and out of the night.

The sound came again, and we both knew it for what it was. Tenderness quavered out of Jenny's throat in a whispered, half-sung cry. "A kitten. It's a kitten." She went blindly from me towards whatever dark place she thought the sound came from, crooning, "Here, kitty, kitty. Here, kitty." I could hear, in the quick, breathless callings, that extravagance of love which was Jenny's gift and liability and which poured from her toward any small furred thing she ever saw.

Plaintive, haunting mews were coming in answer to her calls. Then both murmurs and mewing ceased, and Jenny stood beside me, holding something against her chest. "Look at him, Berit. Oh, look at him, how tiny he is."

I could not see the kitten in the darkness but she couldn't keep him, anyway. She knew that. She was always bringing home hungry cats, and Father never let her keep one. "Put him down, Jenny. Come on. We have to go in."

"He's so tiny, Berit. Look. He's lost, Berit, poor little thing."

I heard the small, rich thrum, the purring. I started up the steps saying, "Put him down, Jenny," and she came after me and didn't put the kitten down. I stopped outside the door, the knob cold and damp in my hand.

"I'm going to ask," Jenny said. The dark prevented seeing; but I knew from the sound of her slow, soft words that in her wide eyes there was that look of determination I was never able to defeat. I wiped my palm against my skirt and pulled open the door.

The weathers of my father's nature blew violently from sublimity and joy to outrage and despair. His knobby, sharp-boned face was seamed and creased by his moods, as lands are marked by their climates' demands. To hear my father angry did not astonish. To hear him shouting at Mother gave room for apprehension. But she, who usually would not speak to him unless he was calm, was answering his anger with anger equal to his own, her voice raised to a near shout. In bewilderment, we both stopped on the dark side of the dining-room door.

"Don't be so unreasonable, Emma!" he shouted. "It has to be done."

"No. I will not let you."

"We have to live. It's that simple. What do you think we'll eat? Leaves off the trees, perhaps?"

"Not the house," Mother cried in a loud, sharp voice. "We don't have to sell the house. We're eating. We're not starving. Not the house!" She sat at the table, the light of the dining-room fixture falling on her coppery hair, her face now lowered into her covering hands.

My father paced around her, circling the round oak table, stopping to lean over her bowed body, and shouting into her ears. "Not starving! Not starving, she says!" With each word, he stabbed the air in front of her with a thrust-out forefinger. "Women! Masters of logic! We'll live in a nice house. We'll walk around with empty bellies, and then, when it's too late, we'll lose the house, anyway. We'll see the day the bank forecloses, that's how it will be!"

From the dark kitchen we watched, trying to find meaning in the storm of words. Why would we sell the house? How could you lose a house? Where would we be if we were not there in that house?

My mother dropped her hands from a pale face in which her eyes were two places of darkness. Then she stood up and put that white face close to my father's red knotted one and shouted, "No. No. No."

His mouth snapped like a trap. His lids slitted down against his eyes' fury. His brows were one black streak across a blazing forehead. Overhead, the light fixture still trembled with the shouts, which had frozen now into total silence. Under the flickering, fragmented light, they stood dumbly unyielding, unforgiving, sudden hate flung up between them that grew into a wall of silence, from which neither could move and which neither could destroy.

In that cold, walled silence, the breaths I drew shook past a thick tongue and a closed throat. Against my arm, Jenny's arm trembled with dismay, and we stood locked, two small girls caught on the outer edge of their anger.

Then, in Jenny's arms, the kitten stirred; lifted a small, sleepy head; mewed faintly.

Both faces turned toward the door, turned from anger to remembrance and surprise.

"What are you girls doing here?" My father's bellow was a lesser anger. "Why aren't you in bed?" Then his black brows rode up, up on his corrugated forehead. His eyes pulled wide open. "What's that?" he shouted. "Get that cat out of here!"

In spite of all, Jenny's desire gave sufficient courage. "I thought we could keep—" she ventured, on a high, frail note.

"Get that cat out of here!" He plunged around the table toward us.

We stumbled back toward the safe dark behind us.

But Mother had already wheeled from her place, and she came to us with her arms spread, like a winged, red-haired angel. She swept both of us away in the white arc of her arms, away from my black-browed, bellowing father, crying over her turned, sharply defying shoulder, "Stop shouting at the children." His huge fist crashed upon the shining table as she herded us through the kitchen to the back door, where Jenny lowered her arms and gave up the tiny kitten to the larger, cold night.

Upstairs in our bed, we lay cradled in each other's comfortless arms. Jenny's tears dampened the pillow beneath my cheek. Her questions—"Berit, where will the kitten go? How will we lose the house, Berit? Foreclosure, does that hurt much? Berit, do you think the kitten will die?"—went with us unanswered, threatening, even as we moved hopeless, helpless, into the distance of sleep.

I awakened to total quiet. The light of a late-rising moon had taken our room. Black shadows of quivering leaves flickered in changing patterns against the white wall. Even before I reached out, I knew that the place beside me was empty. Jenny was gone. I listened. I felt the empty space. I raised up on one elbow, looked about the room. "Jenny?" I whispered.

No answer. Had she gone for a drink? To the bathroom? I listened for the sound of running water, for the flush. I heard no sound. I shook the sheet from my legs. I got up. Gooseflesh fled along my arms, between my shoulders. I tiptoed around the bed. My shadow grew long and strange upon the white wall and moved before me as I left the room. I went along the hall, down the stairs, stopped at the bottom. From my parents' room, the usual deep-drawn breaths issued in forgetful counterpoint.

"Jenny?" The whisper met with consuming silence. I dared once more. "Jenny?"

There was a tick of noise in the kitchen. A door? Opening? Closing? Then I heard the tiny, singing wire of sound. The kitten. I slipped over the smooth, moon-sheathed linoleum floor to the back door.

The moonlight lay like water upon the concrete steps. Its light made a clearness deprived of detail, sharper than reality. Jenny crouched on the step, her long hair fallen past her face so that its ends swept the glittering steps. Her arms were lifted from her sides, and the curve of her hands was shaped to the saucer's circle. The tiny kitten, spraddle-legged and quivering, looked frail and blue in the moon's light, fumbling at the offered milk.

She had not heard me. I looked down on her and the kitten, set there like a carving in the wash of light. I gave up a giggle. "Jenny," I scolded, "what are you doing?"

She turned her face to me, looked at me, not surprised, but with absolute assurance, as though getting up in a deserted, half-finished night to feed a stray kitten she could not keep was an entirely reasonable and expected action. "He's hungry." Her lips fluttered between smiles and woe. As she turned back to the kitten, the silvered sheath of her hair fell again over the curve of her cheek, hiding the look on her face as whispered petals of love and comfort fell from the kitten's peaked, attentive ears. The fear and unhappiness from which we had taken our sleep were gone. Watching her there, sturdy and strange in the moon-whitened gown that covered even her human feet, I took from her the tiny blue kitten, the lapping tides of stirring moon-watered air, forgetfulness and wonder for myself.

But in the day that followed, and in the long, tense days following it, there was little such relief. A great silence stood between my mother and my father, and it was not peace. Whatever occasional dialogue went between them began abruptly, ended impotently.

Each day, Father walked the long way to the Loop. Late in the afternoon, he pulled open the back door, shrugged his coat from weary, humped shoulders, and dropped it to the bench in the breakfast nook. Like someone very old, cautious of his aches, he lowered himself down beside it. Mother set a dishpan full of water on the green linoleum floor in front of him. He tugged at stiff shoes, sticky socks. He dropped his hot, abused feet into the water, moved his toes, groaned. He leaned his elbows on the table, his head on his hands, and growled out tales of jobs gone, homes lost, businesses closed. "America, America," he muttered, with contempt and bitterness clogging his throat. "Land of broken promise." On the radio, Father Coughlin's speeches, dreary stock quotations, glum news reports fed his despair.

And Mother turned only silence against his words. Hearing his grim, unpatriotic speeches, she suffered, perhaps, the pain and embarrassment burning in me. When he was away, she attacked her chores as though she were fighting a battle involving dust mops and laundry tubs and vacuum cleaners. She didn't walk; she ran, as if victory depended on vigilance, and I knew the battle she waged somehow involved her differences with my father. Buddy was cutting his molars, and when she sang comforting, foolish rhymes to him, rocking him toward rest he could not find, her own face held weariness and pain.

But that she hid from Father. She turned toward him a cool, impersonal mask, and he showed her a constant, impersonal and frowning bitterness. They remained if not enemies, antagonists, keeping mind and flesh and soul to resistance.

Jenny paid no attention to their warfares. The kitten had claimed her, and there was room in her thoughts only for it, how to care for it, how to keep it for her own. The Saturday morning after that moonlit night, she found a cardboard box in the basement. She sneaked rags out of Mother's ragbag. She tucked the box with its nest of rags in a green hollow of the wild honeysuckle crowding the corner of the empty lot next door. She smuggled milk out to it.

From then on, each morning when we started down the alley to school, I had to wait on the damp concrete, shivers riding up and down my legs, while she crept through the dew-wet branches to see the kitten and leave it bits of her lunch.

When we got home in the afternoon, she poured herself a glass of milk and went out on the back steps to drink it. In a few minutes, she brought the emptied glass back to the sink, and then she was gone. I knew she was going to the kitten's hiding place with a jar of milk held against her stomach. And the kitten seemed to know. At least, it made that bush its home and did not betray Jenny by following her home, as kittens usually do.

At first, the necessary deception cost Jenny something. There were fever and shyness in her darkened eyes; a deepened color burned her cheeks, and it seemed that the demands of conscience gave off the same signs of danger as disease. Or perhaps the burning of cheek and eye was, even in the beginning, not the mark of guilt, but only a sign of the heart's whole mission. At any rate, she was changed, and I thought someone ought to notice other than me. No one did.

The passions my parents themselves were enduring took from them their ordinary perceptions. Jenny went her dedicated, deceitful way. I warned her, and scolded her, and worried, and Jenny ignored all that.

On the last Sunday in May, I went down the stairs into the kitchen full of morning sun. I felt at once, in spite of that wealth of brilliant light, that the air was drained and empty. My mother stood by the stove as though she leaned on the spoon moving slowly through the pan of oatmeal. In the heaviness of lids lying over her inward-looking eyes, in the droop of her head, there was defeat.

My father leaned over the Sunday paper, spread out upon the trestle table. He looked up; his brows lifted; his teeth gleamed in a showy smile. "Well, there's a fine sleepyhead!" His laugh was loud and not free.

I knew the fine show was for Mother and she was getting no comfort or amusement from it. I could not laugh and only blushed. Father picked up the funnies he never allowed us to see until after we were home from church. He gave them to me, and I held them and looked at the gaudy, foolish colors and didn't feel like reading them.

"When is he coming?" my mother said, her eyes not lifting from the spoon.

I looked up from the funnies and out the window at the quiet yellow morning and saw Jenny wandering down the alley in her red sweater, her head bent toward the kitten in her arms.

"This afternoon," Father answered, and he looked out the window and saw Jenny, too. "Whose cat is that?" he shouted, his anger easier and truer than his joy had been.

I jumped, hesitated, and found deception easy enough to practice. "I think it's Carrie Wallstrom's," I murmured, and, suffering, went and took Buddy, where he leaned from Mother's hip, drooling on his fresh shirt. "Stop that, Buddy," I fussed, and wiped away the bubbles he blew from his wet, laughing mouth.

My father studied the paper again. "Stop acting as though it's my fault!" he suddenly shouted.

My mother's hand dropped the spoon and fell to her side. She stood with her head lowered to her chest and turned away from us. My father stood up, looked at her, and stomped out of the kitchen, down the basement stairs, banging the doors behind him . . .

It was noon, and we were eating lunch in the breakfast nook when the doorbell rang.

"That will be Johnson," Father announced. There was warning in the river of his voice. His brown eye shone at Mother.

She did not look up to see it, but the spoonful of custard she was lifting toward Buddy's wide-open mouth stopped in midair. Buddy's mouth stretched a wide and wider O. Suddenly it blared out a great, wounded bellow. Mother jumped. She popped the spoon into Buddy's mouth. The howl split off. Father went from the kitchen, and Mother began to shovel the filled spoon at Buddy's mouth faster than he could swallow.

"Hurry, girls," she rushed us. Her red head dipped toward the dining-room door. "Shush, girls," she hushed us.

The voice joining my father's was a high-pitched man's voice, with a singsong motion to it that hid its sense.

But Father's bugle-noted words came clear. "The floors," he said. "The floors are of first-grade oak. And the hardware. Throughout the house, the finest. Look at that fireplace. Wisconsin stone. Had the best mason in the business lay that fireplace. See how those edges join? Beautiful. The dining room," he said. "Fourteen by sixteen."

They came into the kitchen, my father walking with arms folded across his chest, the rolled sleeves of his shirt showing the muscle lying smooth and heavy beneath the browned skin, his jaw out, his mouth stern and glad. Beside him was a taller man, thin in the body and loose-looking under the pin-striped cloth of his suit. His long legs lifted and dropped in a slow, light step, like the legs of a water spider. His oiled cap of gray hair lay flat and smooth over a crown that was as oval as an egg.

"Mr. Johnson, my wife." My father's smile was for Johnson, his frown for Mother.

"How do you do," my mother answered, and her tone was light and armored. She moved from table to sink like a dancer, with dirty dishes in her hands.

Mr. Johnson looked down from his high place. His face slipped into and out of a quick, promising, unreliable smile. His small, light eyes ran from corner to corner, taking in the whole room.

"Inlaid linoleum," my father said, looking coldly at my mother's straight back.

"Ah, yes." Mr. Johnson paused. "The stove should go with, of course," he said. "It fits so nicely there."

There was a jerk in the arc of my mother's arm as she lifted plates from the table. "We'll keep the stove," she said.

Johnson looked at my father. His smile, tolerant and fluid, slid over his face.

A band of red flared across my father's high-boned cheeks and took his ears. "There are plenty of cupboards," he said. "Look at this large storage closet."

"That comfy breakfast nook should catch someone's fancy." Johnson's chant was comforting.

They went to tour the bedrooms.

Afterward, my father came back to the kitchen. He sat down on one of the benches by the trestle table in the nook and looked out the white-curtained window at the leaves of the one great oak tree, holding the sun sharply on their scalloped edges. He looked at the leaves as though he needed to study the intricacies of their twined and shadowed shapes. And he said nothing at all.

My mother went to the table. She put her hands on the table's edge. Now she looked down on Father as though she were a teacher and he a recalcitrant student. "Well, what did he say?"

My father looked not at her, but only into the dense clusters of leaves. "Forty-five hundred. He says forty-five hundred."

My mother's hands dropped from the table's edge, went to her sides, came up again, and sat on her hipbones in the shape of fists. Her lips pouted with contempt. Her chin lifted. She stared down at Father. The light in her eyes snapped out at him. Her hair and cheeks looked on fire. She stood there growing straighter and taller and blazing more vividly with each short moment until she burst into rocketing words.

"Forty-five hundred? Forty-five hundred dollars? Why, that's ridiculous! It cost that much to build. That doesn't even allow for labor! What about that? Isn't your labor worth anything? If that Mr. Johnson thinks we're going to sell this house at a price like that, he's mistaken, that's what he is! Why, I'll sit here till doomsday before I let you give away this house for forty-five hundred dollars!"

But her indignation didn't touch Father. Neither the day's heat nor the last of her words affected him. He sat on the bench, looking out at leaves, as though some cold winter had frozen him to the spot, and when the flare of Mother's words faded, it seemed that gray, dreary smoke drifted down over us all, darkening my mother's face so that what had been marvelously brilliant became paled and drained before our eyes. But Father didn't see that, either.

"Axel, you can't sell for forty-five hundred," my mother whispered at last.

"Mortgage, twenty-seven hundred." (He was counting only to himself.) "Rent, probably twenty-five a month. That's three hundred. Food, a hundred a month. Fifteen hundred. One year. It'll do for one year. Perhaps stretch it some. By then, maybe—"

And then he turned from the window and looked at Mother; but she bent from his haunted, calculating look, down to Buddy squeezing her knees. She lifted him up and went away with him, murmuring, "Don't cry, Buddy. There, now. Don't cry."

Johnson came and went at irregular intervals. He brought one or two prospective buyers, who went through the house in a desultory way and did not return. My father still walked to town each day and returned with hurt feet and a bad temper. Jenny was in the empty lot almost all the time. She named the kitten Tiger, though he had a gray coat with a white bib. Mother was quiet and remote. The frown between her fair brows seemed a permanent record.

Then it was late June, and we were out of school. The blue days were long and unseasonably hot. Mornings we played in the shade of the oak in the back yard, and afternoons we retired to the damp coolness of the basement and played there. Mother answered an ad in the paper and began to do piecework for a knitting mill. She got twenty-five cents for each finished sleeve. It took her six hours to knit one sleeve. Father forecast total disaster. "Democracy," he intoned. "A beautiful intention. Failed!"

We went to Powderhorn Park on the Fourth of July. We sat on high hills ringing the small pond and watched the fireworks spray across the close, dark sky. At the end, a box of fireworks blew up, and the show ended precipitously in a wild spatter of sound and brilliant, confused flares, rockets, Roman candles, and fire fountains. "Fourth of July," Father shouted. "Last rites."

In the middle of July, the middle of the day, we were in the basement, canning peaches. Jenny and I had slipped the wet, limp skins from the fruit. Mother had halved them, stoned them, slid the yellow rounds into the green Mason jars that stood in rows on the newspaper-covered table. On the small, two-burner gas stove, sugar syrup simmered over a blue flame. The cool air was heavy with sweetness. Mother lifted the pot of syrup from the stove.

The doorbell rang.

"Shoot. Who can that be?" She set the pot back on the stove, lifted the corner of her wet, stained apron, and wiped the fine beads from her forehead. "Berit, run up and see."

I ran up the stairs, through the shade-drawn rooms to the front door. As I reached the door, the flat, dull buzz repeated. I pushed down the latch, pulled at the heavy door with both hands, and almost fell forward into the blast of white light.

"Well, hello, little girl, is your mother home?"

I recognized that high voice. I peered into the sun and up. Behind Mr. Johnson I saw another form, a large bulk of darkness, someone strange, a woman. A buyer. Important.

I banged the door shut and ran back through the dim rooms and down the stairs, shouting, "Mother, it's Mr. Johnson. And someone else."

Upstairs, the doorbell buzzed. Mother dropped her hot pad and towel, ran ahead of me up the stairs, through the house to the front door. "Excuse me," she said, when I pulled the door open again. "Please come in."

Mr. Johnson looked at my mother as though he towed behind him a cargo of untold value. His face was several shades brighter than usual, his grin wider and looser. "This is Mrs. Faulk." He flapped his hand like a flag.

She had a forward-thrusting, presumptuous bosom, a chin

tucked forbiddingly back toward a stiff neck. Her black eyes looked all around coldly, possessively, taking everything in and giving nothing out. She swayed into the living room behind the shelf of her bosom like a captain looking over a ship's bridge. "The shades," she commanded.

Mr. Johnson rushed to a window and jerked at the hoop on the string of the shade.

"I'll do that, Mr. Johnson." My mother's voice was new, and I turned and saw that she had learned in one swift lesson the art of condescension. She went from window to window, her back and mouth stiff. The hot sunlight broke into the room's summer shade.

"Wisconsin stone." Mr. Johnson gestured grandly toward the fireplace.

Mrs. Faulk exhaled audibly through her thin nose. She pushed at the carpet with the perforated toe of her black oxford.

Mr. Johnson stooped and flung the carpet back. "Good— excellent condition, the floors," he cried. "Fine housekeeper, fine, fine."

Red spots marred my mother's cheeks. Her lips closed in upon themselves. "I will leave you, Mr. Johnson. Excuse me." She turned away with her chin high, signaling indifference. She shooed us children down the stairs ahead of her into the basement. She lifted the syrup from the burner and poured it into the jars filled with mounded peaches. White steam rose around her. She blew a long breath up toward her hair, lifted an arm, wiped her forehead.

"Is she going to buy the house, Momma?" Jenny looked toward the stairs, as if she expected to find those cold black eyes staring down on her.

Mother didn't answer . . .

We were to move to a duplex on Cedar Avenue. It was a high, narrow, scabby-looking building. Its brown paint was flaking. Black screens on the windows and front porch gave it a sinister aspect. The patch of ground that was its front yard was burned dry, and the bushes flanking the steps were woody and tangled. Traffic was steady down Cedar Avenue. At regular intervals, streetcars roared through its steady hum.

"It's temporary," Father repeated, as we toured the empty, high-ceilinged rooms.

My mother eyed inadequate closets; high, narrow windows.

"I can put shelves over the stove," Father said, as we trailed through a small kitchen. "The children can sleep three in one room for a while," he asserted, standing in the center of a lightless bedroom. "After all," he shouted at my silent mother in the small, square living room, where dark woodwork looked soft and disintegrating under too many coats of varnish and stain, "what do you expect for twenty dollars a month?"

"Who's complaining?" my mother said, and walked out the door and out to the car at the curb.

But whatever anxiety and pain touched the rest of us still did not touch Jenny. She went about with her face looking like a flower with sun on it. As long as she had the kitten to be sometimes cuddled, sometimes played with and murmured to, nothing else affected her.

But I knew, if Jenny did not, that her strange impregnability was doomed. Time, which she ignored, was still inexorable. Days dawned and turned and passed into swift, forgotten nights. When six or seven more had gone, Jenny would have to abandon her kitten to his makeshift home in the empty lot, and her present happiness would shatter into loss.

On the last day of July, early in the morning, Father's friend Lars arrived at the house with an old truck. Draperies were down, folded into huge cardboard cartons and covered with sheets. The rugs were rolled into cylinders. The house echoed when we spoke.

Father was furious with energy. He shouted at all of us. "Get that box out of there. Berit, open that door. Let's get that chest next, Lars. Emma, bring the hammer. Berit, get Buddy out of the way."

Everyone but Jenny hauled and shoved and carried and ran. She was not around.

It was past noon when they went off with the first load. Lars was driving. My mother sat beside him, smudged and disheveled, holding Buddy on her knees. My father stood on the crowded platform of the truck, leaning his elbows on the cab's roof. I was left behind to watch the house.

As soon as the truck rumbled out of sight, I ran to the empty lot to find Jenny. The high, covering weeds were dry. They scraped at my legs as I ran. At the far corner of the lot, the tumble of honeysuckle shimmered where sun touched it. The tiny yellow blossoms gave off light as though of sun themselves, and as I came near the lit place, the air was suffused with fragrance.

"Jenny?" I whispered, as though the place would be marred by ordinary sound. She did not answer. "Jenny?" I moved a branch, and in the deeper light, I saw her there, lying face down on the patch of ground smoothed with use. Her long fair hair was tumbled over her neck and face. The gray kitten jumped about her, hissing softly and clawing at the strands of her hair. The light was golden upon them, and in its dapple, they seemed private and privileged.

"Jenny!" I said harshly, though why I scolded her I was not sure.

She flung back her hair and looked at me.

"Jenny, come on home," I commanded, though when I came, I had no plans for ordering her away. The sight of that much happiness somehow made it seem necessary to save her from it.

Jenny sat up and took the kitten into her arms. It lay in the folds of her smooth arms, a soft gray bundle collapsed into comfort. The kitten's wide eyes narrowed down, and a lush rumble of purring filled the shady den. Jenny looked at me, her own eyes grown heavy-lidded with secrecy and willfulness. She shook her head. "I'm not coming. I'm going to stay here."

"Jenny, come on. They're coming back. You can't stay here forever."

Jenny looked only at her kitten. She stroked it, and her face began to assume a look of dreams and separation. Then she stopped, shook the hair from her face, sighed. "I'm hungry, Berit."

I could do nothing but go back across the burned grasses to the disordered kitchen and make peanut-butter sandwiches and take them to her with a glass of milk.

I watched while she ate the sandwiches and drank the milk. She stopped drinking before the milk was gone. She held the kitten and tilted the glass, so that he could lap up what was left. I sat and rested and did not say all the things I had already said too often. Now, even more than ever, she would not listen to what I said, and if I felt sorrowful and full of foreboding, perhaps by now I also envied her for being able to give so wholly what I, possibly, could never give—a desire and love so entire that it could not conceive disaster, though what it risked challenged all realities.

Perhaps I guessed, too, that for one like Jenny, so much more possessed by what she found within herself than I, that it was not a matter of choice. Even if she admitted that she would lose her kitten and her believed-in unreality within a few short hours, that knowledge would not diminish or alter her commitment, and she would have to accept and endure the suffering which was the price of her gift.

Then I heard the truck's faulty motor clattering up the avenue. I left Jenny in the honeysuckle and ran back to the half-emptied house before Father and the gloomy-faced Lars climbed out of the truck.

I ran with them from room to room, as they heaved and hauled the rest of the afternoon.

It was after five, and the hot day was dulling down toward a ruddy evening when Father wearily brushed his hands on his haunches, looked around the emptied rooms, said, "Well, I guess that's it. Let's go."

He closed and locked windows and doors, strode out to the truck, and was halfway up on the seat behind the steering wheel when I grabbed his sleeve.

"Jenny. We have to get Jenny."

Surprise sent his eyebrows high up his sweaty forehead. "Jenny? Where is she?"

I pointed to the empty-looking lot. "Over there."

"Well, go get her." He pulled his leg up and settled down behind the wheel. I shook my head. "Hurry up," he shouted, and I ran again over the weeds, knowing what would happen.

After he called the third time, I trudged back to the truck. "She won't come."

"What do you mean, she won't come? Where is that girl?" Father demanded.

I pointed to the corner of the lot. "Over there. In the honeysuckle bush."

He jumped out of the cab and went down the walk and across the vacant lot, shouting, "Jenny, Jenny," in a huge voice, his long legs pumping furiously. I ran after him and saw him rummage through the tangle of branches and stand tall and momentarily arrested when he uncovered her there.

Color and weariness and anger deepened in his face as he looked. He took it all in at once—the nest in the box, the tin for food, the look of custom within the den, Jenny kneeling there on her cleared ground, her kitten against her breast, her eyes at last barren with fear. There was that moment of silence, each one looking, disbelieving, upon the other.

Then Father burst into rage. "What in God's name are you doing here?"

With that shout, Jenny changed, stiffened, turned adamant with desire. In eye and mouth and uptilted chin, her will was pitted against his own. "Go away," she shouted. "Go away!"

A snarl like anguish rolled from Father's throat. With flaming face and burned eyes, he bent and grabbed the animal from Jenny's arms. He held it by the neck in one hand. The kitten's body arced and twisted. It spit and clawed. Its pointed teeth yearned in the arched red mouth. The claws whipped at Father's arm.

Jenny flew at Father. She beat on his chest with hard fists, kicked wildly at his legs. Leaves and light shook over the three of them in a whistling, spattering storm.

The fury on Father's face became a look I had never seen. That snarling sound repeated in his throat. He wrapped a large, wrenching hand around the kitten's wild, twisting form and turned it fiercely away from the hand that held the kitten's head.

The tiny crack broke through the spitting and the hissing and Jenny's crying, and, in immense silence, the kitten fell from its single, violent shudder and lay broken, looking only like a dirty rag, upon the ground.

With one long cry, Jenny fell upon it there. Father reached down and grabbed her and flung her over his shoulder. He plunged through the fragrant, blossoming branches and ran toward the truck.

We were not what we had been. What was known was gone. What was new was strange. The darker light and limited space of the place in which we lived robbed even the furniture of familiarity. But if the place in which we lived was bleak, it was less than the bleakness each of us found within himself. For Jenny and I could not forget. We would never forget; we knew that. And we could not understand at all.

Those summer days, Jenny sat on the chipped concrete steps in front of the duplex and looked at the paper-littered, track-scarred street and did not see what she looked at. Not even the abrupt, paining roar of the streetcars changed the flat disinterest on her face.

If Father saw her there, her small round chin held on one upturned palm, unwilling or unable to play, his frown pulled blackly across his face. "Let her sit," he'd say roughly. "She'll get over it." But in his eyes there was a distance that had not been there before.

On a leaf-strewn day in October, Jenny and I walked home from our new school. Early evening already blended shadow to dusk. A skinny, half-wild cat darted out at us from the shelter of a low tree. Jenny screamed when she saw it, and ran, terrorized and sobbing, the long block home.

When I went into the kitchen, she stood in Mother's arms, crying and shaking, her dropped books scattered across the floor. Mother looked at me for the explanation Jenny could not give, and Father turned the same mystified and worried look from where he was, half up from his chair at the table.

"A cat. She saw a cat."

The look then that went from Father to Mother, and from her to him, was so stunned and so cold, so knowing and so burdened with recognition, that I stood in the center of it, a prisoner in its harsh winter.

Then my father turned away. He laid his arms and head upon the table. His shoulders heaved and humped; but I would not have known those shaking sounds were sobs had he not suddenly pushed away the chair and fled from the house out into the fallen dark. When he rushed by, I saw the tears runneling his face.

And so there was, in time, forgiveness. We lived through those years to years more comfortable. We knew again times of happiness, and of love. Looking back, one can say if Mother had needed that house less, or if Jenny had been a less willful child, or Father a less passionate man, or the times easier, there would have been less hurt. But where we live and where we love, we must, it seems, bear a plenitude of pain.

Gordon Parks

from A CHOICE OF WEAPONS

Gordon Parks' career has been one of astonishing breadth. Probably best known as a photographer, Parks has also excelled as composer, musician, and writer. He was born in Kansas of a poor black family, much like the one in his novel The Learning Tree. *At the age of sixteen he was sent to St. Paul to live with a married sister, but because of his irascible brother-in-law Parks soon moved out on his own. Subsequently he earned his living as bellboy, flophouse cleaner, and pianist. Eventually one of his compositions attracted the attention of an orchestra leader at the Hotel St. Paul; it was orchestrated and Parks was launched on his career as composer. Just before the outbreak of the Second World War he received a Rosenwald grant for his photography and was hired as a photographer by the Farm Security Administration.*

On the journey to his various accomplishments, Parks was constantly challenged by "a choice of weapons" offered to him by life. After witnessing an execution he wrote: "No, fleeing through the gate, my own scarred past stretches out before me. I recall that elaborate conspiracy of evil that once beckoned me toward such a death, and I am afraid. . . . And I am almost frightened into running, but I will not, call it vanity, bravado, pride or whatever. Only I know it to be something different—a faith in weapons I hold to rout such fear." The following selection is taken from his autobiography, A Choice of Weapons.

S EVERAL THINGS happened that spring which would brighten the coming summer. Three older sisters—Lillian, Gladys, Cora—a brother Jack, and later my father came to live in St. Paul; I got a job as a bellboy evenings after school, at the Minnesota Club, an exclusive establishment for St. Paul's wealthier men; and I fell in love with Sally Alvis.

That March, Herbert Hoover, in his inaugural address, said that all Americans should be bright with hope, that we should have no fears for the future. And I began to think that my good fortune, as small as it was, somehow reflected his thinking. Now, happy at being part of a family again, of working and eating regularly, of tasting the indefinable warmth of a first love, I brightened considerably.

By this time Cora was divorced and working to support her two children. Lillian and Gladys were both married, with children. And Jack had just taken on a wife in Chicago. Poppa would stay with Lillian, and I would remain at the rooming house. I had gone with my sisters to the station to meet him the day he arrived, shrunken into himself, still grieving the death of my mother. He had lowered his chin and eyed me over the upper rims of his spectacles. "Well, boy, how have things been going?" he asked. His manner and tone hadn't changed. It was as though he were inquiring about firewood for the night.

"Just fine, Poppa," I said, straightening, smiling, attempting to appear the embodiment of health and happiness.

"You're skinny as a jack rabbit. Been eatin' enough?"

I lied again and answered yes. I told Poppa about the new job I had, and he was very pleased. Then we all went to eat supper at Cora's.

The world inside the Minnesota Club was one of spacious rooms with high-beamed ceilings, of thick carpeting, of master and servant, of expensive wines and liquors, of elegant table settings and epicurean tastes. Influential men like Frank Kellogg, Justice Pierce Butler and Jim Hill of the Great Northern Railway sat about smoking long cigars and ornate pipes in the overstuffed high-back chairs of the mahogany-paneled library. And I, dressed in a suit of blue tails, white tie and striped red vest, would stand near them discreetly listening to their confidential talk of financial deals, court decisions, their wives and children, boats, politics, women, the Stock Exchange—and the weather. To most of them, I was invisible and unhearing, a sort of dark ectoplasm that only materialized when their fingers snapped for service. I used to stand at the door and take their coats; and the camel's hair and the velvet-collared chesterfields felt good to my callused hands. Their suits were well cut and well pressed, their oxfords and grained brogues discreetly shined. Their faces looked scrubbed; their hair was always neatly trimmed and smelled of barber's soap and bay rum.

In time I got to know all their mannerisms. The way Justice

Kellogg's teeth clipped his cigars intrigued me. He measured and bit in one quick motion. And I, timing that motion perfectly, would have the match lit; then I would nearly gag from the smoke as he puffed away. And Justice Butler's slumping in one of the mammoth leather chairs, his legs crossed and stretched out, his chin resting on his clasped hands, was, I thought, a picture of grace.

There was always the aroma of good food. The great silver platters of roast pheasant, duck and guinea hen banked with wild rice, the huge buttered steaks, served on planks of wood and garnished with steaming vegetables, the spicy cakes, rum sauces, ices and creamy desserts kept my appetite at its peak. And after such dinners, when the great sitting room filled with pipe and cigar smoke, I went about serving little toasted cakes and brandy. I was never hungry during those days.

There was a lot an unlettered black boy from Kansas could learn here. And what I learned I tucked deep inside, determined meanwhile to put each lesson into use whenever I could. I began to read more, slipping newspapers, novels and books of poetry from the club library. And soon a whole new world was opening up, one that would have been impossible to imagine back in Kansas.

One day I heard Justice Butler complain to another member, "I'll be damned if I can remember his name. He wrote *Arrowsmith*." And, before the other man could reply, I gulped and said, "Pardon, sir—if you don't mind—it's Sinclair Lewis."

"Lewis. Sinclair Lewis, that's it." And he went on speaking, I thought, without ever realizing where the name had come from. But a few days later he handed me a small package. "It's for you," he said.

I tore off the paper. It was a first edition of Edith Wharton's *The Age of Innocence*, dating back to 1920. I thanked him warmly. That book would always have a very special meaning for me. And I told him so. The rest of that week I walked around school with it, showing it to my friends.

George Berry and Woodford Mills were in most of my classes, and they soon became my closest associates in most of the things young men do. A few weeks before Easter, the three of us went to Ben Myers' tailor shop to be measured for new suits. Our forest-green outfits were to be exactly alike, even down to the double-breasted vests that I had seen some of the club members wearing. The suits cost thirty-two dollars and fifty cents apiece. I was only making fifteen dollars a week. Each of us paid ten dollars down; Ben would get the rest when he caught up with us. Meanwhile we scraped up the rest of the accessories: brown-and-white spectator oxfords, striped stiff-bosomed shirts, green ties and gray snap-brim hats.

On Easter the three of us met at George's house, where we spent at least an hour before the mirror. Then Woodford quipped, "Come on, fellows, let's go up to Dale and Rondo and give the world a break." And it would have been impossible to convince us that we weren't doing just that, standing there in the bright Sabbath sun like three peacocks. Everything went well until Woodford's shoes began to pinch his toes. But he was determined not to give up; propping himself up against a building, he stood for nearly two hours on his heels trying to relieve the pressure. But finally his heels gave out, and George had to go fetch his father's Essex to haul Woodford home. He walked from the car to his door in his stocking feet, the rest of his day ruined.

That same evening, through a blind date George arranged, I met Sally. She had a dimpled smile on her pale beige face when he introduced us. I smiled back and said that I was very glad to meet her. She had soft black hair that swept back into a knot at the nape of her neck. Her dress was powder blue silk. We didn't talk much as George drove time and again around Lake Como, whispering softly to his girl. At first I thought Sally looked like Claudette Colbert; then, after she had let me move closer, I decided she was prettier. She lived in Minneapolis. After George's Essex had finally chugged to a stop in front of her house, we sat there, not knowing how to say goodnight. When the front door of her house opened, she said, "It's Mom. I'll have to go now." She pressed my hand gently, quickly, got out and ran up the steps. And from that moment on I was in love.

Most of the boys I got to know in Minnesota had never hunted, trapped, ridden horses, watered circus elephants, raided peach and apple orchards, fished for perch and catfish, gathered walnuts, gone on hayrides, swum naked in rivers or done any of the wonderful things I had. When I talked about persimmon and mulberry trees, it seemed as foreign to them as the twang of my Kansas voice. And since they didn't know about such things, I often entertained them with tales that stretched far beyond the truth.

"Come on, Blue," using the nickname they had given me, "tell us about the time you caught a bear in a skunk trap," they would plead. "Hey, Blue, did you ever fight any real Indians?"

"Hell," I'd counter, "I used to fight along beside them. They used to call me Chief Blackfoot." And, while the laughter was at its height, I would concoct a roaring tale to back up my lie.

Yet seldom, if ever, did I recall the tragedies. A boyhood friend of mine, Cleo Anderson, had gotten his leg cut off beneath a freight we used to hop back in Kansas. I remembered he had not cried as he lay alongside the track looking crazily at his amputated limb, that the accident never changed his wonderfully funny ways; it was as though the misfortune had not befallen him. But such truths were not for entertainment.

The Minnesota boys smoked, drank, shot pool, played cards—and even drove automobiles—things I had never attempted back in Kansas. No boy in our family had smoked until he had moved away and started a family of his own. Even then, when Momma was around, they stuck their pipes away. A cigarette was out of the question, at any age. Only Poppa was allowed a half pint of sweet wine once a year. "It's to wash out any evil that's got into your Poppa's soul," Momma used to say. Pool and cards were strictly for sinners. No self-respecting Christian would be caught playing such games.

Neither were these new friends as militant as we back there had been. The lack of racial conflict here made the difference. Minnesota Negroes were given more, so they had less to fight for. Negro and white boys fought now and then in the Twin Cities, but the fights never amounted to much. Some Negro boys dated white girls without any major outcry. The most resentment came from Negro girls who refused dates to anyone "slipping out with Paddy girls." The Negro boys indulged, now and then, in a sort of satiric gallantry. One night a white man approached a group of us at the corner of Dale and Rondo, our favorite hangout. He quietly asked us where he might find a nice-looking colored girl.

We all looked at each other solemnly for a few seconds, then Leroy Lazenberry, a tall, bespectacled boy, shook his head regretfully. "Well, sir," he said with disappointment in his voice, "we're terribly sorry, but we just don't know where to find you any colored girls"—a long regretful pause and more shaking of the head. "But I tell you," he went on, his face brightening up (the man suddenly more hopeful), "we know where we can get you several nice-looking white girls—without any trouble." The man flushed and took off hurriedly without another word. And we, our insides nearly bursting, could hardly wait until he was gone before breaking into laughter.

We weren't subtle with restaurants that used to burn our hamburgers, oversalt them and serve our drinks in unwashed glasses. The White Castle chain was probably the most notorious for this; but after ten of us dumped our sandwiches on the floor one night and doused them with water, the practice stopped, at least at that restaurant.

There were exceptions, but Minnesota Negroes seemed apathetic about the lynching, burning and murdering of black people in the South. The tragedy taking place down there might just as well have been on another planet. And they didn't press vigorously for rights in their own communities.

Until the late 1920's only one Negro, Bob Marshall, had played on the university football team. The thought of one playing in the backfield seemed impossible—the white boys just wouldn't block for him, everyone said. This seemed odd when white boys were already blocking for Negro boys on many high school gridirons in the state. What, I wondered, happened to the white linemen's attitudes in the three months between high school and college? And, though Negro boys played high school basketball throughout the state, and an iron-clad Big Ten rule prohibited their making the Minnesota varsity, scattered grumblings were the only protests.

One Negro newspaper existed, the *Minneapolis Spokesman—St. Paul Recorder*. It had a small voice and a small Negro circulation. Its publisher, Cecil Newman, was as militant as the climate would allow—but the climate wasn't allowing much. My young friends didn't talk about these conditions very often. They seemed at times content with their lot. Or perhaps they were just awaiting the right voice or situation to jolt them into action. Even I, who only a few months before had faced starvation, had all but forgotten the frightful winter. Contentment was the word now, in the pleasant summer of 1929.

June burned into July. And July burned into August. By September I had saved a little money, received a two-dollar raise and fallen deeper in love; and on the ninth day of that same month I enrolled at Central High School. Working evenings and weekends at the club, I overhead talk of Hoover, A. T. & T., General Motors, U.S. Steel, General Electric, the Federal Reserve

Bank and other such names. And, though I didn't know what the conversations really meant, I sensed a certain optimism in them.

On the fifteenth of October, I asked Sally if she would marry me. She only blushed, laughed and explained, "Why . . . I must finish high school before thinking about such things." I felt a little crushed; but she hadn't refused outright. Furthermore, common sense warned me to finish high school too, before taking on a wife. I opened a savings account, anticipating the day, a year later, when we both would graduate.

The employees' locker room at the club was unusually quiet when I arrived at work one Wednesday that same month. Waiters who had known each other for years were sitting about as though they were strangers. The cause for silence was tacked to the bulletin board. It read: "Because of unforeseen circumstances, some personnel will be laid off the first of next month. Those directly affected will be notified in due time. The management."

"That Hoover's ruining the country," an old waiter finally said. No one answered him. I changed into my suit of blue tails, wondering what had happened.

By Thursday the entire world knew. "Market Crashes—Panic Hits Nation!" one headline blared. The newspapers were full of it, and I read everything I could get my hands on, gathering in the full meaning of such terms as Black Thursday, deflation and depression. I couldn't imagine such financial disaster touching my small world; it surely concerned only the rich. But by the first week of November I too knew differently; along with millions of others across the nation, I was without a job. All that next week I searched for any kind of work that would prevent my leaving school. Again it was, "We're firing, not hiring." "Sorry, sonny, nothing doing here." Finally, on the seventh of November I went to school and cleaned out my locker, knowing it was impossible to stay on. A piercing chill was in the air as I walked back to the rooming house. The hawk had come. I could already feel his wings shadowing me.

Henry Rowe Schoolcraft

MANABOZHO

Henry Rowe Schoolcraft, who has been called "the father of American ethnology and folklore," pioneered in collecting and popularizing the oral literature of the American Indian. Born in 1793 in New York State, he worked in glass making in Vermont until the collapse of that industry. After that he traveled extensively in the west. The published results of this trip drew him to the attention of John C. Calhoun, then Secretary of War, who appointed him official geologist to the expedition to Lake Superior and the headwaters of the Mississippi with Governor Lewis Cass. In 1822 Schoolcraft was appointed Indian agent at Sault Ste. Marie. There he met and married a woman who was part Chippewa. After learning the language of the Chippewas he gathered their legends in a series of volumes. His publication of the exploits of Manabozho, or Hiawatha, provided the basis for Longfellow's poem.

The myth of Manabozho was the most prevalent one found by Schoolcraft. "There is scarcely a prominent lake, mountain, precipice or stream in the northern part of America which is not hallowed in Indian story by his fabled deeds." He is both divine and mortal, and not a constantly benevolent god, often resorting to trickery. Sagacious, cunning, persevering, and heroic—Manabozho exemplifies all the traits needed in the hunting world of the American Indian.

The following selection is from Schoolcraft's Indian Legends, *edited by Mentor L. Williams, published by Michigan State University Press in 1956.*

MANABOZHO WAS LIVING with his grandmother near the edge of a wide prairie. On this prairie he first saw animals and birds of every kind. He there also saw exhibitions of divine power in the sweeping tempests, in the thunder and lightning, and the various shades of light and darkness, which form a never-ending scene of observation. Every new sight he beheld in the heavens was a subject of remark; every new animal or bird an object of deep interest; and every sound uttered by the animal creation a new lesson, which he was expected to learn. He often trembled at what he heard and saw. To this scene his grandmother sent him at an early age to watch. The first sound he heard was that of the owl, at which he was greatly terrified, and, quickly descending the tree he had climbed, he ran with alarm to the lodge. "Noko! Noko!" he cried, "I have heard a monedo." She laughed at his fears, and asked him what kind of a noise it made. He answered, "It makes a noise like this: Ko-ko-ko-ho." She told him that he was young and foolish; that what he had heard was only a bird; deriving its name from the noise it made.

He went back and continued his watch. While there, he thought to himself, "It is singular that I am so simple, and my grandmother so wise, and that I have neither father nor mother. I have never heard a word about them. I must ask and find out." He went home and sat down silent and dejected. At length his grandmother asked him, "Manabozho, what is the matter with you?" He answered, "I wish you would tell me whether I have any parents living, and who my relatives are." Knowing that he was of a wicked and revengeful disposition, she dreaded telling him the story of his parentage, but he insisted on her compliance. "Yes," she said, "you have a father and three brothers living. Your mother is dead. She was taken without the consent of her parents by your father the West. Your brothers are the North, East, and South, and, being older than yourself, your father has given them great power with the winds, according to their names. You are the youngest of his children. I have nourished you from your infancy, for your mother died in giving you birth, owing to the ill treatment of your father. I have no relations besides you this side of the planet in which I was born, and from which I was precipitated by female jealousy. Your mother was my only child, and you are my only hope."

He appeared to be rejoiced to hear that his father was living, for he had already thought in his heart to try and kill him. He told his grandmother he should set out in the morning to visit him. She said it was a long distance to the place where Ningabiun lived. But that had no effect to stop him, for he had now attained manhood, possessed a giant's height, and was endowed by nature with a giant's strength and power. He set out and soon reached the place, for every step he took covered a large surface of ground. The meeting took place on a high mountain in the West. His father was very happy to see him. He also appeared pleased. They spent some days in talking with each other. One evening Manabozho asked his father what he was most afraid of on earth. He replied, "Nothing." "But is there not something you dread here? tell me." At last his father said, yielding, "Yes, there is a black stone found in such a place. It is the only thing earthly I am afraid of; for if it should hit me or any part of my body, it would injure me very much." He said this as a secret, and in return asked his son the same question. Knowing each other's power, although the son's was limited, the father feared him on account of his great strength. Manabozho answered, "Nothing!" intending to avoid the question, or to refer to some harmless object as the one of which he was afraid. He was asked again and again, and answered "Nothing!" But the West said, "There must be something you are afraid of." "Well! I will tell you," says Manabozho, "what it is." But, before he would pronounce the word, he affected great dread. "Ie-ee—Ie-ee—it is—it is," said he, "yeo! yeo! I cannot name it, I am seized with a dread." The West told him to banish his fears. He commenced again, in a strain of mock sensitiveness repeating the same words; at last he cried out, "It is the root of the *apukwa*." He appeared to be exhausted by the effort of pronouncing the word, in all this skillfully acting a studied part.

Some time after he observed, "I will get some of the black rock." The West said, "Far be it from you; do not do so, my son." He still persisted. "Well," said the father, "I will also get the apukwa root." Manabozho immediately cried out, "*Kago! kago!*" affecting, as before, to be in great dread of it, but really wishing, by this course, to urge on the West to procure it, that he might draw him into combat. He went out and got a large piece of the black rock, and brought it home. The West also took care to bring the dreaded root.

In the course of conversation he asked his father whether he had been the cause of his mother's death. The answer was "Yes!" He then took up the rock and struck him. Blow led to blow, and here commenced an obstinate and furious combat, which continued several days. Fragments of the rock, broken off under Manabozho's blows, can be seen in various places to this day. The root did not prove as mortal a weapon as his well-acted fears had led his father to expect, although he suffered severely from the blows. This battle commenced on the mountains. The West was forced to give ground. Manabozho drove him across rivers, and over mountains and lakes, and at last he came to the brink of this world.

"Hold!" cried he, "my son, you know my power, and that it is impossible to kill me. Desist, and I will also portion you out with as much power as your brothers. The four quarters of the globe are already occupied; but you can go and do a great deal of good to the people of this earth, which is infested with large serpents, beasts, and monsters, who make great havoc among the inhabitants. Go and do good. You have the power now to do so, and your fame with the beings of this earth will last forever. When you have finished your work, I will have a place provided for you. You will then go and sit with your brother Kabibboonocca in the north."

Manabozho was pacified. He returned to his lodge, where he was confined by the wounds he had received. But from his grandmother's skill in medicines he was soon recovered. She told him that his grandfather, who had come to the earth in search of her, had been killed by Megissogwon, who lived on the opposite side of the great lake. "When he was alive," she continued, "I was never without oil to put on my head, but now my hair is fast falling off for the want of it." "Well!" said he, "Noko, get cedar bark and make me a line, whilst I make a canoe." When all was ready, he went out to the middle of the lake to fish. He put his line down, saying, "Me-she-nah-ma-gwai (the name of the kingfish), take hold of my bait." He kept repeating this for some time. At last the king of the fishes said, "Manabozho troubles me. Here, Trout, take hold of his line." The trout did so. He then commenced drawing up his line, which was very heavy, so that his canoe stood nearly perpendicular; but he kept crying out, "wha-ee-he! wha-ee-he!" till he could see the trout. As soon as he saw him, he spoke to him. "Why did you take hold of my hook? Esa! esa! you ugly fish." The trout, being thus rebuked, let go.

Manabozho put his line again in the water, saying, "King of fishes, take hold of my line." But the king of the fishes told a monstrous sunfish to take hold of it; for Manabozho was tiring him with his incessant calls. He again drew up his line with difficulty, saying as before, "Wha-ee-he! wha-ee-he!" while his canoe was turning in swift circles. When he saw the sunfish, he cried, "Esa! esa! you odious fish, why did you dirty my hook by taking it in your mouth? Let go, I say, let go." The sunfish did so, and told the king of fishes what Manabozho said. Just at that moment the bait came near the king, and hearing Manabozho continually crying out, "Me-she-nah-ma-gwai, take hold of my hook," at last he did so, and allowed himself to be drawn up to the surface, which he had no sooner reached than, at one mouthful, he took Manabozho and his canoe down. When he came to himself, he found that he was in the fish's belly, and also his canoe. He now turned his thoughts to the way of making his escape. Looking in his canoe, he saw his war-club, with which he immediately struck the heart of the fish. He then felt a sudden motion, as if he were moving with great velocity. The fish observed to the others, "I am sick at stomach for having swallowed this dirty fellow Manabozho." Just at this moment he received another more severe blow on the heart. Manabozho thought, "If I am thrown up in the middle of the lake, I shall be drowned; so I must prevent it." He drew his canoe and placed it across the fish's throat, and just as he had finished the fish commenced vomiting, but to no effect. In this he was aided by a squirrel, who had accompanied him unperceived until that moment. This animal had taken an active part in helping him to place his canoe across the fish's throat. For this act he named him, saying, "For the future, boys shall always call you Ajidaumo."

He then renewed his attack upon the fish's heart, and succeeded, by repeated blows, in killing him, which he first knew by the loss of motion, and by the sound of the beating of the body against the shore. He waited a day longer to see what would happen. He heard birds scratching on the body, and all at once the rays of light broke in. He could see the heads of gulls, who were looking in by the opening they had made. "Oh!" cried Manabozho, "my younger brothers, make the opening larger, so that I can get out." They told each other that their brother Manabozho was inside of the fish. They immediately set about enlarging the orifice, and in a short time liberated him. After he got out he said to the gulls, "For the future you shall be called Kayoshk for your kindness to me." . . .

After having finished his term of fasting and sung his war-song—from which the Indians of the present day derive the custom—he embarked in his canoe, fully prepared for war. In addition to the usual implements, he had a plentiful supply of oil. He traveled rapidly night and day, for he had only to will or speak, and the canoe went. At length he arrived in sight of the fiery serpents. He stopped to view them. He saw they were some distance apart, and that the flame only which issued from them reached across the pass. He commenced talking as a friend to them; but they answered, "We know you, Manabozho, you cannot pass." He then thought of some expedient to deceive them, and hit upon this. He pushed his canoe as near as possible. All at once he cried out, with a loud and terrified voice, "What is that behind you?" The serpents instantly turned their heads, when, at a single word, he passed them. "Well!" said he, placidly, after he had got by, "how do you like my exploit?" He then took up his bow and arrows, and with deliberate aim shot them, which was easily done, for the serpents were stationary, and could not move beyond a certain spot. They were of enormous length and of a bright color.

Having overcome the sentinel serpents, he went on in his canoe till he came to a soft gummy portion of the lake, called Pigiu-wagumee, or Pitchwater. He took the oil and rubbed it on his canoe, and then pushed into it. The oil softened the surface and enabled him to slip through it with ease, although it required frequent rubbing, and a constant reapplication of the oil. Just as his oil failed, he extricated himself from this impediment, and was the first person who ever succeeded in overcoming it.

He now came in view of land, on which he debarked in safety, and could see the lodge of the Shining Manito, situated on a hill. He commenced preparing for the fight, putting his arrows and clubs in order, and just at the dawn of day began his attack, yelling and shouting, and crying with triple voices, "Surround him! surround him! run up! run up!" making it appear that he had many followers. He advanced crying out, "It was you that killed my grandfather," and with this shot his arrows. The combat continued all day. Manabozho's arrows had no effect, for his antagonist was clothed with pure wampum. He was now reduced to three arrows, and it was only by extraordinary agility that he could escape the blows which the Manito kept making at him. At that moment a large woodpecker (the ma-ma) flew past, and lit on a tree. "Manabozho," he cried, "your adversary has a vulnerable point; shoot at the lock of hair on the crown of his head." He shot his first arrow so as only to draw blood from that part. The

Manito made one or two unsteady steps, but recovered himself. He began to parley, but, in the act, received a second arrow, which brought him to his knees. But he again recovered. In so doing, however, he exposed his head, and gave his adversary a chance to fire his third arrow, which penetrated deep, and brought him a lifeless corpse to the ground. Manabozho uttered his saw-saw-quan, and taking his scalp as a trophy, he called the woodpecker to come and receive a reward for his information. He took the blood of the Manito and rubbed it on the woodpecker's head, the feathers of which are red to this day.

Sheila Alexander

from WALK WITH A SEPARATE PRIDE

Born in Davenport, Iowa in 1918, Sheila Alexander moved to Minnesota as a child, lived in Kansas and Iowa, and returned to Minnesota during her high school years. She studied at Hamline University and under Sinclair Lewis and Robert Penn Warren at the University of Minnesota. It was the pervasive atmosphere of death during the Second World War that moved her to write of a young woman about to give birth to her first child in her novel Walk with a Separate Pride. *Alexander won the Eugene Saxton Award for completion of her second novel,* King's X. *Her poetry has appeared in the* New York Times Book Review, *the* Northwest Review, *the* Western Review, *and* American Poetry. *Of her writing she has said: "If you come to poetry first you are going to approach prose in the same sort of way. You have some different rhythms to contend with. . . . But no matter what you write—a short story, a novel, a play—the important thing is the juxtaposition of one word in relation to another."*

S HE HAD TO WAIT for the car going to the west side. The pigeons blew about in a soft brightness over the hotel signs and perched on the movie marquees. The stupid sun-eaters sat with their wet bubbling of content in their throats. Nessa stood in the same stupor of warmth, her sensory being swinging now toward, now away from, the living street. But her eyes carried on a process of selection independent of thought and she saw all the women with the long ferment of curled babies in them. Her glance would slide out swiftly as a snake's tongue, absorb the woman, and retreat. She thought of how women carry their pregnancies: some as disfigurements, their faces crippled by a mousy shame; while others walk with a separate pride, in distortion but with true balance, making a path before them out of their importance, thrusting their ripe, stretched marvels before them like a temporary fame. Their eyes signaled to her a thin, shining communication strung in the air until destroyed by intervening bodies.

When her streetcar came, she climbed the steps slowly. She paid her fare and walked back to a seat, sieving everyone quickly through her glance. She knew the thing to do was to keep your face clean and hard as a soap carving and keep yourself out of it because, sometimes, if they thought you were listening, they would freeze up and everything would be spoiled.

Two twelve-year-old boys and one about ten had to stand holding on to the backs of seats. They stood near Nessa and she directed her acquisitive glance out the window.

"Aw hell, I can swim easy a hunnerd yards. Is that all they want? I can easy swim a little ol' hunnerd yards," the small boy said scornfully.

"Okay, Tarzan, but just don't ask your girl to come and watch ya swim," said one of the older boys.

"Why not?" asked the smaller one.

"You lunk-headed dope!" said the other, and the third boy began laughing. "At the Y no guy wears a suit." They laughed together at the small boy.

"Aw hell," he said archly, and stared at the brassiere ad above the window.

"Chuck Wells broke his leg again," said one of the older boys.

"That's five times, ain't it?" asked the second.

"Four."

"Five."

"Four."

"Five. Once he fell off a railing, then the darn guy fell out of a tree, and twice he just folds up and breaks his dumb leg, and now he's runnin' on the track out at the Ag School and wham, gets his doggone leg broke again. Five times. I never seen such a crazy guy." The three boys laughed because they could see it was very hilarious about the goofy guy that broke his leg five times.

"Guy's bones are haywire," said the first boy, and they fell into a silence.

Nessa kept her face turned to the window. You get along with people very well sometimes. They're having fun and don't care, and when they bump into you they say I'm sorry, and it's all right with you. It's like that at the State Fair, next to the Ag School. You walk up the Midway and the sun is hot and the tanbark gets into your shoes and you remember somebody saying that the guy that had the tanbark concession sure made his dough easy, but nobody really cared, just kicked at the stuff and laughed, and everything costs too much, but they don't care about that either, just walk around the Midway looking at the cheap, mangy come-on shows, listening to the barkers and believing everything they say, not really, of course, but wanting to. And when a barker begins *Sex, Sex, Sex, Love and Sex, all our models from life*, they press in to see the exhibit, feeling foolish because they know they're going to be taken in, and when they see the worn-out foetal exhibition with the specimens, dark and broken-looking, they don't even mind because they're very interested anyway, and the terrible mooncalf baby in his formaldehyde solution, born of normal parents in Bavaria, makes them gasp, and they go out listening to the barker yelling *Sex, sex, love, all our models from life*, and they walk away without saying anything. And you see all the marvelous scrubbed girls with their artificial sexy screams on the thrill rides hiding their faces in the chests of the big kids with them. It's wonderful and warm being that way and everybody else being that way. In the stock shows the people walk around and look at the rams with the heavy furry scrotums almost touching the ground, and the bulls', pink, and amusingly obscene. A woman will pinch a man's arm, and they will laugh and feel a suffusion of blood to their parts and go on to watch the stallions relax and swing their supple, dark-skinned organs and urinate, and they will laugh again. They will timidly pat the satin rumps of the mares who are so absurdly female, and watch the silly coach dogs running about. And the farmers and horse breeders sit outside their horses' stalls, or stand around, not being fooled for a minute. They know why the people come to see their animals. At the art exhibit they say, what's so good about that, and so that's art. And everybody eating ice cream cones and candy floss, paying too much for food and not minding it, really, because they're having fun and want to believe in everybody. That's the way you like people to be, relaxed and dressed up, wanting to believe all the ballyhoo even though they know better; or like these boys, easy, with the unconfined eyes and laughter. It was the way you liked them, people, paying to have their weights guessed, their ages guessed, their fortunes told, their horoscopes cast, their handwriting analyzed, people drifting back to the stock buildings.

She pressed the bell. The conductor held her arm to steady her when the car lurched to a stop, and he had a warm, silly look on his face. Nessa smiled and said thanks and got off trying to feel very gay and hopeful for Colin's sake. She'd have to hurry and get some meat for dinner if he was leaving at two for the three o'clock shift at Northern Aeronautical.

The butcher had the warm, silly look in his eyes when he gave her the meat. "It must be pretty hot for you," he said. His voice was tender and silly too and she felt better than she had all day.

"It's not so bad," Nessa said.

"Well, I guess it won't be long now," he said, almost to himself, and was embarrassed when she laughed because he hadn't meant to be improper and she hadn't meant to laugh. She picked up her package wrapped in pink paper and smiled to show she wasn't offended. She felt that she would be quite cheerful when she got home to Colin.

As she walked up the long hill, toiling in the sun like a pack animal, her thighs aching with the baby's weight, her breath pushed up high in her lungs, she heard the laughter of small boys and smiled to herself. They stood in an alley way, and the way they laughed warned her. She stopped and then walked on stoically, pretending not to notice them. The little boys drew together for the attack.

"Hey, Harry! It's a duck, it's a cow, it's a hippopotamus!"

"Name it after the old man!"

She was at least glad she was far enough ahead of them so they couldn't see her face. Why did they have to do that? she kept thinking feverishly. Just when I was feeling so good, why did they have to do that? She was afraid when she felt the first tear because then she knew she'd start to cry about everything else. That's the way it started, and then it was for everything. She kept her head down when a woman passed, and knew that the woman turned around to look at her because the woman's footsteps stopped for a moment and then went on. Cry then, you baby, cry your damned head off, she scolded herself as she walked on up the hill.

When the first teary shock was gone she felt angry, and then began to be amused, remembering what they said almost as if it weren't she who was involved any more. Of course it was funny, like breaking a leg five times. It must be very funny and offensive and frightening to small boys to see her gross thrust-and-hitch walk. She opened her purse and took out her mirror. She didn't look so bad, though her upper lip was swollen the way it always was when she had cried. She walked slowly so her face would be all right when she got home.

She walked around to the back of the house, and as she passed could see the heads of four of Mrs. Wilson's girl friends through the kitchen window. She smelled coffee and heard their shrill, improbable shrieks of laughter. If I can just get up the stairs without her seeing me, she thought, but I suppose she'll have her door open. She opened the back door carefully and saw that the apartment door was open.

Mrs. Wilson, with an elaborate show of surprise, pounced on her and led her into the kitchen. She suffered herself to be stared at and said hello. The five women tried to pick the lock of her bland, empty face, but she held them off, and they contented themselves with starting at her feet with small, nibbling glances, working up to her belly and shaking their heads slightly, and so on up to her hair. They seemed to hate her hair. It was beautiful and young, a child's hair, and they hated her breasts and her great offending body. Their hair was machine coiffed, gray or becoming gray, and one woman's hair was henna-ed. She disliked the round, panicky spots of rouge and the Night of Sin perfume drifting from their bosoms, and their red and green shoes. But she wouldn't have disliked them at all if she hadn't seen their eyes and how they really hated her. I'm lucky if I get out of here alive, she thought, hysterically amused, and she noticed how their hips and thighs overflowed the kitchen chairs and thought how she wouldn't even have noticed if they hadn't hated her. All but one of them wore glasses, and it gave their eyes an extra flash and glint of cold direction. She flushed and looked out the window.

"Lydia has told us about you and your young husband," said the one without glasses.

Nessa's eyes swerved for a moment to Mrs. Wilson who was pouring coffee imperturbably.—So it was you, Lydia. I'll bet you talked. Do we disturb you at night? The bed is noisy and we've gone onto the floor, because it seemed so stupid and middle-aged, the tattling bed . . . Only now it's over. The world breaks your life into two equal parts . . . And you talk of young husbands . . .—

"It's too bad you have to go through it alone," said the woman with the desperate red hair.

"We always go through it alone," said Nessa in a calm, savagely wary voice, and balanced her cup in its saucer.

"It might have been wiser . . ." The woman's voice trailed off meaningfully.

"Well, we couldn't wait," said Nessa, and looked straight at the woman. She carried on the sentence to herself,—and we had to go to bed and ripeness is all, and all.—

"I understand, my dear, but a baby! I'd have been terrified, simply terrified to have a baby alone like this," said the red-headed woman.

Now for it, thought Nessa grimly, now for the business.

"But you're so young, and you don't know the terrible things that could happen. Why, I could tell you some things, they actually happened . . ."

"I think I know," said Nessa coldly.

"No you don't. Why, I had a neighbor once . . . The baby was born in pieces, in pieces I tell you . . ."

Nessa's face felt stiff with the effort to seem calm.

"I know a woman that had a friend whose first baby had to have his head . . . He couldn't be born, and . . they cut off his head. Of course, nothing like that would be very apt to happen in your case, probably, but I'd be awfully scared too," the first woman with glasses said, and her voice was sleek and innocent but she knew what she was doing.

Nessa almost reeled. She stood up, and their middle-aged, spinsterish hate gathered itself up to hurt her. "My husband's expecting me," she said, and put her cup down on the table.

"Must you go? Well, it's been nice meeting you," said the henna-haired woman sweetly.

"I'm sure it has," said Nessa, and went to the door and closed it very quietly behind her. She put her hand on the stair post and leaned her face against it. Her forehead felt hot to her hand.

Don't remember. You're not an idiot. You knew all these things, mother and the dead child . . . craniotomy . . rare . . it only happens once in a great while . . so terrible . . beheadings . . no . . no . . . Don't think or remember. They only hated you because you're loved and they've seen Colin, maybe the way he walks, with his big, hard hands, so gentle. That's it, think of Colin, think of going to bed, the blood rising, and the blindness. Because it can't really happen. It can't. Oh, dear baby, be all right, don't die. They never are born in pieces. I know it. They never are. Dear, don't be.

She raised her head. Colin had come half way down the stairs and he looked at her, searching first one eye and then the other. He picked her up without a word and carried her up the stairs. He pushed the door shut and carried her into the bedroom.

"Colin, I'm just . . ." she began, and kissed the side of his neck quickly.

"Shut up. I knew I should have gone with you this morning. Next time you'll do as I say. Good God, what will you do when I'm not here?" He was quite angry, and angry because he was afraid and had seen the white, staring face look up into the stairway and the little, strained wincing of her face when she saw him, like a child who has been hurt.

Nessa was glad he didn't know why she had stood there. "Does it make you feel any better to know that I probably can't live without you, without you being somewhere, alive?" She whispered the last word as though she hadn't meant to say it, but it was already formed and all she could do was whisper it to make it seem less ominous.

"I feel lousy." He took off her clothes and began to rub her arms and legs and back like a masseur.

Nessa turned her face to the wall.—Don't die. Please, baby, don't die. Colin, don't die. Nessa, don't let yourself die. Everybody's dying, but don't, don't, please, die.—After a while she turned her face back to him and he was smoking a cigaret, and she raised up to kiss him because when his mouth smelled of tobacco it excited her.

"Nessa, we mustn't," said Colin, and she tried to kiss his hands before they touched her. She loved his hands by themselves.

"We must, we simply must . . ."

Later, she almost believed that none of them would die. She raised an arm languidly and dropped it. Colin groaned drowsily and put his leg over hers.

We aren't going to die, after all, not one of the three of us, she thought.

Emilie Buchwald

GETTING AND SPENDING

Emilie Buchwald has taught English at the University of Minnesota, poetry writing at the Loft, a center for literature and the arts in Minneapolis, and courses in writing for children in numerous writing workshop programs. Buchwald was born in Vienna in 1935, came to the United States in 1939, and grew up in New York City, where she received her B.A. from Barnard College and her M.A. from Columbia University. In 1960 she moved to Minnesota, obtaining her Ph.D. from the University of Minnesota in 1971. Her work has been awarded an Amy Loveman Poetry Prize, a Lyric Memorial Award, and a Chicago Tribune Book Award, and has been anthologized in an O. Henry Awards collection, in The Anthology of Magazine Verse, *and in* When Women Look at Men. *She is the author of* Gildaen, *a medieval fantasy for children.*

NOON SUN WARMED the table, warmed Margaret's sweatered arm. The table, she thought, had worn well, better than she had. The porous oak needed only a daily polishing with lemon oil, while she required not only a moisturizer for her needy skin but the tinted make-up to veil imperfections and produce the desired illusion that she spent time in the sun.

Molly methodically broke crackers into her tomato soup, pausing to admire the effect she had created before she took up her spoon. Beneath her dangling feet, Rocky slept, his paws twitching in a dream pursuit.

"You're not telling it!" Molly protested.

"Yes," Margaret said, but she resisted speech, thinking of her face in the bathroom mirror, the face that time was debauching.

"Go on," Molly prodded. Television had conditioned her,

Margaret thought, to expect instant response when she wanted to be entertained.

She luxuriated in the contrast between the comfort of the room and the snow scene outside the window. Smoke rose slowly, very slowly, straight up from the Olsens' chimney. "The prince led her to the center of the dance floor," she said. "Everybody stared at her."

Molly listened to the story, ate her soup and nodded her head occasionally when Margaret supplied a familiar detail. Once told, a story was unchangeable and must always be retold in exactly the same way. The little hairs at the nape of her neck had once again escaped the confinement of the elastic band that held her straw-colored pony tail. The pathos of the scrawny pony tail and the delicacy of the fine limp hairs made Margaret want to put her arms around the little girl, to breathe in the good flesh smell of her neck. But Molly would resist and struggle. She would protest that she was not a baby to be hugged all the time. Stolid and self-assured, Molly measured the affection of others by her own needs.

"How could she have glass shoes?" asked Molly when she was struggling with her snow boots. "Could I get some?"

Margaret squatted down beside her in the back hall to help her. She rummaged through her memory of high school chemistry, a junkyard of irrelevant fragments. Wasn't glass made from a special kind of sand? Wasn't it sand that was heated to high temperatures?

"Could I have a pair?" Molly asked again.

Margaret buttoned the top button of Molly's snowsuit and thought how like Steven she looked when she wanted something.

"Maybe, someday," she said, holding the storm door open for Molly.

Why do we do it? What purpose does it have? she silently asked as she backed the car out of the garage, avoiding the large snowbank at the corner of the house. But to ask was futile, to think of purpose was futile. After all, what choice was there but to go back and forth, back and forth in robot imbecility, doing what was expected?

Today, the houses crowded close to the flanks of the highway came sharply into focus for her. They weren't so ugly now that their roofs and lawns were camouflaged by snow.

One saw and did not see. When Steven came home at night she tried, sometimes, to see him objectively. Then he spoke to her or stooped for Molly who liked to fling herself at his coat, and the moment was gone, his features merged with what she felt for him. It was impossible to know, any more, what he really looked like. Even when she met him downtown for dinner the veil of habitude descended too quickly for her to study him; the tall middle-aged man who smiled at her was no longer an observable stranger but the subject of her fantasy.

"Play music, mommy!" Molly demanded from the back seat.

Margaret pushed buttons, punching in one station after another, one voice after another urging her to buy! buy! buy! She settled for a station that featured diluted rock and roll, not too distracting, not too unpleasant. Molly bobbed up and down in her own counterpoint with the music.

Driving called for only a fraction of Margaret's concentration on this familiar road that led her to the usual destinations, the shopping center, the bank, the supermarket. She lowered the flap of the sunshade to reduce the glare of sun and snow and caught unexpected sight of herself in the make-up mirror clipped to its underside. Her eyes flicked back to the road, but she could not forget that there were faint webbed hatchings beneath the eyes in the mirror and a slight puckering of the skin. The woman in the mirror had—jowls—or perhaps one might call the folds the beginning of a double chin. It was a used face. Behind her shoulder Molly's face had flashed for an instant in the glass, her skin poreless and unmarked as a department store dummy's. She must always, she thought guiltily, renew her makeup before she left the house. She was no longer a girl. She could no longer throw on her clothes, run a brush through her hair and think no further about her appearance. The mirror ought not to find her so unprepared, so vulnerable.

Yet she was healthy and strong, and she should be grateful when almost every day she heard of a death or an illness. She felt the sharpness of fear, the knife thrust in the bowels that came whenever she was forced to remember death, her own inevitable death or that of someone she cared about. I must live, must live! she prayed silently, until the children are grown. If only Steven and she could live until life became uninteresting, a burden willingly set down! But did that moment ever come? Even Aunt Minna whose digestion was ruined, who sat for the better part of every day in a chair that looked out on a brick alleyway, was unwilling to give up living and its miseries. When a death announcement came in the mail, she inked out the name of the friend who had died, adjusting her address book with grimly pursed lips; still, there was something triumphant in the deliberate stroke of her pen. She had survived. Metaphorically, she marked on, while another had fallen from the parade.

Was this grasping and clutching inherent in the species, this desire for more of everything — more food, more money, and, above all, more life? The eccentric rich chose to have their bodies frozen in the hope of a resurrection in the future when the appropriate cure for their disease was discovered. What cure was there for this avarice of the spirit? She herself was greedy. She couldn't deny that she hoped for an indefinite continuation of this great middle plain of her life. Day after day she drove her wastefully inefficient commodious machine, filling the car with groceries, driving her children to their lessons and appointments. She held a handful of moments for herself, discarding others by a deliberate dulling of her senses, a woman willingly submerged in her comfortable life. Time flowed around and through her, a seamless medium, pure and irresistible. Usually she was as insensible of time as a flounder is of the sea in which he swims. But there were days when the passage of time seemed to press upon her. The minutes ticking away on the dashboard clock took part of her life with them and she knew that the days of lists and errands would come to an end. These years would recede into the past.

"You can park over there!" said Molly, pointing to a place in the parking lot.

Molly slammed the car door and ran ahead. "Open!" she commanded, stretching her arms imperiously, leading the way through the heavy door that swung open when their feet touched the electronically monitored threshold. Molly had looked forward all morning to this outing, to this treasure trove of colors and shapes in seemingly inexhaustible variety. Molly brought her a shopping cart from the stack next to the cash registers.

"Just a minute," Margaret said. She reread her shopping list. Without the list she felt unarmed and, even when she had it to consult, the supermarket confused her. The fluorescent lights played caressingly on the film of plastic enclosing the fresh fruits and vegetables, the wedges of cheese, the trays of meat. Everything looked attractive, tempting, worth buying. Even the canned goods, stacked with satisfying precision, achieved an appeal to the eye, here in their proper environment. The music that flowed from unseen speakers drugged her pulse into a false sense of leisure. She found herself strolling down the aisles more slowly than she intended. And although she recognized what was happening to her, she was often mesmerized. In Steven's office building the same methods were used to produce a slightly different result. Beyond his executive privacy, an entire floor of secretaries and billing clerks bent to their work under a similar pseudo-summer fluorescence, steeped in a continuous gas of melody. The music was soothing but the tempo was brisker, the pace livelier. The place reminded her of a modern hen house where placid chickens produced eggs on a predictable schedule.

"Look," said Molly, "there's that lady." She pointed to a white-haired woman picking out fruit in the produce aisle. Margaret moved her cart toward Mrs. Mulholland, their former neighbor who had turned and acknowledged them. She beckoned them closer.

"Good to see you!" she said, taking Margaret's hand in both of hers. The backs of her hands were deeply veined, blotched with brown-pigmented spots. They were hands toughened by exposure to dirt and sun, by work in her garden from early spring until frost blackened the last mums. "The earthworks are closed for the winter," she'd say, mulching the beds with hay and with her neighbors' raked leaves. The summer he could first climb over the boundary fence, Tom had disappeared into that garden. He became guardian of the vegetables. He picked caterpillars off the young broccoli leaves. He emptied the jar lids of their morning cargo of slugs drowned in beer. Day after day he patiently aimed a fine stream of water from the hose into the mulch that separated the vegetables. A few times that summer Margaret had carried him home asleep, his cheeks and forehead sun-flushed, black humus etching the creases of his palms and dug deep under his fingernails.

"How are you?" Margaret asked. She turned her cart out of the traffic of the aisle.

"I can't complain. I see that little girl there is growing up. She's no baby any more."

Molly leaned forward with sudden interest. "Peppermints?" she asked.

"Molly!" said Margaret.

"That's all right, that's all right. 'Shows she's got a good memory." She pulled a roll of mints from her pocket and held it out to Molly. "How's Tommy? Does he do yard work for the neighbors?"

Margaret smiled, but she found it painful to answer. "Maybe if we still lived next door to you, he would," she said.

The two women took stock of each other. They had been good neighbors. Mrs. Mulholland had never assumed friendship, although she merited it. She lived alone without demanding or inflicting guilt.

"You're looking good, Margaret. How's your husband?"

"Steven's fine. Working too hard, as usual." She wondered what to say. They had taken no recent trips, there were no events worthy of reporting, and the day-to-day anecdotes which a neighbor might find amusing were too fragile to survive retelling to someone not familiar with the circumstances.

"Carol does a lot of extra-curricular work, clubs and chorus. Tom's made varsity hockey."

"Good. Keep him out of doors. Better for him than sitting in front of the T.V."

Molly crunched the last of her mint. "Mommy, let's buy doughnuts now," she said, pulling at Margaret's sleeve.

"That's right. You keep on with your errands. I've got to get moving myself," the old woman said. "Come and have coffee with me when you have time." She moved her cart forward a pace or two, beginning their ritualized leave-taking.

Margaret continued the formula of departure. "You must come and see the new house." But the house was no longer new. They had politely discounted these mutual invitations for four years. Margaret knew that Mrs. Mulholland would not come, nor would Margaret stop at her house for coffee. Their real relationship was over. The bond of remembrances was not strong enough to carry them through more than these few minutes of conversation, trading tokens of a shared past. And yet, they liked each other. There was warmth between them. The tides of the day swept them onward in separate directions. They exchanged a last smile and nod. It was too bad, Margaret thought. There was so little time. If they met again beside the paper towels or the dog food, another smile and a sentence or two would suffice. Civility had been served.

She bought doughnuts absent-mindedly. While Molly ate her

sugar doughnut, absorbed in watching the butcher slide the slicing machine back and forth, Margaret stared at the unmoving lobsters displayed on a bed of kelp and crushed ice. They were as close to death as any living thing could be. The casual savagery of this lingering death disgusted her as much as the boiling alive did, but she ate lobster when it was offered to her and considered herself fortunate to get it. What was that among a thousand hypocrisies in a world where everyone saw selectively—had to see selectively in order to survive? Hardness of the heart began with hardness of the eye. She hardened her eye against the lobsters and thought how well the merchants of food had succeeded in abstracting cause from effect; the meat counter displayed no bloody carcasses mantled by flies, nor did the dairy or produce counters retain mouldy cheeses or rotting vegetables. They abetted the fiction that food was made out of clean plastics in a clean factory. Molly might believe something of the sort.

The butcher waited expectantly. Veal was high but everyone liked it. She could freeze it for the weekend.

"Two pounds," she said, pointing out veal steak already sliced for scalloppini.

Molly held her sugary hands up and shook them at Margaret. "I'm thirsty," she said belligerently.

"Yes, I know," said Margaret. She took her packages from the butcher and wheeled her cart to the drinking fountain. She wiped Molly's hands and face with wet kleenex and held her while she sucked greedily at the water spurting from the fountain. At the end of these outings, Molly's fragile covering of civilization fell from her. She was a tired little animal.

Molly leaned heavily against her at the check-out counter, her thumb already in her mouth. Margaret wrote out the check entitling her to the groceries she had collected, the hoard of desirable goods which a week would transform into fodder for the plastic trash can liners she used.

Daylight seemed poor and wan after the splendor of the supermarket lighting. The afternoon had lowered a hostile ceiling, a warning that more snow was coming. The grocery boy arranged sacks around Molly until she was securely barricaded in the second seat.

"Lean back," Margaret said coaxingly.

"I don't want to take a nap," Molly mumbled.

"I do," Margaret said under her breath. Her head ached. Her

legs felt as if they were stuffed with sawdust. Numbly she turned the key in the ignition, avoiding a glance in the truth-telling mirror. Who's the fairest of them all? I'm not! To see one's unprepared no-longer-young self in a mirror was dangerous, a frightening confrontation with the future. Her cousin, she realized, made up her lips without looking at the rest of her face in her compact. She wondered how many of the weary uncouplings of their friends, a process as common now as children's chicken pox had been ten years ago, began with a speculative look in a mirror?

Her car sped westward, a mechanical ant bearing supplies to the nest. In an hour this road would be swarming with cars struggling toward the suburbs. She tried to imagine what they would do, all of them, once the fossil fuels were finally siphoned and drilled out of the ground. She tried to imagine what the landscape would look like. Instead of the sprawl of lights, the double ribbon of neon signs, there would be dead buildings in a winter twilight.

Molly sucked her thumb noisily, not quite asleep, and Margaret thought about the groceries to be unloaded and put away, the dinner to be made, the evening to be survived before she could rest. The routine stretched inexorably before her. If she could talk to Steven she would feel better, regain her perspective, perhaps even her sense of humor. The thought was a talisman. She imagined herself calling his office, hearing Jean's "Just a moment, Mrs. Lowe," and then the click that placed her call on "hold," the limbo of telephone geography, until Steven picked up the receiver. And then, what would she say? "I called just to hear your voice. I love you. I know your worth." The idea was ridiculous! Telephone calls to places of business must have a reasonably business-like purpose to justify them.

What response did she expect from him? What if he had been called away from a meeting for her call? What if he was racing to meet a deadline? What if a client was with him in his office, listening? If she felt even the slightest cloud of his impatience cross her horizon, the purpose of the call was defeated. She felt thwarted, although she understood perfectly that she and Steven shared the same dislike for the unexpected, for people who dropped in without calling first, for events that broke the pattern of their lives. The other night Carol had said to her, brushing her hair in front of the bathroom mirror, "I'm never going to follow silly rules once I get out of high school!" She had smiled at her reflection, brushing, brushing the dark hair that fell in glossy straightness past her shoulders. Spontaneity was the privilege as well as the province, Margaret thought, of children.

The snow began to fall just as she pulled the car into the driveway. Molly leaped out and darted past Tom who opened the back door for them. Unasked, he fetched in the heavy sacks before he went back to the sandwich he was eating at the kitchen counter.

"Are you almost through? Will you help put away the groceries?" Margaret asked, carefully, purposely keeping her face expressionless.

He exhaled, the dramatic sigh of one who is always put upon. She had plucked the sun from his sky and trampled it under her authoritarian feet.

She watched him, the boy who had been angry if she did an errand without him, and words failed her, bitterness was in her mouth. For how could she say, I do this for you and that? I wash your clothes, I drive you to hockey games, and, not too long ago, I wove the fabric of your days. To say anything would turn the acts to dust. To say—you should be grateful! you must be grateful!—was impossible, as impossible as calling Steven at his office. The etiquette of love, her etiquette, forbade the calling up of debts. Tom ought to know, to feel, what was right. He should want to help her with the rock that had to be rolled up the hill each day, and without the necessity of words between them.

But he felt only the imposition on his time, time which rightfully belonged to his friends. They waited for him on the school rink, streaking tirelessly back and forth across the ice, breaking into groups which grappled and fell apart and flowed again as one magnetic unit until it was time to go home.

He ate a pickle, wiped his hands on his jeans and knelt down beside the cupboard; he stacked cans in neat arrangements, moving one grocery bag after another toward him. He flattened and folded the empty bags, holding them secure under his knees. He was methodical when he wanted to be, she thought, and extremely efficient.

"How was school?"

"O.K. The same," he said. Behind his brown paper fortress he was guarded, unapproachable.

She remembered to take aspirin. The big bottle on the kitchen shelf was half-empty and she wondered how long they'd had it.

Voices and shrieks of mechanical laughter roared out of the family room.

"Turn down the television, Molly!" she called.

The baked potatoes should go in now. She turned on the oven, gathered up the potatoes and scrubbed them. "Mrs. Mulholland was at the store today," she said.

Tom's head came up. "Yeah? What'd she say?"

"She asked about you. What you're doing. You were always her favorite."

He smiled and shook his head, obviously pleased.

"You could go see her, you know," she suggested, curious to hear his response.

He flattened a brown paper sack before he answered. "I kind of like to think of her the way I remember her. You know?"

She did know. Mrs. Mulholland staking tomato plants in her garden, Mrs. Mulholland feeding him toast with strawberry-rhubarb jam of her own making in the kitchen, these images were part of his past, as unalterable as the fabric of myth. He wanted to retain them unaltered, the landscape unfading, the figures unchanging, the Grecian urn of his childhood. If he visited the Mrs. Mulholland of today, truth might impinge upon the cherished fantasy.

His hair fell over his brow as he continued to thrust cans back into the cupboard. What was he thinking about? Was he remembering those summers? Or was he anticipating the moment when he had laced up his skates and was ready to attack the puck? Once she would have known. Not so long ago, he would have told her.

"I'm done," he said. His look added, "it wasn't so bad."

In his passage to the back door he grazed her shoulder with one gloved hand, not quite a pat.

"Have you got your face guard?" she asked.

"Sure. Don't worry."

Rocky followed him to the door but Tom stepped in front of the old dog. "No Rock. Sorry." His skates clanged against the door-frame as he closed it behind him and made his escape.

She took the pan of green beans to the sink and watched him cut across Olsen's yard and disappear behind the row of spruces. She sliced the beans as quickly as she dared, to be done smelling them, wondering why it had to come so abruptly, the self-awareness that was both barrier and shield. It kept her from him, but it was necessary, a protection. What had been exquisitely transparent about him was now opaque. Better so, the way people were.

She took down the pepper and the onion powder from the spice rack and brought the meat from the refrigerator. In time he would learn what to keep safe for himself and what he could risk to others. Now he took no chances, and she had to learn to be patient. Behind the carefully expressionless mask, her son was still waiting, cocooned, changing.

She added bread crumbs and ketchup to the meat, then shook in salt and the other spices. The lacerated skin around her fingernails burned as she worked the meat. Not all of the damage could be blamed on the winter dryness or the fact that she did the housework without wearing gloves. She caught herself picking at cracks in the skin around the cuticle, tearing at the loosened flap, rolling it back until she had made a wound. Some people gave themselves ulcers; she brutalized her hands. The state of her hands was an index of the state of her world.

Kneading the chilly mound of meat to a uniform consistency, she wondered why it had to be so painful, so mysterious, this confrontation with self, the self that had to be embraced in conflict before one could turn outward, towards others. There were those who never came to the end of that struggle, whose whole strength was drained by it. She might have been one of them. She might have, without Steve. She shaped the meat into a rounded red loaf, staring out at the unremarkable winter twilight, thinking of Steven. Anticipation and desire focused in her pelvis, a sensation of fecund softness, and the consciousness of a rhythmic pulse that flowed from her genitals to every part of her body, unsuppressable. A child or a neighbor who opened the door and observed her there preparing a workday supper in her kitchen would have no suspicion that her body clamored irrationally and hopelessly for satisfaction, that she wanted her husband's body on hers with an acuteness that bordered on pain.

How ludicrous, she thought, how humbling! Her body had forgotten its programming and made her the victim of an inappropriate impulse. She thrust the meatloaf angrily into the oven above the rack of baking potatoes and set the automatic timer. Tonight, after the ritual of Molly's bedtime had been observed and the older children gave up the struggle to stay awake for one more television program, she was free to yield to passion. Tonight, after the dishes were put away and the counter wiped clean for the final time that day, she could succumb to tenderness. Tonight, after they watched the late news warily side by side on the couch, two beanbag dolls, it would be appropriate for them to fall upon each other with a show of animal appetite.

She poured lotion on her wounded hands, thinking, thinking. They had managed to survive years of living together. They had survived in a captivity of their own making, a captivity that they cultivated, because routine was essential to their lives, a rhythm to move to, as necessary to them as it was to any other animal, a safeguard against the chaos of living.

A smear of orange in the dusk caught her eye. The last school activity bus pulled away from the corner and Carol, her coat flying open, ran up the driveway, books clutched to her chest. Margaret tried to visualize her daughter's face before she could reach the door. The image which came immediately to her mind was that of Carol at the age of two, the girl whose picture, framed in silver, stood on her dresser, not that of the girl walking in the door whose face seemed to change with every alteration of hairstyle, the Carol in quest of a public self.

"Hi!" she said, slamming the door behind her. Snow was netted on her hair, melting on her scarf and the shoulders of her coat. The wind had stung her fair skin a mottled red. A self-possessed human being looked at her and Margaret thought, how strange, she's my daughter. Carol dropped her books on the counter, tossed her coat negligently on a chair back and sat down to take off her wet sneakers.

"Smells good in here!" she said, spiralling the sneakers accurately down the hall in the direction of her room.

Margaret compressed her lips to keep back the reproaches, the commands. She felt her irritation, her aggrievement, mounting. These possessions thrown everywhere! this carelessness! this thoughtlessness! The kitchen, perfectly neat moments ago, was strewn with Carol's debris.

"Your new coat!" Margaret said. The words escaped her, charged with her sudden, ferocious anger.

Carol glanced at her. "So what?" she said, but good-naturedly. She brushed casually at the wet coat collar and thrust the coat in among the others in the back closet. The action was conciliatory but condescending. The look said—"that's what you care about."

It was expedient to ignore the look and accept the conciliation. "How was your day?" Margaret asked.

Carol brought out coldcuts, bread, cheese, mustard from the refrigerator. "Not too terrible," she said. "Are the nuts down in this cabinet? I got a B on the physics quiz. I almost died of shock." She pursed her lips as she sliced cheese for her sandwich. The expression was a mirror of her own, Margaret thought. Little bits of her would live on in these children; fragments of her habits and gestures would survive.

"I've got a good novel for book report this time," Carol said, "not like that gross *Mill on the Floss*." She shook a handful of nuts onto her plate.

Carol carefully balanced her plate atop her stack of books. Food still occupied the chief place in her pantheon of gods, Margaret thought, not yet displaced by sex.

Margaret watched her walk down the hall to her room, a serious figure in flare-leg pants that brushed the carpeting and covered her gym socks.

Outside the window the homeward-bound procession of cars turned past their street. The freeway disgorged them in clusters, like invoices materialized from a pneumatic tube. Each driver, each passenger had his private misery, his canker. Sympathy, literal sympathy, was deadly. How many people could one give to? One had to draw a circle around a few and say, "not beyond this, not beyond these people." Otherwise one would be overwhelmed, drowned in the sorrows of others, useless to everyone.

"I'm hungry," Molly whined.

Margaret turned. Molly leaned against the doorframe, one cheek red, the fine soft skin corrugated where she had fallen asleep against the tweed of the couch.

"I'm hungry," she repeated, challenging Margaret to do something for her.

"I know you are," she said. "It's almost dinner time." She took Molly's hand and led her down the hall to Carol's room.

Carol was sitting cross-legged on her bed, reading in the spill of light from her bedside lamp. What a baby she looked herself now in her old checkered housecoat.

"Will you watch Molly in the tub, please?"

"Do I have to? Oh, all right, I will! Don't look like that!"

"I don't want a bath," Molly said furiously, freeing her hand from Margaret's.

"See, she doesn't even want to take one," Carol said.

"That's not the point. It doesn't have to be a long one. Use the bubbles."

She closed the door behind her to forestall more complaints, relieved that she had restrained herself from commenting on the clothes piled in a soft mound on Carol's floor and the plate on the floor. It was impossible for everything to be clean and in order; it was irrational to keep trying, against the order of the universe. Windowsills attracted soot; rust stains defaced the porcelain sinks; trash baskets overflowed. After she cleaned the house she had the occasional lunatic impulse to lock the doors and seal the windows. In a world governed by flux, she longed for stasis.

Walking back to the lighted kitchen, she became acutely aware of their possessions in the rooms she passed, the toy animals and dolls heaped on Molly's bed and in her toy basket, the stacks of comic books and plane models on Tom's desk, the silver comb and brush set and the glut of photographs on the dresser she and Steven shared. If a tornado blew everything away, the furniture, the matched appliances, the hoard of clothes in chests and closets, the German crystal she had bought glass by expensive glass, the tangle of hoses in the basement, the tires, bicycles, and lawn equipment stored in the garage, the house itself (would they still be liable for the mortgage?), what would become of them? Who would they be? And what if they couldn't get the money to replace these things? Then it would be simpler, she thought tiredly, if they were blown away as well.

Tom should be home by now. She sighed and looked out again, aware of her own breathing and the crackle of fat in the meatloaf pan. It's going too fast, she thought, feeling herself moving quickly in the current of her life, feeling the familiar wonder that she, too, would grow old and die. She reached out for the salt cellar, which would outlast her and float on in the flux of material objects long after she had need of a salt cellar. But she tried to dismiss that certainty and to disregard the sudden knife-twist of visceral fear. She shook salt into the boiling water and tossed the green beans into the pot. Everything could be taken away. Everything hung upon a thread. Happiness was maintained by deliberately suppressing that knowledge. The smell of the baking meat was a defense, and so too was the warm room with its persuasion of order. These were ancient guarantees of survival, meat and warmth, body fuels.

She glanced at the clock and realized that Steven was late. Her physical desire for him was quenched, but now she longed for his presence more than before, for the reassuring everyday comfort of his presence.

Rocky raised his head from the mat. He ran to the back door and barked, demanding to be let out, forgetting as he did every evening that he was an old dog with arthritic hips. She saw the headlights and then Steven's car in the driveway. When the car was safely in the garage she released the dog quickly and closed the door. How incredibly cold it was!

Tom appeared out of the darkness and waited beneath the garage overhang. He began talking to Steven even as he helped him pull down the garage door, gesturing with the hand that held the hockey stick. The blades of his skates flashed as they arced away from his shoulder. The two of them, equally tall, equally slender, came slowly toward the house, and Margaret tried to think of them as strangers approaching, tried to see what they really looked like. Steven noticed her there, nodded to her, and she gave it up, turned from the door, gathered the plates to warm them in the oven.

Tom threw open the door. Cold air and a sprinkling of snow blew in around them. They stamped their feet on the mat.

"I could get a really good trade-in on these," Tom said, more eagerness in his voice than Margaret had heard in a long time.

"We'll see," said Steven. "You just got them this season, re-member?"

Rocky clicked into the kitchen, snow-furred, and shook him-self. Tom ought to clip his nails, Margaret thought.

"Close the door!" she said. Everything could be taken away; everything hung upon a thread. But the room would soon be warm again and dinner was ready.

Ann Chidester

MRS. KETTING AND CLARK GABLE

Ann Chidester, a descendent of early settlers of Stillwater, Minnesota, was born and grew up in that city. She attended the College of St. Catherine in St. Paul and graduated from San Jose State University in California. Scribner's well-known editor Maxwell Perkins recognized the quality of her work when she was an unknown writer. Chidester has published six novels and many short stories, a number of them now anthologized. The Long Year*, set in High Falls, Minnesota, evokes a community in the grip of the Depression in 1933. Currently, she lives in San Jose with her husband and two daughters.*

M RS. KETTING'S APARTMENT WAS A SIGHT. Dust lay over everything, thick on the chipped window sills, stifling and heavy in the early morning air. A litter of old movie magazines was spread around the day bed and the big mohair chair. All of her children had moved away except her youngest, Clark Gable Ketting, who was now fifteen and considerably younger than the others. She loved him best and yet she did not know him nor know the smallest way of showing him her love.

Mrs. Ketting was a short woman with a heavy bland face and a slow expression. Her clothes were too tight, too bright and much too short. She wore little-girl sandals and on Saturdays, when she went downtown to mill around in the shopping crowds, she wore a red ribbon in her hair though she was now fifty.

As soon as she rose in the morning, surveying the careless day, she at once put on her violent purple lipstick. This was even before she removed her heavy face cream, worn chin straps and rusted curlers. She crossed to the bedroom door, barefooted. Her son slept here, and she always knocked three times and let it go at that. "I don't nag my boy," she told Gertrude Buckley, her best friend and daily companion. "I believe in psychology like in that English movie, *The Seventh Veil.* You got to be careful how you talk to kids because they got delicate minds. I let my Clark alone."

Now she beat on the door three times, calling, "It's just about seven-thirty, honey boy." She returned to the day bed, muddling the bedding into the compartment under the bed. She made herself some strong black coffee in the kitchen, returning to recline on the day bed to drink it and to listen to a breakfast-club program which was broadcast from New York. Usually she fell asleep again and did not wake until Gertrude called at eleven. Today, however, while she was sipping away, Clark came out of the bedroom. He was already dressed, a tall, thin boy with a nervous habit of sniffing and wiggling his nose like a rabbit. His hands were restless and beautiful, and he took wonderful care of them. He had big calluses from the clarinet. He wore a tannish shirt, wrinkled and soiled, green tweed trousers and a grimy black sleeveless sweater.

"You got to get a new suit," Mrs. Ketting said at once. "I don't care what we go without, you get a new suit. A good one, too."

"You working now?" he asked in a rough voice that was hoarse from smoking and lack of sleep.

"Not right now, son, but I'll work two, three days at the Bijou next week, and then you got your job after school."

"Oh—yeah."

"What I mean is you got to look well groomed, Clark."

"Umm." He nodded and went out to the kitchen and returned with a cup of coffee and a stale doughnut. He ate standing up and staring out the dusty window.

"How's the new clarinet?" she asked during the radio commercial.

"Okay, I guess."

"Pretty good buy for six bucks, I say." She was proud of the canny bargains he had been making lately. True, nothing he bargained for was of any real good to her since he was interested only in musical instruments, but he had brought her a geranium plant for Easter and also provided her with all the nylons she could use.

"The clarinet's okay," he said nervously and set his cup on the window sill beside one he had used several mornings ago. "You ought to open a window in here sometimes." He looked around the apartment. "It looks crummy in here. I couldn't bring anyone to this place."

"Now, son," she said plaintively in her Greer Garson voice, sufficiently aristocratic to flatten his ego but at the same time wise and warm. Everyone should be warm and friendly, that was her philosophy. But the place looked terrible, and she was going to do something about it just as soon as she had a moment.

"Okay," he said, "have it your way."

"School fine?"

"Umm."

"You feel good, son?"

"Sure, sure."

He went into the bedroom and came out again with his clarinet, which he carried gently and carefully in its case. She was not truly interested in the clarinet, though she bragged to Gertrude Buckley about his playing. This whole conversation was unusual for them because they seldom spoke in the mornings. It was a bad day, too. There was nothing to see in the way of a double feature unless she went all the way downtown and sat in a small, drafty theater which always made her bones ache. She and Gertrude had had a slight quarrel, an old quarrel, about Ginger Rogers, and she didn't want to ride all the way downtown with Gertrude, who would certainly never give in. Not Gertrude Buckley.

"What's your new piece now?" she asked, gently, because sometimes she never knew how he would answer. Often he spoke angrily about his music, and this frightened and confused her. She wished now she could change his name to Gregory, but it was too late. In the old days when he was small, she had not called him anything but Baby. Clark Gable was her favorite then, and she finally named him that, hoping it would bring him luck.

"It's a stinky piece," he said sullenly. He was standing by the door, ready to leave. Suddenly his eyes widened, brightened, and he smiled nervously.

"Got a name, son?"

"Yeah."

"What kinda name?"

"Well, I made it up."

She turned abruptly to see him more fully. "You made this here piece up yourself?"

"Sure."

"I'm blessed if you aren't the real artiste type. I always felt you were a lot more than a horn player, son. You were born under a good sign and at the right time of day, early in the morning when the heavens was most favorable." She sighed, pleased with herself. She had a destiny like Ingrid Bergman and Joan of Arc had a destiny. "Tell me the name of this piece of yours."

"I call it *Me and Little Moses*."

"Funny kinda name. *Me and Little Moses*. The picture people don't like things from the Bible. Can't touch them with a ten-foot pole. Maybe you could call it something like *Blue Skies*?"

"No."

"Well, then, make it sound more like Cole Porter. He turned out to be awful rich."

"I like it the way it is."

"But what does *Me and Little Moses* mean? It sounds like it's about little colored people, a spiritual song. What does it mean exactly?"

He frowned and flushed. "I don't know exactly." She wished he wouldn't pick at the skin around his mouth. "It means I'm like Moses, sitting around in the bulrushes for someone to come by and pick me up and treat me fine." He swallowed and, opening the door violently, ran out into the hall and down the stairs.

She puzzled over this, her coffee growing cold and the sound of the radio unheard. She wished so much that she knew the right people, people in the movie business who could give her boy, her youngest child, a break. The Industry, she called it. Her other children each sent her ten dollars a month, and she had put some by for herself while her husband was living and working for the railroad, but there was certainly never enough to buy all the things she coveted in the big downtown department stores, never enough to live the way she wanted to live with a hostess gown and a glass wall in the living room and a red leather bar and an apartment with two bedrooms and a bathroom all its own. It hurt her pride to share the hall bathroom with those noisy Portuguese people next door.

At the car stop, she had to wait for Gertrude, and she thought she just might not go today. She might go home and fix up the place a little for Clark. She felt queer about everything. Gertrude had a pretty steady income from sitting with babies in the evenings. She knew all about what people had in their dresser drawers and medicine chests and closets and desks. She always ate a little of everything and drank just the smallest bit from each opened bottle, and in this way she got very wise about a lot of people. When she saw Gertrude coming at last, she resolved not to talk about Ginger Rogers. She believed Ginger was a fine dancer and ought to stay in that field, as *The Barkleys of Broadway* well proved, and she had written Ginger several letters to this effect, but she was not going to argue about it today and have Gertrude go into the merits of Ginger's dramatic abilities.

"Know what?" she said at once. "My boy made up a fine piece of music for himself."

"Horn music?" Gertrude asked.

"Yes. Like Harry James. I'm thinking I best copy it down in a real nice folder, bright blue or green, and then I'll send it out to Warner Brothers at Culver City."

"M-G-M's at Culver City," Gertrude said haughtily. She was partial to M-G-M.

"Well, Burbank, then. It's all the same thing."

On the streetcar Gertrude said she had to be back at six. "We can sit through the double feature and have a thick malted and maybe go into the Emporium and look for hats."

"I got all day," Mrs. Ketting said. "I'm going out to dinner, though, with Mr. Hugh Barker." This was something she had over Gertrude. Men still asked her to go places. Her boy was full grown and had been taking care of himself for over three years now so that she was free to do as she pleased. Gertrude was too thin for her taste and she had an Adam's apple like a man and she did not know how to dress with any kind of style—that same old faille suit, shiny in the fanny, she had worn for at least six years.

"What year's your boy?" Gertrude asked sharply.

"Second year high school."

"Seems slow to me," Gertrude said placidly, but she had no children, and her husband had run off with a drive-in waitress about seven years ago. Gertrude said good riddance, but she was ashamed of this.

"He's not slow," Mrs. Ketting said stiffly, and she thought how she would get home early this time and have a nice hot meal for him tonight. "He's the artiste type."

"They're a wild lot. Wild Youth," Gertrude advised.

"Poof," Mrs. Ketting scoffed. "You never know a thing about men or boys, Gertrude." The only thing was that they took Clark away from her too soon, these school people, and she did not understand what went on in school because she had never liked it in her day and she could not remember much about it. It was as if they had taken him from her bit by bit. Still, she did not have problems like Gertrude had. She was perfectly happy so long as she had movies and shopping and little dinners. She didn't hate a living soul and she tried to improve herself all the time by reading what the doctors wrote in the papers, by doing whatever the astrology book advised each day and by making friends around the neighborhood, especially among the Theosophists. That was her plan and philosophy of life.

In the late afternoon, after seeing the double feature, she returned to the apartment house without going to look at hats with Gertrude. She was set on straightening up the place and maybe getting a steak for Clark. The movies would not change programs until the following day. Besides, she felt full up on Gertrude's company. The apartment manager met her at the door, thrusting his face toward her.

"Miz Ketting," he droned, "some lady she been lookin' fer ya up at yer place. Says she's from the boy's school, an' I let her wait."

"Looking for me?"

"Betcha, yeah. Said she'd wait an hour."

Some teacher who had discovered Clark's great talent and wanted to take him abroad! That was what it would be. Climbing the four flights of stairs, she spent the money from such a project and moved in a world where she was the mother of a famous movie and radio personality like Harry James and the Dorsey brothers. The woman from the school was sitting in an old kitchen chair near the window. She was a stiff kind of woman, scarcely wanting to touch anything or look at anyone. An uppity person like the housekeeper in *Rebecca*, that was the type, nasty and snoot-nosed, too proud to breathe the common air.

"Mrs. Ketting?" she asked. She stood up, holding her handbag by the strap.

Mrs. Ketting smiled. She took off her little hat with its red veil and bright red ribbons and smoothed her hair and made a graceful motion for the woman to sit down again. "Excuse the place, the way it looks. I've been awful busy."

"I'm Miss Hobson from the Education Department. I've come about your boy, Jimmy, Mrs. Ketting."

"Jimmy?"

Miss Hobson opened her great brown leather bag and took out a notebook and read from it. "You *do* have a boy, James Clark Ketting, aged fifteen?"

"Well, *we* call him Clark Gable, but I guess he doesn't want to show off about it. You see, Clark Gable was a close personal friend of my late husband when they worked in lumber camps together. Naturally, we named the boy Clark Gable, then." This one was not going to be uppity with her or her boy no matter what. She lit a cigarette grandly and blew out the smoke with a healthy lift of her chin, holding her fingers curved, examining the angle and grace of her wrist.

"Mrs. Ketting, I'd appreciate it if you'd answer a few routine questions for our files."

"Certainly. Glad to co-operate whichever way I can," she said with a slow, elegant smile.

"You have a position?"

"I write," she said easily. "That's why this place is in such a mess. My son and I are both the artiste type, as you probably know." It was true that she had once borrowed a typewriter from the corner cigar store and tried to write a scenario, but after three days she found it too difficult. Still, being a writer would impress this woman, and she was not going to have her looking down her nose at Clark.

"I see," the woman said. She did not write in her book. "And you do not work at home?"

"Certainly not. I have a studio place."

The woman moistened her lips. She did not look directly at Mrs. Ketting. "The reason we are interested is that your boy has not been in school the past six weeks. We have tried to reach you, but none of the notices has been answered."

"You must have some other boy in mind," she said. "My boy's the real artiste type, a little eccentric, you know. You can understand that?" Her heart had begun to beat so that it hurt her ears, and the whole room looked ugly and bare, and there was nothing to hold onto in the violence of her beating heart.

The woman continued. "Not only has he not been attending his classes, Mrs. Ketting, but also he has been hanging around the apartment of a woman named Clara Davidson, a night-club person. He and four other boys eat there and sometimes sleep there. They smoke and drink and carry on generally in a manner that is really dangerous and improper."

"No," Mrs. Ketting said carefully. It was a dream, a tragic unreality that had absolutely nothing to do with her. She was carrying off her own end of this scene admirably. In a moment, she would show this sharp-nosed woman to the door. Now. At once.

"Yes," the woman said. "At this moment, we have your boy and four others down at the superintendent's office. It seems that these five boys have been holding up various music supply stores. They've stolen quite a large quantity of goods over the past six months. Instruments, sheet music, anything musical they felt they needed. Several boxes of nylons——"

"Nylons?"

"Yes."

"Why—my boy wouldn't get himself into trouble like this," she said. She sounded harsh, like Marjorie Main playing a Western type of woman trying to defend her robbing son. It startled her to hear her voice like that. "My boy told me only this morning he made himself a piece out of his own head. He's a good, smart boy. He called this piece *Me and Little Moses.*"

"Yes," the woman said quietly. "We know all about your son's musical ability. He plays very well, though I never liked that sort of music. And I think your boy is smart, too, Mrs. Ketting, but he has put himself in a bad position." She rose. "We have him down at the office right now. Perhaps you'd like to——"

"You bet," she said stoutly. She was full of anger and purpose. "I'll go down there and get my boy out of that office. The idea! I always saw that my boy had everything he needed. Really, it's fierce how the forces of law and order try to take one's own boys from you."

She had never been to the school and she did not know where it was, but she was impressed at once with its size and cleanliness, and she resolved to go home with Clark as soon as they could and straighten up the place and have dinner with him. Maybe he could have a few friends in to play that music he liked. She held herself erect, her head held high like Bette Davis so that her throat would have a good line, her stomach sucked in flat. She followed the woman through an outer office into a larger one where a big man in a dark suit sat behind a desk. Miss Hobson introduced him, and he stood up and held out his hand. Mrs. Ketting would not take it.

"If you're the head here, Mr. Farnum," she said grandly, "I want you to know you've made a pretty terrible mistake about my boy Clark."

"I wish we could believe that, Mrs. Ketting." He talked like Lewis Stone in the Andy Hardy pictures, and she felt instant respect and confidence in him. She went with him into another room, like a small library. Clark and four other boys were sitting there with a man in a dark brown suit and a cop in uniform. They all seemed embarrassed. When she saw Clark, she went to him at once, but he stood stiffly when she put her arms around him, and she was unable to touch or reach him at all. She had not expected he would be like this with her.

"Cut it out, will you?" he muttered. "Will you be kind enough to please cut it out, Mother?"

One of the other boys snickered softly. They were all heavier than Clark and better dressed. The two men stood near them, but Clark stood in one corner by himself, holding his clarinet.

"Mother wants to help you, son," she said. She blinked, and the image of him shifted and rose and fell and she blew her nose loudly. Her boy, her Clark, her last son.

"If you want, you can figure a way to pay for this clarinet," he said. "No one's taking this from me. You can pay sixty-five dollars for it."

"Yes, dear. All right. I'll do that right away."

He seemed to relax. He flushed and lowered his eyes and sucked on his lip. "Well, gee——"

"You didn't stick up no music stores, did you, son? I know you wouldn't do that."

"You bet he did," the biggest boy said. He needed a shave and his eyes were watery. "We're all in this deal together. He did as much, maybe more than we did. It was his idea to take stuff we couldn't even use. Sayin' we could learn to play a flute even! A flute!" He stuck out his jaw.

Mrs. Ketting looked at each of them. Then she looked at Clark. "I don't believe it, son," she said proudly. "I don't believe my boy would——"

"Cut it," he said sharply. "I did what they said." He seemed to grope for words to tell her something that was important. He went over to the leather chair by the reading lamp and sat down quietly, holding his clarinet across the sharp points of his knees. He looked away from her. The superintendent took her arm and led her back into his office.

"A bad business," he said.

She was silent.

"We'll do everything in the world we can. They have to hold them for seventy-two hours and then the case will come up before the juvenile court. You can come to the hearing. I'll call for you myself, Mrs. Ketting. We'll do everything we can."

"I must go home. I've got to clean house," she said dully. She sniffed and blew her nose again. She felt the little ribbons on her hat bob as she moved. She went out of the office and when she came down the wide front steps of the fine building, she saw two police cars drive up. She felt awfully cold in the dusk. The sidewalk was wet the way it was after a rain, only brighter and colder. She did not know the way home, and she would not wait for that uppity woman to show her. She walked to the corner, past the food market and the ice cream bar, past the rows of dark, dreary apartments.

On a smaller street, someone had already turned up the soft neon lights of the movie house. She stood on the corner shivering and alone and looking at the blur of light, and she thought about going home to the empty apartment, the dirt and clutter of things, going out to dinner with Mr. Hugh Barker, and she did not like any of it. She walked toward the movie house and paid for her ticket. Clutching the stub, she entered the warmth and darkness where a few early, lonely people now sat together looking at the shadowy screen. It was a movie about a woman whose daughter had gone bad. For the first time, Mrs. Ketting really cried about Clark, crying openly there in the darkness. She did not cry for herself very long and she did not cry for Clark or for her life or for this fierce confusion which caught at her throat. She was involved in another story, and she felt terribly, terribly sorry for Barbara Stanwyck with a daughter like that. She cried in the leisurely, rich way she enjoyed at sad movies. She had forgotten everything except the problems facing Barbara Stanwyck. And she stayed for the feature picture a second time.

Lon Otto

I'M SORRY THAT YOU'RE DEAD

*Lon Otto's fantasy "I'm Sorry that You're Dead" brings to Minnesota
literature a refreshing collage of several generations of a family on a
fishing trip. Otto was born in Missouri in 1948. He received his B.A.,
summa cum laude, from Pomona College, Claremont, California in 1970
and his Ph.D. in English literature from Indiana University in 1974.
While in college and graduate school he wrote poetry primarily, first
publishing in literary magazines in 1970. He began writing stories after
moving to St. Paul in 1974. In 1977 the Minnesota State Arts Board
awarded him a grant for fiction writing. Otto's collection of stories,* A
Nest of Hooks, *from which "I'm Sorry that You're Dead" was drawn,
won the Iowa School of Letters Award for Short Fiction in 1978 and was
published by the University of Iowa Press.*

"THAT'S RUBBISH." My uncle says, "that's just bunk." And
my grandmother tells him, "Hush now, shut up," and
he shuts up. "Thank you," I say to her and continue my explanation. We had gathered in my apartment to begin the trip back to
the lakes in northwest Minnesota that were my family's fishing
lakes sixty years before. We are using an old map, old sixty years
ago, a huge map of oilskin that hangs in my study taking up half a
wall, floor to ceiling, an 1883 map of Minnesota and edges of
Dakota, Dominion of Canada, Wisconsin, and Iowa. It is detailed,
cross-hatched mile by square mile, except for Indian Lands,
which are mostly blank, unceded.

Most of us are dead; that is the only way we could all squeeze
into the little room. Even so, it is crowded, and my grandfather
complains. He was a crotchety, irascible man. "Keep your shirt
on," I tell him, "we'll be out of here in a few minutes." He takes a

First published in *Chance Music: Gallimaufry 10 & 11* (1977). © 1977 by *Gallimaufry*
and Lon Otto. Included in *A Nest of Hooks* by Lon Otto. Reprinted by permission of
the University of Iowa Press.

slow swing at me with the patent, spring-loaded gaff he has been carrying around, along with his newspaper-wrapped casting rod, ever since getting off the train. He has had the gaff for many years, and keeps its four incurving steel talons razor sharp and the spring steel oiled. Landing nets are unreliable, he says, effete.

Vergus, the town we are heading for, is about two hundred miles from St. Paul, an easy four or five hour trip on modern highways. But there are for us only a series of very bad roads, following the Mississippi north to Fort Ripley, then northwest, roughly following the Northern Pacific Railway. The map, of course, is thirty years older than we need, but it is all I have. The roads hadn't changed much in that short time, I argue, but my uncle is disgusted. He has always thought me soft-headed. But there is no other way. Besides, everyone over sixty, those alive and those dead, believe they remember the way.

It took us thirteen hours, including a picnic on the church lawn of one of my grandfather's old seminary classmates, and frequent stops for repairing the tires on the Model T, and many wrong turnings, before we arrived. It was a good trip, though, and my tiny, fierce grandmother kept everyone in line, the living and the dead, those present and those away; it makes no difference to her. She had seen an angel once, it had appeared to her during the tornado that mashed flat their parsonage and church in Omaha, and ever since she has been able to stand up to anyone. She could before, too.

Everyone finally in bed after the long drive, my grandfather studies me as we sit at the oilcloth-covered table in the big cabin. I am still wearing the broad-brimmed felt hat that had annoyed everyone so much in the crowded car. My hair, uncut for a long time, curls out like a brush fire. My fingers comb restlessly at my beard as I try to get some writing done. "You look like a fool," my grandfather says, still angry at me.

I put down my pencil. "I am a fool, Grandpa," I say. You talk pretty straight to a man who has been dead for nine years. He gives his high, pleasant laugh.

"Well, my boy," he says, adjusting his gold-rimmed glasses on his gaunt face, "at least you're honest. And there are worse things than being a fool. As Paul says, we are fools for Christ's sake." Meaning St. Paul, in Corinthians.

"Grandpa," I say, "you and St. Paul may be fools for Christ's sake, but I'm afraid I'm just plain a fool, for chrissake." I laugh, hoping he will appreciate the little joke, which in fact is my father's little joke, from his seminary days.

"Well," he says. "Well, well, well." His hawk's face and straight, still-dark hair and metal-rimmed glasses nod over the table at me. We are having a little of his favorite brand of California port, very cheap. "Well," he says, "well, well, well." Elastic bands above his elbows keep his sleeves the proper distance up his skinny, liver-spotted wrists. Finally he smiles a little, a small, cracking smile. Then he frowns again. "My boy," he says, "at least take off that blasted hat."

And when we arrived in Vergus we were coming from the north, from Manitoba, from an anniversary celebration at the church my grandfather had started in 1902. The church was in Landestreu. Landestreu, meaning faithfulness to the land, a name changed by war wisdom in 1914 to MacNutt. "From Landestreu," he says, the word cradling on his tongue, "to MacNutt!" two hard, wart-like syllables. "Oh my, oh my, oh my," he sighs. "Oh my, oh my," shaking his said hawk's face. In World War I, when his brother Paul, a runaway, wildman living alone in a shack in the Canadian wilderness, was made a Mountie to patrol against German invasions. Such as my grandfather, who one time made the trip north, alone, to check on his brother, and was arrested as a spy at the border. "Oh my, oh my, oh my." Paul, drafted into the Royal Canadian Mounted Police, whose only companion was a big dog named Bismarck.

For we had heard the fishing was good around Vergus, on Loon Lake, famous for bass, and thought we could rent a cabin from someone. "SCHATTSCHNEIDER, THE GERMAN BUTCHER," said a sign when we first came into town, and that's where we went, and he set us up on Sybil Lake (no cabins on Loon, then), in a very primitive cabin. Schattschneider, who bartered eggs and bacon and butter for our gunnysacks of surplus fish, which went to his smokehouse, which has outlived Schattschneider.

And the first morning my grandfather and Walter, the oldest, went off to Loon to get the big bass there, leaving behind Ewald and my father. We seined some minnows, E. and I, and pushed out in the old, rotting boat that came with the cabin. Afterwards we showed him our gunnysack, as heavy as his, but not with bass. "Pa," we asked, "what are these fish with the great eyes?" He took one long look, struck his forehead with his hand, and announced with reverence in his voice that the fish with the great eyes was the walleyed pike, about which nobody had bothered to tell him. "The walleyed pike," he said, arranging them one by one on the still-wet morning grass beside the dock, "is the finest eating fish on this earth. Equalled, perhaps, by the great northern pike. To which it is not related, as you can see."

"Grandpa," I plead, "sit down. Dad says I have to row in if you start standing up." He glares at me from the back of the flat-bottomed boat, rocking gently, his antique steel casting rod poised in one hand, the other fingering a sopping cigar butt. Ancient preacher's coat hanging long and loose on his stroke-racked frame.

Once, when my father was still-fishing at age five, he flukishly hooked a big northern which his cane pole somehow held until it could be secured with the new patent gaff. Now, my grandfather was not one to display his catch; it was nobody's business what he was bringing up, which could lead to other questions, and then encroachment on favorite spots. He kept his fish in wet gun-nysacks, and the world saw nothing but lumpy burlap and a particular degree of strain in the arm carrying it. But the boy pleaded, and was surprisingly allowed to carry the northern up, dangling from a piece of rope. Two city fellows, elaborately tackled, met the child and fish climbing up from the dock, the fish as long as the child, and asked him where he had gotten it. They knew better than to ask his pa. The boy answered, in German, "Der liebe Gott hat ihn mir gegeben," and his pa, poker straight, translated for the blank-faced city fellows, "He says the good Lord has given it to him."

"I mean it, Grandpa, I promised, dammit." Almost in tears. The language is acknowledged and ignored. The old man sits down with a snort. "Well, then, get us in closer." He gestures angrily toward the weedline; relieved, I work the boat in carefully. The rod comes back in its great sidearm sweep, I dodge, the monstrous triple-jointed plug flies out toward the scalloped, heavy line of lilies, lands with a crash several inches from the table of flat green.

We ate together every evening that summer. The bowl of steaming pink soup passes down our long table, our two picnic tables set up outside. This is The Fish Soup, the one real fish soup, my grandmother's grave-held secret, unduplicated since. A good chance to finally get that recipe, I think, and am about to ask her for it, but she goes into the cabin to get something. Heads of great northern pike were in it, that we know. The bowl is passed to me. An eye floats up, looks at me flatly. The child leaves the table, is sick behind the cabin, leaning against a birch tree.

My father and his brothers get up very early to reach the narrows before first light. Too young, too old, we listen to their preparations, and go out ourselves after the sun is almost up. "Promise me. Or you can't go out. Don't let Pa stand up, come in if he starts. Watch his backswing. And wear a hat. And don't overtire yourself, take it easy. You're taking your pills, aren't you?" Because of his stroke the winter before. Because of my "fainting spells." Because of all that waiting to break loose in our heads again.

"You and I," he said once, tapping his glasses after I had first appeared with mine, monstrous, "we are weak-eyed but very smart. Smarter than any of them, you and I." But all that hell, those two species of hell, there, waiting to knock us silly again.

There was one summer, on Sybil, when the walleyes grew to enormous proportions, and would bite on nothing but little green frogs, which were abundant then: cold wet locusts on the shore. After we had filled two gunnysacks the old man sat back; addressing the blue mid-morning sky in his great preacher's voice he asked, "When will this unprecedented slaughter cease?" Not that summer, though no one else caught much. They would watch us, from a decent distance at first, then gradually move toward us in their boats as we caught fish after fish, until finally we had barely room to throw out our lines. But it wasn't the spot, it was the frogs, which no one could believe. It ceased later, though.

And when we went into town to buy provisions or go to church, Pa would stop to talk to a man emptying trash cans or shoveling horseshit and would talk for fifteen minutes about how much horseshit accumulates per day in a town of that size, depending on the season, and how long the man lived there, and were his folks from around here, and what did they do, and who was the mayor and who was the best barber. And we would say, "Pa, come *on*, dammit, we want to get back and go swimming," though not, of course, so he could hear us. He found out some funny stuff. He learned that the local name for the big, blue-gray wading birds we saw stalking along the water's edge was "shikepoke," and spent hours in the library when he got back to

Omaha, and later he wrote me with indignation that shikepoke was a variant of shitepoke, from the bird's practice of defecating when startled—a disrespectful name, he thought, for the great blue heron, which was what the bird was. It was always the great blue heron, the largemouth and the smallmouth black bass, the great northern pike, the muskellunge. They were lords, they deserved their proper names.

In a fishhouse, twenty-two years later, cleaning fish, a man remembered him. "Your grandpa always carried his fish up in gunnysacks," that's what he remembered. "He was a hell of a fisherman."

He was. And that day he and I caught five bass over three pounds, though we had gotten out late, and my father and uncles came in with just one bass and a pair of hammer-handle northerns. My father laughed hard about that, and my Uncle E. was too disgusted to speak.

This is northern water we are in now: a long, sharp point of pickerel reeds on a submerged sand bar that extends far out into the lake. Grandpa sits in the back, bent forward, tying on a long wire leader, to which he snaps a battle-scarred, triple-jointed wooden minnow. "It's a little late for northern here," I say. He continues his operations in silence, tying a triple knot, testing it savagely, then stands up shakily to cast.

"My boy," he says, "you can never tell. You can never tell." He says it, as always, in a high, chanting voice, and repeats it at odd moments, like the one remembered phrase of a good song. "You can never tell."

"Why don't you stay down, Grandpa; I can get her in closer," I say, but he remains as he is and begins the great sidearm backswing that brings the armory of treble hooks perilously close to my ear, then snaps it forward. There is, of course, no reason to argue with him about it any more. It was his heart that got him, finally, not the old enemy, stroke. But habit is a part of love and lives along with it stubbornly.

I sit at the oars, and watch the old wrists twitch the plug through the tall, slim reeds. There is an explosion, a good one, a northern's long body, green, white bellied, going berserk, trying to dig now into the bottom weeds, he whoops crazily and jerks the square steel rod back, doubled against the pike, skinny arms straining out of the floppy coat, reel screeching against his oblivious smoking thumb. And slowly he makes a little headway, working him in a little. I have the oars in, the landing net already in the water, and he screams, "The gaff! Use the gaff!" and I think maybe he's right, it's too long for the net, so I cock the damn thing, spreading its curved talons till they gape open in a line, but I'm not sure exactly where to hit him and he's going to be lively when he sees the boat, and so I drop the cocked, dangerous gaff and go for him after all with the net, digging deep in to the water as he brings him around, turns his head into the net, and I scoop him out, keep him diving into the mesh, his long thick body half out and drop him tangled into the boat's bottom.

We sit there a moment, staring down at the fish still thrashing on the wooden slats. Thirteen, maybe fifteen pounds, thick as an anaconda. My grandfather's mouth works strangely, then he realizes what is wrong, and spits out the chewed-off cigar and reaches into his coat for a fresh one. His dark mottled skinny hands are shaking a little. I begin warily to untangle the crocodile-dangerous northern and the mass of hooks from the knotted cords of the net. We are both laughing and talking nonsense at once. "Hot damn," I say, "hot damn."

The serious fishing of the morning over, my father leans back and laughs till there are tears in his eyes. He is telling stories about his seminary days, and his rough boyhood in Omaha, and his Uncle Paul, who became a sort of mountain man on the Canadian prairie, who had to leave home after blasting his old man's prized crystal doorknob off the door of their outhouse, hit it with a twenty-two from a block away, his old man crapping inside. He laughs so hard he cannot talk, the boat rocks, we don't care if we catch anything more that morning.

"Grandpa," I say to him, hoisting the heavy, rope-tied burlap bag over the edge of the boat. It hangs there cool and dark, the murderous fish curved inside. "Grandpa," I say to him, "I'm sorry that you're dead." He leans forward, cups his thin hands against the wind, lights his cigar in the brief flash of the match. Then he looks at me narrowly, sun glinting off his fragile glasses. He grips the worn cork handle of his rod, sets his thumb on the reel of wet black line. We have drifted down the reed line. He studies the line of reeds, notices a pocket, a little bay in the line of reeds. He stands up, and I steady the boat for him.

Norval Rindfleisch

IN LOVELESS CLARITY

Although Norval Rindfleisch lives in Durham, New Hampshire, he continues to think of Minnesota as his spiritual home. This is reflected in his stories, set primarily in Minnesota, which have appeared in a number of literary magazines. Rindfleisch's forebears were pioneers in Dakota County and it was his maternal grandfather who as county commissioner initiated and executed the plan for the Mendota Bridge. Rindfleisch was born in 1930, was raised in South St. Paul, and attended schools there and in St. Paul. He received his A.B. and A.M. from the University of Chicago. He is an instructor in English at the Phillips Exeter Academy in Exeter, New Hampshire.

I

THE CITY OF ST. PAUL is built like Rome on seven hills along a river. The hills are rather puny, and the river, dirty with refuse, is narrow and unimposing except at flood time when it overflows its banks and carries in the breech of its current massive slabs of ice. Each morning in the summer sewers flush the night's accumulation into the river, and contraceptives like unweighted parachutes (from that citadel of Black Protestantism upriver, Minneapolis) toss and turn and swivel languidly just below the surface. The mighty Mississippi in the childhood of its length has just begun toward the Gulf of Mexico, yet it is already, glacially speaking, senile and shrunk to a rivulet. Its thin trickle is mocked by the distant valley ridges which were once the lips of a gigantic flow that drained a continent.

The West Side, built on one of those hills overlooking the river (dominated by that section euphemistically called Cherokee Heights after the Indians and the high bluffs), is perhaps the most uniformly dreary residential section in that traditionally drab and sleepy city. It slopes ever so slightly away from the Mississippi to the limestone cliffs and then continues to slope gradually for about two more miles to the farthest limits of the old river's edge, to the Dakota county line and the countryside beyond. There are huge caves carved in the limestone cliffs which reveal in their echoing emptiness the prehistoric energies of primitive man, and stored in some of the caves for aging are barrels of beer and quantities of cheese and mushrooms which reveal in their organization and arrangement the genius and practicality of civilized man.

It is Sunday noon. We are going there, to the West Side, (up from the river, past the caves) for dinner, to my father's childhood home now occupied by his older sister, Aunt Esther, her husband, Uncle Otto, and my cousins, two girls, Roberta and Marlys, and a boy, Donald, who at seven years of age is the shame of the family and the only evidence of Aunt Esther's failure at anything large or small.

When my father was raised on the West Side far above the limestone cliffs near the city limits, the house was relatively isolated. The few acres they had with two cows and some chickens formed a kind of quasi-farm. My grandfather had emigrated from Germany in the 1880's and continued his trade as a tailor in this country. He never bothered to learn English except for those few words necessary to carry on business. He wisely married an American bride, some twenty years younger than he, who served as his interpreter and point of stable adjustment in the new and alien world which he would have preferred to remodel along the lines of old country discipline and order.

They had three sons and a daughter. The sons married early, but the only daughter, Aunt Esther, remained at home, became a proficient legal stenographer, and supported her parents in their retirement and nursed them in their sicknesses. Then she married Uncle Otto, to everyone's relief, in her middle thirties and before it was too late had three children in quick succession. Grandfather was hit by a car at eighty-nine years of age and when Grandmother died six years later, Aunt Esther for services above and beyond the call of duty (and after all the forgotten wounds of childhood had been reopened), inherited the old house and assumed the leadership of the family.

Now the old home and Aunt Esther's uncontested leadership

have become the focus of family unity. She has forged a reluctant coherence with these Sunday dinners. Once a month from late fall through spring we go home, as it were, to her unity dinners, one brother and his family at a time. Her feasts represent our cloistered line of defense against a crumbling world first of depression and now of war.

The struggle in Europe and the Pacific has been raging for a little over a year now. Sugar and meat are rationed; tires are impossible to buy. Gasoline quota stickers decorate the lower righthand corners of every car windshield and a red C sticker can lend a new prestige and dignity even to a dilapidated Model A Ford. Everything that seems of value is scarce or conscripted and the adult world, that outer world of business and doing things, has been either channeled into the war effort or has been patriotically, reverently suspended out of respect for the holy madness that has seized the world.

That feeling of having been left behind, of having been cheated out of some grand destiny pervades my family's spirit. The depression turned the national sympathies inward toward the midlands, and this concern made significant the prosaic terms of daily survival. The war has suddenly redirected those sympathies outward toward foreign lands. While everyone else has gone to sea to engage the enemy in the death struggle, we watch from the safety of a distant shore. No one in my family is old enough or young enough to serve. We have become peripheral.

Winter is entrenched, has taken a deep hold in the earth so that it seems that spring will never come. We are in the fifth layer of snow since November. It is packed tight of its own weight, and the crust has crystallized. It seems that all beauty, and joy, and love have been banished by the arctic blasts which sweep down through Canada and grip a nation already caught in fury and terror.

II

Although it is bitter cold, my father's old Plymouth surprises us by starting. My brother, Hank, and I are pleased that we do not have to shove it. We drive the four slippery miles across town with deliberate caution. When we arrive, my father, who does not presume upon good fortune, leaves us off at the path shoveled in the plowed snowbank below the front entrance. He drives two blocks farther so that he can park the car on a downhill slant.

357

The house is narrow, with unpainted shingles and a sharp peaked roof; it is set back on a lot which rises thirty feet above the street. The houses across the way are built on a street level and their back yards fall away to the alley of the street below.

Hank, now an honors senior in high school and the pacesetter of our generation, solicitously assists my mother up the slippery steps. Although Uncle Otto has shoveled and sanded the walk, they proceed cautiously gripping the pipe railing on the right. I try to run up the steep embankment. My mother tells me to stop. She is afraid I will ruin next summer's lawn.

Out of habit we go around to the rear entrance although we are expected to arrive at the front door on formal occasions. Besides, the front door sticks and the wind whips strongly around the corner of the house. The stoop is precariously small, exposed, and has no railing.

Uncle Otto greets us in the entry. He opens the door from the kitchen and stares at us as he looks for my father.

"Where is he?" he says. "Where's the Republican?"

He squints and looks behind me pretending my father might be hiding there. He shakes his head, bemoaning my father's absence.

We stamp the snow from our feet. My mother insists we take our overshoes off in the entry so we won't track the kitchen. We bump into each other leaning over.

"He was afraid to come. I know. I understand. He can't stand defeat," he mocks. Then he turns to me as I take off my coat.

"Your father is a high-strung, sensitive man. The other night on his way home from work he dropped by for an argument and left like a whipped dog with his tail between his legs."

"Don't worry, Uncle Otto. He'll be here. He just went to park the car on a hill," Hank says. "He wouldn't miss an argument with you for anything."

Uncle Otto wears a white shirt open at the collar. He is short, thick-chested, and bandy-legged. It seems as though the lower half of his body is either under-developed or wasted away. His pin-striped trousers hang loosely from his hips.

He has already been drinking beer, but he looks to my father's arrival as justification for whiskey which they will drink secretly, as is their custom, either in the basement or in the back entry out of sight of all children. He fidgets uneasily, eagerly spoiling for a debate. He has probably remembered an important point or learned a new argument since his last encounter with my father.

Uncle Otto has been a carpenter and furniture maker from his childhood, but he dates the beginning of his moral and political existence (they are the same with him) from the moment he joined a union and registered in the Democratic Party. He has a narrowness of sympathy—for the common man only—which the depression made broad through massive unemployment.

He is a craftsman of great skill. His knotty hands work with that infinite slow plodding patience which tolerates no errors. His deliberate caution, his slowness of intelligence is often mistaken as mature thoughtfulness, and his occasional obtuse insensitivity is often interpreted as self control or moderation, but the opposite is true: he is quick to anger especially when the issue is politics.

Uncle Otto loves the popular radio culture of Jack Benny, and Fibber McGee and Molly. He is humble before the brilliance of Dr. I.Q. and overwhelmed by the Lone Ranger and the frontier justice he dispenses daily to the common man of the days of yore. In Uncle Otto's mind there is a singular parallel between the Lone Ranger and Franklin Delano Roosevelt, his greatest and only hero, the defender of the widow, orphan, and laboring man.

My father is Uncle Otto's logical opponent. He is a white collar worker, an accountant and bookkeeper who has found it convenient to subscribe to the politics of his employers. He has had three jobs in the last ten years, but he has never been unemployed for very long.

He is a Republican in the fullest sense of the word. He is still intensely loyal to Herbert Hoover and holds John L. Lewis in supreme contempt. Just as laboriously as he tries to find a foreign cause for the depression (it *must have* been caused by foreigners—there is nothing wrong with the American economy—it is after all *American*), he tries to find a domestic cause for the war. It is the warmongers, Jews, and Easterners who have delivered the national destiny into the hands of the Communists and the Anglophiles.

For a while he was a follower of Father Coughlin. We used to go to mass at the Cathedral (located across the river at the foot of Summit Avenue where the Hills and Weyerhaeusers still reside, or rather where they still exist in a state of transcendental endowment) which was one of the few places where the *Social Justice* was available. But my father had too much good humor to follow Father Coughlin all the way. He drew back from the brink of reactionary involvement before Pearl Harbor.

In their arguments my father attacks the power and corruption of unions; Uncle Otto defends collective bargaining to the death. According to Uncle Otto the struggle against the Axis powers is a smoke screen to divert attention from all the really important domestic issues. Hitler and Hirohito are pansies to be fought with one hand while the rest of our massive strength is to be directed toward an immediate confrontation with the National Association of Manufacturers.

Political debate is a game to my father. He has been effectively emasculated by his relatively full employment and the status of his white collar. He does not feel with the power of his whole being like Uncle Otto the real consequences of any political or economic policy. He has never been on strike or relief; he has never cringed in anguish and fear before an arbitrary boss.

His detachment has made him more nimble, more flexible. He wins most of the points in their arguments, but he never wins the argument. His intelligence is quicker and he has read more than Uncle Otto, but he loses every debate because he has no moral right to argue. He fends, he bluffs, he has moments of triumph, but he always capitulates, acquiesces, to the moral and emotional force of Uncle Otto's proletarian earnestness.

Aunt Esther enters the kitchen and greets us individually with her best sales smile. She cups her hands under my chin and tilts my head upward. Then she turns abruptly to her dinner preparations. My mother volunteers to assist her and we are chased out of the kitchen. My father enters and is quickly ushered by Uncle Otto to his work bench in the basement.

We are all somehow diminished in Aunt Esther's presence. We have been intimidated by her energy and strength. She has the largest of the large noses that are characteristic of my family. We grow older each year in continual apprehension that maturity will prove we are indeed the children of our parents. Hank is already beginning to look like a loser.

After her late marriage and the children, Aunt Esther grew restless, especially during those times Uncle Otto was on strike. She never shared his absolute faith in collective bargaining and the duties of a housewife did not fill the void left when she relinquished her professional responsibilities as a legal stenographer.

She began selling greeting cards shortly after Roberta's birth and the business has grown steadily over the years. Her technique, of which she is justifiably proud, is to establish a "plant," one of the girls in an office of twenty or more workers, whom she will supply with free cards. The duties of the "plant" are to circulate the sample boxes of cards and then to take the orders which Aunt Esther quickly fills. Low prices, personalized service, and the uncanny ability to pick the right girl as a "plant" have been Aunt Esther's secrets of success. As a consequence of hard work and her system, she controls the sale of greeting cards to the office staffs of perhaps thirty large companies throughout the city. She has recently diversified into cosmetics and has already developed a considerable clientele, many of whom call her at home to place orders.

Aunt Esther was one of the last to have her hair bobbed when that was the style. It is years now since bobbed hair went out, but she persists, has made it her own—the unforgettable signature of her personality—and it along with a calculated formula of colorless clothes and hats gives her the appearance of dignified shabbiness so necessary in her kind of sales work. The girls who buy from her feel they are helping someone worthy of their patronage.

She has been remarkably successful. It is rumored that she makes more than Uncle Otto. My mother is quietly envious of her success especially since her recent purchases of wall to wall carpeting, new living room furniture, and a spinet piano. The piano is especially galling to my mother who has considerable musical talent but only the dilapidated piano of her childhood upon which to perform. Neither Roberta nor Marlys plays despite the several years of intensive lessons which Aunt Esther has lavished upon them. In hopes of getting full value for her purchase, she encourages my mother to play whenever we visit, but my mother often refuses to go close to it, protesting that she just doesn't feel like playing. Aunt Esther never pushes or nags. She does not understand the artistic temperament. She believes that all artistic achievement results from inspiration. She respects the unpredictable vicissitudes of feeling in my mother because she knows she will get her money's worth in the long run.

Aunt Esther has her own form of inspiration. She is intensely religious. Each morning after she has disposed of the children either to school, or into the hands of a responsible neighbor or baby sitter, she attends mass. For the rest of the day she trudges about town on foot or via streetcar selling her wares, believing each moment of her waking hours that true faith will be rewarded with material success. But she is not a fool; she knows that God helps those who help themselves. The profits over the years have vindicated her faith, although my mother spitefully murmurs that child abandonment is too high a price to pay for economic security.

III

Now we are summoned to dinner. Aunt Esther stands beaming at the head of the table directing each of us to our assigned places. We stand obediently behind our chairs waiting for Uncle Otto and my father whose footsteps we hear on the basement stairway. As the basement door opens, their voices burst forth in good-natured argument.

When they have assumed their places, we all clasp hands in a circle of unity and Uncle Otto says grace. I have been placed between Roberta and Marlys. My father sits at the foot of the table; across from me sit my mother and Hank. Aunt Esther and Uncle Otto sit tandem on the piano bench at the head of the table.

Donald has been fed in the kitchen and has been banished to the living room where he plays strange games no one seems to understand. Donald's manners are bad enough, but the main reason he has been fed early is that his toilet habits are unpredictable. Aunt Esther, believing that to presume a desired effect will produce it, has obstinately refused to put rubber pants on him. He cannot be trusted at a table with guests.

As Uncle Otto stands to carve the roast, Aunt Esther returns to the kitchen and in a flurry of trips completes the conveyance of food, still steaming, to the table. The dinner is always the same; we are having green gelatin with grated raw carrots imbedded in thickened suspension and topped with mayonnaise. Only my mother and Aunt Esther will eat this salad. The quality of the pot roast is beyond her control; it is a war cut from a canner cow— tough and stringy. Aunt Esther has overcooked it to make it palatable. It has been roasted hard, the meat has shriveled away from the bones, which have been bleached white (with blackened marrow ribs) by the heat. The potatoes have been peeled and cooked whole and the carrots have been partially boiled, then put in with the meat to brown. They are not thoroughly cooked, however, and they skitter unpredictably across my plate when I try to slice them with my fork. Crowning the meal is that thick, pasty, mucous pan gravy that Uncle Otto pours indiscriminately over his entire plate.

Everyone is hungry. There is little talk the first half of the meal—only the sounds of eating. Uncle Otto eats at a furious pace, his mouth not three inches from the plate. He holds his fork as if it were a hammer and occasionally loads food on his knife and stabs it into his mouth. My mother catches my eye and directs me toward Uncle Otto. 'Don't shovel,' she says with her eyes. She considers all of my failures as reflections upon her. After ten minutes we begin to slow down as though to catch our breath. The rate of our eating diminishes. Uncle Otto cuts some more roast and we pause to pass our plates. Aunt Esther begins her casual table talk.

We rarely talk about any of our uncles or their families. All recent information has already been exchanged. Aunt Esther tries to direct the conversation along lines of personal interest, away from public issues or controversies. She knows that my father and Uncle Otto will argue about anything just for the sake of arguing.

When she turns to Hank, I know before she opens her mouth that we are going to consider again the various aspects of the joint theatrical project of Christian Brothers' High School and St. Margaret's Academy entitled "The Lady of the Veranda."

"Now what was it again that you did in the opera, Hank?" she asks.

"It was an operetta," he corrects her. "I was the stage manager."

"Weren't there quite a few youngsters that we know in the production? I thought I recognized some names on the program, but I couldn't tell who was who with the wigs and costumes."

"Well, I think you know Fritz Ehrling and Buddy Scheffer. They're from the West Side. Then Rita Mertz and Joanne Carstairs." He blushes when he mentions the girls' names.

"Is that the Carstairs family that lost their son at Guadalcanal?" Aunt Esther asks.

"He was Joanne's older brother, a Marine. She says he was reported missing in action. They still think he might be alive," Hank says.

"I heard he was killed in action," my father says bluntly between bites. Hank flushes.

"I only know what Joanne told us. She says he was reported missing in action. She said the telegram said *missing in action*."

"That's probably what they told her," my father says. "But I know the boy's father and what *he* said. Bob Carstairs was killed in action." My father fights a piece of meat.

"Well, whether he was killed or is missing in action, it's tragic. I feel with all my heart for that poor mother," Aunt Esther says.

"He could be missing," Hank argues, angry that he has been repudiated by a more reliable source of truth. He is ashamed that he may have accepted uncritically a story of romantic wistfulness. My father rises to Hank's pitiful challenge.

"Awful goddamn small island to get lost on. You can almost throw a stone across it."

"I mean, they could have got dog tags mixed up. He might still be alive. Somebody else might have been killed and they thought it was him."

"And I suppose he got hit on the head and has amnesia or thinks he is somebody else and that's why he hasn't written for close to a year now."

"Leave the boy alone," Uncle Otto says. "He might be missing in action. You don't know for sure."

"Well, if he is missing, then it's because they can't find all the pieces," my father replies brutally.

"Rudy. For heaven's sake. We're eating dinner," my mother cries. "If you must wrangle, go down the basement."

But my father is angry.

"I'm just getting sick and tired of him contradicting me every time I say anything. This is just one of a dozen times in the last week. If he wants to enter adult conversations, then he'd better start thinking like an adult and not like some moonstruck fool."

"He was just telling us what this girl told him," Uncle Otto says.

There is a silence. My father does not answer. He begins to eat again. Hank picks at his food to cover his humiliation.

The serving bowls are passed around for seconds. When Marlys takes more potatoes, Aunt Esther says,

"Marlys, eat everything on your plate. You haven't touched your meat."

"I can't chew it, Ma. It's too tough."

"Either eat your meat or there will be no more potatoes," Uncle Otto says with sudden anger. Marlys reluctantly begins to stuff her mouth with the meat. Her jaw moves up and down, exaggerating the difficulty of chewing. Aunt Esther resumes the discussion of Hank's operetta.

"It certainly seems a shame that with all the work you put in on the play you could only have four performances."

"Somebody suggested that we put it on for another weekend and it was almost set. Some parents agreed to guarantee the expenses, but Brother Anthony put the kibosh on the whole thing. He wanted to know if the parents were going to guarantee our homework done on time, too."

"What's a kibosh?" Roberta asks, but before Hank can answer Marlys chokes and gags. Her mouth opens wide and she rushes her head over her plate and delivers a round, symmetrical ball of chewed meat and potatoes. She smiles sheepishly and brushes the tears from her watering eyes.

"Marlys, if you are not hungry, you may leave the table now," Aunt Esther says. Marlys gets up from the table without a murmur and shoves her chair in, then turns on her heels for the living room. She does not seem unhappy that she is being disciplined. As she leaves my mother looks at me again and throws me a glance which says, 'There, but for the grace of God and my vigilance go you.'

"What exactly are the duties of the stage manager?" Aunt Esther asks, knowing that continuity is the only way out of her embarrassment.

"Well, actually the stage manager is the most important single person in any production. Once the show is ready for the stage, the director turns everything over to the stage manager who is the absolute boss. He is responsible for every prop, every cue, every scene change, every actor being at the right place at the right time . . ." Hank exults in his importance, in the knowledge that everyone on the production looked to him as the real star, the unsung hero of "The Lady of the Veranda."

"Besides that I sang in the chorus and helped design the set," he continues eager to seize this opportunity.

We hear a scream from the living room. Marlys races around the corner. She holds her nose delicately as if she is politely drinking a cup of tea.

"Pew, pew. He's done it again, Ma," she tattles. Aunt Esther tightens her lips, pressing her face into a frozen smile. "He's gone to the bathroom in his pants again."

Roberta jumps from the table, dashes into the living room at her sister's heels. She spells loudly and emphatically.

"P.U. P.U. It's Number Two."

They return to the dining room. Roberta's voice is full of disgust. She begs Uncle Otto.

"Pa, you got to do something."

Uncle Otto sits bent in suspended fury. He swallows the food he has been chewing. Then he thrusts back from the table.

"Goddamn that kid. Goddamn him. Goddamn him." Spittle sprays across his lips and his eyes bug wildly.

We sit stunned by his violence. Aunt Esther prays aloud in bold supplication to cover his blasphemy (or is it to protect herself from the backwash of his damnation?).

"God's name be praised in our house. God's name be honored in our house. God's name be praised in our house."

With each incantation she makes the sign of the cross. She smiles her set smile and continues to eat as though nothing has happened, or rather she continues to chase the remnants, the minute fragments of food, across her plate, catching them and pressing them in the crevices of her fork.

Uncle Otto wraps Donald in a newspaper and carries him upstairs to the bathroom. Roberta sits down again at the table. Her face is ugly with anger. She blurts,

"He does it on purpose. He saves up all day so he can make everybody *sick* at dinner."

"That's enough, Roberta. We'll talk about something else." Aunt Esther smiles her tight smile. She addresses my brother again.

"How did you make the stage so misty for the last scene when the mysterious lady leads Sir Michael to the lost family treasure? It was a really fine effect."

"We dropped this big curtain made out of something like cheesecloth from the deepest batten on the stage. It's called a scrim. Then we set the lights up at different angles. The Lady of the Veranda danced slowly across the stage behind the scrim." He pauses. "That created the effect of mist and shadows that everyone admired so much."

Roberta is too humiliated to be still. She interrupts, turning to us in pleading explanation.

"He did it at school all the time because the little snot didn't want to go."

My brother is annoyed.

"We set the lights at about thirty different combinations and angles before we got just what we wanted."

"Then Sister sent a messenger to my room and I had to take him to the girls' bathroom and clean him up and then take him home," Roberta continues. Aunt Esther's smile disappears. She glares at Roberta who seems to wither before our eyes. But she persists in her explanation, weakly.

"He can't go to *any* school. Even the public school expelled him and the nuns won't take him back."

Her voice breaks and trails off. She jumps from the table and runs wailing up the stairs to her bedroom.

We hear the stinging slap of leather on flesh and Donald's howls. After several licks my father stirs apprehensively in his chair and then pushes himself away from the table. He goes into the living room and yells up the stairway.

"Otto. Otto. Do you want coffee with your dessert?"

The thrashing stops. We hear Uncle Otto's footsteps. My father shouts again,

"Do you want coffee with your dessert?" Donald's simpering moan trails down the stairs.

Suddenly Aunt Esther bolts upright, her mouth sagging in alarm.

"Oh, has he hurt my boy? Has he hurt my little Donnie?" She runs from the room past my father and calls ahead of her as she stumbles up the stairs.

We sit silently for a few moments. Then Hank says,

"Now that all the dirty work is done, she can be the loving mother again."

My mother nudges him to be quiet. She stands up and begins clearing plates.

"Well, Marlys honey, would you like to help Auntie Bea serve desserts?"

Marlys follows my mother into the kitchen. Uncle Otto, his forehead covered with sweat, returns and sits as my mother and Marlys serve the desserts and coffee.

Now all is predictable, automatic. My mother has a headache and goes into the living room to lie down on the sofa. Uncle Otto disappears upstairs for his nap and my father draws a chair close to the radio where he will sit all afternoon through the concert and the Catholic Hour.

Aunt Esther returns once Donald is securely asleep and begins the preparations for tomorrow's calls. Roberta, Marlys, and I finish clearing the table and begin the dishes in the kitchen after which Aunt Esther will give us enough money to go to the movie and have a treat.

Hank is going to the third reunion of the cast of "The Lady of the Veranda" to be held at the home of the soprano lead over on the East Side. He borrows carfare money from my father and hurries to the car stop three blocks away lest he be late and fail to share those poignant moments of recall which a resinging of the entire score is certain to evoke.

When we go into the dining room to collect from Aunt Esther, she requires a last chore before she will let us go. I must carry a stack of card boxes from the small bedroom off the dining room (which she has converted into a storeroom) to the dining room table. She makes several groupings of the boxes in a spatial arrangement which corresponds to the order of her Monday deliveries. When we receive the money, Aunt Esther puts me in charge and adds a bonus of a quarter to our total which we in turn squabble about all the way to the theater.

Now we eagerly seek the refuge of the darkness which we know will dispel the clarity of the winter's sun and where we can hide our glaring shame. We abandon ourselves in this plot of others' joys and woes with the certain knowledge that we shall be delivered from all impending calamities, from every haunting doom.

It is the story of a beautiful night club singer who has a depression trauma: she wishes to marry for money rather than love. Her mother made the foolish mistake of marrying for love and both her parents worked themselves to death supporting the products of their love.

Two men are in love with her. One, the worthy lover, happens to be a fine dancer and this talent along with the heroine's production numbers adds variety to the progression of the plot. The other lover is the hat check boy, unworthy of her love by talent, looks, and station in life. The hat check boy is in turn loved by the cigarette girl who deadpans her way through the entire movie.

The plot thickens when the hat check boy wins the Irish Sweepstakes and suddenly becomes wealthy. But he does not wear his new affluence well. He makes an ass of himself and we are asked to believe that because he did not "earn" his wealth, he does not know how to spend it.

He sets out to court the lovely singer who now realizes that she is caught in a conflict of heart and head. Her heart yearns for the dancer who has gone off somewhere with his pride. Her head dictates that marriage to the newly rich hat check boy will end her depression trauma forever.

But the heart wins out over the head. The hat check boy realizes that money cannot buy love unless you are worthy of it to start with. He finally accepts the cigarette girl who has chased him without respite throughout the movie.

Honesty is rewarded; perseverance is rewarded. The dancer marries the singer; the hat check boy marries the cigarette girl and the two young husbands sing and dance themselves to a recruiting office and are last seen marching in uniform out the other side into a hastily staged sunset. They are joined by the girls in a grand finale of patriotic songs and although I get the message (am convinced even of its truth) I wonder why two single, thirty-year-old men haven't been in the service all the time.

IV

And now the sureness (and accuracy) of my vision falters.

It is growing dark as we leave the theater. Street lights have been turned on. The descending shadows seem to soften the cold hardness of the winter's glare. There is no wind; a stillness has settled on the streets. As we make our way along the icy paths and streets, I feel a gradual release from the bondage of my shame.

Perhaps it is not the darkness alone which has mitigated the cold, yellow objectivity of a Sunday afternoon. Because we cannot long sustain the clarity of a loveless gaze, we seek to transfigure the squalor of our lives as if we had always believed in the mythic, Perfect Circles of our better selves, or as if we had never doubted the final triumph of the Ideal over the Real.

From the entry, where we are hanging up our coats, we can hear the drone of voices. Although we have missed the Catholic Hour, we have arrived in time for the Rosary broadcast from a local station. In the living room Aunt Esther kneels before the radio. Uncle Otto is behind her and my mother half sits, half kneels on the edge of an easy chair. We reluctantly join in the antiphonal prayers for peace. We squat behind my father who kneels at the far side of the room from Aunt Esther. My lips mumble the words without conviction, but when I look at Aunt Esther, I see her head thrust in forthright challenge and I am impressed. It seems as though she is looking God squarely in the eye. She answers the voice of the priest loudly in precise, clearly articulated phrases. I decide that if she does not have a faith to move mountains, she has incredible gall, either quality to be greatly admired. We are in the fourth joyful mystery.

The prayers are over, the radio returned to an obscure station where Uncle Otto has recently discovered yet another transcribed repeat of a complete episode of *The Lone Ranger*. Uncle Otto and Donald have already settled in chairs close to the radio. Aunt Esther and my mother, who is now fully recovered from her headache, go into the kitchen and begin moving the platters of food from the refrigerator which Aunt Esther has already prepared. She has sliced the pot roast and added lunch meats and cheese. There is a bowl of potato salad and the several gelatin salads now cleansed of mayonnaise. My mother carries an armful of bottles—olives, pickles, mustard, ketchup, mayonnaise—from the refrigerator. Then she begins to whip the cream for the desserts. It is all arranged smorgasbord style. When Aunt Esther carries the pitcher of nectar to the table, we realize with delight that we are having a summertime picnic in the middle of the winter.

My brother arrives from his afternoon of happy recapitulation of the finer moments of "The Lady of the Veranda." He is still flushed with excitement and sings as he hangs up his storm coat. The song, from the third act, reflects the radically masculine posture of the male chorus in opposition to the radically feminine female chorus. The occasion of plot which justifies this explosion of emotion is an argument between the hero and the heroine over the probable and preferable sex of their children if and when they marry. The blocking of this scene was his masterstroke as stage manager. All the boys were to one side of the stage and all the girls to the other; they faced each other in physical and symbolic confrontation.

Hank acknowledges our presence with dignified condescension, then he crosses the kitchen to the table of food. He rubs his hands in eager anticipation (as well as in imitation of the manner of the villain of "The Lady of the Veranda"). He surveys the food carefully and proclaims loudly,

"Ah, thrift, thrift, Horatio. The funeral meats are set forth coldly at the wedding feast."

He quickly steals a slice of cold beef before my mother can stop him. Roberta, who has been watching him in admiration and bewilderment, says,

"What is *that* supposed to mean?"

"It is a line from Shakespeare, from *Hamlet* to be specific, which I have rather cleverly applied, extemporaneously, to our picnic supper." Hank is in a rare mood.

"Well, what does it mean?" she says.

He raises his hand to signal her attention.

"Object lesson to illustrate." He picks up one of the green gelatin salads and a knife from the table. "First, your mother, my dearest Auntie," he bows toward Aunt Esther and clicks his heels together, "slicks the mayonnaise onto the left-over potatoes." He pretends to flick the blade across the top of the shivering mass. Then he snaps his wrist, directing the imaginary mayonnaise into an imaginary bowl.

"Next, we smother the naked salad with whipped cream."

He goes over to the table and ladles three heaping tablespoons from the bowl which my mother has placed behind the nectar pitcher. He selects a spoon and holds the plate before him and raises his eyes toward heaven as though he is making an offering to appease the angry gods. Then he presents it for our inspection.

"Lo, the bitter salad of despair hath become the sweet dessert of hope and nothing hath been wasted." He adds a dramatic aside behind his hand and out of the corner of his mouth so Aunt Esther won't hear. "The mayonnaise hath already found its way into the potato salad."

He spoons a mouthful. Some whipped cream catches on the tip of his nose. He stretches his tongue and licks it off, a talent of such prodigious dexterity that I am awed and envious each time he does it. Roberta giggles and my mother pretends to scold him for making off with a dessert and an excessive amount of whipped cream. He swaggers slowly into the dining room, eating as he goes. He turns in final commentary on his explanation.

"It's like transubstantiation," he says obscurely to Roberta who has no idea what he is talking about.

We pile our paper plates high and with our silverware and glasses of nectar carefully make our way through the dining room to the card table which Uncle Otto has set up just inside the archway in the living room. Roberta places her food on the table and goes to get a deck of cards. It is our unspoken custom that we will play cards as we eat. We do not mention the game because we always argue about its proper name. My cousins call it Rap-rummy and I call it Thirty-one.

Aunt Esther approaches and from a coin purse withdraws fifteen cents for each of us and places the coins in neat piles on the table. She leaves three nickles in the fourth position for Hank who she knows will join us in his good time. He will eat alone and then kibitz at my father and Aunt Esther's game for a while, but he has not yet been invited to play with them so he will reluctantly demean himself by joining us.

My father sits at the end of the dining room table eating and warming up a deck of cards for his game with Aunt Esther. They will play Sixty-six, a strange hybrid of Euchre and Pinochle. Uncle Otto and Donald sit by the radio eating from plates balanced unevenly on their laps. The women are the last to eat. Aunt Esther takes her plate to the dining room table. As she sits, she vows to give her baby brother a lesson at cards as evidence that she is still the boss around here. We laugh when she calls my father a 'baby brother.' My mother takes her plate into the living room, places it on a side table and then sits at the piano and begins running scales, quietly so as not to disturb anyone, to loosen her fingers.

We begin our game. In our first two hands I rap quickly and catch Marlys without even a matched pair. Hank joins the game, but as a concession to Marlys' losses he must place a nickel in the kitty before she will deal him in.

My mother now bursts into song. She plays a rhythmic virtuosity piece, "Kitten on the Keys" to warm us up and then we hear the thunderous chords of her rendition of "Bye, Bye Blues." She plays the first several notes slowly with majestic pomp and emphatic repetition. It is a false start, though, for she suddenly changes tempo and rushes through the song in happy release from the despair to which the lyrics bid a fond farewell.

We can tell from the 'card German,' the only foreign language spoken in my family, that my father is defeating Aunt Esther in their first game. She has called upon the Lord in heaven to assist her, and she has damned the Jews, the universal scapegoats, all to no avail, but she smiles despite her bad luck. As my father deals a new hand, she leans across to our table and says to Roberta,

"Ask Aunt Bea to play 'The World is Waiting for the Sunrise'."

It is her favorite song. Perhaps she thinks it may have some influence on the cards. Roberta excuses herself from our game and walks across the room to my mother's side. As my mother continues to play, Roberta whispers in her ear, and my mother nods her head, but I know she will not honor Aunt Esther's request for at least another song or two.

After "Alice Blue Gown" and "Beyond the Blue Horizon," (we are in the 'blue' period of my mother's musical development) we are bathed in the idealism and hope of a new dawning. My mother embellishes the piece with occasional runs and rhythmic improvisations. Aunt Esther says, shaking her head in admiration,

"She plays that song with *such* feeling."

When my mother is done playing, she takes up her plate and silver and begins to eat. Her timing is perfect, for as the last notes of the piano are fading, the trumpets on the radio proclaim our return to the days of yesteryear. Uncle Otto turns the volume up. He puts his glasses on, an odd habit apparently intended to assist his hearing or to keep his imagination in proper focus, and then he leans closely to the radio.

As we continue our card game, I listen out of the corner of my mind to the unfolding plot. The Lone Ranger and Tonto are camped outside of Canyon City in a secluded clump of trees. Tonto is out rustling up wood when the Lone Ranger, busily administering to Silver's needs, is surprised from behind and told to raise his hands. He discovers that the rifle aimed between his shoulder blades is wielded by a boy of fourteen years, who mistakenly has concluded that the Lone Ranger is one of the outlaws who has been harassing his family in a thinly veiled attempt to make his widowed mother sell her homestead quarter.

At this point in the dialogue young Jeff is surprised from behind by Tonto who unarms the youth and holds him awaiting orders from the Lone Ranger. In his understanding and great compassion, the Lone Ranger orders Tonto to release the boy, who, overwhelmed by this unexpected mercy and already convinced of the essential goodness of the masked stranger, unburdens his difficulties to the two attentive listeners.

They ride together to the boy's home where the Lone Ranger, with that marvelously resonating baritone, quickly wins the confidence of the boy's mother and his sister. The rest of the exposition is completed. It seems there is a range war in the Canyon City area. Jeff's father was killed fighting for his right to be a free yeoman farmer in fulfillment of the dreams of Thomas Jefferson, after whom his son is named. The villain appears to be a certain cattle baron, Rancher Gillis, who has hired outside gunslingers to do his harassing while he poses as the sympathetic neighbor willing to pay a fair price for the land.

Then the Lone Ranger sends Tonto to town to buy supplies as a pretext to eavesdropping. Tonto overhears the villains and reports back to the Lone Ranger.

"Me hear Rancher Gillis talk to tough hombres," Tonto says. "Him say him buy mortgage from bank. One missed payment and him foreclose."

Their suspicions are confirmed.

And then the Lone Ranger in that deep, reassuring voice says, "Listen to me, Tonto. I have a plan." His voice trails off into a crescendo of music. We return to the present.

During the commercial my father on the verge of another triumph shouts across the room. "Hey, Otto. I hear the Lone Ranger shot Tonto last week." He plays a card following Aunt Esther's lead.

Uncle Otto turns the volume down and takes off his glasses. He stares at my father. "What are you talking about now, Republican?"

"It's true, it's true. He shot him right between the eyes with one of those silver bullets." He points his forefinger between his eyes and flicks his thumb hammerlike, then lands with a trump on one of Aunt Esther's aces. He leads back the ten of trump to break up her forty meld.

"I heard about it just the other day," he laughs. "After all these years the Lone Ranger finally discovered that 'Kimosabe' actually means sonovabitch."

He breaks into his stuttering donkey laughter as he completes Aunt Esther's downfall. My mother admonishes him to guard his language before the children.

"Aw, Pa, that joke's as old as the hills," Hank complains.

Uncle Otto returns to the radio with an unsympathetic "humph" which reflects his utter contempt for my father's sense of humor. But Hank, catching my father's spirit, points his thumb toward Donald, bent with his father in profound involvement, and announces our reconciliation.

"Anyone who listens to *The Lone Ranger* can't be *all* bad," he says and even Roberta smiles a partial forgiveness.

"Why do they call him the *Lone* Ranger?" Roberta asks. "Tonto is always with him and he has a nephew, too."

"Indians, even good ones, are not counted as people in American history," Hank says cynically, "and Dan has been tossed in as a sop to the moronic twelve-year-olds who listen to the stupid program."

Uncle Otto does not appear to hear him.

"Notice that he is the *Lone* Ranger, not the *lonely* Ranger," my father says. "My guess is they call him *Lone* to emphasize that he is unmarried, free of burdens and responsibilities."

Roberta does not seem satisfied with either answer.

We move quickly now toward resolution. The Lone Ranger's plan works perfectly. The Rancher Gillis falls for the ruse and discovers himself trapped. In fact, the plan works so well that the Rancher Gillis unwittingly reveals himself as the greedy villain. When all seems lost, he resorts to his gun which is instantly shot out of his hand by the Lone Ranger. The hired gunslingers prove to be cowards, and the Sheriff, who has been too weak to confront the wealth and power of Rancher Gillis in the past, is now able to jail the whole gang until the circuit judge arrives to conduct a fair trial.

That would be enough, but there is one final scene. The widow, her children, the good townsfolk, and the Sheriff assemble to thank the Lone Ranger and his faithful Indian companion. Someone, however, is still confused. A voice asks,

"And who is the masked stranger?"

The Sheriff answers (with a touch of impatience and disbelief in his voice),

"Why, *that* was the *Lone* Ranger."

We hear the Lone Ranger's final distant urgings to the great horse, Silver. As his voice fades once again into the past, a shiver goes down my spine and I am swept along by this scene of recognition and farewell. It seems as though, through the power of this fiction, we have all been somehow wondrously translated into a remote allegorical drama. As I look about I see my father, Good Humor, braying laughter and my mother, Fine Arts, returning to the piano. There is Aunt Esther, Ambition and Industry, waiting patiently for the ever renewing possibilities of a new shuffle, cut, and deal, and Uncle Otto, Common Man himself, leaning over Radio listening to the Good News of Eternal Justice.

And I, now helpless to resist, am moved to believe (if only for the moment) that Truth and Beauty and Peace and Love (Ah, Love) reign upon the face of the earth.

Monica Krawczyk

TOKENS

After Monica Krawczyk died in 1954 someone said that if the angels in heaven didn't know Polish Monica would teach them. Krawczyk was born in Winona in 1887. After her education at Winona State Teachers College, the University of Minnesota, and the School of Social Work in Chicago she became a pioneer in settlement social work and for years was a visiting teacher at several Minneapolis public schools. During the 1930's she founded the Polanie Club, an organization of women dedicated to learning about and sharing their Polish background. Her involvement in a number of Polish-American associations and her ability to reach out to the very poor people in Northeast Minneapolis gave Mrs. Krawczyk an unusual vantage point from which to view Polish-American life. She fashioned this material into short stories which like the following selection were first published in magazines, and later she brought them together under the title If the Branch Blossoms and Other Stories.

S HE CAME TO ME ON MONDAY. She was a little bit of a woman, freckled, light-haired, of regular features, a face fit for a cameo.

"I come to invite you to shower," she said brightly, with a foreign accent, after I offered her a chair.

"Oh, no, I no can sit down. I have to call at twenty-nine more places."

"Well, who's getting married?" I asked. I could not remember that Mrs. Futerko had any daughters.

"My son. You cannot guess which one," she teased.

I couldn't guess. Louis was eighteen and the other two were too young.

"Louie, of course!" she asserted. "He is the one. He is to be married!" she said, with happy emphasis.

"But you don't mean . . ."

"Yes, I do. Well, what's wrong? He is of age!"

"But he's so young!"

"Young? He is old enough. When I was sixteen, he was born. And look at me, or at him! What's wrong? He find a girl, and I'm helping him out. He is a full-sized man! There is no stopping him now!"

"And what about the girl?"

"Oh, she's a plain little girl,—nice enough,—but poor, very poor. She's the youngest, and the mother is an old lady, who licks a beer mug every time she can get it. That's why she won't give the wedding. But that don't bother me. I have no daughter, and I can do for a son what any mother can do for a daughter. That's why I'm giving the shower. I have one hundred and twenty names on my list. And everybody is promising to come."

"But do you think, . . ."

"Don't worry. He'll be all right."

"Has he a job?" I asked.

"No, he ain't. But my boss promised to take him on for extra next week. It won't be so bad. I'll help them a little from the start. But you must come to the shower! You . . . his teacher. It will be at . . ." She handed me a slip of paper upon which was written an address and a date. "Now don't forget. Put this slip in a sure place. I really must hurry. Oh, I nearly forgot. Do you need car tokens?" She brought out a soiled handkerchief, untied the knots, and held it out. "You see I sweep street cars on night duty, and I find these. I sell them fourteen for a dollar. Oh, what a help they are! Last month I sold eight dollars' worth. You see, these tokens are very important to me, because it was this money that gave me a chance to deposit five dollars on the hall for the wedding, and three dollars for the orchestra."

I bought some car tokens, realizing fully that my dollar was to be a deposit on some other part of the wedding.

"Really, Mrs. Futerko, you shouldn't. . . ."

"Don't you bother your head about Louie. Just come over to the shower. You'll see, everything will be all right."

The shower day came, and I had not had time to go. So the following day I called to give my regrets and incidentally to see if my parcel had been delivered.

"Oh, yes, your bath towels was a nice present," Mrs. Futerko assured me. "Too bad you don't come. Seventy-five ladies came, and the rest all sent their presents. Every room was full. And we took in twenty-seven dollars in cash!"

"Then they are to be married for sure?"

"Oh, my yes. Yesterday I draw out some of my savings and I buy their rings."

"You bought their rings?" I was dumbfounded.

"Certainly. Louie ain't working. And I know what's proper. Wait. Sit down a little. I'll show them to you."

She rummaged in a dresser drawer and brought out two small white leatherette cases.

"I paid thirty-five dollars for the engagement ring. I made Louie give it to her so she can wear it before the wedding. Of course I told them that the ring cost a lot more! It looks like a real diamond! You'll see it! Ain't these wedding rings pretty? I paid ten for hers and twelve for his."

She was like a little girl, getting ready for a big doll party. Her face was enthusiastic and most happy as she told me of one thing and then another.

"So you have bought the rings! Really, Mrs. Futerko, Louis shouldn't get married. He is so young, he has no job, he . . ."

"Oh, it's too late to back out now. I rented the hall and the orchestra, and this morning I took out the rest of the savings and I bought their outfits. Wasn't it nice that I had that money saved up? Really, my last three years sweeping cars will give them the start. Wait, let me show you the outfits."

Out of a closet, she brought out the new purchases.

"This is his suit. Twenty-five dollars! It's nice goods, don't you think: And this little white suit is for our Frankie. He will carry the rings. Now here is her dress,—nice satin and lace—cost me seventeen dollars! Then I bought her wreath and veil and all the other extras that she needs. Her bill alone is close to fifty dollars, but won't it be nice?" She held the dress against her own body, as though she were to be the bride. "When I got married, nobody made a big fuss about me, and I know how that feels. So I'm going to see to it that Louis and Jennie has everything they need."

What could I say to her? Nothing could stop the wedding.

"And here's the pillow for the ring-boy. I made it myself. Not expensive,—the lace at the Dime Store,—and the ribbon too. Don't you think the blue ribbon is nicer than the pink?"

"Oh, of course! And you made it?"

"Yes, I did. I missed my sleep yesterday forenoon, and didn't

378

do my ironing. But that can all wait. Just so Louie's wedding comes off."

"I don't know. I am still worrying. You know Louis is so inexperienced . . ."

"Why should he wait? I've washed his shirts and called him mornings long enough! Let some one else do it now!"

What more could I say!

"Don't worry. He's a man. Let him start his own nest."

"And what does your husband say?"

"He has nothing to say! He is helping me. He has already arranged with our baker,—you must know him,—Blazik,—he's delivered us bread for twelve years,—well, he's to do all the baking. And then my husband ordered the drinks and he saw the priest."

"And who'll pay for all that?"

"Oh, that will come out of the bride dance. You are surely coming to the wedding! I think the young couple is coming to your house tomorrow. We are inviting one hundred families. It's lots of work. I go right with them, and I make them talk right up to the people. They are very bashful, you know. And we hire a man with a car to take us around, and then we have to go evenings to find the folks in, and Louie gets a chance to treat the men with cigars."

"You know Mrs. Futerko," I shook my head, "knowing Louis as I do, such a boy . . ."

"He's much smarter now! I sometimes think it was my fault that they was bad when they was small. I used to leave them alone so much. You know, I was young when I got married, and I wanted pretty things in my house. My husband,—he don't earn enough in the coal yard,—so I went to work, and my children was out on the street. But, they all learn. Louie knows better now!"

"But how will he support his wife?"

"The boss called him for extra help today. They won't have to pay for rent. They will live upstairs,—right in my house! The rooms are empty. Come on up and see them."

I followed the slight figure of Mrs. Futerko up the rear hall and stairway, which was littered up with a sack of potatoes, a broken stepladder, a pile of old clothes, and a discarded organ.

"Just these two rooms,—the kitchen and the bedroom. The stove and the bed we bought at the Salvation Army Store, and this table and chairs I gave them. We have too many. Look," she pointed to the closet off from the kitchen, "the stuff they got at the shower. And these dishes,—ain't it a pretty pattern,—they got that at Cohen Brothers for nothing! Everybody that gets a license gets these dishes free! And all this bedding they got at the shower."

"So they have their license already?"

"Oh, yes, you know, we can't wait. Really, they won't have it bad here,—and when they get rich, they can move! I gave them a pretty lamp for the shower, but as long as they don't have a parlor, we keep the lamp downstairs. You know we have a little radio, they can visit with us evenings."

"Well, you're surely good to them," I remarked as I turned to go.

"Oh, before I forget, maybe you could use some more car tokens?" She was pulling out her handkerchief. "Every dollar comes in handy. And be sure to come to the wedding!"

It was a big wedding,—the church ceremony taking place in the morning,—then there was the visit to the photographer,—then the return to the hall for breakfast. It was served in the spacious dining room, where there were long tables heavily laden with platters of meats and sausages, mashed potatoes, green peas, and sauerkraut, cheese cake, *chroscik*,—salads,—and many pies. There was the bar room, in which Mr. Futerko officiated, knowing whom to serve pop, beer, and wine,—and whom to serve, with a wink of the eye, a small glass of *vodechka*. Men, in their Sunday best, button-holed with a flower, stood about in groups. Women, in their freshly starched dresses, or their bright silks, stood about, gossiping about nothing. Children were chasing each other from one room to another. And upstairs, in the dance hall, were the young people in gay colors, dancing to the orchestra's loud music. The bridal couple stood near the entrance door.

I met them there, as I entered late in the afternoon of the wedding day. The groom, a pale lad, rather tall, fair-haired and straight of feature, like his mother, smiled and greeted me awkwardly. The bride, a slight little girl, no older than Louis, ordinary in spite of the satin, lace and veil, shook hands with me and invited me to dinner.

"Oh, I'm so glad you came!" Mrs. Futerko was at my side. "Isn't it nice here? And you were so worried! They are married already!" She pointed to the couple that stood like two children beside her.

I watched Mrs. Futerko as I ate of the delicious chicken and the crisp *chroscik*. She was dressed in a dainty flowered silk thing over which she had tied an apron, and the long pearl earrings and the rose in her hair made her very festive.

"You'll excuse me if I can't stay with you long. You see everything is on my head. We are short one dishwasher; so I must help out when they get rushed. Oh, here, you must have a flower." She looked about at the tables, but the bouquets long ago had been robbed,—only sprays of leaves remaining. She pulled the rose out of her hair and offered it to me. "I haven't any more left," she explained, noticing its withered petals, "but it smells nice."

"No, you keep it," I insisted.

"Excuse me, see, how they are calling me! They can't get along without me!"

Two months later, on a Monday morning, I dropped in to see Mrs. Futerko.

In the kitchen, the new bride, in a bright flowered wash dress, was doing the family washing.

"My mother-in-law ain't up yet. You know, she works nights."

"And you're doing her washing?"

"Yes, I work, but my boss gives me off on Mondays, so I do the wash."

"And where is Louis?"

"Oh, he's doing the house work upstairs. He got laid off from his work." She turned toward the bedroom door. "I think my mother-in-law is calling you. You can go right in."

I went into the bedroom where Mrs. Futerko was sitting up in her bed, her head propped against many pillows.

"Well, good morning, Mrs. Futerko," I greeted. "You have it easy now."

"Yes, I have to rest up. I worked hard for the wedding. And Jennie is young, she can do the washing in two hours." She shoved her flaxen locks back of her ears.

"Now that Louis is married your worries are over," I said.

"Oh yes, everything came out all right. The bride dance brought in about three hundred dollars. After my husband paid the wedding expenses, he had about forty dollars left for the couple. That paid for their wedding photographs, a half of a ton of coal, and groceries for about a month."

"And what about Louis' job?"

She yawned ever so carelessly and tapped her mouth with her hand.

"He has a job promised," she answered. "But if he doesn't get it, I'm going to ask my boss to let Louie take my job. Starting a new family like that, he needs it more than I do. Oh, say, before I forget, I have some more car tokens to sell . . . Will you buy some?" She placed her finger on her lips, and then whispered. "I have to save for the new baby. Oh, yes," she smiled, "Louie told me!"

Patricia Hampl

LOOK AT A TEACUP

Patricia Hampl lives in St. Paul, where she was born. Her first book, a collection of verse entitled Woman before an Aquarium, *was published in 1978 by the University of Pittsburgh Press. Her poetry has appeared in literary magazines, including* Paris Review, American Poetry Review, Antaeus, *and* Iowa Review, *and she has had an essay in* Ms. *Hampl has taught at the University of Minnesota and in various community programs, including that of Poets in the Schools.*

S HE bought the teacup in 1939, of all years. It was on sale downtown, because it was a discontinued pattern. Even on sale, it was an extravagance as far as her new in-laws were concerned; it set her apart. She used to say how she just put the money down on that counter and let Aunt Gert sigh as loud as she pleased.

1939. My mother was buying dishes that had come from Czechoslovakia, because they made the best china and she was marrying an American Czech. Most of the teacups are still unbroken. They're mine now, because I'm her daughter and she cleaned out her china cabinet last week. Each piece has a tiny "Czechoslovakia" stamped on the bottom. The cup is thin—you can almost see through its paleness when it's empty; right now, there's tea in it, and its level can be gauged from the shadow outside. The cup is the palest water-green imaginable. Sometimes, in certain lights, it is so pale it doesn't seem green at all, just something not white. It is shiny, and there are thin bands of gold around the edges of the saucer and cup, and again midway down the bowl of the cup and at its base, which is subtly formed into a semi-pedestal. There is also a band of gold on the inner circle of the saucer, but it has been worn away, after so many years, except for a dulled, blurred line. There is no other decoration on the outside of the cup—a bland precision of lines and curved light.

But inside the cup there are flowers, as if someone had scattered a bouquet and it had tumbled into separate blossoms, falling in a full circle around the inside. Some have fallen faster to the bottom of the cup, while some are still floating. The blossoms don't seem to be pasted on the surface like decals, they really appear to be caught in motion. And now, for the first time, alone in my own house (I've never been alone with one of these cups before; they were her company dishes), I see that no two flowers on the cup or the saucer are the same. Each a different flower— different colors, different altitudes of falling, nothing to create a pattern. Yet the cup and saucer together are pure light, something extremely delicate but definite. As refined as a face.

My mother's face, which has fallen into sadness. Nothing tragic ever happened to her—"nothing big," she'll say. I am the one who has wanted something big.

"I know the most important thing in the world," I told her when I was ten.

"Well, what is it?" she asked.

"Work. Work is the most important thing."

Her face showed fear. "Oh, no," she said quickly, trying to sweep away the thought. "No. Family is the important thing. Family, darling." Even then, her voice was sounding a farewell, the first of all those goodbyes mothers say to their daughters.

Or maybe our parting began one day when Dad came up behind her in the kitchen. He kissed her on the back of the neck. She thought they were alone, but my brother and I had followed him into the kitchen. He kissed her neck just where the hair stops. She turned from the sink like a swaying stem, with her hands all full of soapsuds, and put her stem arms around his neck. Her eyes were closed, her arms heavy and soapy. Pure and passionate soap arms of my mother. He drew her down suddenly in a swooping joke of an embrace—a Valentino bend, an antic pose for us giggling kids. He swept her in his arms and gave her lips a clownish kiss. We giggled, and our father laughed and turned to grin at his audience. "My dahling, I *luff* you!" he said to her soulfully. Her body struggled awkwardly, her eyes flew open, and she tried to rise from his clownish embrace.

"No, no," she said. No, no to any joke. She stood at the edge of her red-petalled life. There are buds that never open. "Just let me up," she said. "I've got these dishes to do. Let me *up*." And she plunged her hands back into the dishwater. Every night, she swam with her thoughts in that small sea.

In the cup, amid the bundle of pastel falling flowers at the bottom of the bowl there is another firm, thin gold circlet. It shines up just below the most deeply submerged flower, like a shoreline submerged by a momentary tide of morning tea. The engulfed flowers become oranges and violets—those colors. Above the tea-line there are green leaves and several jots of blue flowers, not deep and bright like cornflowers but a powdery, toneless blue, a monochrome without shadow or cloud. Also, there is the shape of the flowers. Some are plump, all curve and weight. There is a pale lavender rose on the saucer, with a rounded, balled-up cabbage head of petals; and on the opposite side a spiky, orange dahlia-like flower. None of the flowers looks real. They are suggestions, pale, almost unfinished, with occasional sparks of brightness, like a replica of memory itself. There is a slur of recollection about them, something imprecise, seductive, and foggy but held together with a bright bolt of accuracy— perhaps a piercing glance from a long-dead uncle, whose face, all the features, has otherwise faded and gone.

In 1939, in Chicago, my mother was a bride. That was the first year of the war, when Europe began to eat itself raw. In the newspaper picture announcing the marriage, her head had a halo. A golden light was around her head.

"I wasn't one for buying a lot of stuff," she tells me. "You only need so much. I bought what I needed when I got married." In the past few years, she's been giving me many of those things, piece by piece. Every time I go over to visit, she says, "Well, you might as well take the yellow tablecloth." Or there will be a pile of silverware she'll want me to have. These teacups. I'm always walking off with something.

I try to get her to talk about her life, but she won't do that. It's not that she thinks I'm prying. "Well, honey, what do you want to know?" she says. "I mean, what's there to say?" And she pushes her hair, which is still more blond than anything else, away from her face, and she looks really beautiful. I start talking fast, saying how everybody *knows* the world has changed a lot since the Second World War ended, and she was alive when Hitler was in power, for God's sake, and she's lived through something, and it's part of history.

"It wasn't *that* long ago," she says, and flips her honey hair again and lights a cigarette. "Besides, you'd have to talk to somebody from Europe about all that. They lived through it." Once she told me that in high school she'd had an assignment to write an essay about why Hitler was good for Germany. "Personally, I never liked him," she said. "We were always Democrats. But we had that assignment."

So I go over to visit, and we talk and I ask all these questions and she says, "You sound like one of those oral-history projects," and I say, "No, really, I'm interested." I'm always telling her, anything you can remember, any detail—it's really important. Everybody's life is important, I say. I'm interested. I can't even explain why.

Sometimes she says things like "You know, I bet you won't believe this, but we girls, way back—and this wasn't in the country, either—we used to use cotton strips all bundled up, instead of Kotex. And we'd wash them out and use them over again." Or, "The first pair of nylon stockings I bought, they lasted two years. Then stockings started not lasting." Once, she looked across the kitchen table at me and said, almost experimentally, as if she wanted to hear how it would sound aloud, "You know, one time your father came home, just an ordinary day, and I looked up and I wasn't even thinking, it just darted into my head: Someday he'll walk in and I just won't be here, I'll just leave. But it never happened."

None of it amounts to anything, though. Her details don't add up to a life story. Maybe that's why she's been giving me all these things the past few years—her possessions, everything she bought in 1939, the year of her marriage. This teacup, which I look at closely, for a long time, sitting at my own white-and-yellow kitchen table, alone, across the city from her.

The teacup was made in a country far away, of which other countries knew little. An English politician (but you can't go just blaming *him*, my mother says) shook a nation away as he tightly furled his black umbrella. A country lost its absorption in peaceful work, lost its pure science of flinging flowers onto the sides of teacups.

I tell her I believe that something could have been different. What would have happened if someone with an important black umbrella had considered the future of teacups, if powerful men bowed their heads at the difficulties of implanting the waxy tulip on porcelain? Old questions—certain people have tried to answer them, there are books. But many of us still live with the details; the souvenirs of some places are never broken. This cup is a detail, a small uncharred finger from the mid-century bonfire.

I visit my mother. We sit in her blue-and-white kitchen. My mother stands up for the future. "Life goes on, you can't keep going over things," she says. "It's the *flow* of life that counts." She wants me to ride forward into the golden light that she says is the future and all its possibility. "Look ahead," she tells me.

I try, but everything drives me into the past that she insists is safely gone. How can I ride forward on her errand when all the world, even the smallest object, sends me back, sets me wondering over and over about our own strange life and country, always trying to understand history and sexuality. Details, however small, get sorted into their appropriate stories, all right, but I am always holding out for the past and thinking how it keeps coming back at us. No details are disparate, I tell her. Mother, the cups were discontinued because a country was discontinued.

"Oh, but now you're talking politics," she says, and clears off the kitchen table. "Over my head, over my head," she says.

But it's not. That's what makes me mad. She *knows*. They all do, those brides who chose their china in 1939. Many things fell that year, for those brides—not only flowers into teacups. Their bodies fell, paired with other bodies, on beds together for the first time. "But that was no tragedy," she says, smiling, with her hands on the back of a chair. Smiling because she knows after all our talks that I think something was wasted when she first fell. Because I have refused to fall. "Some people just don't want to get married—I know that," she says broadmindedly. But she knows I'm saying marriage isn't *there* anymore; the flowered flannel nightgown isn't being hung on a peg in a closet next to a pair of striped drawstring pajamas anymore. We don't get married anymore, Mother. Don't blame me; I didn't think it up.

"Don't talk like a sausage," she'll say. "Some people—there are always some people who do not *want* to get married. I understand this. I understand you. You don't want to get married. Fine. That's just fine. It's fine. Many people live . . . that way."

Her own marriage, I agree, was no tragedy. It was the old bow pulled across the cello, making its first sexual sound again. Another generation joining the long, low moan. The falling of flowers down the sides of teacups, the plunging bodies on white sheets—I know people could take any amount of this pain. But the falling of the other bodies, the rain of bodies in Europe, that happened that year too, Mother.

Marriage, that's one thing; we agree that for her it was no tragedy, wasn't the end, really. But Europe was already broken, broken for good; there was no replacing a nation of glassblowers. Bodies fell that year in Madrid, too. In the cities of Spain, women looked up at the sky in terror. In Barcelona, almost for the first time in history, a woman carrying home a branch of forsythia wrapped in waxed paper ran for cover, hiding from the air. In that war, bombs fell on women from the air, and it was planned.

My mother says she can't get over how I'm always connecting things.

"Everybody I know talks this way," I say. "Does it embarrass you?"

"No. Just—well, tell the truth."

"I will. I'll try to."

The only real difference between us, between my mother and me, is all the talking I do. Her cello voice was drowned somewhere in the sound of falling flowers, in marriage, in the new thought of bombs falling on women with flowers, with teacups. But this particular teacup and its golden shoreline escaped, and she and I have both sat with it in our kitchens. She gave it to me.

Mothers know their daughters go to their bedrooms and try on the strange clothes women wear and look at themselves in the full-length mirror, trying to understand the future, the lipstick, the bras. Is there a mother who gives a daughter a teacup and thinks it is not also inspected?

"Mother," I said last week when I was over to visit and she was putting red tulips in a vase, talking about how everybody she knew smoked and how she was glad I'd never taken it up. "Mother, everybody I know, they're always talking about their parents, trying to figure out their mothers. Did you do that? My friends, we all do that."

"No," she said. "We didn't, I guess. We didn't talk the way you do. We didn't, you know, have *relationships*." Then she remembered about the teacups, and we changed the conversation.

If she were alone having a cup of tea, as I am now, she would be smoking a cigarette, staring dreamily out the kitchen window, absently rubbing her index finger over the nail of her thumb (she still uses nail polish) in circle after circle. The smoke would be circling around her head of honey-and-smoke hair. Just sitting. I can see her.

This afternoon, though, it is my finger looped in the ear of this European cup. She is not the only submerged figure I see—she and this buoyant cabbage-head rose. There is so much sinking, no hand can hold all that has happened.

We sit around a kitchen table, my friends and I, and try to describe even one thing, but it flies apart in words. Whole afternoons go. Women often waste time this way. But history has to get written somehow. There are all these souvenirs in our houses. We have to wash and dust them. They get handed down when there's no way of explaining things. It's as if my mother has always been saying, Darling, look at the teacup. It has more to say.

Sinclair Lewis

from CASS TIMBERLANE

Sinclair Lewis, the first American writer to receive the Nobel Prize for literature, was born in Sauk Centre, Minnesota in 1885. An astigmatic and awkward boy, Lewis made few friends in his native town, an experience repeated when he was a student at Yale College. There, however, he started writing fiction. After his graduation in 1908 he began to search constantly for the right place in which to live and work—a search that never really satisfied his restless, querulous nature. Lewis's temporary homes were to include New York City, Hartford, Minneapolis, St. Paul, Duluth, and Excelsior, Minnesota. He died in Rome in 1951.

During his apprentice period Lewis worked for a publishing house in New York, quitting when his stories began to sell to the better-paying national magazines. It was his novel Main Street *that established him as a major writer in 1920. Quite obviously modeled on Sauk Centre, it outraged inhabitants of many American small towns, with its satire that shades over into caricature. In subsequent works Lewis took on the middle class businessman in* Babbitt, *religious credulity, charlatanism, and commercialism in* Elmer Gantry, *and the upper middle class chase after spurious culture in* Dodsworth. *In* Cass Timberlane *Lewis examines the institution of American marriage, and the following selection treats one example in the city of Grand Republic, a fictional Duluth.*

THE RETURN of Judge Timberlane to his court room was marked by an impassive "Glad to see you back, Judge" from Humbert Bellile, the bailiff, a hand-shake from the clerk of court, and "Now we can get going—nice trip, Chief?" from George Hame, the court reporter.

They were quiet and competent men, though bored, and it appeared evident from seeing them run the court machinery that they had nothing so disturbing in their lives as wives to hate or trust, daughters to be worried about, ambitions to be defended; nothing more complex than the conduct of dull agricultural arson cases.

Hame and Bellile went, after court, to the Cockrobin Bar, and had comforting conversation with Ed Oleson, the barber, and Leo Jensing, the electrician.

"See your boss is back from his honeymoon, George," said Oleson.

"Looks fit 's a fiddle. Incidentally, the best judge in the State. Born professional."

"What kind of a girl he marry?"

"Cute little trick, bright 's a dollar. Hope she appreciates him."

Jensing yawned, "Those rich guys that belong to the Federal Club certainly do marry the swellest dames. Well, they can have 'em. I'll bet they're all a bunch of headaches. My old woman and I—I always tell her she looks like a constipated chicken, and she says I look like a stubble field—she's dumb and she was brought up a Seventh Day Adventist, but we get along like nobody's business. I cuff the kids and send 'em off to bed and then I get a can of beer and we strip down to our undershirts and sit around and tell lies and yap about what rats our neighbors are and generally enjoy life. The Judge can keep his cutie, and that goes for all the fat boys in the Federal Club. Say, ever been in that club, George? What kind of a dump is it?"

Mr. Hame explained, "I often take papers to the Judge there. It's a pretty swell joint, at that! All wood paneling and the bar's like a chapel, stone arches and floor. But you know what you can do with the whole club! Lot of landlords telling each other Roosevelt is a Communist, like it was a piece they learned at school."

Ed Oleson was eager. "You ask *me* about the Federal Club! I go there all the time, to shave the upper-bracket crooks when they got too big a hang-over to walk. Oh, a lot of 'em are okay; Webb Wargate is a real constructive citizen, and Judge Blackstaff—he's just as good a judge as your boss, George, and tips you four bits, like a gentleman. But Prutt, the banker, he never gives you a cent—explains they don't tip, in a club. Hell, I ain't a club servant; I got my own independent business and I don't have to shave any cactus-faced old gentleman-virgin unless I feel like it.

"But the worst guy there is that Boone Havock. Say, why decent people ever let him in their houses is beyond me. I've been called in to shave that cut-throat when he was so drunk he couldn't go home and had to take a room at the club, and he told and volunteered and told me that he'd spent the night with a tart in a shack down in the South End and then got her cockeyed and cheated her out of her five bucks, and he boasted about it.

"My son Tracy, that works for Wargate, has got more brains and financial savvy than the whole club put together. By the way, Tracy knows Judge Timberlane's bride; says she's a high-class girl. And talking of wives, I'm like Leo here: my old girl and I have a swell time, especially now the kids are grown up. We go out hunting and canoeing like a couple of Indians. That's the kind of a wife I like."

George Hame rose, jeering, "Glad to hear there's so many square-shooting wives around this burg. I congratulate you boys."

The bailiff, also rising: "Same here. Fellows that 're out from behind the matrimonial eight-ball like you two must have money to spare. We'll allow you to pay for the drinks."

Jensing crowed, "Just to prove it, I *will* buy 'em!"

"Any time you're in for rape, Leo, just remind me that I used to know you, and I'll get the Judge to let you off with life," said Hame. "Good night."

Bailiff Bellile, as he entered his brown Cape Cod cottage, waited for his wife to say, "Have you wiped your feet? I try so hard to keep things nice here, and then you come home drunk and get everything all dirty."

She said it.

She waited for him to say, in echo of his days as a lumbercamp teamster, "I wish to God I *were* drunk, and maybe it wouldn't make me so sick to look at you."

He said it.

Ed Oleson went noisily into his upstairs half of a two-family house, and his aging wife chirped, "It's the old master himself. Have a good time with the boys?"

"I'll say! Wish you'd been along."

"Whyntcha invite me?"

"Juvecome?"

"Try it and see! Bet I would. Smell something nice?"

"And how! What is it?"

"Real Hunky goulash."

"Now you don't tell me." He kissed her.

"Nice time in the shop today?"

"Fellow here from Rochester, New York, he told me all about how we'll lick the Japs with a secret weapon we got. Say, I'll bet Tracy 'll be in the war, and be a major."

"If his lungs are all healed up. Golly, Ed, aren't you proud of that boy!"

"Say, don't you quote me and don't let the newspapers get hold of it, but I'm nuts about him. The damn little hick—think of him—headed for the top of the Wargate Corporation some day!"

"And let me tell you, Mr. Ed Oleson, they'll be lucky to get him!"

"I'll say. How about lassoing that goulash now?"

"I think you got something there, Mister. Let's go!"

There was no ugly noise between George Hame and his wife, Ethel, when he came coldly into their freight-car of a house, but only an uglier silence. That was agreeable to him, because there was for him a poisonous boredom in what he considered her spiritless and hopeless fussing, her whimpering demands for money.

He looked at her over the Dumas he was always reading. She was hemming a pot-holder made of red calico.

"Much too bright for her," he muttered.

"What?"

"Nothing . . . You certainly will drive me nuts."

"What say?"

"Nothing."

Then another baby yelled. They had five of them, and all unwanted. But there was also their fifteen-year-old daughter, Betty, whom he loved.

He said placidly, "All I exist for is to supply you with brats and lactation."

"And whose fault——"

"Yours. If you'd take a little care of yourself——As Montaigne observes, this place is always obscene with new dripping babies, and smells like wet death."

She knew enough then not to speak. When he mentioned Montaigne—pronounced Montaigny—he was likely to hit her with his seal ring.

Betty came in, round and pert as a bouncing tennis ball.

"Hello, Daddy," she said, as she raced for the stairs, and "Hel-low, sweetheart" he answered, looking up after her new nylon stockings and old shoes.

His wife was afraid not to speak now. "George! I will not have you looking at Betty that way!"

"So you will not have it! So what?"

He returned to Dumas.

Some day, he thought, Betty and he would run off together to France, to the shrine of Dumas. She looked much older than fifteen, didn't she? He dreamed about this always, and always knew that he would never do it. He knew that he would hold to his wife. She irritated him, but he was lonely without her on the evenings when she was visiting her incessantly sick relatives and Betty was out with one of the neighborhood boys whom he hated. He was lonely not because he had no treasures in himself, for he could renew them out of Dumas or Scott or Washington Irving, nor because he could not take comfort in solitude, but because he was afraid that when Betty discovered how he felt toward her and vituperatively left him forever, then no one in the world but Ethel would stay by him, no one else would blame it on Betty.

He guessed that Judge Timberlane would kick him out, if the Judge discovered his thoughts about Betty, and he was sorry, because, though he considered the Judge a little too naive, he also believed him to be the Archangel Michael.

With the firmness of the will to death, he waited for Betty to come down and pass through the room again. The other children panted in and out, but their noise was so blurred that it was to him like an absolute silence.

"Don't you want any supper?" grated his wife.

"What? I suppose so. I never thought about it . . . . Oh, Betty, going out? Get home early now, sweetheart. I'll sit up for you."

"Swell, Daddy," she condescended.

Then he felt gay, and he looked amiably at his wife. When he saw her expression, he froze and returned to Dumas.

Carol Bly

GUNNAR'S SWORD

*Carol Bly was born in Duluth in 1930, and was graduated from Abbot
Academy, and from Wellesley College. She lives in Madison, Minnesota
and is active as a poet, translator, book reviewer, short story writer, and
creator of custom-made crossword puzzles. However, she is probably best known in Minnesota for her incisive essays in the "Letter from
the Country" column of the* Minnesota Monthly. *Her letters are
marked by their questioning of the vague and easy generalizations that are
too often used when real solutions to complex social problems are painful.
She has served as an area theme planner for the National Endowment for
the Humanities and Farmer's Union project. Her work has included
managing the* Fifties *and* Sixties *magazines, the* Sixties Press, *and the*
Seventies Press. *Her writing has appeared in the* Nation, *the* Minneapolis Tribune, *the* New Yorker, Poetry Northwest, Ironwood, *and*
American Review. *The following selection appeared in* American
Review #19.

As she climbed the hill to the Home, Harriet White felt the
town falling away behind her. She usually despised the
town in a casual, peaceful way, the way adults sometimes despise
their parents' world once they've left it. The mind simply remembers it as something unpleasant, but dead. Right now she felt
annoyed with the town in general because she had begun a quarrel with the Golden Age Auxiliary women about the quilts they
were making: they were using old chenille bedspreads for cen-
ters, since the center can never be seen, and then doing elegant
patchwork covers. The pastor had held the quilts up at service
and praised the ladies. These quilts, which looked cosy but didn't
keep out the cold, were then sent to Lutheran World Relief. Harriet was irritated with these women's ethics, which often seemed

First published in *American Review 19*, January 1974, © 1974 by Bantam Books.
Reprinted by permission of the author.

like little more than an uneasy suspension of local pastors' remarks and the inchoate strictures of their husbands in the VFW
Lounge.

She had lived all her adult life with her husband and son on
their quarter section, where a half mile in every direction was
theirs: when she came to the Home, she had somehow to shrink it
all to the size of her room. Some people managed that by stuffing
all the furniture they could bring from their old houses into the
tiny rooms of the Lutheran Home; Harriet managed it by working
away at her pastimes with a fury. The crafts room was full of her
output; she was like a factory; she turned out more sweaters and
afghans than 20 residents together. But when it snowed, even
during the tiresome snows of late March, she felt a settling inside
her, as if her mind lowered and glided outward, like the surface
of a lake. She would fetch her coat and overshoes and walk about
the ordinary, dreamless town as if lost in thought on her knees,
someone who has been dealt with cordially.

Harriet's neck was ropy and knotted, in the way of old people
who have got thin. She forgave herself that. As a little girl, and
later as a young woman, she had feared the degradation that age
might bring. She remembered watching the hired girl, who had
cared for her over weekends when her parents went to their club,
pulling on her stockings. Above the knee, Harriet had seen the
white meat of the thigh swelling and she had sworn, I shall never
let my legs look like that! And later she had sworn, I shall never
let my chin sag like that! Or, I shall never lower myself to *that*!
Now, as she swung fairly easily up the hill, she thought she was
less discontented with her body, and self, than she had been at
any time earlier. She was 82, but she kept a jaunty air, some of
which was gratitude when her right ankle didn't act up. She
climbed firmly, noting how soundless the cold air was, except for
traffic in the town below. The elm treetops were broomy and
vague; the smoke from the Home power plant piped slowly
straight up. She hoped it would snow.

On the upper sidewalk at last, she saw Arne, the Home's driver
and man of all work, helping Mr. Solstad, the mortician, wheel a
casket out of the east entrance. Harriet paused, partly for the flag
that lay over the coffin, and she knew it was the body of Mr. Ole
Morstad whose funeral was to be down at the church that afternoon. She was not sorry that he was dead; he had been taken

up to the infirmary floor on third more than three years ago. Then, rather than now, they had recognized his death; her roommate, LaVonne Morstad, had cried and Harriet had held her shoulder and hand. "He will never come back down into second!" cried Vonnie then. And so he hadn't.

Arne and Mr. Solstad eased the casket off its wheeled cart into the hearse. Then Arne came over to Harriet, with his workingman's sidewise walk, blowing on his hands. He smiled at her. "Morning, missus," he said respectfully, as he always did. Inmates who were very feeble or not very alert he tended to call by their Christian names. "Will you be wanting a ride down to the services this afternoon, Mrs. White?"

"I'll walk, Arne—it isn't so cold!"

"Not for you maybe," he said admiringly. "But some of 'em, they wouldn't go if they had to walk."

"I bet you won't be taking down storm windows today after all," Harriet said, remembering an announcement over the public-address system that morning.

"Feels like snow," he said, swinging his head northwest, where the tiny cars ran along on the cold gray highway. "Weather don't seem to scare you none though."

They both paused as the hearse drove by them carefully—and then they gave each other that odd farm-people's signal, as they parted. It was a slight wave with the right hand—half like a staff officer's from his jeep; half like a pastor's benediction. Harriet went in.

She avoided the reception entrance, with the residents sitting about looking hot and faint, and the few children inevitably hanging around the TV sets instead of going up to the grandparents they'd been sent to visit. She marched straight off to the back, where the crafts room was, and had the good luck to find Marge Larson, the therapist, there. The room was full of half-finished products at this end—but at the other end, divided by a Sears Roebuck room divider, was the "shop" where the finished hot pads, napkin holders, aprons were on sale. The Golden Age Auxiliary members came by regularly and bought. Harriet's work was known because it was fair isle knitting, in western Minnesota called Norwegian knitting. Not everyone could do it. Harriet also helped Marge with other people's unfinished work, or work that needed to be taken out and remade, which she kept quiet about.

Together they discussed some of the projects lying around on tables. Some weren't any good. An old man was in the room, too, but it was Orrin Bjorning who could not hear and could not work. He sat utterly still, and the dull light came in off the snow so that the skin on his forehead and cheeks looked like a hood—as if a monk sat there frozen—instead of like a face. He insisted on spending whole mornings in the crafts room, his fingers bent around a piece of 1 X 1. He never stirred. When the PA system announced dinner time, he would shake himself and slowly leave, never speaking.

Harriet and Marge walked around the room, touching and lifting Orlon, felt, acrylic, cotton. Harriet promised to return in the afternoon, and work a little on that Mrs. Steensen's rug. Mrs. Steensen had started braiding. Marge often placed new lots of nicely stripped wool in the woman's lap and Mrs. Steensen always looked up and said energetically, "Yes—good, thanks then, Marge!" in her Scandinavian accent. "*Ja*—I've been needing just such a blue—now I can get on with my rug!" And then all morning, her hands made little plucking gestures at the rags in her lap. Marge and Harriet together worked up two or three feet of the braid from time to time and Mrs. Steensen seemed not to notice. "Rug's coming along pretty good!" she would shout, when Marge came by.

At ten Harriet left. She still had her coat to hang up, and she had to write a short speech. Later she would have to help Vonnie Morstad dress for the funeral.

But she stopped at the second floor landing because Mr. Helmstetter and Kermit Steensen were sitting by the elevators.

"Thank you very much for that little rabbit favor, missus," Helmstetter said. "I gave it to my granddaughter—the one they called Kristi. Kristi is for Christine, that's her aunt on the other side, then Ann for the middle name. I suppose it's for someone. She was very pleased."

"*Ja*, I suppose you told her you made it, huh," Kermit said, one of the Home wits.

Helmstetter blushed. "She wouldn't have believed that, I guess. Where you going in such a rush?" he said to Harriet. "You're always rushing. Chasing. This way, that way. Such a busy lady."

"Busier'n Jacqueline Kennedy," Kermit said.

Harriet sat down beside them and they all faced the aluminum elevator doors. "I can sit down a moment."

"Work'll keep," Helmstetter said.

"Work don't run away," Kermit Steensen said in a witty tone: again they all laughed, all of them more heartily than they felt like, but they all felt pretty cheerful for a second. Harriet rose to the occasion.

"Well, how's 'Edge of Night' coming?" Harriet asked them. She knew that they all listened to television drama serials during afternoon coffee in the coffee room. In the morning the sun didn't come into the coffee room, so it was empty save for the candy-stripers' carts and a slight odor of dentures. In the afternoon, however, the lace curtains were transformed and a light fell on the people as they were served their "lunch"—the western Minnesota word for the midafternoon snack. Sometimes the sun was so gorgeous that they had to squint to make out the dove-pale images on the TV set. Helmstetter and Steensen and a couple of other men—and nearly all the second floor women—kept track of the dramas. From time to time, Harriet asked them about them.

"We don't watch that anymore," Kermit told her. "'Splendor of Our Days' is what we're watching now."

"This young fellow has got an incurable disease and he is trying not to tell his girl about it, but she knows. She wants to talk it over with him so she can help him."

"Oh, that isn't the point!" Kermit said sharply. "The point is he doesn't want her to find out he's scared to die. He wants to keep on laughing and joking right up to the end. She belongs to the country club that his folks want to get into."

"There's an old Viking story like that," Harriet put in. "Do you remember that old legend about how the Vikings believed you must make a joke before you died, in order to show Death you were better than he is?"

Letting the *Lutheran Herald* sag on his knees, Helmstetter said courteously, "How'd that hang together then?"

Harriet said, "There was a particular young Viking and he and his friends had a grudge against a man named Gunnar. So one day they decided they would put a ladder up to the loft where Gunnar slept, while he was away, then they'd hide in there and then kill him when he came in at night. So the friends helped the young fellow put up the ladder, and up he went, with his knife between his teeth. Just as he was heaving himself over the windowsill, however, Gunnar, who happened not to be away after all, leapt off his straw bed and ran his sword right through the young Viking. The Viking fell off the ladder backward, and of course his friends raced over to where he lay, with the blood coursing out of his chest.

"'Oh—Gunnar is at home, then?' they asked with astonishment.

"'Well now,' the young man said as he died, 'I don't know if Gunnar is home but his sword is.'"

Helmstetter and Steensen hesitated: they weren't sure they got the point of the story, yet they felt moved. "Pretty good, pretty good," they both murmured. There was a polite pause, and then Kermit Steensen fidgeted and brightened and said, "Not to change the subject, you see this girl belongs to the country club, but the boyfriend isn't interested at all, but all the time his parents are anxious for him to belong and they keep throwing him together with this girl."

"But she's really interested in that other fellow—the doctor fellow!" cried Helmstetter with a laugh.

"She isn't either!" said Steensen. "That was all over weeks ago. In fact they've dropped him; you don't see him anymore."

"I seen him on there just yesterday!"

"You see lots of things!" Helmstetter said.

Harriet rose after a moment, and said, "Are you going to be in the dining room at 11?"

"What for then?" Both old men were very anxious not to be forgetful of any part of the Home schedule.

"We're having coffee in honor of Marge Larson, you know the woman who helps us with crafts? It's her birthday. We'd do it this afternoon but there's the Morstad funeral."

"Oh, *ja*, then," the men said. When Harriet left, they fingered the church magazines on their knees in a distracted sort of way, and Kermit began deliberately snapping over the pages.

Harriet looked forward to getting to her room. She not only had two books going at the same time but she also had one small bit of knitting—a patterned complicated sweater for little Christopher. She had not used a pattern, but had counted the stitches there were to be across the shoulders, at front and back, and then, using the same number of squares on light-blue-inked graph paper, she had made up her own pattern. She blocked in the colors with crayons, trying different combinations. It was immensely satisfying, because she not only had the problem of what colors and shapes would look well in wool, but also, she wanted, if possible, to make up a pattern that would work in the different colors in any one row at least as often as every fifth stitch. If a row were to have blue and white, for example, she made sure the blue yarn was used at least as often as once in five—or the white, conversely. This way she prevented "carrying" yarn for more than an inch in the back. Long, carried yarn tended to get caught in buttons and baby fingers. Harriet laughed at herself for her love of knitting—you are simple-minded, she told herself—yet it sustained her in a way that would have surprised her years before. For example, during the meals—as in most institutions meals were a weak side of life at the Home—she could keep cheerful and even hold up a sort of one-handed conversation, by reminding herself that the orderly, beautiful knitting lay waiting upstairs. Sometimes the thought of her knitting even came to her during Larry's visits. I do hope, she told herself, I won't get so my own son is overshadowed by a pair of worsted mittens. She felt certain that the best defense of one's personality, against everything—senility mostly, and worse, later—was one's humor. And hers was intact. Or at least, so people assured her.

"You have a wonderful sense of humor, Mother," Larry had told her on one of his visits from Edina. "When did you develop it? Was it when you married Dad and went into farming?"

She opened her top bureau drawer to take out the lined paper to write the speech for Marge on, and found Larry's last letter. "I'm hoping to get out to Jacob over the weekend, hopefully Saturday," he wrote. Ghastly usage, Harriet thought affectionately. "I'll call Saturday around noon if I do. Are you having a cold horrible March? The city is a mess—mud and melting snow. I don't know why we Minnesotans complain about winter, spring is what's horrible. See you soon. Love from us all, a kiss from that wonderful little Christopher—Larry." Harriet read it over again, and then laid it under her notebook.

She began work on the speech. "We are gathered here this morning in honor of Marge's birthday," she began. "But it seems to me it would make a lot more sense if she were gathered here in honor of *our* birthdays—we've had so many more of them." She sat back, staring at the smudgy storm window that Arne had not removed. "What drivel," she thought, glancing at her speech again. She crossed it out. Even first-rate jokes didn't work particularly well at the Home—and second-rate jokes went very badly. She visualized the dining room—the bleached foreheads, held motionless over the plates full of desserts, the stately, plastic flowers. She bent to the job again, forcing herself not to hope that Larry might offer her a ride out into the country to look at the farm. She worked away at the speech, finished, shortened it, and had just thought to check the time when Vonnie came in.

The young girl volunteers called candy-stripers had put curlers in Vonnie's hair for her. On the first floor was a shampooing room, where once a week a few members of the Jacob Lutheran Church—the Golden Age Auxiliary—laid their heavy coats on the steel-tubing chairs, and washed and set the hair of any of the women who cared to come down. In between those Tuesday afternoons, the candy-stripers would sometimes do it. The residents preferred the services of the Golden Age women, most of whom were in their fifties and could remember how hair "should be done nice"—meaning, with bobby pins screwed to the head, dried hard, and then brushed and combed, leaving discernible curls. The young girls, on the other hand, believed in either back-combed hair—or more recently, in simply straight "undone" hair. Vonnie came into the room scowling, and Harriet supposed she wasn't pleased with the way the candy-stripers had done her.

"Shall we lay out our clothes for this afternoon?" Harriet said, closing her notebook.

Vonnie grasped the arms of her rocking chair, got ready, and then jammed herself down into it. "You lay out *your* clothes!"

"Can I help?" Harriet said gently.

"I can lay out my own clothes; I can get into my own clothes. Next thing you'll want to rinse my teeth!"

"Going to the dining room for the birthday coffee for Marge?" Harriet said after a pause.

"To hear your speech you mean!" snapped Vonnie. Her cheeks shook.

"Vonnie!"

"Oh, *ja*, Vonnie! Don't Vonnie me!" cried the woman. "I am sick of you doing everything like you were better than everyone else. Speech for Marge! Why couldn't we of got a printed card like everyone wanted? A nice printed card, with a nice picture, a photo of some roses, on nice paper with a nice poem on it, they got hundreds now, at either one of the drugstores—you're always going on them walks, you could of walked to the drugstore and you could have got it and you could of read it aloud to us, and then we would have the cake and it would be real nice. But oh no, you got to do some fancy thing no one ever thought of—oh, *ja*, it had to be something—a speech!"

"Ridiculous," Harriet said. "A woman like Marge gets a hundred cards like that a year. The idea is to do something more personal."

"Whose idea? Everyone else thought a card would be real nice!"

Vonnie turned around and faced Harriet—the day's full light on her stretched forehead. "And I got something else to say to you also! My knitting! You can just keep to your own and leave my work alone! When I want your help with my work, I'll ask you for it."

"Oh, Vonnie," Harriet said, "all we did was take out back to the row where the increasing was supposed to start, and do the increasing every second row—and then you take over again from there."

"Don't you have any of your own to do? Why don't you do your own increasing and your own decreasing and leave mine be."

They both stood up and stiffly began taking fresh stockings, their better shoes, their dark print dresses out of their closets. If they dressed now, they wouldn't be caught dressing later when LaVonne's relations began coming in to pick her up to go down to the church. They had a half hour before the birthday coffee for Marge.

When they both were dressed, there was a pause. There was a problem they simply had to solve, Vonnie's hair. Harriet finally took the lead. "Vonnie," she said as efficiently and impersonally as she could, "let's get your curlers out now—because now's when we've got time to get it combed out before LeRoy and Mervin come."

The widow grumbled, but let herself down in her chair, with her eyes pointed coldly into the mirror. "I don't want it brushed out too much. I don't like the way that one candy-striper girl does it. No sense of how hair should be done."

"The one called Mary?" Harriet asked. Standing behind Vonnie, she began gently taking out curlers.

"*Ja*. Now that other one's a real nice girl. Friend of the Helmstetters. My Mervin married a Helmstetter." Slowly the curlers came off—LaVonne Morstad kept one trembling wrist raised, to receive them one by one from Harriet. Talking to each other in the mirrors, the two women pulled together again, a little.

The chaplain's voice now came over the PA system: his voice was rusty and idealistic. In his Scandinavian accent, he said: "If everyone will please come straight down to the dining room, we will be having a coffee hour in honor of Mrs. Marge Larson. If everyone will please come down to the dining room, we will be having a coffee hour in honor of Mrs. Marge Larson. *Vil De vaer så snill å komme til spisesalen; vi skal ha kaffe . . ."* continuing in Norwegian. He did not give his announcement in German, for in the Jacob area most of the German-Americans were Catholics. There were only a dozen or so in the Lutheran Home.

Harriet left Vonnie muttering over the funeral programs. The widow had the conviction something had been printed incorrectly, and she kept running her big finger across the lines again, pronouncing the names, the thou's and thee's, in a hoarse whisper.

Harriet found Marge and Arne dragging the PA system hookup over to the standing mike, near the diabetic table. Now the younger residents came in briskly, glancing out at the snow-lit window, nodding to one another. The more aged people followed, looking like the wooden carvings of Settesdal valley and the Jotenheim: Over the shuffling slippers, the stooped backs were immobile; you were aware of the folds and creases of sleeves, the velvety skin coating elbows that looked sore, the huge blocky ankles of the old, like knots of marble. Harriet listened, a little nervous as always before she addressed a group, aware of rayon rubbing, now chair legs being dragged out. Finally everyone was seated—even old Orrin Bjorning sat gazing at his right hand cupped over his left. Harriet was delighted to find Kermit Steensen and some of the other men sitting where she could see them; if you had just a face or two responding, you could carry the others.

"Harriet," Marge said, "would you read off the birthday list for this month? We were going to do it for Golden Age this afternoon, but since most of them will be down at the funeral, we thought we'd better do it this morning."

Harriet flattened the typed yellow sheet over her clipboard, rapidly checking the names for those she might not pronounce right. Three were crossed through—she recognized the names of two men who had died in the past few weeks, and of a woman whose relatives had moved her to the Dawson Nursing Home. Mr. Ole Morstad's name was still on. "Shan't I pencil through this?" Harriet asked, pointing.

"Oh my goodness—thanks!" cried Marge, leaning across Harriet to run her ball-point through it. "I'm glad you caught that!"

They stood together, planning the next few minutes—odd, Harriet thought, this stupid 15-minute affair, a two-minute speech for a birthday, and yet it had all the trappings of the hundreds of meetings she had presided over. It had also the old lilt to it—the sense that she herself was exciting, someone who could bring off things, someone to be relied on; if little difficulties arose, she could back and fill. She was a leader. Color came up into her face and she knew it.

As Arne knelt at her feet tinkering with the extension cord, Harriet thought, I used to believe that as I got old I'd feel closer to people of all sorts of backgrounds. I thought there was some great common denominator we'd all sink to—and I'd feel *more* affectionate toward clumsy, or unexperienced people. But it hasn't worked out. I don't! I am perfectly resigned to being among people who never read or reflect on anything but I don't feel close. And less than ever can I understand how they can bear life with one another. She looked out, now, over the whole dining room because Arne was through, and her birthday list, touching the mike, gave a hoarse rattle, showing the current was on.

"Good morning!" she said, remembering not to duck to the mike. "We are gathered together this morning in honor of someone who means a great deal to every one of us." She went on, faces turned toward her. Quietly, at the edges of the room, the kitchen staff with their red wrists carried in coffee urns and set down plates of dessert. Harriet noticed with the speed of eight years' residency that the dessert was sawed slices of angel food with Wilderness Cherry Pie filling and Cool Whip on it. She was aware of Marge herself, modestly perched on a chair at the diabetic table. When the speech was over, and the gift received, Marge would be off again—flying around doing the dozens of chores she somehow accomplished during a day—pushing a wheelchair to the shampoo room, helping a church women's group plan their surprises for the infirmary trays, even helping to tip the vats of skinned potatoes in the kitchen. Harriet mentioned some of these tasks so graciously done—and she heard the warmth fill in her voice. It had its effect, too. She had the people's attention: the moment she saw that, she felt still another warmth in her voice: the warmth of success. So she wound up with some lilt, made Marge stand, handed over the gift, excused the roomful of people from singing "Happy Birthday" because she knew they hated it—the sound of their awful voices—and she read the birthday list, after which everyone clapped. Then she said to Marge, "We all say, bless you, Marge," and retreated from the microphone.

Harriet settled herself in a folding chair by the maid's serving stand, to hear Marge's thanks but Siegert, the head nurse, was bending over her shoulder: "It's your son, Mrs. White. He's waiting for you in your room. I said you'd come up, but surely you can stay and have your coffee . . ."

"No, no!" cried Harriet. "I'm coming! Larry! No, I don't want any coffee! Thanks, Mrs. Siegert!"

The nurse smiled. "Tell you what, I'll bring up some of the dessert for both of you—and some coffee, how's that?"

"How nice you are," Harriet cried, and hurried out.

She wanted to go the fastest way, which is to say, up the staircase, but then she would be short of breath when she arrived and then Larry would worry. So she pressed the stupid bell and waited for the poky elevator to sink all the way down from the infirmary on third.

She found room 211 full of Morstad men. They were milling about in the tiny space between the bureaus, the two rocking chairs, the beds—in heavy dark overcoats flung open in the hot air of the Home. They were shaking hands, in turns, and then prowling about the room, trying not to bump into one another or the radiator. Vonnie herself stood rummaging in the top drawer of her bureau. Her rocking chair kept rocking as one man or another struck it with his ankles. Harriet paused a moment, daunted by the crowd, and then entered, and shook hands with each person separately. They were in their good clothes. "I think I ought to know yer face . . . Mervin Morstad's my name. My brother LeRoy, Mrs. White. He's from the Cities—over in Edina. Well I guess you know our mother all right." (Sociable laughter.) ". . . Deepest sympathy." "Oh, thank you now. . . . Yes, he was. He sure was—a blessing in a way, if you get how I mean. . . . Here—mother, never mind—it don't matter. . . ."

But Vonnie was furious. "Don't matter! I'll say it does. Look, right there, in print, and we paid for it, too!"

Both her sons, Mervin and LeRoy, huge men with gleaming, round cheeks, tipped their gigantic shoulders like circling airplanes over the card she held. She handed it to Mervin, and he read aloud: "Olai Vikssen Morstad. Born 14th April, 1886, Entered into Eternal Rest, 9th March 1971. 84 Years 1 Month 6 Days!"

"Well, it ought to be five days, shouldn't it?" Vonnie shouted.

"Oh, Mom, it doesn't matter," the son called LeRoy said.

"Oh doesn't it! Well, people will just sit through the services, you know what people are, and they'll count that up and they'll see just as sure as anything someone didn't add straight. There'll be talk."

"Come on, Mama," Mervin said. "Here's your coat . . . hat." Harriet found and gave him Vonnie's black bag, her gloves. "Come on, Mama," Mervin said, helping her. "They've got a real nice dinner down at the church—and Corrine's are all there already and they want to visit with you. And Mahlin's—all except Virgil, he's away at school yet—" And gently he went on, listing the various relations who had come for the old man's funeral, and now were being served a hot luncheon by one of the church circles. The big men followed poor Vonnie out of the room—Mervin taking her arm in the doorway. LeRoy hung back a minute and said civilly, "I know what you done for our ma, Mrs. White. All these years. She wouldn't get by near as good without you being so good to stay by. So thank you then!" A final view of his huge blushing face.

"Oh, Larry!" Harriet cried. "It's so good to see you!" For her son was there; all that while, he'd been waiting in that crowded room, quietly sitting on the edge of her bed near the far wall, glancing through her books.

They hovered a moment, hugging each other, in the middle of the room; "Mama," he said delighted, like a boy: "Look what I brought!"

There was a huge bundle of what looked like used clothing on her bed.

"You can hold it if you're good!" Larry laughed. He picked up the clumsy package, unwinding some of the clothes.

Harriet darted over without a word. Trembling, she undid the rest of some old padded jacket the baby was wrapped in, loosened his knit blanket—not without noticing through her tears, though, that it was one she had knitted. She carried Christopher to her rocking chair, and sat down. For a moment baby and great-grandmother made tiny struggles to get sorted. Harriet had to get her good foot, the left, which never gave her trouble even recently, onto the ground, to use for pushing to make the chair rock. The baby had to move his tiny shoulders as though scratching an itch, but in actuality, finding where and how this set of arms would hold him. He didn't pay much attention to what he saw out of his eyes: he saw only the dull whitish light off the snow, smeary and without warmth. What he felt in his shoulders, behind the small of his back, under his knees was the very soul of whoever was holding him; it streamed into the baby from all those places. The baby stilled, paying attention to it, deciding, using shoulder blades, backbone, and legs to make the decision whether or not the energy entering was safe and good. Everything now told him it was, so in the next second, he let each part of his body loosen into those hands, and let his feet be propped on that lap, then let his chest be lifted and pressed to that breast and shoulder—his colorless rather inexpressive eyes went slatted half-shut. He made a little offering of his own; he let his cheek lean on that old, trustworthy cheek, and then with a final wiggle, he gave himself up to being held. All she ever said to him was, "Christopher, precious!" but that was nothing to him—that was just noise.

Larry had stood up and gone over to the doorway; someone was conferring with him. He returned with a tray with two cups of coffee on it, and a plate with some white cake with the inevitable Wilderness Cherry filling on it. "That was your head nurse—Mrs. Siegert, isn't it?" he asked, proudly keeping track of the Home staff.

He sat down on Vonnie's rocking chair, with the tray; he shoved Vonnie's Bible over. The lace bureau cloth immediately caught in one corner of it and wrinkled up, and the program for Ole Morstad's funeral, a paper rabbit candy basket, and a tube of Chap Stick fell on the floor.

Larry, sipping his coffee, told his day's news. It hadn't been a bad drive out from Edina, although Evelyn had sworn he would run into snow. One hundred and fifty miles with very few icy patches this time—not like last year at this time! "Met some of your menfolk here, in the hallway, on the way up," he added conversationally. "I told them who I was and they said, 'Oh sure we know your mother! She's a real alert, real nice lady!'"

"I'm a regular Miss Jacob Lutheran Home!" Harriet said.

They both laughed, and he told her Evelyn sent her love. He told her about bringing Janice, his oldest son's daughter, out to see her folks in Boyd, and how he begged the baby away from her on condition he wrap him up well.

"What farm business did you come about?" Harriet said, meaning to ask intelligent questions although in truth she was only holding the baby.

"Oh that—" Larry said, frowning. "Before I get to that, there's something we've been over before, Mother, and I want to say it all again."

"Yes—all right!" She laughed at him ironically, mainly because it felt so marvelous holding the baby. His little eyes were half-open, but she held him so close, up to her cheek, that the eye against her cheek was of course out of focus, and therefore only a dark blur: she thought, I shall never forget that look of a baby's eye when you hold him too close to see—the dark, blurry, soft fur-bunch of his eye!

"You know that Evelyn and I have plenty of room, Mama. We want you, Mama. This is OK"—he gave a kind of wave at the tray of Marge Larson's birthday cake and Vonnie's mirror—"but, Mama, we want something different for you."

"You're right," Harriet said gently, "we *have* been over this before. You know how touched I am you feel that way, Larry. You and Evelyn."

She imagined again their house in Edina. It was one of a Cape Cod development—white, but with the green black shutters hung behind, rather than hinged on top of, the outside woodwork, and therefore straight-away visibly fake. But they had some marvelous rooms in it: a kind of library with a woodburning fireplace and a Viss rug with a light blue pattern, and the dining room. The other rooms had somehow soaked up the builder's ideas, and they all seemed to wail, Edina! Help! Evelyn had done what she could, but the built-in hi-fi cabinet in its fake Early American paneling suffocated the walls.

This wasn't why Harriet didn't go to live with them but she conjured up the picture anyway.

"I know perfectly well you moved in here because that was the right thing for Dad," Larry was saying. "That was *then*, Mama. True he would have been a burden to us—you never said that, but we knew that's what you thought. Anyway it's all different now, and I want you to reconsider. Very carefully."

"There's still your dad to think of, you know," Harriet remarked.

Larry put down his cake. "I don't know if that's true or not," he said. "I mean I don't know if that's the right thinking for you or us to be doing at all. I can't think it would make any difference— and meantime I've got a mother 150 miles away from me that I'd like to have living with me if you don't mind." He spoke a little feverishly—which Harriet understood as slight insincerity on his part.

"I don't know how to thank you," she said. She squinted hard into the baby's sleeping shoulders. His woolly sweater and the upper lip of his blanket she felt clearly on her eyelids. "I expect I could thank you by knitting baby blanket number 234 for Christopher here?"

They both laughed a little but Larry let the laugh fall and quickly took up his point again. "And Evelyn feels the same way, too, Mama."

Harriet was thinking as fast as she could. She had to think: why was Larry feverish? He must be talking excitedly because he didn't really feel so enthusiastic about her moving in with them as he wished to show. Or, that he felt enthusiastic about it now, but that the offer really—very deep within him—was good only so long as his mother was sprightly, alert, a little witty, and so forth. And that he was not giving her the profoundly felt invitation— which would be an invitation to live with him and Evelyn when she might be incontinent, irritable, afraid, or even demented. And perhaps she, like Einar, would have a bad stroke.

As Harriet went through this in her mind, being as systematic about it as she could, she felt this last was the real explanation of Larry's nervousness. It reassured her in her refusal to live with them: even if she should choose not to consider Einar, going to live with her son would mean having to make this adjustment to the Home later—to this one or some other less familiar one she'd have less energy to face it with than she had now.

Having thought this through to the end, she gained her poise. She said kindly, "I know Evelyn feels that way. And I know you do, too—both of you—well, you're marvelous children. I'm going to stay put, I think though. You know I thank you very much."

"Well there's another reason, Mama," Larry said.

Harriet looked up, still feeling the new sense of control from having thought through the whole thing.

410

"You see, Mama, I've actually sold the farm. That's one reason I am out here this weekend."

She felt damaged. This piece of news was like an actual danger to her body. The trouble with being at the end of life, Harriet thought, was that body and mind get too close together: that is, when the mind takes a blow—such as from Larry's selling the farm—the body takes the blow as well. You feel the thing physically. Other times, she had noticed it worked in reverse. When she had originally tripped over Orrin Bjorning's bird-feeding station he left on the floor of the crafts room—a good five years ago now—not only had she hurt her right ankle and toe, but she had felt a kind of damage to her soul. Tears of hurt feelings had come, she remembered. Senility, she suspected, arrived the day you forgot to laugh at these incidents.

Rapidly she now went over Larry's actual words. If he hadn't literally sold the farm, she might convince him not to. But she thought she could still hear his voice saying he had already done it.

He hadn't asked her. She didn't expect to be begged for advice, but it would have been lovely, really lovely, if he had let her in on the various stages of the dealing. He could have told her, I'm beginning to consider offers on the farm, Mama. Or, Well, Mama, two of the buyer prospects look pretty good.

No doubt he had sensed that she would try to talk him out of it! In any case, she gathered herself carefully, meaning to have nothing of the wounded about her.

"You ought to sell the farm, my dear," she said smoothly. "You can't manage a piece of real estate properly unless you're right there, available, when things come up—and goodness knows, it doesn't look as if you and Evelyn are ever going to farm—and certainly Janice and Bob aren't moving in that direction. And I can't really think any of you would want to *retire* to the farm. No, that was probably a good thing!"

Larry gave her a sharp look but she gave away nothing—he surely saw only half old-woman-being-sensible, half great-grandmother-holding-the-baby.

"I don't want you to get around me this time, Mama," Larry said. "I want you to come live with us. We have all that room now. And time. And there'd be congenial people for you to meet. We're not country club people you know! Look, Mama—you've spent your whole life out here!"

The loudspeaker made its electric whine, and the pastor's hoarse, nasal voice came on with the table prayer. *"I Jesu navn, går vi til bords, å spise og drikke på ditt ord. . . ."* It was dinner time at the Home—and the only sound on the second floor was the soft rub of nurses' shoes, as they moved about their duties.

"Let's go to lunch!" Larry said, standing. "Which one of the marvelous French restaurants of Jacob, Minnesota, shall we take in today? McGregor's Cafe or the Royal?"

"Neither for me," Harriet said. "Give me ten more minutes, dear—and then you go because I've got to go to that funeral this afternoon—and I just had cake and coffee. I don't want more now."

On a scaffold outside, Arne was manhandling a large screen frame. Apparently he had decided to start with the taking down of the storm windows after all. Both Harriet and Larry watched him a moment, in the way people who have done any job many times can't help pausing to watch someone else tackle it. They nearly felt the weight in their hands of the storm window coming off—they knew which snapholders had been loosened first; they knew the instant the weight of the glass and wood dropped into the vault of Arne's palm.

"You don't feel badly about the farm then?" Larry said, still looking out the window. Arne's shadow kept sliding back and forth in the room.

"No, dear. It was a good idea. Probably, you should have done it ages ago."

"You used to like it when we drove out there and checked out the old place," he said. "You'll miss that."

"Nonsense. There're hundreds of places I enjoy driving past."

"If you won't come to lunch, Mama, I've got to take that baby back to his mother, I'm afraid. You're sure you won't come?"

Christopher had wet through his clothing a little; his blanketed bottom was moist and warm, but Harriet, whose arm had ached the past half hour, couldn't bear to part with him. This moist, hot weight seemed like a part of her—she dreaded handing him over. She dreaded it. Yet, a minute later, when Larry carefully reached down, she managed a social smile up. Suddenly her breasts and lap were cool. She felt abominable, never to nurse or hold a baby again. Her heart turned really black; she felt her whole body was like a cold andiron.

412

Larry promised to write, to repeat the invitation. They kissed and he left, saying he'd go see Dad on the way out.

Harriet waited until from down the hall she heard the elevator doors open, close, then she hurried out herself.

"Oh, *ja!* there she goes!" cried Helmstetter, sitting in his usual place at the landing. So everyone was up from dinner already.

Now there were four other men taking up all the chairs there, or she'd have joined him. They all looked especially fragile and pale because they had now put on their good suits; the corrugated necks were so thin, they touched their white collars only at the ribby cords. They were all ready for the funeral.

The two candy-stripers were approaching the elevators from the new wing; glasses and pitcher tinkled like little bells on their cart.

"Hullo, Mrs. White!" they both said.

"Hello—DeAnn . . . Mary."

"Oh my," the one called DeAnn said, cocking her head at the men sitting about, "aren't we dressed up all fine and nice! Everybody looking so nice!"

"They're going to a funeral," cried the other candy-striper.

DeAnn swung the light cart about. Mary had to step back, so it could enter the elevator when the doors opened. "Well they all look real nice," DeAnn sang. She pointed her arm at full-length to press the elevator button, and turned her head, with the faultless, groomed hair, to the men. "Mr. Morstad was a real fine man," she sang to them. "And he looked real nice, too, for the services."

"I didn't think he did!" said Mary in a low tone to Harriet, dodging close to make room for the head nurse, Mrs. Siegert, who came up to wait beside them. Looking younger than 14 and very exposed, Mary seemed to gather her bravery and she blurted out, "I didn't think he looked very nice! He looked so tiny and brown and . . ." Her voice faded in terror, for the head nurse, as well as DeAnn, who no doubt despised her, and the four old men in the lounge chairs, now were staring at her.

"And dead," Harriet said, helping. "I agree. But then, the funeral had to be the fourth day instead of the third so the relatives could get here—that's why." Harriet brought out her best, sensible tone: "I remember on the first day he looked rather like himself—only asleep. The second day he began to look diminished, somehow. I remember thinking, that face wants to *leave.* The face is begging us to let it go—like a guest on the porch trying to get away from an officious host. . . . Then, yesterday, I remember—I happened into the chapel coming from my walk, and he looked simply like a dead man—he'd simply lost his distinction. It wasn't that he wasn't preserved or anything like that—but just that he had got generalized—he had become a sampling of death."

The candy-striper's hands came together. "Oh yes!" she cried. "Yes—exactly—that's how he was!" Still the elevator hadn't come down; the light showed it was on three; and they could hear metal scraping and men drawling instructions on the floor above.

The young candy-striper whispered, leaning over the cart toward Harriet, "I even noticed a tear under his eyelashes, Mrs. White."

"Oh for goodness' sakes!" the head nurse snapped.

"That happens," Harriet said. "I know what that racket is," she said to Mrs. Siegert. "I bet Arne's stuffing storm windows into that elevator—"

They had still to wait, half-listening to the scraping noises upstairs as something was fitted into or out of the elevator.

"You girls hold back with that cart," Mrs. Siegert said, when the elevator came. "Let Mrs. White get in first." But when the tall metal doors had slid open, no one could get in, for the elevator was full of men and a stretcher—Arne, now in his good dress suit, and Mr. Solstad, the mortician, both men standing soldierly beside a stretcher cart. The significant mounds and hollows under the white sheet told the mind *A body is lying there*, but such an observation was only academic. Harriet couldn't seriously believe in a human being under there. "We'll be done with the elevator in a moment," Arne said. The doors closed again. Harriet, Mrs. Siegert, and DeAnn watched the first floor light come on, and they all had to listen to the elevator door springs downstairs, being struck open twice. Harriet unwillingly imagined the body on its tray being nudged and guided out.

Harriet and Mrs. Siegert walked down the third floor new wing. The infirmary rooms ran along the north side, so they were walking along in direct light from the tall windows facing south. In the middle of the corridor Ardyce, a very, very old person who had been incontinent for over a year stood urinating on the rubber runner. Feeling the hot liquid course over her great ankles, she had begun to cry. Her bony, caving body gave this shriek like some poor sort of violin.

Mrs. Siegert was not an easily likable nurse but she had her strong side; swiftly she got to Ardyce and had the limp elbow and said, "Don't cry, honey—I'll take you. We'll get cleaned up OK—don't cry"; they wobbled together to the old woman's room.

Two younger nurses were guiding a white-curtained screen out of number 307 on little metal wheels. "Oh . . . it was Mr. Kjerle?" Harriet asked.

One of the nurses bent to wipe up the urine from the corrugated rubber mat, and in a moment all was quiet again. Only mysterious breathing came from some room or another, and a cough like small twigs rubbing from some other room.

Harriet put her head into 307. She had meant to do whatever it is we intend in a place where someone has just died. She meant to give some honor or to wish him luck flying off the earth; she meant to help to lift him far off the curvature of the earth by evening. She wasn't clear about it but she felt somehow obligated. She crept into the room, if only to sense his possible presence. In any case, Harriet had expected the room to be empty. Everyone knew Mr. Kjerle's relatives never came to visit—only a retired piano teacher from two miles west of Jacob used to stop in sometimes. The piano teacher's visits weren't much. He really only prowled aimlessly about the infirmary room, not really visiting the old man, at least not keeping up a conversation. Whenever Harriet was up on the infirmary floor, he would waylay her, talk to her eagerly; sometimes, leaning in the doorway of 307, he would tell her it was cruel the way some of the residents never got any visitors.

Harriet was brought up short to see a woman sitting at the bare little desk under the window. She sat so still, and wrote with such concentration, that in the indifferent northern light, she looked positively spooky. She wore an elegant knit dress of dark lavender—for a second Harriet felt pleased as if for a glimpse of the *grand monde*. Harriet received three impressions in rapid order: first, that this elegant figure writing was the spirit of the dead man; second, that it was some beautiful creature of society set here like a statue, just to give pleasure, and third—and she smiled with simple happiness at this—that it was the doctor.

Dr. Iversen didn't wear her medical jacket; like the other two doctors in Jacob, she avoided looking like a physician when she went to the Home. If you carried a medical bag, the old people snatched at you, telling of new sets of aches or about old prescriptions that didn't help anymore. Right now she had been called to the Home to "pronounce," that is, to legalize, a death. She had been sitting quietly, therefore, making out the certification.

"Hullo," she said courteously, as she saw an inmate pause in the doorway. Then, with the instant calculation, the mental sorting of people that she exercised every day in her job, she added, "Mrs. White. Hullo, Mrs. White."

"How are you?" Harriet said, coming in, shyly. "I'm sorry, I didn't know anyone was in here."

"No, of course not," the doctor said. She had not quite finished, but without showing any haste, she quickly picked up the sheet placing the printed side that read Minnesota Department of Health, Section of Vital Statistics, inward, against her hip. She rose. "How is that painful foot of yours anyway?" she asked.

"It isn't very painful," Harriet told her, gratified to be asked. "When it is, I take those gigantic tablets of yours anyway, and can't tell left foot from right!"

"Most of them," the doctor said, "wouldn't admit that a prescription ever did any good. I wouldn't dare ask how their foot is."

"By most of them I gather you mean most *old* people." Harriet laughed. "Don't talk so quickly! I shall be like that someday—and so will you. In fact, it's too bad you're so much younger—we could sit in our rocking chairs and tell each other what ached, and neither one of us would pay the slightest bit of attention to the other one. In fact, maybe you'll be worse. You'll be tired of listening to other people complain."

"No change, I suppose?" the doctor inquired, nodding toward the wall between the room they were in, number 307, and the next, 308.

"I haven't been in today—I'm just going now," Harriet said.

"It is hard, isn't it?"

"Yes—and I feel so sorry for him," Harriet added, not having planned to say anything like that.

Room 308, like 307, faced north, the cold light seeming simply to stand outside. There was the same little window desk, whose purpose was simply to be a piece of furniture for a sickroom. There was a high bureau, on which stood favors sent up from the public school children. At Christmas there had been paper reindeer with sleighs made of egg carton sections. Now there was an

Easter bunny, stapled to a bit of egg carton, in which one or two of the hard candies that must have filled it remained. Harriet supposed the staff took a candy now and then, just as they gradually were taking the bureau space. In the top drawer were the clothes Einar had worn when they brought him up. But in the other drawers were odds and ends, a few more added right along, a small plastic bag of curlers, some lip moisturizing cream, two magazines read by the candy-striper who spoon-fed patients, half a box of tissues. More and more that had nothing to do with Einar seemed to sift into the room; his small influence, like a little scattering of pebbles, was being buried lightly under other influences.

Harriet spent a second by the desk, her eyes on the fields plowed black and to the north, and the semis moving like little blocks on U.S. 75. Then she straightened and went back over to the bed.

"Hello, dear," she said. She pulled the white-painted rocker over and sat down to talk to him. On the good days he gave a sound, as well as he could, to recognize her; on the other days, no particular sign. Today—nothing; so she settled to talk to him. "A little news for you, Einar," she said. "Larry's selling the farm— probably a very good idea," she went on. "And considering the condition of the buildings, he did very well I think. There's no doubt that was the right idea—selling the farm."

She paused. She pulled herself together and said, "There's no doubt that was the right idea, selling the farm."

She took another pause—pulled herself together again. "I gave him the go-ahead on that. . . ." She was trying to remember other things to tell; she remembered in the crook of her elbow, with the palm of her hand, the feeling of Christopher in her arms, but the memory was still too personal. In fact, it was not yet a memory, but still part of herself and therefore couldn't be told. "I gave another speech this morning," she went on cheerfully. "Anyway"—she smiled—"the speech went off all right. About the only other news is I've fairly well planned little Christopher's sweater now, so I'll start the knitting of it soon. Oh yes—and the men said to give you their best. That Helmstetter whose first name I never can remember—and Kermit—they both said to greet you. They were telling me about television. They don't watch 'Edge of Night' anymore, they said. They watch something called 'Splendor of Our Days.' It sounds dumber than the other one, but

I expect if you kept track of it all the time, it would begin to seem real—you'd begin to care what happened to those people. . . . But those television characters don't seem like real people at all—and you know, they never show *where* the people are— they're always in a room somewhere—you never see a real place that counts, like a farm or anything like it—it's as if none of them had any place to belong to. Did I tell you, Larry sold the farm, Einar? Yes—very good idea, too!" She talked to him some more, and then rose saying, "I'll be back at five again to help you with your dinner, dear," and she went out.

She had spoken truthfully to the doctor in saying her right foot was not painful. When she finally got outside with her hat and scarf and gloves, she swung along well, and drew deep breaths of the cold burdened air. It definitely was going to snow. She lightly dropped down the hill to the traffic circle, noticing all the cars and the hearse parked in the church lot. She turned west on 11th Street and was still moving freshly and gladly when she came to U.S. 75, with the closed Dairy Queen building and Waltham's Flower Shoppe.

When she turned north, on the right-hand shoulder of the highway, the wind struck her forehead. It wasn't bitter, but it was colder than she had hoped for. She turned away from it, long enough to pull her scarf up about her neck better, and now the buildings of the town, even the hasty gimcrackery of the Dairy Queen, looked protective and familiar. Well, I don't have to walk all the way to the farm on the ugliest day of spring, she told herself wryly, but she turned into the wind again, bending her head. Under her feet the dozens of pebbles on the road's shoulder underfoot looked shrunken and abandoned. She tried to set up her walking motion into a kind of automation, the way she and Einar and Larry had done for years and years when they were tired from the farmwork. At first you grew tired, then you grew so tired you felt you might cry, and then, by not feeling any pity for any part of your body, by not weakening those parts, that is, with pity, you actually exacted from them more character; once the ankles, back, shoulders, wrists, learnt to expect no mercy of you, they began to work as if automated. Then you weren't exhausted anymore, and you could sift fertilizers, or lift alfalfa, or shovel to an auger for hours and hours, until, with their head-lights glowing like tiny search beams, coming out of the fields as if out of the sky itself, the tractors came home with the men who had been hired—and everyone could quit. Thus the tiredness could be held back until you all leaned over the salmon hot dish, and reached for the bread.

Harriet did the same thing now, looking up only once really—taking in a field of corn that someone hadn't gotten plowed, or even disked down at all. It'd do it good to snow a little, she thought of the scenery critically. So she was delighted like a child when the first flakes blew at her, around three-thirty.

It took her another two hours to get to Haglund's Crossroads, and a half hour to the farm from there. This last half hour was the township road running east, however, so the steady snow, that had been hurting her forehead, now struck only her left cheek, and she took her second wind cheerfully. When she reached the corner of her farm, she felt surprised: her old land, not ten feet from her now, across the ditch past the telephone company marker, looked just like all the fields she had been walking past. When she had sat on the porch in the hot evenings, all the dozens of years she and Einar had had the place, she certainly never would have thought those particular sights—Elsie Johnson's barn with the louver-window towers, Vogel's run, the Streges' line of cottonwoods to the south—would lose their distinction. When Larry had taken her out for rides, she always knew the place. Yet now, this late afternoon, she felt no particular recognition.

"Well, but the house will make the difference—when I can see the house," she said. Because the driveway lay another quarter of a mile to the east, she decided to cut across the plowing instead. She paused and then went down into the ditch, some pebbles falling into her boots, and then slowly up, and began working along the headlands of the field. Her forehead was tight and silky now with cold, and the skin gave an unpleasant sensation of not being close to her head. Harriet moved carefully, not just because she was exhausted, but because it was borne in on her that she was a very old woman and she would make a fool of herself if she fainted out here in the middle of nowhere, with night coming on.

The plowing was coarse, and from her height—as she imagined herself an airplane passing over it—it became a chain of harsh, tumbled mountains, with peaks turning floury but the smooth sides, scoured by the shares, still gleaming black. At last the farmhouse, or at least some dark, square, blessedly man-made shape stood out 100 yards ahead. Its lightless windows, broken, its tumbledown porch seemed friendly and very memorable. It had been a marvelous idea to come—marvelous!

Harriet's fingers, particularly on the right hand, were starting to freeze, but she put them in her coat pocket and went forward quickly. She also planned ahead, using her common sense: she would stay in the house or around it, but not for more than half an hour. She wasn't a fool; it would be difficult to explain why she'd come, but if she left soon and got home she might not even be missed.

The rough plowing ended; she stepped into the spineless pigeon grass, and emptied her boot. The snow stopped, but enough was down so the farmyard, with the L-shaped old house on it, rose a pale, glowing mound. Harriet went happily up.

The front door was half-ruined and stood open. She decided that it would be depressing inside the house so she sat down gratefully on the edge of the porch, feeling sorry for its beautifully milled railing posts wrecked and lying in the snow. She crossed her hands in her lap—a trick she had had all her life—in order to think deliberately, and get things right.

Immediately her mind and body seemed to have opposing wishes. Her mind wanted to go over favorite memories—it wanted to swoon, to graze, to be languid, and to rove over things that are delicious, such as her old loves. Her own mother and father, for example, whom she visualized dancing in their club, or drinking with faces yellow from the firelight at home. The mind wanted to go over how she loved them although she had despised their shallow, rich, greedy, life; how much she loved her parents and would like to know what they were thinking now . . . . It wasn't a new line of thought but her mind wanted so very much to go over it again. But her body, or her soul, whichever it was, was thoroughly excited and seemed to be urging, something very strange is about to happen! It was alerted like an animal—it refused to let her dream along the old intelligent reflections—it wanted to get the scent of something, it seemed to send fingers out beyond the broken porch. Oh—she thought, holding these two parts as well as she could—it is definitely something spiritual, something about to happen! And not from inside me! All these years I assumed it was all inside me—but apparently it isn't!—and I am afraid! In any case, it was in the outer circle of darkness now, rising over the Haglund Road maybe; anyway it lay outside the farm, and was lifting and falling, coming in closer, without any excitement of its own, simply waiting, not crouching nor threatening—something calm, but mortally large. She needed to invite it, Harriet felt, if it was to come in any closer.

Then a third thing happened: headlights were moving along the snowy road to the south, going east the way Harriet had come, and then going past the place where she had turned up through the field. Now the invisible car presented its red taillights for a moment but then, in the next, the headlights swung left and were quartering on Harriet. So they knew she was gone and had figured she might do just this—walk up here; and they were coming, to save her from the cold and dark. Her hand, particularly the fingers, hurt enough; she nearly leapt forward gratefully.

Wait a moment, she thought, sensibly: there are three different things I can do. I can still run behind the house—it isn't too late—they would call about a little here and there, but they wouldn't think of the old chicken house we had used for lawn mowers. Then, whatever that part of her was that wanted to invite the huge mortal thing outside, would have a little more time to do it in. But no, Harriet thought intelligently, they would see her footsteps in the snow and she would be tracked like an animal, and she would never recover her pride—not ever, after that. Now the headlights were fully turned in her direction, and as soon as the car tipped up to make the rise, the lights would flood over her, as the lights of all their visitors always had, blinding anyone on the porch. It was going to be unpleasant, whatever happened; but she tried very hard to think of some little speech to give that would not let them think she was old and out of her wits—something to pass it off lightly—but how? For she didn't feel she had any light touch at the moment at all: more and more, her soul was being engaged by the gigantic, mortal thing waiting in its wide arc outside; one minute it seemed to offer to go away, and leave her with her ordinary life in her hands again: this she couldn't bear, not now that she'd once seen it. She had a taste for it now. The next minute, however, she found she was still too mortal, too frightened by far, and she would agree to marry any sort of dullness rather than to join whatever that was. She couldn't toss off anything with a laugh now. If she herself were so deadly serious, how could she hope to make whoever was driving up in this car take the whole thing lightly?

Now the headlights were brilliant on her, so she had to look down at the wrecked railing and posts, that lay like a ladder thrown down in the snow. The headlights came no closer: the car must have stopped, and she heard the incredible confidence of an American automobile engine idling in neutral. Doors clicked open and shut—men were tramping in the darkness behind the headlights—someone in a low tone could be heard saying, "It's her all right!" Another voice—"You all wait. I'll go up!" Then a gigantic black profile of someone came at her, shielding her from the beams.

"Hi, Mama," the man said.

In a flash Harriet was angry at this grown Larry—a shallow thing he seemed, no matter that he was her son, no matter he was being dear and dignified and not talking at her, helping her step over the smashed banister in the snow. But she thought, how different he is from the baby he was, with the dark, blurry eyes so close to her face, for now he was only a grown son—predictable, and wrapped around with his health and sense.

Other people sat in the car. As Harriet got into the front seat, she saw all their faces in the light from the car's ceiling—Arne, it was; Larry; Siegert, the head nurse; some other nurse she had seen but didn't know—and she felt comforted, partly, by this lighted little circle. Outside the car, in a much wider circle, the mortal presence still wafted lightly. Harriet felt very definitely that it was offering to lap forward toward her again; she felt she could rally it and offer to go out with it, like something bobbing on lumpy, stale seawater in the darkness; she felt it wouldn't take her quickly, it would lap forward and receive her, but for a while it would let her look back to the tiny car, with the tiny circle of human beings; but they were all she knew, so she fled into the front seat, and let herself be walled up with Arne's shoulders on one side, moving as he went into reverse, and Larry's great shoulder on the other side. And from the back seat came low, special voices—the nurses talking to each other professionally. Harriet hoped she had not lost individuality from their viewpoint: now she was a woman who wandered off from the Home and had to be brought back at a good deal of inconvenience, and on such a busy day. She must be very careful to be light and sociable. "So good of you all," she murmured. "It was very cold."

She was very grateful for losing the sensation of God being close—or perhaps she had made up in her mind the whole impression of something in the darkness. In any case it didn't matter. She hadn't the slightest curiosity to think it over, for something much worse occupied her. Squeezed between these kind men, with the car heater blowing hot breath into her face, and with her eyes full of the dancing needles and blue tiny fires on the dashboard, she was sharply aware that she wasn't safe with these protectors. Her hand was in great pain now, from the freezing: but suppose *all* of her were in pain, and suppose death did come, and not some death she chose to conjure up and call upon, but plainly death himself, the real one—she would flash down like silk between these men, past the glittering dashboard without leaving the slightest impression, the way the pebbles in the road were blown off by the speeding car. I'm simply not going to be able to do anything about it, she thought with surprise.

They were driving rapidly down the Haglund Road—she felt the millions of pebbles of gravel that had always lain there, unwrapped, which no one pays any attention to, all the millions of things that lie about unbound to the millions of other things. With a tremendous burst of humility and joy Harriet thought: what a tremendous lot I have failed to think through! Yet I always thought I thought through things so well!

From a mile and a half north, the Jacob Lutheran Home suddenly stood up, with its three stories of lighted windows. It was difficult to visualize the shuffling heels moving about near bureaus, or to believe in the cartful of magazines parked idle for the night in the coffee room. The Home looked at least like a mighty office complex where far-reaching decisions are made that affect common people without their even knowing it. It was difficult to believe in Einar up there, lying lightly gowned in white, scarcely touching, like a bit of string, as he had lain for 14 months. Harriet thought, And I shall lie up there, too, and from month to month, because I will no doubt get less amusing and I will get more frightened, there will be fewer and fewer visitors, even this huge man next to me, Larry, my son, will come much less often, and perhaps my death will rock forward and backward on its heels waiting a long time, and I shall be so diminished by the time it comes even the staff won't feel anything personal. There will be none of the old recognition . . .

Now they were approaching the confident little town.

Harriet was very surprised to find that she hadn't spent 82 years in love with all there is, and tiny things like pebbles, which were in some strange way her equal; pebbles were her equal; she was astounded she had missed it! Now she needed every possible second, even if it were to be spent in a daze. How could she ever have said, "It is cruel that so-and-so's life drags on like this!" or, "It is a blessing that death came to so-and-so!" Or, "I certainly hope I shall go quickly when I go"—as if it were a question of being fastidious.

The heat of the car did not help her frozen hand. The pain was frightful—but her thoughts seemed so much more frightful to her that she deliberately gave in to the pain. From the back seat came kind voices: "Soon there, Harriet . . ." and "You're not the only one to go out walking, you know," and "We all do it, Harriet . . ." And in the front seat, her son's shoulder jerked a little next to hers and he stared ahead, silently, through the windshield.

When they were up in room 211, the doctor examined her fingers carefully. "We'll have you knitting again—it won't be long," she said. "She can have something to help her sleep," she said pointedly to the head nurse, who paused in the doorway.

Larry sat on Mrs. Ole Morstad's bed, with his knees spread, his hat thrown up on the pillow. He was turning over Harriet's alarm clock, and he looked very tense and bored. Harriet, too, felt very strained and bored.

"If you would *please* reconsider, Mama," Larry was saying— still asking her to go live with him. A second ago her heart had leapt—but only for a second. She would love to leave this fate! She would love to go to him! Again she imagined his house, the flowery rug with its wide edge of sky blue that looked like a cool, ancient summer all the time, and the marvelous tone of the Vivaldi on his record machine; Janice would come on weekends, perhaps, and bring the baby, and Harriet would rock with the baby, and look at all the woolen yellow flowers in the rug.

Larry was making the offer, but she heard a new apprehension in his voice. I am a very old woman apparently, she told herself, and I've wandered off in a snowstorm, but I'm not going to add this to my other sins. As she turned him down, she smiled quite genuinely, because the pill she'd been given was taking effect— her hand no longer hurt—and everything looked peaceful and colorless. From time to time, the upper echelon of the staff and residents looked in and greeted her—Marge Larson the therapist even stopped a moment, Kermit Steensen nodded from the hall—the candy-stripers had long since gone home or she knew Mary would have greeted her.

Tomorrow morning, word would have got around the whole community, and the simpler, the very aged, or the less acquainted people would take to hobbling by room number 211. They would want to have a look at someone who had stirred the community by getting a notion to go back home. From their flagged, lifeless expressions it would be hard to understand that actually their hearts were rather aflutter by this Harriet White's doings—the way the hearts of young women feel roused, and unstable, and prescient, when the first of their friends is going to marry.

J. F. Powers

KEYSTONE

Born in Jacksonville, Illinois, and educated at Northwestern University, James Farl Powers came to Minnesota in the 1940's. In 1946 he married another writer, Betty Wahl of St. Cloud, and since then they have lived on Cape Cod, in Milwaukee, in Northampton, Massachusetts, and for a dozen years in County Wicklow, Ireland, the scene of Mrs. Powers's novel Rafferty & Co. *But they have always returned to Minnesota, and have lived for extended periods in Avon, St. Paul, St. Cloud, and Collegeville, where Mr. Powers now teaches a writing course at St. John's University. His short stories have appeared in the* New Yorker, *as have Mrs. Powers's, and his have been collected under the following titles:* Prince of Darkness, The Presence of Grace, *and* Look How the Fish Live. *His novel* Morte d'Urban, *set in rural Minnesota, received the National Book Award in 1963.*

A T HIS DESK IN THE CHANCERY, the brownstone mansion that was also his residence, John Dullinger, Bishop of Ostergothenburg (Minnesota), was hard at work on a pastoral letter, this one to be read from the pulpits of the diocese in some five weeks. The Bishop was about to mention the keystone of authority, as he did so often in his pastoral letters, that stone without which . . . when Monsignor Holstein, Vicar-General of the diocese and rector of the Cathedral, a lanky man in his late sixties, arrived with the Minneapolis *Tribune* and a paper bag. *"Wie geht's?"* said Monsignor Holstein, and deposited the bag on the desk.

The Bishop peeked into the bag, said "Oh," and, with a nod, thanked Monsignor Holstein for his kindness—for the fine new appointment book. It was that time of year again.

"I hear Scuza's worse, John," said Monsignor Holstein.

The Bishop had heard this, too, but assumed that Monsignor Holstein had later word. New Pilsen, where Father Scuza lay dying, was Monsignor Holstein's hometown.

"A bad month, John."

The Bishop sighed. He figured to lose a couple of men every December, and had already lost one that year.

"Another foreign movie coming to the Orpheum, but I can't find out much about it—only that it's Italian," said Monsignor Holstein.

The Bishop sighed.

Monsignor Holstein, who had rolled up the Minneapolis *Tribune*, whacked himself across the hand with it, but did not sit down. On mornings when there was clear and present danger in the diocese—a dance for ninth-graders scheduled for the Eagles' Hall, *Martin Luther* coming to the Orpheum—Monsignor Holstein sat down and beat himself about his black shoes and white socks with the Minneapolis *Tribune*, while the Bishop, a stocky man, opened and shut his mouth like a fish, and said, "Brrr-jorrk-brrrr." On such mornings, by the time the Bishop got the paper it was in poor shape, and so was he. But this wasn't going to be one of those mornings. Monsignor Holstein was about to depart.

"Like me to take that over to the printer?" he asked, looking down at the pastoral letter.

"Not finished."

When Monsignor Holstein was halfway to the door, he saw that he had the paper in his hand, and came back to deliver it. "Like me to wait a few minutes?"

"*No.*" There was more to writing a pastoral letter than getting it to the printer—a lot more than Monsignor Holstein would ever know. He'd never make a bishop.

"Hello, Tootsie," said Monsignor Holstein when he opened the door, addressing the housekeeper's kitten, whose name was not Tootsie but Tessie—and the Bishop wished the man would remember that. "*Raus*, Tootsie!"

"It's all right," said the Bishop, and the kitten came over to Monsignor Holstein's shoe, kicking up her heels.

While waiting for the kitten to come and sit on his lap—Monsignor Holstein had upset Tessie—the Bishop checked the helpful data in the new appointment book, as was his custom each year. He was sorry to see that the approximate transit time from New York to Minneapolis by air was still given as seven hours, which took no account of jet travel, and that among the cities with population over fifty thousand there were more places than ever that he hadn't heard of, most of them in California, and that Fargo, North Dakota, which he regarded as his hometown, though he'd been brought up on a farm near there, was still not listed. Perhaps next year. He saw that young Kennedy was now among the Presidents—the youngest ever, except Theodore Roosevelt, to hold that high office—but that Alaska and Hawaii were not among the states. Otherwise—postage rates, stains and how to remove them, points of Constitutional law, weights and measures, weather wisdom, and so on—everything was the same as in the previous edition, including nicknames of the states and the state flowers (Alaska and Hawaii missing). Then, as was his custom, the Bishop examined his conscience:

Good Rules for Businessmen
Don't worry, don't overbuy; don't go security.
Keep your vitality up; keep insured; keep sober; keep cool.
Stick to chosen pursuits, but not to chosen methods.
Be content with small beginnings and develop them.
Be wary of dealing with unsuccessful men.
Be cautious, but when a bargain is made stick to it.
Keep down expenses, but don't be stingy.
Make friends, but not favorites.
Don't take new risks to retrieve old losses.
Stop a bad account at once.
Make plans ahead, but don't make them in cast iron.
Don't tell what you are to do until you have done it.

To the extent that these rules could be made to apply to him—and all of them could, to an extent—the Bishop was doing pretty well, he thought. Presently, with the cat on his lap, he took a call from the editor of the diocesan weekly, Father Rapp, who said that Monsignor Holstein had just left, after giving him an argument over the spelling of "godlessness." "I told him we never capitalize it," Father Rapp said. "'Then you better begin,' he told me."

"Don't capitalize it," said the Bishop, and returned to the pastoral letter.

Father Gau, the Chancellor, who had put through the call, entered the office, saying, "I thought I'd better let him talk to you."

428

"Took care of it."

"Is that ready to go over, Your Excellency?"

The Bishop looked down at the pastoral letter. "No—and what's the big hurry?"

"No hurry, Your Excellency." Father Gau smiled in that nice way he had. "I guess I just wanted to read it."

* * *

Three days later, the episcopal Cadillac went to New Pilsen for Father Scuza's funeral. Father Gau was at the wheel, the Bishop and Monsignor Holstein in the back seat, where there was some talk, on the Vicar-General's part, of possible successors to the deceased. The Bishop was careful not to commit himself. St. John Nepomuk's, where Father Scuza had been pastor, was one of the most important parishes in the diocese, and the Bishop intended to take more of a hand in such appointments. Every pastor in Ostergothenburg, where there were three churches besides the Cathedral, was one of Monsignor Holstein's men.

After the funeral, on the way back to Ostergothenburg, Monsignor Holstein raised the matter again. "We were down in the church basement, and Leo"—who was Monsignor Holstein's choice for pastor of St. John Nepomuk's—"says why not heat the rectory from the church? Run a pipe underground, and convert the rectory from hot water to steam. Not a bad idea."

The Bishop said nothing.

"I was worried about the radiators in the rectory, but Leo says they're sound. Just have to watch your joints when you go to steam. And switch from oil to gas, Leo says. That's one thing Leo understands—heating."

The Bishop liked Leo well enough. Leo might easily have had the job in days past, but he was one of Monsignor Holstein's men.

"House needs a lot of work," said Monsignor Holstein. "As usual, curates don't give a damn. Saw their rooms—nails in the walls and woodwork, and so on. Whoever goes there will have plenty to do. I'd say Leo's your man, John."

The Bishop said nothing.

As if he'd settled that matter, Monsignor Holstein moved on to the next one. How did the Bishop feel about relocating the big cross in the cemetery so that it would be visible from the new highway? "John, wouldn't it be fine if, next summer, people driving north on their vacations could see the cross?" Then, not mentioning the argument he'd had with Father Rapp, although Father Rapp was present now, riding up in front with Father Gau, Monsignor Holstein got onto the spelling of "godlessness." He said he could see how the word, under special circumstances, might not be capitalized. A heathen of no faith at all—and there were many such in ancient Rome, by all acounts—might be said to be godless as well as Godless. "But, of course, when we use the word, we don't mean anything like that, do we? I don't know whether I make myself clear or not."

Father Gau and Father Rapp, no longer conversing, seemed to be listening for the Bishop's response. It was the Bishop, after all, who had said, "Don't capitalize it." Later, the Bishop had checked the dictionary and found himself right, but as he saw it now the dictionary was wrong. He said nothing.

Father Gau glanced around and, smiling, said, "How would you spell 'atheism,' Monsignor? With a capital 'T'?"

By tradition in the diocese of Ostergothenburg, whoever became chancellor had to be a good, safe driver. Always before, with his long confirmation trips in mind, the Bishop had taken a young man a few years out of the seminary—a practice that might have been criticized more if the diocese hadn't enjoyed the services of a very able, though aging, bishop and a strong vicar-general. For a number of years, Monsignor Holstein had had a lot to say about who should be chancellor, but Father Gau had been the Bishop's own choice for the job. He had come to it at the ripe old age of forty, after years spent entirely in rural parishes, ultimately as pastor in Grasshopper Lake, a little place that hadn't been much in the news until he went there—until, to be more exact, Father Rapp, a classmate of Father Gau's, took over as editor (and photographer) of the diocesan paper.

In May, on a confirmation trip to Grasshopper Lake, the Bishop had had a chance to see some of the wayside shrines he'd been reading about (and seen pictures of). They weren't as close to the road as he would have liked them, but Minnesota wasn't Austria, and the highway department had to have its clearance. The figurines in the shrines were perhaps too much alike, as if from the same hand or mold, and the crosses had been cut from plywood. But, garnished with the honest flowers of the field, as they were in May, these shrines—these outward manifestations of the simple faith of simple people in a wide and wicked world—were a very pretty sight to the Bishop. When he'd pulled up at the church in Grasshopper Lake, little children had suddenly appeared and, grouping themselves around his car, raised their trained voices in song, pure song. The Bishop had never heard the like. "First time I ever heard angels singing, and in German at that!" he told the congregation before beginning what turned out to be a good, long sermon.

Late in August, returning from a trip that had taken him to the northern border of the diocese, the Bishop had paused at Grasshopper Lake. It was the day of the parish's harvest festival. Such occasions still had meaning in the Ostergothenburg diocese, the Bishop believed, and he did all he could to encourage them, only asking that they be brought to a close by sundown, that there be no dancing, and that pastors keep an eye on the beer stand. Father Gau was doing this when the Bishop arrived, and was *not* tending bar, which was something the Bishop didn't want to see, as he'd said time and again. Together they had strolled among the people, the Bishop smiling upon the pies and cakes and upon the women who had baked them, and occasionally giving his hand to a man for shaking. To the grownups he'd say, "You earned this. You worked hard all year," and to the children, "Give us a song!" And, since he was still a long way from home, he had kept moving, in time with the little *Ach-du-lieber-Augustin* band that played in the shade of a big tree, until he was almost back to his car—in which his chancellor of the moment sat listening to the Game of the Day. After asking whether Father Gau's driver's license was in good order, and hearing that it was, the Bishop had said, "Like to live in Ostergothenburg, Father?"

"I'm happy here, Your Excellency."

"I can see that."

"What parish, Your Excellency?"

"I'm looking for a new chancellor."

"Gee," Father Gau had said. "Gee, Your Excellency."

In September, Father Gau had moved into the Cathedral rectory. He handled the routine work at the Chancery, drove the Bishop's car, heard confessions at the Cathedral on Saturdays, and said two Masses there on Sundays. He also organized a children's choir—this at the earnest request of the Bishop. All went well. Then, with the Bishop's consent, Father Gau formed a men's chorus, and there was trouble. Mr. McKee, the director of the Cathedral choir, a mixed group, said that if male members of the choir wanted to get together on purely social occasions and sing "Dry Bones," that was one thing, but if they were going to sing sacred music, that was something else. The men's chorus would be a choir, and a choir couldn't serve two directors, said Mr. McKee and Monsignor Holstein backed him up. Father Gau took no part in the controversy. In fact, he offered to resign as director of the men's chorus, or to disband it, or to turn it over to Mr. McKee—and the children's choir as well, if that would help any. The men of the chorus wouldn't have this, nor would the mothers of the children. The Bishop said nothing—wouldn't discuss the matter with anybody, not even Monsignor Holstein. In the end, in a surprise move, Mr. McKee resigned. And so Father Gau, who already had enough to do, was obliged to assume the direction of the choir. But what the Bishop had feared, an all-out choir war, hadn't happened, and for this he was grateful to all concerned.

Then, a week before Christmas, soon after Father Scuza's funeral, the men of the chorus put on bright tights and sweatshirts and, thus attired, went caroling through the streets of downtown Ostergothenburg. The Ostergothenburg *Times*, whose editor Father Gau had already got to know better than the Bishop ever had (the Bishop didn't like the man's politics), printed a very nice story about the minstrels in their colorful medieval garb. The Bishop had just finished reading the story when in came Monsignor Holstein, who said he'd spotted the men in Hokey's, the town's leading department store, and complained bitterly that they had been singing pagan-inspired drinking songs. The Bishop listened to him but said nothing, and Monsignor Holstein went away. Did it matter to Monsignor Holstein that the minstrels were important men in the community, that they thought they were engaged in a good work, that the *Times* thought so? Monsignor Holstein had just plunged in, as was his habit—a very bad habit. Monsignor Holstein was a rash man, an unsuccessful man, and even when he was right, as he sometimes was, there was something wrong—something wrong about the *way* he was right. However, the Bishop did feel that jolly songs shouldn't be performed under his auspices during Advent, which, as Monsignor Holstein had said, was a penitential season second only to Lent, and so Father Gau was asked to see that such songs were dropped from the minstrels' repertoire, the Bishop citing "Jingle Bells," and another that, to quote Monsignor Holstein, went "Ho, ho, ho, the wind doth blow!" When Father Gau heard these words from the Bishop's lips, he smiled, and then the Bishop, too, smiled. Until then, he had been worried that Father Gau might think that the Vicar-General was running the diocese. Father Gau, though, had made a joke out of the incident—and, to a certain extent, out of Monsignor Holstein.

In January, after Monsignor Holstein left town—he was appointed pastor of St. John Nepomuk's, in New Pilsen—the Bishop and Father Gau were often seen together in the evening, in the main dining room of the Hotel Webb. The food was good and plentiful at the Webb. The tables weren't placed too close together, there was light enough to eat by, and there was music. In fact, the organist, a nice-looking middle-aged woman who didn't use too much make-up, was a Cathedral parishioner.

These evenings at the Webb, topped off with Benedictine and Dutch Masters, were great occasions for Father Gau (who called himself a country boy), and this was a good part of the Bishop's pleasure in them, although he also did most of the talking. He spoke of his youth "in and around Fargo," of his years of study at home and abroad, of his ordination at the hands of a cardinal in Rome. Back and forth in time he journeyed, accompanied by Father Gau, who now and then asked a question. One evening, the Bishop spoke of the curious role the number two had played in his career: curate in two places, pastor in two, chaplain to the Catholic Foresters for two terms, fourth Bishop of Ostergothenburg (and four is the square of two), and consecrated on his forty-second birthday, on the second day of the second month. "In 1932."

"Gee."

On another evening, the Bishop said, "I couldn't have been more surprised if I'd landed St. Paul or Milwaukee, or more pleased." The Ostergothenburg diocese might well be what it was sometimes called, "the biggest little diocese in the world," for you really couldn't count Europe and South America. There might be dioceses to compare with it in the French part of Canada, but had the faithful in those dioceses been completely exposed to the temptations of a high standard of living? Ostergothenburg, and all the roads around it, blazed with invitations to drink, dine, dance, bowl, borrow money, have the car washed, and so on, but let the diocese stage a rally of some kind at the ballpark and there wouldn't be much doing anywhere else. Oh, of course, if you looked for Ostergothenburg on the map, or judged it by any of the usual rules of thumb—population, bank debits, new construction—you might not think it was much of a place. It had no scheduled air service and no television station and it had lost its franchise in organized baseball. But if you looked at the *diocese*—well, pastors in Minneapolis and St. Paul, who might compare their situations very favorably with those of bishops in barren sees to the north and west, knew they weren't in it with Dullinger. Catholics outnumbered non-Catholics by better than three to one in the diocese. The Bishop had a hundred thousand souls under his care.

"We're well *over* the hundred thousand mark, Your Excellency."

"When I first came here, we were under seventy thousand."

"Gee."

Another man arriving in such a diocese, with no previous experience as a bishop and only forty-two years old, might have chosen to leave well enough alone. This the Bishop had not done. He had twice voted for F.D.R., had backed the New Deal in all its alphabetical manifestations, and, in general, had tried to do what the government was already doing for the common man, only spiritually. "My words were widely quoted. I was referred to as 'the farmer Bishop.' Some thought it sounded disrespectful. I didn't."

"I don't."

But then had come the war and prosperity. The Bishop went out as before and spoke to gatherings, not so large as before but interested. After the war, to combat the changed times—changed for the worse—the Bishop had reached into the faculty of the seminary for Monsignor (then Father) Holstein.

"We were all sorry to see him go," said Father Gau, who had been a seminarian then.

"A good man, in his way."

Monsignor Holstein had done well with public events of a devotional nature—field Masses, "living rosaries," pilgrimages, and processions. And he had stamped out the practice of embellishing the cars of honeymooners with crude sentiments. But in too many ways he had failed. There had been no change at the Orpheum, and at the normal school some smart alecks who hadn't been organized before—before Monsignor Holstein—now made themselves heard on the slightest provocation. When the second Kinsey report had come out, Monsignor Holstein had played right into their hands, telling the *Times*, "Only an old priest with years of experience in the confessional should write such a book, and he wouldn't." This, though true, had looked silly in print.

The Bishop was glad that the troublesome postwar, or Holstein, period was over. Father Gau had been stationed at some distance from the front during this period, and might have been interested in a firsthand account of the fighting, but he seemed to understand that the Bishop didn't care to talk about it.

Father Gau was very understanding. The organist in the main dining room at the Webb did not forget the Bishop's one request—for "Trees"—and night after night played it, sometimes at great length, which was all right, but when she took to rendering it as a solemn fanfare to mark his arrivals and departures, the Bishop wasn't sure he cared for it, but he said nothing. After a while, the organist abandoned the practice, and Father Gau, when questioned by the Bishop, admitted that he'd asked her to do so.

During the day, too, on trips and at the Chancery, Father Gau saw to it that the Bishop's will was done—sometimes before the Bishop knew what his will was. "Just say yes or no, Your Excellency," Father Gau would say, offering a solution to a problem the Bishop might not have been aware of, or to one he'd regarded as tolerable.

One such problem had to do with the regulations for fasting, which, of all the regulations of the diocese, were the ones of most concern to the laity. Monsignor Holstein, trying to make these regulations perfectly clear and binding wherever possible, had gone too deeply into the various claims for exemption—youth, old age, poor health, pregnancy; "But if you *can* fast, so much the better!"—and had shown an obsessive preoccupation with "gravy and meat juices," the abuses of which were subtle and many. The regulations had been "clarified" until they were in need of codification and took a good half-hour in the reading. Father Gau, with the Bishop's permission, let the wind out of them, and took up the slack with the magic words "If you have any questions, see your pastor."

Father Gau suggested other changes. "You know what, Your Excellency? People don't *know* you." This couldn't be helped, the Bishop felt, but he was interested, and after listening to Father Gau, and seeing that the greater good of the diocese was involved (something he hadn't always been sure about when listening to Monsignor Holstein), the Bishop did promise to be seen more in public. He attended a Bosses' Night banquet given by the local Jaycees, going as Father Gau's guest and giving a talk on "My Boyhood in and Around Fargo," which turned out very well. He kicked off the Red Cross campaign, which hadn't had direct support from the diocese before, and won the approval of non-Catholics, who, economically and ecumenically, were not to be sneezed at, as Father Gau pointed out. The Bishop was even seen at concerts at the two Catholic colleges, which, in recent years, he had visited only when necessary, for commencement exercises, and had departed from as early as he possibly could, as soon as he'd said all he had to say against the sin of intellectual pride. The Bishop really got around. On some nights, returning home, he fell asleep in the car and had to be roused, and it was all he could do to get into his pajamas. But he often retired with a sense of satisfaction he hadn't experienced since his New Deal days.

In his pastoral letters he became more and more humane, urging the faithful to drive carefully, to buy a poppy, to set their clocks ahead for daylight-saving time. Formerly it had been his custom to visit the orphanage once a year, at Christmastime, with six bushels of oranges. He hadn't gone oftener because it always made him feel bad—and mad. Now, at Father Gau's suggestion, he went every month, and found it easier. "They wait for you, Your Excellency," said Father Gau, and he was right.

There were other changes. For some years, the Bishop had had his eye on a certain large family, had noted the new arrivals in the birth column of the *Times*, and had inquired of the family's pastor whether there was any improvement otherwise. (The head of the family was an alcoholic, his wife a chain smoker.) There was no improvement until Father Gau, fighting fire with fire, found the father a job in the brewery. Miraculously, the man's drinking and the woman's smoking fell off to nothing. "There's your model family, Your Excellency," said Father Gau, and the family's pastor agreed. So the Bishop dropped in on the family one Sunday afternoon with a gallon of ice cream, and was photographed with the parents and their fourteen children for the diocesan paper.

436

And there were other changes. In June, Father Gau, who had been acting rector of the Cathedral, became rector in fact, and a domestic prelate.

"Gee," said Monsignor Gau after the colorful ceremony—at which the choir had performed under the direction of Mr. McKee, whose reappointment had been one of the first official acts of the new rector. "Gee, Your Excellency."

"Just call me 'Bishop.'"

The next day, a scorcher, it was business as usual for the Bishop and Monsignor Gau at the Chancery. In the afternoon they drove out to the cemetery, where the big cross was to be relocated so that it would be visible from the new highway across the river—the Bishop had noticed many out-of-state cars in town during the past week. He had hoped to escape the heat by coming out to the cemetery, but the place just *looked* cool. He walked along the edge of the low bluff, below which ran the river, until he found a spot he liked, and Monsignor Gau marked it with a brick. Then the Bishop gazed around the cemetery with an eye to the future. "I give it ten years."

"If that," said Monsignor Gau.

The Bishop shot a glance at the adjoining property, a small wilderness belonging to the Ostergothenburg Gun Club.

"It's a thought," said Monsignor Gau.

But that evening at the Webb, which was comfortably cool, Monsignor Gau said he doubted if any land at all could be had from the Gun Club, and also if purchasers of cemetery lots would care to be any closer to the activities of the Gun Club. As for buying the Gun Club lock, stock, and barrel (to answer the Bishop's question), even if that could be done, it would be a very unpopular solution. The center of population had shifted north since the war, people following wealth and the river as closely as they could, and now, all along the river, right up to the cemetery and continuing on the other side of the Gun Club, there were these large estate-type houses, while back from the river the prairie was filling up with smaller but still very nice houses. "The Gun Club's holding the line against us, as some people see it, and they'd take us to court if we could get the Gun Club to sell—*if*."

"I had a chance to buy that property long before it was the Gun Club's, and I wish I had," said the Bishop.

"Things go on there at night," said Monsignor Gau.

"What kind of things?"

Monsignor Gau didn't seem to know how to put it. "Shenanigans," he said.

The Bishop just looked at him.

"Cars drive in and park," Monsignor Gau explained. "In fact, there have even been trespassers in the cemetery."

The Bishop sighed. He had heard that such things happened, but not in Ostergothenburg. A high wall? A night watchman? He thought of the cost to the diocese, and sighed again.

"Bishop, don't say yes or no to this right away," said Monsignor Gau. Proceeding slowly, with great caution—as well he might, if the Bishop understood him—Monsignor Gau offered a solution to the problem. For the sake of the town and the diocese, for the sake of the living and the dead, said Monsignor Gau, the Bishop should *move* the cemetery.

"No, no."

"Frankly, I don't see what else we can do, Bishop," said Monsignor Gau.

"Wait a few years," said the Bishop, finally.

"I just thought now, rather than in a few years or ten years from now, might be better, all things considered."

Monsignor Gau, it seemed, hadn't given any thought to the possibility that the Bishop might not be around in ten years. This was comforting, in a way, but it also forced the Bishop to recognize, as he hadn't before, clearly, that it had been his intention to leave the problem of the cemetery to his successor, and, seeing this as a defect in himself, he took another look at Monsignor Gau's solution. No, all the Bishop liked about it was being able to thwart the desires of trespassers. That was all. That, however, appealed to him strongly. "Where?"

"I was thinking of the old airport—high, level ground, good visibility from the road. Hilly, secluded cemeteries were all right in the past."

The Bishop just looked at Monsignor Gau.

"Think of the mower, Bishop."

When the Bishop noticed where they were in the conversation, he didn't want to be there. "The cemetery's consecrated ground," he said.

"Yes," said Monsignor Gau—and did not (which was wise) point out to the Bishop that consecrated ground could be deconsecrated and put to other use in case of necessity. Instead, he spoke of the capacity crowds on Sundays in all four churches in

Ostergothenburg, and of the parking problem he had at the Cathedral, which he could do nothing about because of his downtown location. "Oh, I'm not at all *enthusiastic* about moving the cemetery." (The Bishop hadn't realized that they were coming back to that, and sighed.) "Still, if it has to be done, it has to be done."

The Bishop agreed with that statement, in principle, but gave no indication that he did.

"Bishop, don't say yes or no to this right away," said Monsignor Gau, and, having offered his solution to the problem of the cemetery, now offered his solution to his solution: on the consecrated ground, once the mortal remains of the dead had been removed to another location, the Bishop should raise a great church and make *it* his cathedral.

The Bishop said nothing.

"Don't say yes or no right away, Bishop."

No more was said on the subject that evening.

The next morning, at the Chancery, Monsignor Gau entered the Bishop's office saying, "Oh, Bishop, about relocating the cross in the cemetery . . ."

"Better hold off on that. Yes," the Bishop said.

That very day, the Bishop called on Mumm, of Mumm and Muldoon, lawyers for the diocese, and went into the legal aspects of moving the cemetery. It wasn't an easy interview, for Mumm, a man as old as the Bishop, kept coming back to all the paperwork there'd be, as if that were reason enough to abandon the idea. But since the diocese owned the cemetery land, and the graves were only held under lease, subject to removal in case of necessity, there was nothing to stop the Bishop from doing what he had in mind. "Legally," said the old lawyer sadly.

At the Webb that evening, Monsignor Gau, who was working with Muldoon of Mumm and Muldoon, said that Muldoon, whose hobby was real estate, had learned that the old airport could be purchased for only a bit more than the going price for farmland in the area. "Dirt cheap, Bishop. But renting those big earth-moving machines is something else again. We'll need 'em at the old cemetery."

"There'll be a lot of paperwork," the Bishop said, preferring to think of that part of the operation. "And, of course, I'll have to get in touch with Rome."

This he did the next day—entirely on his own, because of a

slight difference of opinion with Monsignor Gau over the means to be employed. The Bishop had been going to write to the Apostolic Delegate in Washington, but learned (from Monsignor Gau) that the Apostolic Delegate was in Rome. "Better cable," said Monsignor Gau.

"No, it might give the wrong impression," said the Bishop, who had never, so far as he knew, given Rome that impression.

"To save time," said Monsignor Gau.

"No," said the Bishop, and did not cable.

In his letter, however, he did request that a reply, if favorable, be cabled to him, in view of all that had to be done and the earliness and severity of winter in Minnesota.

After ten days, the reply came. The Bishop let Monsignor Gau read it.

"We're in business, Bishop," said Monsignor Gau. "You *asked* them to cable?"

"To save time," said the Bishop, and their relationship, which had gone off a few degrees, was back to normal.

Things moved quickly then. Letters to the nearest living relatives of those buried in the cemetery and to those, like Mumm, who had contracted for space were drawn up by Muldoon and Monsignor Gau, approved by the Bishop, and dispatched by registered mail. After two weeks, the paperwork was well in hand. During the first week, Muldoon and Monsignor Gau purchased the old airport for the diocese, and the following week it was measured for fencing—galvanized chain link eleven feet high and, as a further discouragement to trespassers, an eighteen-inch overhang of barbed wire. "That should make it as hard to get in as to get out," said the Bishop.

Next, Monsignor Gau and Muldoon, who had been seeing a lot of "the boys at the Gun Club," came to the Bishop and proposed an agreement under which the diocese, soon to have more room than it would need for a new cathedral and perhaps a school later, and the Gun Club, soon to transfer its activities to a location farther up the river, would, for the sake of getting the best price, sell off two contiguous parcels of land as though they were one, as indeed they would appear to be when cleared and leveled, this tract to be restricted to high-class residences only and to be known as Cathedral Heights, with thoroughfares to be known as Cathedral Parkway, Dullinger Road, and Gun Club Memorial Lane. This agreement—over his protests against having a street named after him—was approved by the Bishop. So it went through June, July, and August.

And then, with September and cooler weather, came the hard part for the Bishop, although people who stopped him in the street would never have guessed it. Under his steady gaze, the question that was uppermost in their minds changed from "How could he?" to "How would he?" The Bishop didn't say that he had responsibilities that the ordinary person was neither able to face up to nor equipped to carry out, but he let this be seen. "What has to be done has to be done," he said, "and will be done with all due regard and reverence." And so it was done, in September.

Trucks and earth-movers rolled into the old cemetery, and devout young men from the seminary did the close work by hand. The Bishop was present during most of the first morning to make sure that all went well. Thereafter, he dropped by for a few minutes whenever he could. The Bishop also visited the old airport, now consecrated ground, where clergy in surplices, as well as undertakers and seminarians, were on duty from morning till night. Everything had been thought of (Monsignor Gau, with his clipboard, was everywhere), and the operation proceeded on schedule. After twenty-two days, it was all over, and there was a long editorial in the *Times*.

The Bishop was praised for what he'd done for his town and his diocese, and would do. It didn't stop there. On the street and at the Webb, the Bishop began to see people who had been avoiding him, among them old Mumm, who said, simply, "I got to hand it to you."

And the clergy, too. Men who had stayed away from the Chancery all summer came in again, and some of them, perhaps mindful of the assessments to be levied for the new cathedral, talked up the next parish as they never had before and belittled their own. Some of the Bishop's callers found him not in but at the site of the new cathedral. As long as he had them there, he thought it well to put them in the picture. Pointing to one of the big yellow machines, he'd say, "That one's costing us over two hundred dollars a day. I don't know where it's all coming from, do you, Father?"

On the good days in October and November, the Bishop spent many happy hours at "the job," as it was called. Had bishops in the Middle Ages been so occupied, they might have saved a few

441

years on cathedrals centuries in the building, he thought, for it seemed to him that the men accomplished more when he was around. Some of them he knew from other jobs, and called by name, and others he got to know. One day, he took aside a young workman who was to be married the following morning and spoke to him on the purpose of sex in God's plan, and was so pleased by the response that he gave the young man the rest of the day off and also a cigar, which, since it was a good one, he advised him to save for his honeymoon. Others he spoke to on the purpose of work—a curse, yes, but also a means of sanctification—and cited the splendid example of St. Joseph, a carpenter, the patron of workmen, or workingmen. (The Bishop preferred those words to "worker.") To give additional substance to his remarks, the Bishop spoke of the manual labor he had performed in the years when, home from the seminary for the summer, he'd driven an ice wagon and worked on a threshing crew, and also, though briefly, as a section hand on the Great Northern. "Between Barnesville and Moorhead—until I was overcome by the heat."

By December, the foundation had been poured, the structural steel was in place, and the walls were rising—so slowly, though, that it didn't pay the Bishop to visit the job daily. The men he knew were gone. A few masons drew $4.05 an hour. The Bishop was reluctant to interrupt them. Inside, the air smelled and tasted of oil. Outside, the ground was frozen. By the end of December, the architects—Frank and Frank, of Minneapolis—and the contractors—Beck Brothers, of Ostergothenburg—were feuding.

The Beck brothers (there were four of them) said that Frank and Frank, also brothers, were making too many changes in the plans. If Beck Brothers had known this was going to happen, they wouldn't have bid on the job, they said. They hadn't really wanted it. The plans called for a church such as Beck Brothers had never built before, or seen. "Too goddam modern," they said.

None of this reached the Bishop directly, and almost all of it he discounted, having dealt with contractors for many years, but one evening at the Webb, early in February, he mentioned the part that did bother him.

"Frank and Frank are modern, all right, but they're not *too* modern," Monsignor Gau explained. "Contemporary" was the word for them. They believed in beautiful but simple structures, less expensive, but more impressive structures, and churches

442

were their specialty. They'd done churches in such places as Milwaukee, Dallas, and Fargo, not to mention St. Paul and Minneapolis. "They're tops—and so, locally, are Beck Brothers," said Monsignor Gau.

"Yes, I know," said the Bishop.

"I can tell you what the trouble is, but you can't do anything about it."

"No?"

"Frank and Frank are from Minneapolis, if you know what I mean."

The Bishop did. More than once, he'd heard the contractors refer to the architects as dudes.

The feuding continued into April. In April, the Bishop was planning to fly to Rome.

By then, the cathedral was beginning to look like something—a chasuble, said the architects; a coffin, said the contractors. It looked like neither, the Bishop thought, and it never would unless you viewed it from above, from an airplane. The Bishop thought that the little model of the cathedral in the contractors' shack could be blamed for much of the trouble—it *did* look like a chasuble or a coffin—and so, on his last visit to the job, before leaving for Rome, he carried it off and locked it in the trunk of the car.

That evening, in the main dining room of the Webb, which he wouldn't see again for perhaps a month, the Bishop got a pleasant surprise, for there, not too close to the organ, having a drink, and soon to break bread together, it seemed, were the two architects and the four contractors. Monsignor Gau was also there, but the Bishop had expected him.

"Well, well," said the Bishop, joining the party. He sat at one end of the table, Monsignor Gau at the other. On the Bishop's right sat an architect, on his left a contractor, and on Monsignor Gau's right and left there was one of each. The seating arrangements had been worked out by Monsignor Gau, the Bishop felt, but how had Frank and Frank and Beck Brothers been brought together?

Presently, this question was answered for the Bishop—and for the Beck brothers, too, to judge by their faces. An architectural journal of excellent repute and wide circulation was planning an article on the new cathedral. If it followed the usual pattern of such articles, said one of the Franks, there would be photographs of the new cathedral and of those intimately associated with the job. "All of us here."

"Why me?" said Monsignor Gau, with a surprised look that didn't fool the Bishop, for obviously Monsignor Gau had heard the good news earlier, had talked it over with Frank and Frank, and on the strength of it had arranged the evening.

"You're rector of the Cathedral—that's why," said the Bishop.

"But why me?"

"It's your church," said Monsignor Gau. This was true. In fact, without the Bishop it wouldn't be a cathedral.

The evening now went better. The Beck brothers, who were rather shy men away from their work, opened up as they hadn't before. Frank and Frank said that the food at the Webb surpassed anything Minneapolis could offer and, a little later on, that they wished there were contractors like Beck Brothers in Minneapolis. At that point, the Bishop called for a round of Danish beer, a new thing at the Webb, and they drank a toast to the job.

The Bishop, trying to hold the attention of those at his end of the table, said that they might be interested to know that he had at one time given some thought to building the cathedral out of fieldstone. Yes, plain, ordinary, everyday stones, just as they came from the hand of God and were collected by farmers from their fields. The true and special character of the diocese and its people might be expressed in a cathedral of fieldstones. Monsignor Gau, however, had more or less discouraged the idea, saying that he doubted if fieldstones would look good in a structure of such size, or if fieldstones would hold together as well as, say, bricks. The Bishop had had nothing against bricks, but for a cathedral he preferred stone—good, honest stone. Yes, he was happy with the grey stone that had been chosen. He had wanted a rough finish, yes, until he had learned that this would be too hard to clean, and now he was happy with the smooth. For some reason, perhaps because of his romantic ideas about cathedral-building, he was sorry that the walls wouldn't be solid stone—that the stone slabs, which were being anchored to the steel structure, were only two inches thick. Yes, he'd have reason to be sorry if the walls of the cathedral *were* solid stone—no air space, no insulation. He knew how buildings were constructed now, and wouldn't have it any other way. He wasn't complaining. Yes, he knew that they were doing things with stone that had never been done before, using it as if it were plywood, saving time, labor, and stone, and he was happy. He wasn't complaining. Why should he? He was getting everything he'd ever wanted in a cathedral. It would be ideal for processions—wide aisles, assembly space, space to maneuver in. He was getting landscaped parking lots. He *wasn't* getting as high a structure as he'd wanted at first, but, as Monsignor Gau had pointed out to him, the site would do a lot for the cathedral. From across the river, from the new highway, it wouldn't look anything like Mont-Saint-Michel—another idea the Bishop had had in the very beginning and recognized as crazy even then. In short, he was getting a fine contemporary building with a distinct Romanesque flavor. He was getting real arches. "Oh, I've entirely given up the idea of fieldstones. I wouldn't want 'em now if I could have 'em. But from what I know now, I think it might have been possible."

"Anything's possible, if you're talking about the facing," said the architect on the Bishop's right. "What counts in a building, be it skyscraper or cathedral, is the steel. That's *all* that holds it together."

"Oh, it's *safe*," said the contractor on the Bishop's left. He must have seen that the Bishop could use a little reassurance on that point. "It'll be good for fifty, seventy-five—maybe a hundred—years."

The architect nodded.

* * *

Driving up to the job on his return from Rome (where, except for the Holy Father, nobody had seemed very glad to see him), the Bishop was pleased to note how much had been accomplished in his absence. But then, getting out of the car, coming closer and looking up at the arches, none of which had been completed when he last saw the cathedral, he couldn't believe his eyes. Going inside, he found, of course, that what was true of one arch was true of all—those over the windows, those along the aisles, the one over the baptistery, and, worst of all, the one over the sanctuary. In the middle of every arch there were *two* stones— *where the keystone should have been there was just a crack.*

Had any of the responsible parties been with him then— Monsignor Gau, Frank *or* Frank, or any of the Becks—the Bishop wouldn't have been able to conceal his dismay. He decided to say nothing. In the evening, he consulted the complete set of plans in

445

Monsignor Gau's office—and wished that he hadn't relied so much on just the floor plans, for the plans he was looking at did show how the stone would be set. But they didn't say why.

The next day, at the job, the Bishop approached a workman and said in an offhand manner, "No keystones in the arches."

The workman said that keystones weren't necessary in *these* arches—that steel was all that counted in a building nowadays. From another workman whom he questioned in the same manner the Bishop received much the same reply, and again did not pursue the matter. The following day, an intelligent-looking truck driver, the father of seven, told the Bishop that keystones in the arches would have clashed with the architects' over-all plan. The Bishop nodded, hoping to hear more, but did not. The next day, the Bishop spoke to one of the Becks about cathedral-building in the Middle Ages, saying in an offhand manner, "I suppose keystones in those arches would've clashed with the architects' over-all plan," and was told that you didn't see keystones much any more. Then for two days the Bishop was out of town, but on his return he tried one of the architects, saying, "You don't see keystones much any more." You did, he was told. You still saw them, and more often than not, if not always, they were ornamental. Out of honesty to their materials and, in the case of the new cathedral, out of a desire to give a light and airy feeling to what was, after all, a very heavy structure, Frank and Frank had rejected keystones. It hadn't been easy to give what was, after all, a very heavy, *horizontal* structure, and a rather low one at that, a *vertical* feeling. That was what the cracks did, and what keystones, apart from being obsolete, would not have done.

That was early in May—a very wet month, as it turned out. At the job, there were signs of erosion and subsidence, and the ground was quickly sodded. Fortunately, the hairline cracks that appeared here and there in the fabric of the structure, and that had to be expected, did not widen.

At the Chancery, there were also signs of erosion and subsidence in the Bishop's relations with Monsignor Gau, but here the hairline cracks (which, perhaps, had been present before) did widen. The work of the diocese went on, of course, but there was much less dining out than there had been. The Bishop didn't enjoy being with Father Rapp, and Muldoon and the others, who seemed to appear regularly at the Webb at Monsignor Gau's invitation, and who, though they gave the Bishop all the attention he could stand, still had a way of excluding him from the conversation. On confirmation trips, more often than not, the Bishop was driven by a curate—the Bishop had given Monsignor Gau a third one for Christmas. Much as Monsignor Gau enjoyed being with the Bishop, driving him and attending him, he could seldom manage it that spring. "Chancellor" was no longer a synonym for "chauffeur" in the Ostergothenburg diocese. Monsignor Gau was chancellor in the proper sense of the word, as well as rector of the Cathedral, building inspector for the diocese at the job, and troubleshooter there and everywhere—no man in the diocese below the rank of bishop had ever been so honored, trusted, and burdened with responsibility. Monsignor Gau also ran the newly created Diocesan Procurement Office.

The D.P.O. stocked, or took orders for, practically everything a Catholic institution required—school and office supplies, sporting goods, playground equipment, sacramental wines. It was saving money for the priests, nuns, and people of the diocese, but it also made demands on Monsignor Gau's time and energy. He had to spend long hours with his catalogues and clipboard in the basement of the high school, and he had to go out of town on buying trips. There had been one or two too many of these, it seemed to the Bishop, who hadn't anticipated any when he authorized the D.P.O., which, though, was unquestionably a success.

However, when the Bishop had approved the sale of sweatshirts bearing his coat of arms to seminarians and clergy, he hadn't anticipated seeing one of these articles, as he did in the middle of June, in front of Hokey's department store, on the person of a well-developed young lady. Immediately, he stepped into the lobby of the Webb, phoned Monsignor Gau, and asked that the stock of sweatshirts be checked. "No more, when those are gone," he said, after he'd got the count.

"Gee," said Monsignor Gau, but he sought no explanation, and the Bishop offered none.

By June, that was how it was with them. During the previous winter, at Monsignor Gau's suggestion, the Bishop had become a columnist in the diocesan paper, dealing with events at home and abroad, and more than holding his own, according to Monsignor Gau, Father Rapp, and others. In June, he gave up his column. "No more," he said, again in a way that didn't invite questions. That wasn't all. For over a year, at Monsignor Gau's suggestion, letters of congratulation had been going out to Catholics in the diocese who had done something worthy of the Bishop's attention—an honor defined with great latitude by Monsignor Gau—and then, in June, the Bishop ended the practice. "No more," he said.

The Bishop was sorry that he couldn't think of better ways to assert himself in his relations with Monsignor Gau, and was quite prepared for the consequences. Total obscurity held no fears for him at the moment—not that that would ever be his fate. He just didn't want it thought that he wasn't running the diocese. Or was it already too late—again—for any but the strongest proof? If it was, did he wish to give such proof—again? Monsignor Gau was a very popular man with the people, as well as a very successful one. Monsignor Holstein hadn't been either. And the Bishop was older now.

The Bishop had never felt so out of it as he did late in July, at the dedication of the new cathedral. For many months, Monsignor Gau had been busy with the arrangements—not only bishops from nearby sees were asked to attend but also several archbishops, whose acquaintance, it seemed, Monsignor Gau had made, or almost made, on his buying trips. Two archbishops actually showed up for the dedication, as did an unimportant and indigent Italian cardinal, an added starter, who had more or less invited himself. This, apart from the expense of flying the man in, round trip and first class, from Syracuse (N.Y.), where he had relatives, was unfortunate. He talked a lot of nonsense about rice, having been informed somewhere that this was a major crop in Minnesota, as it was in his part of Italy, and nobody had the nerve to tell him that the only rice in Minnesota grew wild and was harvested by a few Indians.

At the dedication itself, this Prince of the Church played with his handkerchief and closed his eyes during the sermon—which might have been shorter, in view of the oppressive heat, and would have been if the Bishop's train of thought hadn't eluded him twice. Both times, he covered up nicely by reviewing what he'd been saying earlier, once shot ahead on the intended line and once on another just as good. Trying to appeal to everybody present—clergy, nuns, and laity, Catholics and non-Catholics, and even children—he spoke of the splendid progress made by the Church and the country in his own lifetime, reckoning it in terms of Popes and Presidents, a number of whom he'd met or seen and come away from with varying impressions, which he did his best to describe, ranging back and forth between Popes and Presidents, pinpointing the great events and legislation associated with each and, whenever possible, bringing in the diocese. Such an effort would have taxed a much younger man on a cool day. As it was, with the temperature in the nineties, the humidity high, and the robes of his office heavy on him, the Bishop left the pulpit in a weakened condition.

The tour planned for the visiting prelates—first, the seminary and then lunch under the trees unless it rained, then the new cemetery, then the high school, and then back to the cathedral for lemonade and a look at the residential quarters—went on without the Bishop. Monsignor Gau led the tour. The Bishop spent the afternoon in seclusion, trying to recover. Monsignor Gau phoned. "No, it's just the heat," said the Bishop, and wouldn't have a doctor or an air-conditioner. In the evening, it was Monsignor Gau who presided over the banquet at the Webb.

The Bishop stayed home with the housekeeper's cat. He found it too warm for the cat and the paper, but not before he read that His Eminence (as the *Times* called the wandering cardinal in one place) had landed in "the country of Columbus" with the hope of seeing Niagara Falls and what he could of the frontier, and that he was delighted with Ostergothenburg, which was not unlike Brisbane, with the new cathedral, which was not unlike St. Peter's, with the local clergy and laity, whose good sense and piety were not unlike what he'd been led to expect, and with the Orpheum for exhibiting an Italian film during his visit.

In a black mood, the Bishop wondered whether he shouldn't do away with the D.P.O. Later on, when it must have been about time for cigars at the banquet, and for Monsignor Gau to rise and say once again that though he greatly enjoyed city life, he was a country boy and would be proud and happy to be a rural pastor again, the Bishop wondered whether that shouldn't be arranged. At another point in the evening, thinking he might read awhile, the Bishop went into his office for a book but then forgot why he was there, and stood for some time before a chart on the wall. The chart, which was in the form of a cross, had been made by an artistic nun at Monsignor Holstein's instigation, and showed the spiritual plan of the diocese: bishop at the top of the tree, vicar-general below him, then chancellor, and then to the right, on the right branch, clergy in general, and to the left, on the left branch, nuns, or religious, as they were designated on the chart, and, finally, down the middle, on the trunk of the tree, the laity. The Bishop hadn't really looked at the cross for years, and now saw it as he never had before. What struck him was the favored position of one officer of the diocese. He hadn't noticed it before, or it hadn't meant anything to him before, but the chancellor occupied the very heart of the cross. It seemed to the Bishop that the chart, in that respect, gave a distorted view of the spiritual plan of the diocese. He thought of taking it down. But he didn't. He went back to his bedroom and got into his pajamas.

It rained sometime in the night, and cooled off, and the next day the Bishop was almost himself again.

One night about a month later, in a black mood—it had come to his attention during the day that the senior members of the model family had gone back to their old ways—he was standing before the chart again, and again it seemed to him that it gave a distorted view of the spiritual plan of the diocese. He tried one of the thumbtacks, then another. When he had the chart down, he carried it around for a while, not knowing what to do with it. He didn't care to throw it away. He thought of burning it—respectfully burning it, as one would an old, outdated, or perhaps defective flag. In the end, he rolled it up gently, carried it out to the garage, and put it in the trunk of the car with the little model of the new cathedral.

The next morning, he noticed that the cross was still there, in outline, on the wall, and that same morning he received word that he was getting an auxiliary—something he certainly hadn't asked for and didn't want—and that the man chosen for the job was Monsignor, or Bishop-elect, Gau.

Minnesota Prose

SELECTED READING

The basis for inclusion in the following list was simply a Minnesota setting. Whereas the selections in the anthology itself were chosen principally on the basis of quality, the reading list is more variable, some of it consisting of very good work, where other pieces are of moderate interest. Many of these writers have published works with other settings. Although I have focussed on short stories and novels, I have included a few essays, articles, and autobiographical pieces.

Aldrich, Darragh. *Girl Going Nowhere*. Kinsey, 1939.
———. *Peter Good for Nothing*. Macmillan, 1929.
———. *Some Trails Never End*. Kinsey, 1941.
Alexander, Sheila. *Walk with a Separate Pride*. Itasca Press, 1947.
Allen, Nicoline. *High Threshold*. Vantage, 1953.
Anderson, Chester, ed. *Growing Up in Minnesota*. University of Minnesota Press, 1976.
Bailey, George Ryland. *The Red Mesabi*. Houghton Mifflin, 1930.
Banning, Margaret Culkin. *The Convert*. Harper and Brothers, 1957.
———. *Country Club People*. George H. Doran, 1923.
———. *The Dowry*, Harper and Brothers, 1954.
———. *Fallen Away*. Harper and Brothers, 1951.
———. *First Woman*. Harper and Brothers, 1935.
———. *Iron Will*. Harper and Brothers, 1936.
———. *Mesabi*. Harper and Row, 1969.
———. *Mixed Marriage*. Harper and Brothers, 1930.
———. *The Quality of Mercy*. Harper and Row, 1963.
———. *Spellbinders*. George H. Doran, 1922.
———. *The Will of Magda Townsend*. Harper and Row, 1974.
Beers, Lorna Doone, *A Humble Lear*, Dutton, 1929.
———. *The Mad Stone*. Dutton, 1932.
Bell, John. *Moccasin Flower*. The Book Master, 1935.
Benson, Ramsey. *Hill Country*. Stokes, 1928.
Bloom, Harry. *Sorrow Laughs*. Abelard-Schuman, 1959.
Bly, Carol. "Gunnar's Sword," *American Review* #19 (January, 1974).
Boardman, Neil S. *The Long Home*. Harper and Brothers, 1948.
———. *The Wine of Violence*. Simon and Schuster, 1964.
Boyd, Thomas. *In Time of Peace*. Minton, Balch, 1935.
Brennan, Dan. *Badge of Honor*. Belmont Tower Books, 1974.

———. *Lay-over Town*. Caravelle Books, 1968.
Brink, Carol. *Stopover*. Macmillan, 1951.
Buchwald, Emilie. "Getting and Spending," *Great River Review*, Vol. 1, #3.
Cannon, Cornelia. *Red Rust*. Little, Brown, 1928.
Chidester, Ann. *The Long Years*. Scribners, 1946.
———. *No Longer Fugitive*. Scribners, 1943.
———.*Young Pandora*. Scribners, 1942.
Christgau, John. *Spoon*. Viking Press, 1978.
Chute, M. G. *Sheriff Olsen*. Appleton Century, 1942.
Dahl, Borghild. *Homecoming*. Dutton, 1953.
DeLange, Anneke. *Anna Luhanna*. Greenberg, 1946.
Davis, Kenneth S. *In the Forests of the Night*. Houghton Mifflin, 1942.
DeGrazia, Emilio. "A Minnesota Story," *Red Cedar Review*, Fall 1978.
Dorson, Richard M. *American Folklore*. University of Chicago Press, 1959.
———. *America in Legend*. Pantheon, 1973.
Duckwall, Kristi. "Harter's, Portage Corner," *Minnesota Review*, Vol. 8, #4.
Eastman, Charles. *Indian Boyhood*. McClure Phillips, 1902.
Eastman, Mary. *The Dahcotah: or Life and Legends of the Sioux*. Wiley, 1849.
Ederer, Bernard Francis. *Birch Coulee*. Exposition, 1957.
Eggleston, Edward. "The Gunpowder Plot" *Scribners Monthly*, July 1871.
———. "The-Man-that-Draws-the-Handcart," *Harper's New Monthly Magazine*, February 1894.
———. *The Mystery of Metropolisville*, Thompson and Thomas, 1873.
Elli, Frank, *The Riot*. Coward McCann, 1966.
Ellsworth, Franklin. *The Band-wagon*. Dorrance, 1921.
Ervin, Jean Adams. "Spots of Commonness," *Indiana Writes*, Spring 1979.
Faralla, Dana. *A Circle of Trees*. Lippincott, 1955.
———. *The Madstone*. Lippincott, 1958.
Fitzgerald, F. Scott. "Absolution," *All the Sad Young Men*. Scribner's, 1926.
———. "A Short Trip Home," *Taps at Reveille*. Scribner's, 1935.
———. "Basil: A Night at the Fair," *The Bodley Head Scott Fitzgerald*, volume 6.
———. "Basil: He Thinks He's Wonderful." *Taps at Reveille*. Scribner's, 1935.
———. "Basil: The Captured Shadow." *Taps at Reveille*. Scribner's, 1935.
———. "Basil: The Freshest Boy." *Taps at Reveille*. Scribner's, 1935.
———. "Basil: The Scandal Detectives," *Taps at Reveille*, Scribner's, 1935.
———. "Bernice Bobs Her Hair." *Flappers and Philosophers*. Scribner's, 1959.
———. "Hot and Cold Blood." *All the Sad Young Men*. Scribner's, 1926.
———. "The Ice Palace," *Flappers and Philosophers*. Scribner's, 1959.
———. *This Side of Paradise*. Scribner's, 1920.
———. "Three Hours Between Planes." *The Stories of F. Scott Fitzgerald*. Scribner's, 1951.
———. "Winter Dreams." *All the Sad Young Men*. Scribner's, 1926.
Flanagan, John T. "Folklore in Minnesota Literature," *Minnesota History*, 36:73–83 (Sept. 1958).
———. "Thirty Years of Minnesota Fiction," *Minnesota History*, 31:129–147 (Sept. 1950).
Flandrau, Charles Macomb. *Prejudices*. Appleton, 1911.
———. *Loquacities*. Appleton, 1931.
Flandrau, Grace. *Being Respectable*. Harcourt Brace, 1923.
———. *Entranced*. Harcourt Brace, 1924.
———. *Indeed this Flesh*. Harrison Smith and Robert Haas, 1934.
———. "The Untamable Twin," *The Taming of the Frontier*. Minton, Balch, 1925.
Frederick, John T. *Druida*. Knopf, 1923.
Gifford, Thomas. *The Cavanaugh Quest*. Putnam's, 1976.
———. *The Wind Chill Factor*. Putnam's, 1975.

Gray, James. *Shoulder the Sky*. Putnam's, 1935.

———. *Vagabond Path*. Macmillan, 1941.

———. *Wake and Remember*. Macmillan, 1936.

Greenberg, Alvin, "Footnotes to a Theory of Place," *Antioch Review*, 32, #31 (1973).

Gruchow, Paul. "Pieces of the Prairie," *Minnesota Monthly*, August 1977.

———. "The Prairie Is Like a Daydream," *Minnesota Monthly*. March 1978.

Hampl, Patricia. "Look at a Teacup," *New Yorker*, June 28, 1976.

Hassler, Jon. *Staggerford*. Atheneum, 1977.

Havill, Edward. *Big Ember*. Harper and Brothers, 1947.

Hedin, Mary. "Devourers," *Great River Review*, Vol. 1, #2, 1978.

———. "Places We Lost," *Best American Short Stories, 1966*.

Hinkemeyer, Michael. *The Fields of Eden*. Putnam's, 1977.

Hoffman, William. *Mendel*. Yoseloff, 1969.

———. *Tales of Hoffman*. Denison, 1961.

Hoover, Helen. *The Years of the Forest*. Knopf, 1973.

Hough, Donald. *The Streetcar House*. Duell, Sloan and Pearce, 1960.

Katkov, Norman. *Eagle at My Eyes*. Doubleday, 1948.

———. *A Little Sleep, a Little Slumber*. Doubleday, 1949.

Johnson, Robert Proctor. *A Legacy of Thorns*. Morrow, 1965.

Keillor, Garrison. "Don, the True Story of a Young Person," *New Yorker*, May 30, 1944.

———. "Drowning 1954," *New Yorker*, Aug. 16, 1976.

———. "Found Paradise," *New Yorker*, Sept. 18, 1971.

———. "Friendly Neighbor," *New Yorker*, Dec. 31, 1973.

———. "How It Was in America a Week Ago Tuesday," *New Yorker*, Mar. 10, 1975.

———. "Plainfolks," *New Yorker*, Nov. 4, 1974.

———. "The Slim Graves Show," *New Yorker*, Feb. 10, 1973.

———. "WLT (The Edgar Era)" *New Yorker*, Apr. 12, 1976.

Kolling, Wanda. "The Taste of Oranges," *Carleton Miscellany*, 7:46–55, 1966.

Krause, Herbert. *The Thresher*. Bobbs-Merrill, 1946.

———. *The Ox-Cart Trail*. Bobbs-Merrill, 1954.

———. *Wind without Rain*. Bobbs-Merrill, 1939.

Krawczyk, Monica. *If the Branch Blossoms and Other Stories*. Polanie, 1950.

LeSueur, Meridel. *Corn Village*. Stanton & Lee, 1970.

———. *Salute to Spring*. International Publishers, 1940.

Lewis, Sinclair. *Cass Timberlane*. Random House, 1945.

———. *Free Air*. Harcourt Brace, 1919.

———. *The God-Seeker*. Random House, 1949.

———. "Harri," *Good Housekeeping*, Aug. 1935, Sept. 1935.

———. *Kingsblood Royal*. Random House, 1948.

———. *Main Street*. Harcourt Brace, 1920.

———. *Selected Short Stories of Sinclair Lewis*. Doubleday, 1935.

———. *Trail of the Hawk*. Harcourt Brace, 1915.

Lindsay, Catherine. *The Country of the Young*. Reynal and Hitchcock, 1946.

Lovelace, Maud Hart. *The Black Angels*. John Day, 1926.

———. *Early Candlelight*. University of Minnesota Press, 1929.

Lovelace, Maud Hart and Delos. *Gentlemen from England*. Macmillan, 1937.

———. *One Stayed at Welcome*. John Day, 1934.

McCarthy, Abigail. *Private Faces, Public Places*. Doubleday, 1972.

McCarthy, Mary. *Memories of a Catholic Girlhood*. Harcourt Brace, 1957.

McNally, William. *House of Vanished Splendor*. Putnam's, 1932.

———. *The Roofs of Elm Street*. Hurst and Blackett, 1936.

Malm, Dorothea. *Every Third Thought*. Peter Davies, 1962.

Manfred, Frederick. *Apples of Paradise*. Trident, 1968.
———. *Boy Almighty*. Itasca Press, 1945.
———. *The Chokecherry Tree*. Alan Swallow, 1948.
———. *The Giant*. Doubleday, 1951.
———. *Green Earth*. Crown, 1977.
———. *Milk of Wolves*. Avenue Victor Hugo Pub., 1976.
———. *Morning Red*. Alan Swallow, 1956.
Meigs, Cornelia. *Railroad West*. Little, Brown, 1937.
Milton, John. "An Inner Disquiet," *The Minnesota Experience: An Anthology*, Adams Press, 1979.
Minnesota Statehood Centennial Commission. *A Selected Bio-Bibliography: Minnesota Authors*. 1958.
Neff, Wanda. *Lone Voyagers*. Houghton Mifflin, 1929.
Nye, Bud. *Home Is If You Find It*. Doubleday, 1947.
———. *Stay Loose*. Doubleday, 1959.
Nygaard, Norman. *They Sought a Country*. Longmans, Green, 1950.
O'Brien, Tim. *Northern Lights*. Seymour Lawrence/Delacorte, 1975.
———. "Speaking of Courage," *O. Henry Prize Stories, 1978*. Doubleday, 1978.
O'Connor, William Van. *Campus on the River*. Crowell, 1959.
Ogley, Dorothy, and M. Goodwin Cleland. *Iron Land*. Doubleday, 1946.
Olson, Sigurd. *Listening Point*. Knopf, 1976.
———. *Open Horizons*. Knopf, 1969.
———. *Singing Wilderness*. Knopf, 1956.
———. *Wilderness Days*. Knopf, 1972.
O'Meara, Walter. *Grand Portage*. Bobbs-Merrill, 1951.
———. *Minnesota Gothic*. Holt, 1958.
———. *The Trees Went Forth*. Crown, 1947.
———. *We Made It through the Winter*. Minnesota Historical Society, 1974.
Ostenso, Martha. *The Mad Carews*. Dodd, Mead, 1927.
———. *The Dark Dawn*. Dodd, Mead, 1926.
———. *A Man Had Tall Sons*. Dodd, Mead, 1958.
———. *Mandrake Root*. Dodd, Mead, 1938.
———. *Milk Route*. Dodd, Mead, 1948.
———. *O River Remember!* Dodd, Mead, 1943.
———. *The Stone Field*. Dodd, Mead, 1937.
———. *Wild Geese*. Dodd, Mead, 1925.
Otto, Lon. *A Nest of Hooks*. University of Iowa Press, 1978.
Parks, Gordon. *A Choice of Weapons*. Harper, 1965.
Patterson, Mary. *Iron Country*. Houghton Mifflin, 1966.
Pirsig, Robert. *Zen and the Art of Motorcycle Maintenance*. Morrow, 1974.
Powers, J. F. *Look How the Fish Live*. Knopf, 1975.
———. *Morte d'Urban*. Doubleday, 1962.
———. *Presence of Grace*. Doubleday, 1956.
———. *Prince of Darkness and Other Stories*. Doubleday, 1947.
Proctor, Ellen. *Turning Leaves*. Dodd, Mead, 1942.
Quigley, Martin. *The Secret Project of Sigurd O'Leary*. Lippincott, 1959.
———. *Winners and Losers*. Lippincott, 1961.
Richards, Carmen Nelson, ed. *Minnesota Writers*. Denison, 1961.
Richards, Carmen Nelson, and Genevieve Rose Breen, eds. *Minnesota Writes*. Lund, 1945.
Rindfleisch, Norval. *In Loveless Clarity and Other Stories*. Ithaca House, 1972.
Rölvaag, Ole. *The Boat of Longing*. Harper, 1933.
———. *Pure Gold*. Harper, 1930.
Schoolcraft, Henry R. *The Indian Fairy Book*. Frederick A. Stokes, 1916.
———. *The Myth of Hiawatha and Other Oral Legends*. Lippincott, 1856.

———. *Personal Memoirs of a Residence of Thirty Years with the Indian Tribes on the American Frontiers*. Lippincott, Grambo, 1851.

———. *Schoolcraft's Indian Legends*, ed. Mentor L. Williams. Michigan State University Press, 1956.

Schoonover, Shirley. *Mountain of Winter*. Coward-McCann, 1965.

Seeley, Mabel. *The Beckoning Door*. Doubleday, 1950.

———. *The Crying Sisters*. Grosset and Dunlap, 1939.

———. *The Listening House*. Grosset and Dunlap, 1938.

———. *Stranger Beside Me*. Doubleday, 1951.

———. *The Whispering Cup*. Doubleday, 1940.

———. *Whistling Shadow*. Doubleday, 1954.

———. *Woman of Property*. Doubleday, 1947.

Shulman, Max. *Barefoot Boy with Cheek*. Doubleday, 1943.

———. *Potatoes are Cheaper*. Doubleday, 1971.

———. *The Zebra Derby*. Doubleday, 1946.

Snelling, William Joseph. *Tales of the Northwest*. University of Minnesota Press, 1936.

Sterrett, Frances R. *Years of Achievement*. Penn, 1932.

Stong, Phil. *Iron Mountain*. Farrar Rinehart, 1942.

Swanson, Neil H. *The Forbidden Ground*. Farrar Rinehart, 1938.

———. *The Phantom Emperor*. Putnam's 1934.

Treuer, Robert. "The Mysterious Business in the Waboose Woods," *Yankee Magazine*, November 1974.

———. *The Tree Farm*. Little, Brown, 1976.

Ueland, Brenda. *Me*. Putnam, 1939.

———. "Narrow Escape," *Delineator*, December 1935.

Vizenor, Gerald. *Wordarrows*. University of Minnesota Press, 1978.

Wahl, Betty. "Gingerbread," *New Yorker*, January 28, 1950.

———. "Martinmas," *New Yorker*, November 15, 1947.

Williams, Carlton. *Trailer Doctor*, Penn., 1941.

Wilson, Grove. *Man of Strife*. Frank-Maurice, 1925.

Wise, Evelyn Voss. *As the Pines Grow*. Appleton Century, 1939.

———. *The Long Tomorrow*. Appleton Century, 1938.

———. *Mary Darlin!* Appleton Century, 1945.

———. *Wheels in the Timber*. Appleton Century, 1941.